IMPORTANT: *'The Secret Norwegian' contains material that some may find disturbing. If you are affected by any of the issues raised you should contact your doctor and seek professional advice. I am not a doctor, therapist or a mental health expert. The information is strictly for informational purposes only and is not intended as a substitute for advice from your doctor. You should not use this information for diagnosis or treatment of any health or mental health problem. 'The Secret Norwegian' includes discussions of abuse, racism, discrimination, bullying, suicide, death, mental illness and child abuse which some may find triggering. Except for the Prime Minister, all names and identifying details have been changed to protect the privacy of individuals. Consequently, any resemblance to actual persons, living or dead, or actual events is purely coincidental. A small number of questions have been edited for brevity and clarity, including the removal of certain extreme racist views and/or editing of profanity. The views and opinions expressed in the 'The Secret Norwegian' do not necessarily reflect the views of the author or are the views of the publisher. Discrimination based on race, colour, religion, sex, national origin, citizenship, age status, sexual orientation, disability, marital status, or any other basis is wrong and is fully condemned by the author and the publisher. The individual opinions expressed in this book are in no way an accurate representation of Scandinavia, the country of Norway or the Norwegian people and should not be taken as such. Any such examples or opinions that may be included in 'The Secret Norwegian' are wrong and are including for educational and historical reference only. Discretion is advised.*

THE SECRET NORWEGIAN

Anthony King

Published by Faria Publishing Limited 2020

The Secret Norwegian (First Edition)

Edited by Debz Hobbs-Wyatt
Formatted by Polgarus Studio

ISBN: 978-1-9160887-4-0 (print)
ISBN: 978-1-9160887-5-7 (eBook)

Disclaimer: This book is not intended to be a substitute for the medical advice of a licensed physician. The reader should consult with their doctor in any matters relating to his/her health and well-being. Before continuing reading this book it is recommended that you seek medical advice from your personal physician and follow their instructions only. The information contained within this book is strictly for informational purposes. If you wish to apply ideas contained in this book, you are taking full responsibility for your actions. The author has made every effort to ensure the accuracy of the information within this book was correct at the time of publication. The author does not assume and hereby disclaims any liability to any party for any loss, damage, or disruption caused by errors or omissions, whether such errors or omissions result from accident, negligence, or any other cause.

To all the Norwegians who felt like it was your fault when you were bullied for being different and having a non-conformist opinion... it was never your fault. This book is for you.

VOLUME ONE OF FOUR

Contents

Foreword

This book is a first time, *never been done before* analysis of conversations with hundreds of Norwegians. It is a record based on over 350 interviews and conversations: 500,000 words of transcripts, hundreds of hours of audio recording, many hours of video recording and about 50,000 – 100,000 words of contemporaneous notes. For the first time in many Norwegians' lives, they were discussing, not only things that they had never discussed before, but things that they had never *thought* about before.

My journey took me north, south, east and west of Norway. With a tape recorder, I travelled from Oslo to Tromso to Kristiansund to Trondheim to Kongsberg to Stavanger to Drammen to Molde to Kristiansand to Alesund and a total of fifteen of the major cities and towns, even journeying to Longyearbyen, Svalbard in the deep Arctic 78 degrees north. I also travelled to over fifty small Norwegian towns and villages including Sogndalstrand, Asgardstrand, Bud, Vestfossen, Averoy, Surnadel, Romsdalen and Atlantic Road and many more.

I sat down with native Norwegians but also with Norwegian tourists and immigrants and spouses married to Norwegians. In fifteen months I travelled to Sweden, Denmark and Warsaw and interviewed people there *about Norway* and aspects of Norwegian history. I interviewed the Prime Minister, historians, doctors, teachers, students, teenagers, archaeologists, scientists, hotel workers, fisherman, museum workers, royal property workers and people from all walks of life and all ages. What I discovered is beyond belief. This series is brimming with the conversation transcripts so the reader can read for themselves what was said by hundreds of Norwegians *in their own words*.

You will need to pay very close attention. You need to read the words carefully in these transcripts or you might *miss* what I teased out, a truth I had to work to get, as you will see for yourself. It was clear to me quite quickly that something wasn't right. Something was *off*. Don't take my word for it. Before we go further, here are 100 quotes from 100 Norwegians – taken completely randomly from these conversations: **read it for yourself.**

Authors note:

I would like to acknowledge the generosity and hospitality shown to me in Norway by many people including in particular in Kongsberg and the Kristiansund area. This book in no way is meant to diminish their kindness just as their kindness and generosity in no way are diminishing of the opinions of other Norwegians shared in this book. A country cannot be summarised in a book series. 'The Secret Norwegian' is a collection of individual opinions and these can only tell a small part of the story from the perspective of those biased individuals. Each person has their version of the truth. However, this does not necessarily mean that their perspectives are wrong even if they are indeed only 350 out of 5.368 million people living in Norway. It is for the reader to decide what they may think or feel based on what they read, for themselves.

100 Quotes from 100 Norwegians

1. *"F****** everyone is bullied in Norway!"*
Karsten, Psychology Student, twenty-two years old from Molde

2. *"Norwegians are antisocial… if you see your friends on the street then sometimes you try to avoid them and put your phone up and pretend that you don't see them."*
Olav, Trainee Pilot, nineteen years old from near Trondheim

3. *"One of the main things we want for mental health is a psychologist in every school because people need to talk with someone. Just like you are talking to us now."*
Seline, Student, nineteen years old from the north of Norway

4. *"It's just normal for us. It's just normal for us… we're just more honest… It's also just normal for us…"*
Ole, Student, eighteen years old from the north of Norway
(describing bullying in Norway.)

5. *"When I was younger there was a gang of boys. They would have competitions to see how many butts they could touch in a school day and we told our teachers and our teachers would just say, "Oh they are just flirting with you!" That's like the common… They don't want to "ruin it for the boy." If a girl has been sexually assaulted… it's always, "But he has a future, we can't do anything." We are like taught since we are children that is what boys do!"*
Nina, Student, fifteen years old from the north of Norway

6. *"If a boy sexually harasses you the teacher will almost always say, "That's just the way they are." If you get raped, they will instantly say, "What was she wearing?""*
Emma, Student, fifteen years old from the north of Norway

7. *"The meaning of words is created by the way we use them."*
Aksel, Linguistics Expert, twenty-eight years old, from the south of Norway

8. *"If somebody sexually abuses you, you are supposed to forgive, them the bible says… and in Norway we use the bible as the basis that we want to use for life… and ignore the other. This is my understanding of it. The way I see Norway… you should avoid conflict… you don't upset people… and that is the easier way… we have two types of people here, and one is the victim and one is the perpetrator."*
Nora, fifty years old, from the south of Norway

9. *"We spoke earlier about the issue of "loyalty", as you say, and "respect". It's a word that maybe we do not use so much because (loyalty) is not so common."*
Johan, Businessman, forty-seven years old, from rural Norway

10. *"If you speak to people you don't really know they think you're "crazy" or completely out of your mind… instead of being a nice person you become like a weird person."*
Petr, Student, fifteen years old from near Oslo

11. *"I visited Africa and there are things there which are better than here. They said that I was in paradise (Norway) and I told them, "Yes, in a way, I have won the lottery by being born in Norway." However, in Gambia if your neighbour is hungry they will find a 1kg bag of rice outside their house. I envy that. In Norway, your neighbour could be dead and they'd just complain about the smell."*
John, sixty-year-old, Businessman, near Drammen

12. *"There aren't many good teachers! They are like a paedophile, or they don't really care, they have this thing where they have physical education and they like have couples dancing, the teachers want to dance and like demonstrate with the most pretty girl, like with the best body and the big ass and big boobs because then they can get close. Nothing happens to those teachers. They are not teachers because they love children or do what they love because they want to teach… they are basically a teacher because they did not know what they wanted to be!"*
Julia, Student, sixteen years old, near Oslo

13. *"I think that one of the biggest taboos in Norway and this kind of relates to the Janteloven thing, is that you cannot talk about yourself."*
Julia, Student, sixteen years old, near Oslo

14. *"In our school... when a girl gets a better grade than a boy... the boys will be like "It's just because you are a girl" and if it's a male teacher than it's the same way, "It's just because you are a girl and our teacher is a paedophile." I know that the girls got better grades than the boys, and I know that if there are girls in the class that are like small and don't have the body form – they will get less grades."*
Hanne, Student, sixteen years old, near Oslo

15. *"It's wrong to show emotions."*
Hanne, Student, sixteen years old, near Oslo

16. *"This is the land of the Janteloven, if you want sympathy and compassion you have come to the wrong place."*
Helene, Hotel Owner, fifty years old, near Lillehammer

17. *"It is pretty much bull****! I think that in Norway we have this fake sense of modesty... like we kind of want it so, but deep down we just want to brag about... It's a d*ck-measuring contest."*
Raj, seventeen years old, Student from near Kristiansand

18. *"I think... I know that I am spoilt! Yes... really spoilt... I am! I really am! I think I'm very lucky. When I watch my car out there I feel very lucky. When I go home I feel lucky. When I see my dog I feel lucky because we get everything we want here in Norway (giggle). A Norwegian walking in London, walking down Regent Street, I would say, "We own the street!""*
Ingrid, twenty-five years old, Oil Industry Worker, south of Norway

19. *"It's very racist! But it's not even down to colour. It's any kind of foreigner. I have grown up with that my whole life because I have a foreign surname from my ancestor. So foreigners in Norway often change their name to a Norwegian sounding name... just to get your foot in the door."*
Ragnhild, forty-five years old, Museum Worker, rural Norway

20. *"I think that they know what they're doing but they don't know that it is wrong because they are the generation that grow up and they feel entitled. You have the adults who are kind of spoiling them, considering the background, they grew up with parents that were not so ready to talk about their emotions, the feelings, especially here in this part of the world… is like you keep your mouth shut about struggles."*
Christian, fifty years old, Educational Leader, Oslo

21. *"We only care to know other people when it will profit us."*
Elise, Student, twenty-two years old from Alta

22. *"I think, Norwegians are nice people, and we like to help and also we have the luxury to help in Norway, of course… we have a lot more privilege then most of the world and most of the people, of course, in Norway we know that."*
Karl, twenty-two years old, Charity Worker, More og Romsdal

23. *"The social interaction is Norway is strange because even I find it strange at times. For example, yesterday I was in the supermarket and an old school friend saw me and I saw him. He pretended not to see me and turned away. We both knew that we saw each other but there is this thing where this is done in Norway."*
Julia, twenty-six years old, Police Officer near Oslo

24. *"Norwegians will always tell you what you want to hear when you ask them a question. The second time you ask them they will tell you to go away. The third time you ask when they realise that you won't go away is when they will tell you the truth. I never tell the truth when asked if I am doing fine. I always say that I am doing great even when I am not. In fact, I never feel great but I just say it anyway. I never even think about it because it just comes out automatically. I feel that I am a burden on others."*
Elsa, fifty years old, Management, near Drammen

25. *"(Norwegians) We are not spontaneous because we are stable."*
Helen, forty-seven years old, Tonsberg

26. *"The Norwegian media are very loyal."*
Hector, fifty years old, Computer Programmer (explaining Norway's "Code of silence")

27. *"Norway has always been the underdog – until we got the oil."*
Dr Anon, forty-seven years old, Surgeon from Oslo

28. *"No… they are Norwegian, they don't do that here."*
Kate, forty years old, Jehovah Witness (asked if they are "treated kindly in Norway?")

29. *"If I was raped now I would never go to the police. In Norway the community supports the rapists… it's this thing called Janteloven. It has destroyed my life."*
Anne, forty years old, rape victim, Norway

30. *"I find it hard to connect to Norwegians… they are so weak! I am ashamed of being Norwegian."*
Bridget, twenty-three years old, Office Worker, Stavanger

31. *"We Norwegians are pretty secluded… Like 'OK… Stranger… Stranger danger! I would say that most are pretty racist."*
Nora, sixteen-year-old, Student, near Bergen

32. *"It's this picture of the perfect country. We're Norway! We're rich we've got a lot of money… "Perfect" and nothing's bad in the country… So basically everything that's bad gets covered up."*
Kimmy, eighteen years old, Lifeguard, Trondheim

33. *"I would say that Norwegians are like this: they don't realise that some things they say are offensive… racism is written inside our constitution."*
Henrietta, twenty-five-year-old Historian, Norway

34. *"It makes it easier that I can just not be a Sami… I can just choose to not show it to anyone, or not tell."*
Flora, Sami lady, thirty years old in the Arctic, north Norway (The Sami are the indigenous people of Norway.)

35. *"In Norway we just want to be nice to everybody and we just want to have "friends", and we don't want to have enemies, that's why we don't say anything..."*
Tuva, sixteen years old, near Oslo

36. *"We have like an expression in Norway called "ferlsum" and that means that you are weak, and yeah, you are feeling like you are showing your emotions."*
Hanne, sixteen years old, near Oslo

37. *"The people at the bottom of the scale... I know you don't like the word but we would call them "retards". There are the retards, the middle people and the popular class, so the retards basically they have a great life. The middle classes, they have good friends, they have a good life. The people who have a bad life are the popular people who are not at the top."*
Sarah, sixteen years old, near Oslo, describing the hierarchy in school.

38. *"We are not exactly a culture where we are socially taught how to listen. People in Norway... are really closed off. We don't talk about things. We are more push things under the rug, because of the Janteloven. We want to keep the Picture Perfect, oh Norway, nationalism!"*
Kim, twenty-five-year-old, Student, Tromso

39. *"Nationalism and patriotism... That is the thing about our country too... We won't scream in your face but we will just be passive aggressive about it, in the way that we respond. Everything that is Norwegian (is the best)... And that's just how we are. That's also the way we are with each other..."*
Elle, twenty-five-year-old, Student Tromso

40. *"It is! That's what keeps the country kind of going! Because on the one hand it suppresses you, but on the other hand, my neighbour is just as good as me, that's why it's actually a big support system... when people say that they don't "believe" in Janteloven, they still do it. Because it is taught in this unspoken way. Because children grow up in the way that their parents do things and that's the way they do it. There is freedom of expression here, you can do whatever you want, you can wear whatever you would like, you will never be bullied."*
Kjersti, Museum Worker, twenty-five years old, south of Norway

41. *"Almost every job that a young person has is acquired by family (connections)… almost all young adults. Their jobs are always acquired from family."*
"Miss Anon", Royal Property Worker, twenty-five years old talking about "equality" and how people really get their jobs in Norway

42. *"I used to live in north… I am from the south… So I speak an Oslo dialect but living in the north, we were called "Goddamn southerners!" And one guy told me that "Norway was shaped like a bin bag with all the s*** on the bottom…"I told them that they are a "goddamn Sami!"… because they don't want to be called Sami if they are not Sami."*
Sara, Archaeologist, forty-five years old

43. *"I think it's we are the "best" – period. Not so sure we compare to Sweden anymore. I see this attitude, and I see an arrogance and laziness that we will continue to be the "best". I think we can easily hit the wall here."*
Vilde, forty-five years old, Teacher

44. *"Being a Norwegian, you are brought up with this set of traits of a "typical Norwegian" which you bring with you when you are introduced to somebody new… that is something common for all Norwegians. It's something that you need to have or that you inherently have… we Norwegians, we come with this identity of what Norway is."*
Anon, forty years old, Svalbard University

45. *"I am a proud racist. I don't care. I don't want any Muslims in my country… we have too many already! All of the migrants can go back home, we don't want them here. Our politicians are a disgrace… tactics… it's all a game for them. Send them to the Arabia!"*
Ole, seventy years old, More Og Romsdal

46. *"We are Norwegians, we don't talk… we sit quietly and drink our coffee."*
Passive aggressive, Kongsberg Café Waiter, nineteen years old

47. *"It's like living in hell here. Stay here for some time and you will see. My neighbour is a policeman and harasses me. My neighbours hate me and gossip about me. I don't have any friends here. I want to leave Norway and move to Bali."*
Ylva, thirty-nine years old, rural Norway

48. *"If you assault somebody in Norway you will never go to jail. You will never go to jail for assault or beating somebody up in the street."*
Magnus, Archaeologist, twenty-eight years old, middle Norway

49. *"Never tell a Norwegian the truth. Never! They just want to be told nice things and feel warm and cosy."*
Ola, Kristiansund, Artist, twenty-eight years old

50. *"Norwegians are cowards when sober."*
Eve, Kristiansund, twenty-one years old.

51. *"I'm myself living in the forest because I need peace and quiet... I got burned out a couple of years ago... It's so hard since we get our worthiness in this society by doing and so many people around me are doing the same thing... you know how it is here, quiet, dark, a lot of drunk people."*
Celine, Journalist, twenty-seven years old, Bergen

52. *"We have this abnormal celebration national day. It gets more and more abnormal for each year. Now "The Scream" has taken over us..."*
Magnus, seventy-nine years old, Alesund

53. *"I was born this way and I was born with Sami in my family and my grandparents... And they never learnt Sami because of that (the abuse) they never learnt the language... my grandpa's dad went to Norwegian school where they were they were abused for speaking Sami... and their culture and stuff like that... So he never learnt Sami and my dad never learn Sami... And I never learn Sami from my dad, or, you know... They were talking to me like as if I was a foreign man... I was bullied for that."*
Jens, eighteen years old, Sami village Arctic

54. *"That's the thing about Norwegians... we're cold, we're distant and we just keep to ourselves... here in Norway, we have a saying that if you are on the bus and somebody that you don't know is sitting next to you, instead of asking them to get up when you want to leave you will just continue riding the bus. Because we're so shy and we're so scared."*
Erin, Waitress, twenty-five years old, Longyearbyen, Svalbard

55. *"It's a game. We would never use anything personal against an opponent even if we have something on them. When I see my opponent (redacted), doing (redacted) event and smiling and waving, in the newspaper I laugh because I know that he hates that! It's just a game for press and media and then I will do something in return which he will see!"*
Thor, forty years old, Local Political Candidate, near Oslo

56. *"It's always somebody else's fault in Norway, never your own... always someone else."*
Marie, Jockey, twenty-five years old, middle Norway

57. *"It's not like Norwegian tradition is racism but they want Norway to be the best and they don't want people from other countries to come and ruin the country..."*
Thea, sixteen years old, Kongsberg

58. *"(Bullying)... is everywhere, yes!"*
Nils, forty years old approx., Lofoten

59. *"I say that he needs to walk away but he does not do that. He says, "It's is my job" and I say, "Is it your job to make me feel uncomfortable?" But he says, "No it's my job to help you"... too close to the comfort zone... and we had someone talking to us about a ring zone and if someone breaks it, and you don't feel comfortable, they should walk away... But he breaks it every time and that is why I have to go in the room with the other people."*
Thomas, fourteen years old, talking about his school teacher making him feel "uncomfortable"

60. *"Nope, nothing lost in translation. The further definition of empathy is "from within their frame of reference, that is, the capacity to place oneself in another's position". I still don't think Norwegians are good at being empathetic because we often fail in this part of the definition. A lot of Norwegians do not see things from the perspective of others (within their frame of reference), but tend to instead bring our own point of view into the mix."*
Siri, Teacher, forty-five years old, explaining lack of empathy in Norway

61. *"It's amazing... in minutes you are describing the last fifteen years here exactly! I never tell my neighbours anything personal because I know they will use it against me and gossip to the whole town. I keep myself to myself and am friendly every now and again... but I know never to trust them."*
Mona, Farmer, forty-five years old, rural Norway

62. *"Our teacher bullies a girl who is disabled and in a wheelchair. He makes her do things that he knows she cannot do"*
Linn, Student, eighteen years old, Trondheim

63. *"You're very right about conformism and lack of dissent. Why question a system that's working so well? We're all rich from oil anyway. It's one of the things that just kills me about my culture (I like money. Just really dislike collectivism/complacency). Took a looong time for me to even begin to question whether there could be something wrong with the whole social narrative instead of just me. So now I'm loud, trying to shake my fellow countrymen. Wake up."*
Marius, twenty-five years, Norway

64. *"No... I'm drawing a blank, I'm not sure, I'm sorry."*
Central Oslo Bookshop ("Do you have any serious books about Norwegians or Norwegian culture?")

65. *"Norway can't do real because they're too harsh and so they keep everything comic and light."*
Oslo Airport Bookshop ("Do you have any serious books about Norwegians or Norwegian culture?")

66. *"No, we don't have those. We're horrible people so we have to be ironic."*
Central Oslo Bookshop ("Do you have any serious books about Norwegians or Norwegian culture?")

67. *"No, actually I don't think we have any... we have to maintain an illusion to survive."*
Central Oslo Bookshop ("Do you have any serious books about Norwegians or Norwegian culture?")

68. *"Sometimes I think that I am not Norwegian because I like to express my feelings and I like to be happy..."*
Norwegian Bookshop Seller, twenty-eight years old

69. *"No, no, no. We can't write that. That goes against all of our social laws for us to write it."*
Oslo Bookshop ("Can't a Norwegian write a serious book about Norwegians or Norwegian culture?")

70. *"Very interesting to hear your experience from talking to Norwegians. I get some of the same comments, which indicates that there is something here..."*
Professor Anon, Norway

71. *"Make sure that you double check his sources."*
Bookseller in Stavanger, undermining a professor who wrote a mildly critical book of Norway

72. *"I think overall Norwegians hate talking to people, on average... I think it's very sad actually. Maybe that is a reason why I love travelling? Unfortunately, I have no explanation for why, I also want to know why we/they hate talking to people (I can't relate)."*
Silvia, seventeen years old, Bergen

73. *"I'm Norwegian! We are crazy in Norway."*
Supermarket Worker, twenty years old, Norway

74. *"Bullying is everywhere in this country."*
Cristina, Gallery Worker, twenty-seven years old, South of Norway

75. *"There are a lot of stereotypes about the north in Norway so when you come to the north and you speak to the people, when you speak to people in the south about the people in the north, they're almost always wrong... because they don't understand the culture for us north Norwegians."*
Lars, Student, twenty-two years old, Finmark, Norway

76. *"They don't include us in the history... even though the officials have worked on it the last few years, still there is a lot of discrimination"*
Stian, Student, twenty-three years old, Finmark, Norway

77. *"Finmark has always been isolated from the rest of Norway and if you listen to our parents and grandparents, Finmark has always been excluded from the rest of Norway... when the reparations were paid they said let's not pay Finnmark because they are used to being cold and having a sh*t*ss life."*
Marianne, Student, twenty-five years old, Finmark, Norway

78. *"Norwegians don't open up to anybody. When I came from Hauguesland I couldn't make any friends because people were so closed knit and they didn't let me into their friends."*
Lilian, Academic, thirty-five years old, south of Norway

79. *"...all of this "happiest" and "luckiest" country in the world kind of also makes us think that our problems are not top priority."*
Helene, Psychology Student, twenty-five years old

80. *"We do have a book on the history of skiing (bursts out laughing)."*
Bookshop Seller, Kristiansand ("Do you have any serious books about Norwegians or Norwegian culture?")

81. *"You're so polite... so many "please" and "thank you", we don't get that so much in Norway. They're very polite but rude and stressed out, sometimes they don't say thank you or anything."*
Mohammed, twenty-one years old, Oslo Airport Worker

82. *"I've travelled all over Norway, everywhere in a camper van. In the north they are friendly and open and let me use their shower and park my van but in the south, they just shake your hand and that's it. Much more selfish in the south and more selfish inwards away from the coastal areas. 100% I have seen it and I know it, this is something which I know for sure."*
Stein, Stonemason, sixty years old, rural Norway

83. *"Are we sociopaths? If we are standing at the bus stop there is a very very very very tiny chance that those two will start to talk, or starting to talk with one another, very small, it's like, 'Ooh! I've never seen them before.'"*
Bookshop Seller, western Norway.

84. *"No... I don't think so... people only want to know about trolls and Vikings... I don't think we have one... I don't think we have any in this*

store"
Bookshop seller, Molde ("Do you have any serious books about Norwegians or Norwegian culture?")

85. *"Brown cheese."*
Live, sixteen years old. "Can you name five traits of a typical Norwegian?" (Full answer.)

86. *"Norwegians are afraid to talk to each other; we always stand metres away from each other in queues and use the second seat on the bus for baggage so no one will sit."*
Hilde, sixteen years old, Oslo

87. *"I don't really care if someone doesn't say hi to me… I just let it pass."*
Ruth, sixteen years old, Oslo

88. *"I think we complain a lot because we are used to getting what we need and most of the people living in Norway live a very good life, and when things don't work out the way we want it to, we often get mad and start to complain about it… Something else I think of often and makes us complain is that it seems like it's never "our fault", if you understand what I mean. No matter what happens, many Norwegians always find ways to put the blame on someone else… Another thing we do is for example if we break something in a store. Normally I think people would say that they unfortunately managed to break something, that they are very sorry for it and that they are going to pay for what they broke, but in Norway, many people would just put the thing they broke back where they found it and leave without taking any responsibility for their actions."*
Linn, sixteen years old, Oslo

89. *"A Norwegian man was the only passenger on a bus. An Indian man entered, saw the Norwegian man and all those empty seats. Thinking the Norwegian man must be lonely, he sat down next to him! That of course made the Norwegian man feel extremely uncomfortable and most likely he thought the Indian man was slightly crazy! Typical example of cultural misunderstanding, due to different expectations, different unwritten social norms. We all see the world through cultural glasses. Norwegians feel*

uncomfortable having a stranger sitting so close, they need more space, but it's very different if it's a friend or relative."
Elisabeth, forty-five years old, Artist

90. *"(Norwegians are)... Proud, silent, honest, happy and friendly and in general disappointed that nobody really understand that and actually see it."*
Daniel, forty-three years old, Businessman

91. *"A typical Norwegian would be handsome, nice, funny, arrogant and often sarcastic. I think Norwegians are known for being arrogant."*
Rolf, fourteen years old

92. *"(Norwegians) Don't greet strangers on the street and eats brown cheese."*
Grete, twenty-two years old ("Can you name five traits of a typical Norwegian?")

93. *"I think we (Norwegians) simply don't engage much thought in what we do and how we behave at daily basis."*
Lise, twenty years old, Dancer

94. *"Yes, most Norwegians do not have an emotional response, especially in public view if the emotional response is rational. I talked to my mom the other day, and she mentioned something very interesting about publicly mourning the dead in Norway. When someone dies and make the news, there are often masses of people that go out and show their emotions of pain publicly. The pain they express in tears is not necessarily because someone died, but the death of someone to mourn for is an excuse to express all the sorrows and pain they usually suppress. If all these people were so damn happy and bonded with these people, they would've spent more time with them and showed their emotions for them while they were still alive which is often not the case. There is a disturbing lack of emotional response in the Norwegian society, the most common real emotions are anger and sadness. Most people of course try to hide these too, but when someone gets pushed past a certain point, their emotions will get the "best" of them. It is scary and frustrating that this is how Norwegians react to the truth, they are missing out on the solutions. They might not want to go along with the truth because*

we live in 'one of the best countries in the world.'"
Thomas, twenty-seven years old

95. *"Most people in Norway believe in what makes them feel good. Some few are aware that they are playing a game with themselves."*
Linda, fifty years old

96. *"Norwegian equals proud of being Norwegian, a bit cocky and self-centred, wants to be a World Champion in every field... again, these are too complex issues for me."*
Jenny, fifty year-old, Musician ("Can you name five traits of a typical Norwegian?")

97. *"I think that being poor is such a big taboo that people end up in huge credit card debts because they hide the fact that they are really poor..."*
Mary, twenty-five years old

98. *"Even if we have the cars, we have the money, we have the houses but still we are in a survival mode! We have maybe not come out of the survival mode yet..."*
Ove, fifty years old, Fisherman

99. *"When it comes to that Norway has the worst rape statistics... like one in ten of the cases actually get reported... And there are very few people that actually get jailed for rape..."*
Rape victim, Norway, twenty-five years old

100. *"When it comes to politics, I like to think that I have a self-reflective way about seeing things... I think I can see what's wrong and what's not working, and I think that the school system is horrendous!"*
Petter, seventeen years old, Student

Breaking the Curse of Janteloven

"Anthony, you should write a book about Norway." It was a friend's daughter who first suggested this, as we drove across Norway. I looked at her, at first unconvinced before she added, "You know more about Norway than most Norwegians!" It was true, I had taught a lot of Norwegians and extensively travelled the country, but that didn't mean I had something to say about Norway. At the time I was having a year off: a break from teaching people how to dance in London, and to finish two books, one on *High Functioning Autism Spectrum Disorder* and the other on *Dance History*. As we talked we discussed what I could write about if I *did* write about Norway, a travelogue maybe, a few Norwegian cultural idiosyncrasies? But I decided that I couldn't really add anything to what was already out there. If that was Norway, then it had already been written.

Over the next few weeks, however, I played with some ideas, identified possible subjects; the kinds of things that usually formed the focus of a book about Norway, for example, skiing, trolls, cabins, hiking, Christmas cake, even the way Norwegians behave. I left the list on my table. However, as I worked on my other books, I uncovered something quite surprising. The things that I was writing about in my *High Functioning Autism Spectrum Disorder Book* were frequently the same things that I was observing in a great deal of Norwegians and even often heard Norwegians talk about themselves, inadvertently.

So I consciously made a point of observing *every single Norwegian* I met. I quickly noticed things I had not seen before. I really started listening to Norwegians and not only listening to the *exact words* they were using but also observing their body language and demeanour. I have always known how to 'breakthrough' to Scandinavians. In fact, I've taught many thousands of Scandinavians, both in the Scandinavian countries and in London. Teaching school groups of Norwegian children to team-building for the Swedish to teaching master classes in Denmark and beyond.

I first travelled to the Nordic countries when I was seven years old. I delved beyond the Arctic Circle in Finland and from there to Norway, to Denmark and to Sweden extensively. When you constantly teach groups from all over the world you quickly notice that the Scandinavian groups often have *a totally different method of interaction* than the rest of the world. I have always been cognizant of that, and over the years I have acquired a wealth of experience in how to break down those walls in such a way that many Scandinavians have opened up to me and trusted me, often in a way that they wouldn't do in their day-to-day lives.

To aid my research, I also tried to acquire books that looked at the behaviour of Norwegians, in a social, political, even historical context. I walked into sixty-seven bookshops across Norway, posing the same simple question every time: **"Do you have any books about the Norwegian people and its culture, please?"**

In sixty-six out of those sixty-seven bookshops, I was directed to well-promoted displays complete with stuffed trolls holding Norwegian flags – but no "serious" books. What these displays held were a small number of comedic, humorous and offensive stereotypical books, predominantly authored by non-Norwegians. They were thin volumes, often filled with cartoon pictures; they were certainly not the books on culture or societal development I sought. I'd tell them again I was looking for **a serious book written about the Norwegian people**. This drew blank stares. I was told by one bookseller, "No, we don't have those. We're horrible people so we have to be ironic." I asked booksellers, "Why are you even promoting offensive stereotypes about yourselves? Look at these: you're promoting books that portray Norwegians as unemotional psychopaths, why?" One answered me directly, "Because we are psychopaths." I asked her if I could record our conversation and she, surprisingly, said yes.

I spent hours and hours talking to booksellers across Norway before I decided to travel further. I even walked into eleven bookshops in Stockholm, Sweden and asked them the same question. They had no books to offer me either but they certainly had a lot to say about their Norwegian neighbours… as you will see later.

I set out to find out **what was being hidden about Norway and its people** and why were there seemingly no serious books on Norway and its culture in its bookshops? That's how I came to travel so extensively and interview 350 people: to get to the truth.

It wasn't easy because even trying to simply discuss Norway in any meaningful way often seemed to invoke fear. **But why?**

At first, many people I talked with were **not candid**. In fact, that was almost unanimous, initially. I was aware but I knew how to push through to get to the truth. I simply asked the same question again until they realised I wasn't going to accept a "stock" answer or an untruth. That is when so many Norwegians finally opened up to me. Only then did it seem they trusted me enough to tell me the truth. On so many occasions it was as if they were suddenly liberated from invisible shackles because once they started, they didn't want to stop; what's more, they allowed our conversations to be recorded. As you will see as you read on, I identify in the many conversations defining moments – the turning points or breakthroughs in the conversations when finally we were getting to the truth nearly all concealed so deeply. You won't believe what you read. Remember – these are *their* words.

Many Norwegians often use these adjectives to describe themselves: "crazy", "special" and even "weird"– terms you will see a lot in the transcripts. I've even read foreign authors and bloggers unashamedly portray this as a *positive* thing. This is often propagated by self-proclaimed experts of the often lauded "Nordic lifestyle" within Norway, Denmark, Sweden and beyond. Indeed the one book I've since found – one book – written by an actual Norwegian, describes Norwegians as "special people" in its opening pages. He goes on to say that Norwegians have "developed our own norms, rituals and unwritten social rules". Norwegian author, Elise H Kollerud, tells us that learning these "unwritten laws" is difficult and that "almost no Norwegians will tell foreigners about them". Now we were getting somewhere. But why would this book, called *The 100 Unwritten Norwegian Social Rules* need to be written in the first place and why would any Norwegian intentionally choose not to "tell foreigners" about them? I have also learned there are companies in Norway that actually train people in "working with Norwegians" as doing so, in their own words, may cause "frustration and confusion" in people from other cultures – **why?**

What are the mental health consequences of concealing these Norwegian "unwritten rules" on non-Norwegians or indeed Norwegians? Norway is often voted as one the "happiest" countries in the world; why, then would the Prime Minister of Norway tell me directly, **"From next year there is a law that makes it mandatory for all municipalities to have psychologists"**? If it's the happiest place on earth, why is the anti-depressant medication use so high in Norway?

It seems to me from my discoveries, that there is an open secret in Norway held together tentatively by fear. The ONLY book that has a mild criticism of

Norway that I could find was a book by Norwegian Professor Harald N Røstvik from Stavanger, Norway. It was not available in a single one of the sixty-seven bookshops in Norway that I visited, and it was not available anywhere in Norway that I could find. In fact, when I asked for it in the professor's home town, the bookseller told me unashamedly, "Make sure you check his sources." They don't trust him?

It is not widely known but Norway is actually one of the world's most conformist countries and cultures with the some of the strictest social "rules". A 2011 study entitled "Differences Between Tight and Loose Cultures A 33-Nation Study" even placed Norway amongst Pakistan, India, South Korea and Malaysia. A Norwegian professor said that it was "a surprising result". Associate Professor Vidar Schei is reported to have said to **nhh.no**: "The researchers cannot find a simple explanation of why the social norms in Norway are so strong."

If the professor would have simply looked back into history he would have found that this is not the first time Norway and Norwegians have been categorised in such a way. A 1962 study by one of the world's most renowned psychologists, Stanley Milgram, in his conformity experiments involving Norwegians, stated that he was "puzzled" by the way that Norwegians "often voted with the group" and exhibited "fear" of their private disagreements being known to the "group" even when he assured them that they could answer in confidence and "that the responses would be privately analysed" only. Interestingly, I can find no trace or reference of this experiment in Norway in any capacity. I can find evidence of Stanley Milgram's other experiments, in Norway but strangely not the one that relates to the Norwegians themselves.

There is a Nordic 'code of conduct' called 'Jante Law' or the 'Janteloven'. In short, it's a social attitude governed by rules such as a disapproval of individuality and personal success, an emphasis on adherence to the collective. You can find more information about this if you research. I began to realise that what I was seeing as I met and interviewed the overwhelming majority of the respondents was almost certainly *Janteloven* personified. It may well explain why I was generally finding a country of people living in fear and in denial. So many people I met across Norway seemed to live compartmentalised lives with no awareness of their actual place in the world, of their local community, even of what was going on inside their own families. And perhaps, more alarmingly, unaware of what is going on inside their own minds, as you will read for yourself. I believe it accounts for the way the history of the country is being written, the manner in which it is promoted and explains the ubiquitous bullying, blatant racism and overt xenophobia I have witnessed first-hand in **all** parts of Norway that I visited.

A toxic environment will arise where abuse is normalised and that seemed to be what I was seeing. I also believe that in Norway this is often denied, enabled, and covered up. I have encountered stories of bullying, paedophilia and abuse in almost every place I visited and I have intentionally decided to focus this book series away from the sensational because if I focussed on those it would be a book series merely about abuse.

Despite my findings, generally speaking, I got the impression that so many of the Norwegians are some of the most generous people I have ever met. They are hard-working – I saw this in all ages. I have had the privilege of meeting surgeons who dedicate their lives to helping others with barely any appreciation or acknowledgement. I have met headteachers who hardly sleep so that they can teach their pupils and run schools, again, with nobody to tell them "well done"… they just do it from a sense of duty. I have been overwhelmed by the intelligence of the children of Norway. Their strength, their fortitude and their intellect. They are a credit to their country. But I've seen that brightness snuffed out too many times in my journey.

My hope is that from what you learn here, change can be effected and I believe it must. I believe that the Norwegians that do read these books will be better and stronger for it. I have changed names and removed/disguised identifiers to preserve anonymity **but the words are theirs**. I hope that by someone daring to reveal the truth it will make it easier to reject the indoctrination of the disgraceful unspoken 'rules' of oppression: Janteloven.

I hope that this book series can facilitate the complete eradication of the cursed Janteloven, not only in Norway but in the whole of Scandinavia.

A Conversation with the Prime Minister of Norway

The Prime Minister of Norway, Erna Solberg, was kind enough to briefly answer some of my questions during my visit. I explained that I was writing a book about Norway and she seemed very happy to speak with me. The Prime Minister of Norway is the head of the government and is appointed by the monarch. Erna Solberg is fifty-eight years old, has held office since 16 October 2013; the head of the Conservative Party. She was born in Bergen, which is on the west coast of Norway. Surprisingly the Norwegians, including party members that I spoke to, tended to be rude and derogatory about their Prime Minister, and did so without prompting. I spent significant time socially with local "pillars of the community" in a particularly affluent area and they repeatedly cast aspersions. This did seem odd because the same individuals implied they were friends. They were not aware, and neither was I, that forty-eight hours later I would be meeting and interviewing her. Fortunately for them, I didn't discuss this; choosing instead to speak with her about the most pressing issue that I had seen in Norway: bullying and mental health.

Anthony:
Prime Minister, can I ask you a quick question?
I'm writing a book about Norway.

Prime Minister:
OK.

Anthony:
Mental health. Is that an important issue for the government?

Prime Minister:
Yes, it's a very important issue for the Norwegian Government. We've been having an action plan to work with mental health especially among the

municipalities and among others who have low-threshold activities, so that people can easily get in touch with it… From next year there is a law that makes it mandatory for all municipalities to have psychologists in there.

Anthony:
Yes.

Prime Minister:
Municipality Healthcare… And then we have been working especially focussing on youth health, because we see that the pressure that young people are under.

Anthony:
There is a lot of bullying!

Prime Minister:
Well it's bullying… but it's also about, review of your own body… This…

Anthony:
Yes.

Prime Minister:
And into our schools we will have what we call "life training", which will be part of your—

Anthony:
Curriculum?

Prime Minister:
Curriculum.

Anthony:
Wow.

Prime Minister:
On all levels so, you will learn about mental health and about how mental diseases develop and you can take care of your mental health and understanding more of that into that subject.

Anthony:
Thank you so much, Prime Minister… Thank you.

A Conversation with a Psychology Student

Karsten Magnus is approximately twenty years old and is from Oslo. We were talking at a location some distance from Oslo, on the other side of Norway, which will remain undisclosed. I have changed certain details to protect his identity. What's interesting is that this conversation arose from a *completely* random encounter. Earlier in the day I had carried out six hours of interviews with Norwegians describing bullying and abuse. This interview was with the hotel receptionist where I was staying. When I mentioned what I was doing, she said that she would love to talk with me and share her experiences with me. You will read her story later in these books. However, before retiring to my room, mulling over the day's interviews, I went for a walk to get some food and that's how I met Karsten.

There was a group of three people in the street and I told them of my intentions for the book. They all said they would love to talk to me. I took out the tape recorder and interviewed the three of them right there. One of the three was clearly 'performing'. She was talking about the "plight" of a certain group in Norwegian society. She even said that it was so important to her that she'd love to email me and send me all the information that she had, that she was so passionate about it. Her friends were in agreement with her, but she was leading the group. I was initially convinced by her so I emailed her the following day. She replied: *"What is the intention of this book?"* I wrote that *"I am writing a book about Norway and Norwegians in their own words… so anything you want to tell me, I will listen to."* She then replied, *"I can't help with this. Good luck"*. She was twenty-three years old… this, I had learned was why you also need to speak with people **on their own** and not just in front of their peer groups.

However, during that conversation we had an eavesdropper. After the group walked away, seemingly very pleased with themselves, Karsten Magnus, walked up to me very shyly and said, "Thank you for doing what you are doing." This is that conversation.

Anthony:
We just had a discussion about your trip to England, you told me that you are from Oslo, we discussed where we are right now, you told me some of the challenges you have had, and I told you to be strong and you told me that it was "hard to be yourself in Norway"?

Karsten:
It is hard!

Anthony:
Tell me why?

Karsten:
OK, because in Norway... and I don't know if it's like this in other countries... but whatever it is, if you are different they latch onto it!

Anthony:
And what are the consequences of being "different"? They latch on in what way? What do they do to you?

Karsten:
They f****** bully you! They bully you into the ground! If you have glasses... You are f*****! If you are a little bit smarter than anyone else... You're f*****! You're then the "bookworm!"

Anthony:
Karsten, can I ask you directly, have they bullied you?

Karsten:
They bullied me! Luckily my dad is a Norwegian Air Force soldier! I went to self-defence since I was six years old, so I knew how to defend myself.

Anthony:
Karsten, can I just say that I'm sorry and I'm sorry that you had to deal with this.

Karsten:
Whatever it is... Being in an interview with you right now... It's f****** legendary!

Anthony:
Everybody says that bullying is an issue?

Karsten:
It's f****** awful! Yes! I have been in England and I have heard about the mental health issues in England.

Anthony:
Is it different in Norway?

Karsten:
It's different.

Anthony:
Janteloven? It's "normal" to abuse people?

Karsten:
Yes! That's what it is… I'm going to tell you right now… abuse! My dad is a Norwegian Air Force soldier, so obviously he wanted me to be in the military but if, in Norway, if you have mental health help after the age of eighteen there is zero chance of you getting into the military.

Anthony:
Why?

Karsten:
They don't want to take the responsibility for someone that is mentally handicapped into the military!

Anthony:
That to me sounds like textbook discrimination.

Karsten:
Yes, it is. I went to mental health help for a myriad of reasons, but even if I was just a little bit socially anxious and I went to mental health.

Anthony:
They would dismiss you?

Karsten:
You're out of the f***** book!

Anthony:
Can I tell you something? I have noticed that the empathy level of the people that have been bullied seems to be significantly higher than certain others in Norway?

Karsten:
Yes! Don't you f***** know it!

Anthony:
Because they know how it feels? They don't want to live in that way and treat others like that... am I right?

Karsten:
You are right! When I was in fifth grade they tried to do this like anonymous bullying test.

Anthony:
But what difference does it make when so many teachers are bullies too?

Karsten:
It's f***** true! And I wrote on the back of my test... and it was supposed to be anonymous... but I wrote my identity to try and get my teachers to pay attention to what was going on... nothing was done! I was beat up when I was in fifth grade... It was a f***** gang! A gang ganged up around me and they were like cheering on for me to get beaten up! Since I went to martial arts because of my dad I beat the s*** out of my bullies! Students, they learnt their lesson... but teachers... did not. I had to apologise to *my* bully!

Anthony:
Can I ask you a question, I have observed regularly on my travels and conversations that many Norwegians describe that the "perpetrator" is elevated and the "victim" is undermined on so many occasions... is that true?

Karsten:
100%!

Anthony:
It's the culpability, it's the enabling, it's the community that enables the abuse?

Karsten:
Yes!

Anthony:
Do people make it so it's not a conducive environment for victims?

Karsten:
If you tell the teacher then the teacher doesn't do anything and then the bullies beat you up... expose this! Bullying brought me here... I've had to rise above bullies... I've had to rise above social anxiety... I've had to rise above depression... and I'm studying psychology as a bachelor and I'm going to save the world from the same f****** mistakes!

Anthony:
I need to ask you... I am going to be attacked for talking about these things, right?

Karsten:
I hope not... but of course it's going to happen.

Anthony:
They are going to say that "he found people to say these things... not everybody has been bullied... he has gone out and found the only person that has been bullied... statistics clearly show that hardly anyone is bullied in Norway!" What would you say to those people right now?

Karsten:
F****** everyone is bullied in Norway! It's disgusting, honestly! And the fact that teachers and officials don't do anything about it... It's morbid!

Anthony:
And to the people that deny that what would you say?

Karsten:
I would say honestly... excuse my language... excuse my French... but go f*** yourself!

Anthony:
How do you feel about expressing this to me today?

Karsten:
I think that it's very shameful that it takes someone from outside Norway to expose the atrocities, within accepted Norwegian society. I hope… I hope this gets somewhere, man! I hope that people… I hope that somebody takes hold of this and fixes it, because if there's one thing in Norwegian politics that nobody wants to take hold off, it's bullying.

Anthony:
Which is exactly why I raised it directly with the Prime Minister of Norway.

Karsten:
What did she say?

Anthony:
She gave a Prime ministerial answer.

Karsten:
Exactly! "Trying to do something about it but it's hard to fix bullying"… Yeah yeah yeah!

A Conversation with a Trainee Helicopter Pilot

I sat down to speak with Olav near Trondheim when I paid a visit to a helipad and he explained to me the *ins and outs* of aviation. At nineteen years of age he was a very insightful young man.

I am going to add commentary to the interviews from this point, which will come in the form of an "Author's note or Observation" and subsequent observations labelled as *"(AN – observation.)"*. As you will see I have set out dialogue in a way that I hope makes it easier for the reader to follow as if listening in. I appreciate that the repetition and disfluencies (oohs, hmms, like…) that form part of the normal inflections of speech, usually edited out, are almost always left in, as much as possible, because these are taken directly from the recordings of the actual conversations. This also includes the phrasing when English is not the first language. Again all left in to avoid any misinterpretation. I will point out certain phrases or words which the Norwegian respondents say which may be of specific interest to the reader.

Olav:
Norwegians are antisocial… It's just a general thing.

Anthony:
Tell me more?

Olav:
Well, I can give you an examples… if you sit on a bus; everybody will try to avoid each other as much as possible because no one wants to sit together because we're just not that socially.

Anthony:
Tell me the thought process. The couple that saw me walking just now. They saw me… I saw that they saw me.

Olav:
Yes.

Anthony:
They stared at me and as soon as I looked towards them, they looked away.

Olav:
Yes.

Anthony:
So obviously I said to myself, "OK, they're staring at me" so I just greeted them politely and then they carried on looking away and then really awkwardly... Just muffled, "Hi." It was weird. Is that "normal" here? Is that typical Norwegian behaviour?

Olav:
Yes, actually I would! I actually would.

Anthony:
Tell me more because I'm very interested in this?

Olav:
I just guess that's how our culture is... I don't know... It's even like that with friends sometimes, if you see your friends on the street then sometimes you try to avoid them and put your phone up and pretend that you don't see them.

(Author's note: This is an interesting thing to do, because it's a physical barrier between "you" and "them" but it's obviously not a very efficient physical barrier because it's not large enough to conceal a grown adult. Nevertheless, the respondent describes the action that they carry out regardless of its efficiency or logic... even though they are fully aware that it's an act of pretence. This is something which the majority of respondents I spoke to raised and participated in; pretence. Could a high level of daily pretence have an effect on mental health?)

Anthony:
Right. If there was an actual choice and you were given a choice... do they want to be like that? Is this *compulsive* behaviour or is it *conscious*?

Olav:

(AN – big exhalation of breath.) They don't actually want to be like that but that's *just how our culture is*… nobody wants to be different; everybody wants to be the same you know? And our country is just like that.

Anthony:

So it's very much a consensus and a conformist culture, is that what you're saying?

Olav:

In a way, yes.

Anthony:

So everyone is the "same"… It kind of sounds like… It sounds like avoidance?

Olav:

It is!

Anthony:

Tell me about this avoidance of new stimuli? Does it raise the anxiety level when something "new" appears?

Olav:

From my personal point of view, no, but that's because I am social so it's hard for me to answer.

(AN – Interestingly, note that the respondent prefaced their statement with "from my point of view". I have noticed that many respondents I spoke to prefaced their statements and answered with qualifying phrases like this. I am in a one-on-one conversation… whose point of view does he think I am asking for? Keep an eye out for this i.e. Respondents answering from the viewpoint/position of the collective/others and often not seeming able to explain or describe what they themselves think/feel individually.)

Anthony:

So, do you know that you said that Norwegians are "antisocial"… do you count yourself in that, or do you place yourself apart from that?

Olav:

I am beside that because I sit next to people on buses and I talk to people if I see them in the street.

Anthony:

So let me ask you then… you are a non-conformist person in a conformist society? Would you agree with that?

Olav:

Yes, yes. Totally!

Anthony:

So how do you feel being among people that don't act like you?

Olav:

Well I mean… it's kind of strange. When I go on a bus I see that everyone is standing up and I see a seat which is not taken and I am like "Can I sit down?" And they say "Sure…" *(AN – with an uncomfortable weird look.)*

Anthony:

So they have an uncomfortable look on their face?

Olav:

Yes! But I don't know why… I don't know if that's because I'm Norwegian or not or it's something that other cultures?

(AN – This is incredible. He doesn't know what is normal and what isn't normal? Ironically though, he does reject it and alters his behaviour, so he must realise that on a certain level it is not normal?)

Anthony:

Why are you different? Why are you not socially excluded like the rest of your country then?

Olav:

Because… I don't like to stand on the bus! Literally who wants to do that? There is literally one seat right there… why don't you just sit down? Why? Why?

(AN – The respondent became agitation and animated, raising his voice, when answering this question.)

Anthony:
This is a very good question…

Olav:
Yes… just sit down! It's not *dangerous*! You're not going to get *bitten* or anything… It's just a human being!

(AN – Note the reference to a potential threat and allusion to violence as a potential cost of sitting down on a bus seat next to somebody. You might think that this is an innocuous comment but you would be wrong. Another Norwegian respondent explained to me in an interview why you shouldn't speak to somebody you don't know because they "might be a serial killer"… She was upset and on the verge of tears when she said this. She raised her voice and exclaimed, "I can't take this… This is too much! This is not right! Norwegians don't do this! It's JUST NOT RIGHT!". We will come to that later. However, this perception of people that you don't know as, potential "threats", is actually something which appears to be very real to a great many Norwegians that I spoke to, even if there is no realistic threat, in reality or even statistically. Another Norwegian respondent on the other side of the country, implied that Norwegians are brought up to perceive "strangers" as dangerous, which she phrased as "stranger danger!", but she chooses to ignore this because she likes to meet new people… we will speak to her later.)

Anthony:
So let me ask you something. So the person that doesn't sit down, do you think that its peer pressure? Or if they had a choice, they *would* sit down, but they *feel* that they can't because of social pressure, peer pressure, because they want to conform… if they did it, would it be like they were stepping out of the box and taking a risk?

Olav:
Yes. Actually yes. That is actually exactly what I think because I have gone through that. I was standing on a bus before but I… I guess I just changed… I don't know.

(AN – So now this brings us back to his previous answer and a contradiction. He previously said: "From my personal point of view, no but that's because I am social so it's hard for me to answer" but now reveals that he has indeed engaged in said behaviour. He concedes that he doesn't know why he changed though. It's was an automatic behaviour before? Even when I asked him to think about it, after the fact, he could not and found it difficult to such an extent that he couldn't answer it. This is

very peculiar… I will go on to ask him about that specifically and his thought process at the time. Finally, look at what I asked and look at his confirmation. He has confirmed that a kind of "risk assessment" is made in the simple determination of whether to sit down on a bus. Can you imagine feeling the need to act in this way? A comprehensive risk assessment to simply sit on a bus to determine whether there is a threat to your life or raising of the phone, pretending to hide form people that you don't want to see etc.)

Anthony:
So, in a way you had the courage to push through the barrier, which is called exposure?

Olav:
Yes.

Anthony:
The first time, the first time you said to yourself "I don't want to stand here anymore, I want to sit down" did you feel uncomfortable the first time?

Olav:
Yes! Until I actually sat down.

Anthony:
And then were you like "Oh my God! I did what I wanted to do… and I survived!"

Olav:
(Laugh) Yeah exactly!

Anthony:
Wow! What you have just described to me… part of it is very sad… you chose to sit down and you exhibited a kind of strength by doing that, but the perception is that daring to be different is actually a weakness in this culture? If you act differently then you are weak or for example if you show feelings… something is slightly off and that is not perceived in a positive way, I understand? Would you agree with that?

Olav:
Yes.

Anthony:

So in a way, it's kind of "upside-down" in Norway? If you do something which shows strength and uniqueness then maybe you are perceived as "weak" or "crazy"… that's what it seems like?

Olav:

Crazy I would say, yes.

Anthony:

Tell me why? Why do they think you're "crazy"?

Olav:

It's hard to explain, because they won't directly tell me that I'm crazy when I sit down next to them, beside them… but they will always think "why did you sit next to me?! Why is this guy sitting with me?!" But I don't really care though… I just want to live my life! If I want the seat I will take the seat! If anything I just want to take it… I don't really care!

(AN – He has previously explained that the whole dynamic of the situation confuses him because he doesn't have awareness of whether it is the same in Norway, as in a different country. He has now pointed out that the participants in this "routine" don't assist, because they don't overtly speak about it, they keep their annoyance concealed. We also note that he is frustrated, which is clear by his wording and tone of voice and notice that he is forced to rebel perceiving all this as restricting his life; "I just want to live my life!". We also see anger or frustration which is suggested clearly with, his "I don't really care!" comment.)

Anthony:

Would you say that many Norwegians think about what others think about them?

Olav:

YES! *(AN – Forcefully answered.)* YES! Like, really… yes!

Anthony:

Does anyone ever stand up on the bus and say, "Everybody, you're all acting irrationally, let's just chill out!"?

Olav:

Oh! Nooooooooooooooo! Never! NEVER! NEVER!

(AN – He is raising his voice. Asking simple questions and asking the respondents to think about their everyday life, something as simple and mundane as sitting on a bus often elicits and triggers responses like this… we will look at why this is later. If this is the pressure felt by a simple act like finding a seat on the bus, imagine the internal psychological pressure elicited from the more serious events and issues in life?)

Anthony:
Tell me more. If somebody stood up and said, "Everybody let's just be cool, let's just express our emotions from now on" what would happen to that person?

Olav:
Everybody would just look at him and *ignore* him… It would just be the most awkward situation ever.

(AN – This one comment is one of the most important answers in this book. This sums up the experience of many of the Norwegian respondents that I spoke to, who said that they are often "ignored". This type of withholding of approval and acknowledgement is clearly a device regularly used by some people. I actually encountered it again and again in my discussions and also in my personal day- to-day life in Norway. In addition, we get to see how the respondent "frames" the event in relation to his life and the world… he described something this trivial as, "the most awkward situation ever".)

Anthony:
This is incredible. Do you think that this has anything to do with you being a pilot? Because to be a pilot you have to be confident, you have to accurately assess risk… Do you think that your perspective has contributed to you going towards being a pilot? Do you think that that has helped you think in a different way to others around you?

Olav:
It's really weird to see… but I have never thought about that. It would make sense!

Anthony:
If you are a pilot then you can't play mind games up there in the sky, so it doesn't matter about how you "feel", you can't be like "Oh… I don't feel like communicating today", hide behind a phone or play linguistic mind

games with your co-pilot. You have to just "say it as it is"... stick with reality only... because your life is at stake and you've got passengers' lives at stake. Maybe that attitude informs your day-to-day life too? Now, is there any validity to what I am saying at all? Am I crazy?

Olav:
No, you are not crazy at all. I actually do relate to what you are saying.

Anthony:
With that said, I have been asking the question, who is Norway's Sigmund Freud, to some very intelligent people and do you know what the answer I have been getting?

Olav:
What?

Anthony:
"There is no Norwegian equivalent of Sigmund Freud", they tell me. There is nobody... "no thinkers"... There are no big psychologists, no big psychoanalysis... it's technical engineers and probably just Ibsen... I think that that is very, incredible... because I feel like... *how* can I just come and ask questions that have *never* been asked before in Norway?

Olav:
Yes!

Anthony:
There are these nonsense books about the "rules" of Norway, and I've got four of them...

Olav:
(Laugh.)

Anthony:
They are just superficial stereotypes and I feel that so many Norwegians have listened to people projecting negative stereotypes onto them to such an extent where you believe those stereotypes. For example, earlier when you said "Norwegians are like that"... "Norwegians are antisocial". OK... on the surface *some* may be antisocial but if we stripped them down... you probably don't *want* to be like that. That's how I feel. Some of them do,

but some of them don't, because… some have been bullied and it's like somebody has never told them, "Don't worry, it's OK to be like that"… but I just think that these negative stereotypes have been reinforced over and over again in Norway, telling people what "they" are, that they now just can't be themselves! That's just how I feel. What do you think about that?

Olav:

(Laugh.) You're giving a lot of good points… and it's true. It is the truth!

A Conversation with Norwegian Teenagers (1)

I interviewed "Anita" and "Hanne" who are both sixteen years old. You are going to hear two horrifying accounts of life in Norway from two teenagers that align exactly with what teenagers say on the other side of the country. They will speak in detail about sexual harassment by teachers and how it is encouraged and enabled. They will talk about corruption and how Janteloven destroys people's lives in Norway. The account that you will hear from these two teenagers is an account that I heard all over Norway. In fact, I didn't encounter a single contrary viewpoint in this age group… they all seem to describe exactly the same thing.

Anthony:
So we met and had a conversation a couple of months ago and now we're going to have another conversation. As soon as we met again you immediately said "Anthony we have something to report to you, our social lives are much better now" and then I asked you whether our previous conversation had had anything to do with that and you said "yes!". So tell me what's happened?

Anita:
So, basically it started when we had the talk you asked me whether I felt better, and I was like "no!", because I know that the social setting is not going to be fixed suddenly and she (Hanne), said that she felt better because at least she was talking about it, and knowing now what is up, kind of… but I think that it helped us… for me it felt very relaxing to know that I had other people around me, seeing and understanding the same situation, for example, with our big friend group, it's still kind of the same… we never talk! We have this group on Snapchat and the only time we ever talk is when there is a party, and it's the same people saying the same stuff about if somebody is like hosting the party… and then everybody is like "no"… and that's it. So I think that a lot of people have realised that we're not really friends… we just party together! And then I literally thought about all of my friends separately, because I remember what you told me about the traffic light system… yes, I did that!

(AN – The "traffic light system" is a technique that I devised to help with looking at the people around you in your life and determine how you really feel about them, you can find out more from my book, "Living in a Bubble" or "The Personal development book for Performers".)

Anthony:
You did that?

Anita:
Yes... and now I know what people to invest my time in... and after that it's kind of come back to me more because you know the people that you invest in invest in you back and then you'll get some very close friendships.

Anthony:
Yes.

Anita:
Instead of like twenty fake ones.

Anthony:
Has it helped you navigate some of your issues?

Anita:
Yes!

Anthony:
Some of the issues with your friends that you shared, you realised that you all experienced them? Did it make you feel less alone?

Anita:
Yes!

Anthony:
That's brilliant, isn't it?

Anita:
Yes!

Anthony:
Is there one thing in particular that stood out from our conversation that

you would say really helped? You think about that question Anita and then now I'll ask the same question to Hanne. Hanne, we had our talk. Did it help you in any way?

Hanne:
I remember this very well, because you asked, "Why are you friends with fake people?" and that really got me thinking! Because... it's a really good question! So when I look at my real friends, we have a small group within a big group, these are my closest friends and these are the people that I trust, very very much, so, I feel like when you asked, "Why are you friends with people when they are not friendly with you?"

Anthony:
Yes.

Hanne:
And I really think that that's true! Why invest and energy in somebody that is not worth it?

Anthony:
And just to be clear... those people don't make you feel good about yourself, I think you originally said? So what I was pointing out to you, was that the people that you were describing as your "friends" didn't sound like friends, they didn't sound like they lifted you up in any way or that you even really liked them?

Hanne:
Yes... like honestly... it's just for the popularity. We're not real friends. We're just hanging out for higher status, yes.

(AN – We note that Hanne is 100% aware that she engages in relationships merely for "status"... this has been described to me many times in Norway. Many young people described that they learn that this is a necessary method of interaction to survive in Norway. Can you imagine how reinforced this behaviour will be by eighteen years old and beyond?)

Anthony:
For me the moment that stood out was when I asked you what would happen if you were no longer able to dance, and you said, "I would commit suicide" *(AN – Hanne now starts laughing)*... and I said to you,

"why are you laughing when you say that?" … that was the one thing for me… because then I saw you stop and think about it… and I watched you and you really thought about it and then I watched you realise what you had just said, because you literally were laughing about it… but when you started thinking about it I saw you abruptly stop laughing. Do you remember that and what do you think about it now?

Hanne:
Yes. I still think about it now because it's kind of absurd, to say that if I could not dance I would *kill* myself… really like! *(AN – She burst out laughing.)* It's really dramatic!

(AN – Hanne is missing the point and saying that it's "absurd" that she said it when I am saying that it's absurd that she has been placed in a situation where she would feel that way in the first place.)

Anthony:
But what I would say is, is that that is how you felt at the time. I do think that there is a logical reason for you saying that, because it was an honest expression of pain, thinking about if you lost it… It's not necessarily that you would really commit suicide… But it is an indication of the pain that you might feel, if you were to lose something which allows you to release the stresses of your life. But the thing is though, that you were laughing when you were saying it. Essentially you were saying "it would be sad for me" but then you were laughing. So then you stopped laughing when you were thinking about it… And for me that is so interesting and that's why, it's good to have real conversations because then you can think about the way that you think… When you really start thinking about these things I think that just talking about it can really help. That's what I think anyway. What do you guys think about that?

Anita:
Yes!

Hanne:
Yes!

Anthony:
So was there anything else, Hanne?

Hanne:

Like Anita said… it's now like we have a better connection. We saw better
what was going on. I had never thought about it that much. I had just
thought that these friends were there for popularity and that's just the way it
is!

Anthony:
Anita, did you think of anything that helped you?

Anita:

Yes! It was two things and it's really funny because as soon as Hanne
mentioned the fake friends… that is the first thing that I thought of! Basically
I was talking to Hanne about this and our big group, and I was like then and
there, because you know the top gang leader… *(AN – redacted.)*

Anthony:
OK.

Anita:

And then I heard that she *(AN – redacted)*… and then I was like "I'm out. I'm
out."… I'm not even going to *pretend* to be friends with these people
anymore! I wrote down everyone's name on a list, in front of Hanne and I
haven't thought about that before but I just did it then and there. We circled
the people that we thought were our *real* friends. Then I crossed out the
people that we are not close to and that if we split up would have no contact
with them. When I crossed out the people that hurt us and then after I did
that I was left with one or two people… who are like friendly but not super
close… then I put the people that hurt us… because if we split with them
they would still stay together… Because we have always thought that if we
split our gang then we would be so afraid, to not be popular, because that's
always matters to us…

Hanne:
We were nobodies.

Anita:
Being popular was… if you get what I mean?

Anthony:
I understand.

Anita:

But after we had the conversation I was like, I don't care about being "popular", I want to keep my *real* friends… Because I have more fun with them then my *fake* girlfriends. And when I put it down on paper I looked at the girls in the gang that were being like bad people to us, and I was like "who the hell would like to hang out with them!?" They're not nice! So I think, talking to you, I don't think it came to me immediately after the conversation… but it really sparked my thoughts. You basically got me to start thinking it through myself and then I realised really I actually don't care! I don't care about being popular if it means that I basically have to put up with b*tches that just want to hurt me! They actually want to do you harm! It's not that they just don't care… they actually want to be mean to you! So I'm like "why the hell would I *pretend* that they are my best friends when I know that they actually want to hurt me?"

Anthony:

Incredible. True… and that's the point I was trying to make with you. That it's not logical. It's like just doing things on autopilot?

Anita:

Yes, it is!

Anthony:

But I do think that there is underlying logical reasons for it like fear, stress, peer pressure, bullying. You said that there was a couple of things… was there something else as well?

Anita:

It wasn't one thing that you said; all that we talked about but it was like the whole conversation, just realising that the people around me understood! Just knowing that they saw that and that they understood. That really made me feel good!

Anthony:
That's brilliant.

Anita:

And after that, we had so many brilliant… close conversations!

Anthony:
So do you think that the fact that I made the conditions safe for you to talk openly, without being judged about really important questions, then you realise "Do you know what? I feel really good that I had this conversation with my loved ones and now I can keep talking about these things because now I don't have to pretend that these problems aren't there anymore." Would you say that in a way gave you a new perspective?

Anita:
Yes! Because after we had that conversation I remember saying that's literally the best conversation I've ever had in my life… and now it's probably not anymore… Because it's sparked so many other really good new conversations!

Anthony:
So basically that conversation was the seed leading to other conversations and change in your life and leading to communication with people that you love?

Anita:
Yes! I actually think that I will never forget that! I really think that it helped me even talking with the girls.

Anthony:
That's incredible.

Anita:
We felt an issue for months and months… but we never knew what it was!

(AN – This is something which I have heard all over Norway. People know that there is a problem but can't identify it or its causes because they are "in" it. However, after an hour or so of talking about these issues and lowering barriers, many respondents feel that they have been enlightened and had major life issues identified, which in itself is relieving for them.)

Anthony:
Do you think, that the things that I talked with you about and the points that were raised… is it real? Are these real issues and do you feel that someone has finally given you the answer?

Anita:
Yes! Definitely!

Anthony:
Have you thought about why nobody has ever talked to you about these things before? About why nobody has helped you challenge these things before? About why somebody hasn't expressed these things before?

Anita:
Not really, actually.

Anthony:
So how about now if I ask you? Why has nobody ever said these things to you before? Why has nobody opened up these issues? Why, out of all of your teachers and all of your mentors and all of the people in Norwegian society, why has it been that I have been the one who has opened your eyes or explained these problems in your society and in your life?

Anita:
I actually think that to notice this, you have to be very intelligent. Obviously an idiot won't be able to notice all of this! I had a teacher that I really liked and we talked and she was smart… but I don't think that she would ever do anything about it… I think that the people that are smart enough to recognise the issue are also smart enough to realise that this is too big!

(AN – She is stating that the people who are "smart" enough to see it are also "smart" enough to know that they need to shut their mouths about it.)

Anthony:
Do you think that, in a way, they don't have the courage to fight against the whole system and expose this? It also brings us onto the next subject, which is obviously the fact that I am going to be attacked for exposing these things. They are going to say, "Oh, he only spoke to a few people! He didn't speak to 5 million people in Norway! So it's not representative! He just found some random teenagers! He got them to say that and they didn't really mean it! What do they know!? There are so many happy people in Norway, this is all lies! How can we believe what these people say?! This guy is just raising negativity!" What would you say to those people who would say that to discredit?

Anita:
Just give them facts and that's it… because the people that would attack you for doing something like this are idiots! This is one thing that I have thought of out of our conversations… you actually have to choose what group of people you want to stand up for, if that makes sense? For example, in our situation, there are different types of people in our age group. Some people get drunk and do drugs and there are some people that are nice… You can't stand up as a good person for both groups.

Anthony:
Yes.

Anita:
It's actually impossible!

Anthony:
Of course, you can't both stand up for right and wrong simultaneously. These people are going to say that I am not representing the "big picture" and the true representation of the situation in Norway even though I believe you and have seen it all over the country repeatedly.

Anita:
Yes!

Anthony:
What you guys are explaining is what so many people up and down the country explain to me but I believe that denial is so strong within many in Norway that some people generally do not have the courage to speak about this… even if they know it in their hearts though.

Anita:
Yes!

Anthony:
But they won't be able to admit it. Now we are speaking anonymously, so nobody is going to know who you are but let me ask you, if you were to make a public statement like a public blog… or let's say that you were on NRK *(AN – The Norwegian national broadcaster)* talking about this… what would happen to you guys?

Anita:
I think that if we like spoke openly about it on a big news channel, then I think that people's first reaction would be that we are on the news! I think that they would look down on it to be honest, because it's not cool to be smart… I mean, for example, even me, I am guilty of this. When I see that people are posting on Instagram about that they are spending their whole summer in study camp, then I'm like, "I know you're a really good person and I know you're really smart but that's kind of lame!" And I think that people would think that.

Anthony:
What would be the main response? By the way, I mean public response, not in private, what would they say publicly?

Anita:
Who is "they"?

Anthony:
Everybody! For example, I am guessing that you wouldn't be little "Miss Popular" if you said these things publicly?

Anita:
Well, I think that in our age group I don't think that anyone would actually talk to us about it.

Anthony:
Yes?

Anita:
I think that they would talk s*** about it behind our backs!

Anthony:
In what way? What would they say?

Anita:
I think they would be like "Oh my God! That's kind of lame." (AN – *she puts on a horrible voice.*)

Anthony:
But even though they know that everything you're saying is true, they

would still say that? Because they have to live in this situation and they know you're not lying?

Anita:
Yes! The people that talk s*** about it are the people that cause the trouble!

Anthony:
Indeed! Now, let's turn to the adults and the teachers that basically preside over all of this... what would they say?

Anita:
I think that again it depends... I mean... a "bad teacher"... that's Norwegian! There aren't many good teachers! *(AN – She laughs.)*

Anthony:
Really?

Anita:
A lot of Norwegian teachers are like, really bad.

Anthony:
Bullies?

Anita:
They are like a paedophile, or they don't really care... *(AN – she turns to Hanne)*... some of her teachers are... *(AN – she screams! She then laughs.)*

Anthony:
Just to be clear about what just happened for the audio recording... you put your hands on the chest Hanne and implied that that's what the teachers do to you?

Hanne:
I haven't experienced it but... scary things like touching your hair, massage you, like creepy stuff like that... hmm.

(AN – She is scared to talk about it and I don't believe her when she says that she's never experienced it.)

Anthony:
What happens to this teacher?

Anita:
Nothing!

Anthony:
Did you just say "nothing"?

Anita:
They have this thing where they have physical education and they like have couples dancing… The teachers want to dance and like demonstrate with the most pretty girl… like with the best body and the big ass and big boobs because then they can get close *(AN – her voice start speeding up when she says this)*… these things… but nothing happens to those teachers.

(AN – Almost 100% of the young people I spoke to described that they have experienced this situation almost exactly. From the top of Norway to the bottom. Unanimous! In fact you will hear a young man and many others describe the same thing almost word for word later in this series.)

Anthony:
And nobody stops this and nobody says that this is wrong?

Anita:
Well, obviously the students talk about it…

Anthony:
But the adults?

Hanne:
I think that if your daughter came up to you and said that my teacher is sexually harassing me, then I think that that father will take action.

Anthony:
So, if they saw the same teacher holding you and touching you in that way and laughing I presume that they would just laugh too?

Hanne:
I don't know.

(AN – They have both gone silent now. They are scared to talk about it.)

Anthony:
I am guessing that everybody in the room would have laughed and that nobody would have spoken out and said, "Don't touch her on the breast!"

(AN – I have encouraged her that it's safe to say the truth and then she starts to tell the truth.)

Hanne:
No! They are like laughing! In (redacted) class… it is like Anita is describing: a girl has big boobs and big ass, and stuff like that and the teacher will always, ask her… One because, she couldn't say no.

Anthony:
Right.

Hanne:
And because she had this body… I know that that is really like disgusting! But none of her classmates would like stop him… stuff like that… but they are thinking…

Anthony:
So publicly they have to smile and act like everything is OK but inside they hate it? Is that true?

Hanne:
Yes but… *(silence)*.

Further discussion

Anthony:
Can I ask you both… do you think that this happens a lot? Because Anita, you just literally said that most of the teachers are either paedophiles or "bad"… are you saying that this is basically a big problem in Norway?

Anita:
Yes… My *(AN – redacted)* has talked to me about this and told me that I have to get out of Norway! Because *(AN – redacted)* said that when you grow up

and get a job you will have to basically compete against the international market because the way that we are raised and taught in school is so… not old fashioned… but it's just a really bad way compared to how the rest of the world is doing. It's not efficient and like the teachers… Who are like, especially like the old traditional Norwegian teachers style people. They are not teachers because they love children… Or do what they love because they want to teach… They are basically a teacher because they did not know what they wanted to be!

Anthony:
Are they all like a paedophile or an abuser, you basically said?

Anita:
Yes!

Anthony:
I want you to know something… all of the things that you have been too scared to say… You can say them right now. Nobody will ever know that you said these words… I will say it for you… speak on behalf of your classmates… If you had the power to expose all of this what would you say to the people?

Hanne:
In our school we kind of make a joke about it… But we know that it is actually how it is… So when a girl gets a better grade than a boy…

Anthony:
So just to be clear, you are saying that it's actually a topic of conversation that a girl will get a better grade than a boy, because the teacher finds the student sexually desirable more than the boys? Is that right?

Hanne:
Yes!

Anthony:
Is that what the boys openly say?

Hanne:
Yes.

Anthony:
What do you say back to them?

Hanne:
We kind of laugh back because we don't...

Anthony:
You laugh because it is true?

Hanne:
Well, I can't say that... but we can't argue back logically. (Laugh.)

Anthony:
But you do say that it is logical?

Hanne:
Yes, because if, for example, a female teacher... is like a feminist and you know... "girl power!" (*Laughs.*) Then she will like support the girls, and help them and be more kind and open, to the girls!

Anthony:
OK.

Hanne:
And then the boys will be like "it's just because you are a girl and she is a girl"... and stuff like that and if it's a male teacher than it's the same way... "It's just because you are a girl and our teacher is a paedophile"... I know that I... Our *(redacted)* teacher is like old and he is disgusting and scary... and yeah... and I know that the girls got better grades than the boys, yes. *(Laugh)*... and I know that if there are girls in the class that are like small and don't have the body form... they will get lesser grades.

Anthony:
Can I just say that that is absolutely shocking!

Hanne:
(Laughs.)

Anthony:
That is absolutely shocking! How do you feel when I say that to you right now?

Hanne:
I think it's funny… because I am used to this!

(AN – Note that she states that my shock at the described sexual harassment, child abuse, corruption that she has described in Norway is "funny" because she is "used" to it.)

Anthony:
This is what the book is about… you have told me that many of your teachers are paedophiles and do not act in a professional way with you. Now I am going to ask you, what would people say if you publicly came out and said this?

Hanne:
I think that the teachers would be like, "No you are just making this stuff up, because you got a less grade than your classmate".

(AN – You can't read it clearer than that. It's horrifying that the young victims are aware of exactly how things "work" and that if they ever spoke out they would almost certainly be undermined, attacked and called liars by default)

Anthony:
So basically they would say that you are lying and attack you?

Hanne:
Yes.

Anthony:
Anita, I am guessing that people around you would say "oh you're overreacting", and it wouldn't only be the teachers that are saying that you are lying. What would people say Anita?

Anita:
In our environment?

Anthony:
For example, if you came out and said "ten of our teachers give girls better grades than the boys because of their bodies and touch us inappropriately… we're fed up of it and nobody does anything about it and we want it to stop now!" If you said that publicly what would happen to you and what would people say?

Anita:

I think that this comes back to people not caring enough, for example, I don't think at the school anyone has ever went up to the principal and told him.

Anthony:

But I am asking if it did happen, what would happen? If you publicly said this... let's say that you posted it on Facebook, for example... say that you just told everybody, what would the adults and everybody say? In the town, for example? Would they help you or would they say "oh come on guys stop being dramatic!"... what would they say? Would they respond with sensitivity or would they help you or would they just try and brush it under the carpet?

Anita:

Probably all of the above! (*Laughs.*)

Anthony:

Obviously if that is the case then you would never say anything because you know that you're not going to get any support, is that right?

Anita:

Yes.

Anthony:

Why would anyone ever say anything if they know they're not going to be supported and they're probably going to be undermined, attacked and called a liar?

Anita:

I think that that is the setting in the main schools in Norway (*redacted*).

Anthony:

I'm talking about the main schools in Norway... for example, if Hanne came out and said this, what do you think the adults in her school and community would say?

Anita:

I think that... hmmmm... I think that they wouldn't take it like they should... Sometimes you need a trustworthy close confident person to tell... and you need more people to say it.

Anthony:
Basically if you are alone it would be hard? *(AN – They nodded.)*

Hanne:
In my situation if I went to my principal and told him that my teacher is abusing me and giving me grades blah blah blah… then I think that the boys in my class would laugh at me… The teachers would say, "We understand but we haven't had any other complaints and I think that this will just be OK after all."

Anthony:
Wow.

Hanne:
"Just just… settle down and don't give up"… or some b******* like that!

Anthony:
That is a cover up. That is perpetuating an enabling abuse. Wouldn't you agree that that is covering it up?

Hanne:
Yes!

Anita:
Honestly this is what I think will happen… but this is sometimes the way that they deal with things at school if you have a problem with the teacher… they make you meet with the school and the same teacher.

Anthony:
So you basically have to sit next to the person that has abused you?

Anita:
I feel that they would do something like that, yes.

Anthony:
Wow.

Anita:
And then obviously you would not be then able to say what really happened!

Anthony:
Of course not. This is crazy because the system enables the abuse and doesn't protect you, right?

Anita:
Yes!

Anthony:
There is something that I have noticed in Norway and I'm going to say it directly. My observation in Norway is that on too many occasions abusers are elevated and supported, and victims are undermined and left out on their own… I don't care what anyone says to me that is what I have seen throughout Norway, repeatedly. Do you think that I am right or do you think that I'm wrong?

Anita:
I think that you are right! But in this exact situation with the teachers that are kind of sexual and stuff, I think that's the reason that it always ends up kind of a joke for them… Because I know that they all know that this is going on, but they joke about it. It has something to do with the people that are like being touched… they are kind of *lucky* that it's them if you know what I mean?

Anthony:
Tell me what you mean?

Anita:
OK, I just want to think of a person… hmmm… OK do you remember *(AN – redacted)*? She's like a sweet angelic girl… she's really quiet and really shy and, for example, who would you believe if they said this happened to Hanne or *(AN – redacted)*… it would be more likely to happen to Hanne because she is confident and is more likely to be able to handle it… If they went to the shy people than they would have crumbled. They would have been destroyed definitely.

Anthony:
So this is why it's a real problem that you always have to be "strong" and pretend that everything's "OK"? When *(AN – redacted)* said "we're in the land of the Janteloven now… you're not going to get any sympathy here"… that's a "joke" right?

Anita:
Yes.

Anthony:
But let me tell you something… it's not a joke.

Anita:
What *(AN – redacted)* said is real and it is doctrine… in Norway people say
that they have to be strong all the time.

Anthony:
What it does is it makes the available victim pool bigger because they
know that the victim will never reveal the crime… because they want to
be "strong", so basically this whole system where you have to pretend to
be strong, it basically makes victims and children and teenagers more
vulnerable to be abused by people that abuse, because they know that
their victims will never say anything about it because if they do then their
victims will be perceived as "weak", liars or troublemakers. Is there
anything to that?

Anita:
Yes, I think that's basically true!

Anthony:
But that is really really sick! Why doesn't anybody do anything about it?

Anita:
Because it's too big.

Hanne:
It's too big.

Anthony:
It's *too* big?

Hanne:
Yes.

Anthony:
I am willing to face the whole of Norway on this; it doesn't just happen to

teenagers it also happens to the older people as well. When we started this conversation, I never anticipated that it was going to go in this direction.

(AN – They both giggle.)

Anthony:
It's obviously something which is important to you because that's why you're speaking about it, is that true?

Anita:
Yes.

Anthony:
Is it true that this is actually an everyday part of your existence in school?

Hanne:
Yes!

Anthony:
To be in that situation... don't you think that that's an abnormal thing? It might be "normal" for you in Norway but it's not normal.

Hanne:
For me... it's normal and it's not that big a deal anymore because I'm so used to it. So it's funny to see how you react because of this... because I'm so used to it kind of.

(AN – You can't read it clearer than that. She is stating that abuse is so normal that it's not a big thing in Norway. She even states that she finds my shock at it "funny".)

Anthony:
Yes. Let me describe these people to you. They are corrupt people. What do you have to say about that, Hanne?

Hanne:
Yes.

Anthony:
What do you have to say about that, Anita? Because this is the deepest

type of corruption that you can do. They're not even being teachers to help they're just being teachers to get a pay check?

Anita:
Obviously, this is not all the teachers… I know a couple (of good ones).

Anthony:
But you described before that the majority of teachers are like this, is this true?

Anita:
I think probably… and I don't think that this is making it bigger than it is… or overreacting… I have probably heard from all of my friends from every different school, mention just two teachers that they really like and appreciate. And I've heard their names come up and the rest are all idiots.

(AN – Many young people explained that they'd expect that they will be judged to be "dramatic" or "overreacting". In conversation, the youth in Norway regularly pre-emptively stated that they are not being "dramatic" or "overreacting", in an automatic way, during a disclosure of abuse.)

Anthony:
So basically every single person that you know has only mentioned a few teachers that are good? The rest of them are idiots or abusive or bad?

Anita:
Yes.

Anthony:
And how many teachers would you say are in the pool… 100 teachers? If you had to guess any random guess?

Anita:
Seventy.

Anthony:
If you had to do a percentage of the teachers that you would say are "good" and the teachers that you think are "not good" or abusive, what would your percentage be?

Hanne:
It's a wide scale if you could put it that way but some of them, just bad and nothing good! You just want them gone!

Anthony:
How many of them? Percentage wise...

Hanne:
But some of them are in the middle... sometimes they are good and sometimes they are bad.

Anthony:
OK, let's talk about the ones that actually engage in the sexual behaviour... the ones that touch or the ones that give better grades to certain students... what percentage are they? What percentage are the ones that are wrong and unprofessional?

Hanne:
That's a really hard question.

Anthony:
50%, 70%, 1%, 20%?

Hanne:
Because I feel like it's how you define. Definition...

(AN – This is shocking. An extremely intelligent girl is asking for the definition of "sexual behaviour" which suggests that, as she has stated explicitly already, abuse is so normalised that the definition doesn't even have any real meaning or consequence in her environment. I will now "define" it so it is without any doubt.)

Anthony:
OK, I'll give you a definition right now. A teacher that touches you on your buttocks, for whatever reason, as a "joke" or intentionally or whatever... or touches you on your breasts, a teacher who has made a sexual reference to you in the class, or has fondled touched or given someone better grades, because they like a girl better than a boy... *what percentage of the teachers are those?*

Hanne:
Like really… like really the ones that are really bad?

Anthony:
Not "really bad"… just by the definition which I have just given and even if it was just one time…

Hanne:
(*Giggles*)…30% or 40%… I don't know?

Anthony:
That's OK. Let me ask you this question. Don't you think that that's a crazy high percentage? 30% or 40%!

Hanne:
Yes.

Anthony:
Can I ask you, if we had a conversation like this once a week in your class. Would that help?

Anita:
I don't think so, because it would be like, in a big group of people.

Anthony:
Oh, so people would not tell the truth?

Anita:
Yes.

Anthony:
Tell me more about that?

Anita:
Norwegian people are very scared I think. That's one of the biggest things that we have uncovered here! (*Laughs.*) But I think that, people wouldn't. Obviously in a class. Can't really represent a social setting because as you know some people are popular, some people are really weird… stuff like that… and obviously you won't say that you're feeling pressured by the popular people because they are sitting right in front of you.

Anthony:
Yes.

Further discussion

Anthony:
Anybody that is different or an "outsider"... they just exclude you, is that true?

Anita:
Yes.

Anthony:
If we had a conversation in school once a week like we had before do you think it would help?

Hanne:
If it was just us and one or two people then yes, but if it was a large group then I don't think that it would to be honest.

Anthony:
What would happen to you if you were honest in front of those people?

Hanne:
Then I would be the one that's weird and then I would be excluded.

Anthony:
Would they exclude you if you were honest in front of the whole class?

Hanne:
Yes... It's like... Yes.

Anthony:
Can I ask you why do you have no problem speaking to me about these things?

Hanne:
Once again... To understand these things... you can't be an idiot... And I don't think you're an idiot. You understand and you are the one that helped

us with these problems and I feel like you understand but I can't speak to an idiot about this because they wouldn't understand!

Anthony:
It seems like nobody asks you how you think and feel? Why is it only me?

Hanne:
I think it's really good. Again there is no one else who has the courage.

Anthony:
For example, have your parents ever spoken to you about this?

Hanne:
No!

Anthony:
Have your teachers ever spoken to you about this?

Hanne:
No!

Anthony:
Have your politicians ever spoken to you about this?

Hanne:
No!

Anthony:
What you're telling me is that this is the number one issue in your life that everybody knows but nobody talks about?

Hanne:
Do you know I don't know the English word… but taboo?

Anthony:
Taboo? Yes, taboo.

Hanne:
Yes, taboo.

Anthony:
And here is the thing… there are so many taboos in Norway that even if you mentioned them, then you will be attacked and excluded. Is that true?

Hanne:
Yes! You have these personal taboos if you know what I mean… like you are supposed to hold them to yourself you are not supposed to share them and I feel like, this is one of them… You are not supposed to tell your class about it because you will just be that weird kid.

Anthony:
Tell me what you think about this… I think that there might be a chance that when some Norwegians read this they might say "thank you"… they might not have the courage to publicly… but inside their hearts they know that at least someone said it… and in ten or twenty years' time people may have the courage to talk about it publicly… what do you think about that?

Anita:
Yes.

Anthony:
I think it's possible… but very unlikely…

Anita:
I think it's unlikely… obviously everything is possible!

Anthony:
But in the end the truth always comes out…

Anita:
Yes! In the end if it even ends up not being talked about I think that the people that do read it, find peace with themselves, if that makes sense… even now just after the conversations that we have had and the people around I have now had together… I feel so relieved! I feel like a better person! And I know how to work my life now! It's way easier than it was just a couple of months ago!

(AN – we high five!)

Anita:

So my point is that even if it's talked about or not that the people will really need to hear this! Will be able to find it and take in the information... Even if it is talking about publicly or not... that will help them with their lives any ways. I don't think that they will feel the need... although obviously it deserves to be a public thing.

Anthony:

This is to tell them that someone is hearing them and explaining to them that you are not "crazy" but that it's the whole system that is crazy.

Anita:

Yes... but everyone is involved in this issue. Well, obviously in one way the whole country is connected to it... but I think that it kind of touches the most people like us, because we're not popular! *(Laughs.)*

Anthony:

I will tell you something interesting, this is something that not only people in your age group describe, but also all the people. But let me tell you this... for a taboo to exist, it has to have everybody's involvement?

Anita:

Yes.

Anthony:

It can't just have a couple of people... and that's why everybody is involved. Would you agree with that?

Anita:

Yes. I agree.

Anthony:

At least now we've started the solution because we are talking about it. So that is good. Change of subject... Earlier a person that I interviewed had a very strong emotional reaction because she didn't understand why people in the UK said "how are you?"... This is so similar to some people on the autistic spectrum... When you explain to them that it's just a greeting. Just like "what's up?" It doesn't mean to look up in the air, something is up there... it's just a greeting. My response is that most people should be able to calmly and rationally understand that without getting very upset and agitated. Now, I have noticed that many people in Norway, when they describe this type of thing they get really agitated and really upset, "Why do people in England say how are you all the time?" They get really angry about it. Now me explaining that... would you agree that that is true?

Anita:
Yes, kind of...

Anthony:
They say, "Why do you say how are you all the time!?" They don't just say "you're idiots"... They look really stressed by it... Stressed... We talked about this earlier with regards to having a world view. You said that because you have a world view and are well travelled that when somebody says that to you, you understand it and don't get stressed by it. Can you explain that to me?

Anita:
Can we add the "darling" stuff as well?

Anthony:
Sure, go ahead! So basically we were saying that at the market or street stall in England they might say "alright mate! Do you want a pound of potatoes, mate? Alright love, thanks darling!" Now in Norway that actually stresses people out?

Anita:
Yes! That makes Norwegian people feel *extremely* uncomfortable.

Anthony:
I have noticed that... I have noticed that faces literally contort... go red... literally cannot handle it... it's like an overloaded computer and here is my point: you said that you noticed that in Norway, but that when people say it to you, that you respond in a totally different way. Are you saying that because you've travelled, you've experienced it before and you understand, for example, that they are not saying it *literally*?

Anita:
Yes.

Anthony:
Because you understand that, it doesn't make you feel uncomfortable?

Anita:
Yes.

Anthony:
Why do so many people in Norway take it literally and why do they get so stressed and anxious about it: that is my question?

Anita:
I think that is because, they have never experienced something like it. Because… I don't know… but I have this theory that every super Norwegian… For example, if you ask any Norwegian family "Where do you go on vacation?" they're going to say either "Thailand", "Spain" or like "Gran Canaria"… maybe Croatia… something like that; something very central in Europe or Thailand. And if they go to Thailand then they have been there four times to the same hotel every time! This is so normal! Hanne do you agree with that?

Hanne:
Yes!

Anita:
So normal! People literally don't travel! If I tell people that I travel somewhere other than that then they are literally like "What the hell!?" And I'm like, "No! We just choose not to go to the same place every time!"

Anthony:
And how do they respond to that? Because now you have challenged them with logic. How do they respond to that logic?

Anita:
Well just like the normal Norwegian.

Anthony:
Superficial stuff?

Anita:
Yeah!

Anthony:
What you just described to me sounds very similar to some people on the autistic spectrum because many people on the autistic spectrum like to have the same routines… Change can make some people on the autism spectrum feel uncomfortable. It sounds like many Norwegian people are very set in their ways and it sounds like whenever anything adds change or does something different… It can be kind of shocking and stressful for many of them. Would you agree with that?

Anita:
Yes.

Anthony:
I am a guest in Norway and this whole situation that we have discussed… it's just not normal. It's as simple as that. It's not normal behaviour. Do you relate to that? Does that resonate with you? Do you understand that?

Anita:
I understand… but the thing is… (AN – *large exhalation of breath.*)

Anthony:
It's not normal to have teachers like this, that act like this… and everybody is quiet about it. It's not normal that people are shocked if you've travelled somewhere in the world other than Gran Canaria or Thailand. It's not normal if every single person dresses almost exactly the same. It's not normal that if someone decides to wear something else that everyone will be shocked and gossip about it. You think that's normal?

Anita:
The thing is… For us that is normal. For Norway this is normal!

(AN – *Again, you can't read it stated clearer than that!*)

Anthony:
Just because something is perceived as "normal" here do you think that it is healthy for you and do you like it?

Anita:
No! (*Laughs.*)

Anthony:
Now, why do you think, nobody has ever tried to change or has changed this kind of "normality"? It obviously doesn't help you very much so why do you think that nobody has ever had the courage to change it?

Anita:
I think that the people who are able to make a change, if you know what I mean, I think that they like it because it keeps everyone in check. I don't think that they want it to change… and I think that the people who have the power to change they like it the way it is!

Anthony:
Don't you think that the celebrities and sports stars should be helping in this department instead of talking nonsense on Instagram about the fashion that week?

Anita:
Yes!

Anthony:
With that said… if they benefit from this why would they ever do that? For example, Hanne, if your school teachers at school agree with what you said today, then they also must agree that they have failed you. They have to say "I failed you" because they should have protected you from those teachers. But that's why they don't want to admit it, do you agree with that?

Anita:
Yes! I agree.

Anthony:
Let's talk about *(redacted)*… said that Norway is the "Land of the Janteloven and we don't give sympathy"…

(AN – Further discussion in Norwegian between Anita and Hanne.)

Anthony:
Can I ask you, as a young Norwegian girl how did you feel hearing *(AN – redacted)* say that? So the premise was that we are "Norwegians" and we don't give sympathy because we are the "land of the Janteloven". How did

it feel as young Norwegians to hear that? Those conversations affect me deeply and I'll tell you why. Adults saying "this is the land of the Janteloven... we don't do that here, if you want sympathy then you have come to the wrong place"... proudly saying that in front of adults and teenagers... thinking about that logically I think that that is shameful to say... I'll give you an example why... Maybe you, Anita, have got a private battle that you are fighting... Maybe you, Hanne, have got a private battle that you are fighting... and you hear (redacted) say "we don't do sympathy here". You will say inside to yourself, "I will never speak to these people because I know that I will never get any sympathy from them". That's what I think. What do you guys have to say about that?

Hanne:
Do you remember last time when we were speaking when I said that it was wrong to be compassionate and it was wrong to show emotion? (Laugh)... that's what...

Anthony:
That's what *(AN – redacted)* was saying?

Hanne:
Yes.

Anthony:
OK, let's have a normal conversation and let's talk normally... that's crazy! If you are sitting there in pain or you have got a challenge in your life, you will never trust the adults around you or the people around you like that... You would never share it with them because they have just told you, out loud, that they do not give sympathy here. What I am trying to determine is, how does it make you *feel* to hear them say that?

Hanne:
Like last time that it's wrong to show emotions, that's what they're saying... I kind of wish that it wasn't that way, but I feel that I have accepted that it is that way... that is wrong and that is horrible but it's just the way it is in Norway.

Anthony:
But I'm going to ask you the question again. How does that make you *feel*

inside, emotionally? Think about it right now… "This is the land of the Janteloven, if you want sympathy and compassion you have come to the wrong place"… You heard a Norwegian adult say that… You are a Norwegian teenager… How do you feel emotionally hearing someone say that? Do you feel good, do you feel happy, do you feel sad… how do you feel?

Hanne:
It's sad that if you had a problem then you can't come to the adults, because again… they don't show compassion, they don't care.

(AN – Note that she didn't say how she actually felt but could only state, "It's sad". I have noted this response repeatedly when I often asked people in Norway how they felt.)

Anthony:
Yes… this is what makes it a double whammy for me because obviously they act like that but they have no shame and they will laugh and say it loudly in front of everybody… they act like they are proud of their behaviour! That shows you that they don't even have an insight into the damage that it causes, because it erodes the trust in the people around, because you can't express vulnerability around them because you know that you cannot trust them to be compassionate towards you… That is why a simple comment can actually change somebody's life, because it can turn them away from you. I'm saying that it could be conscious as well as unconscious because the next time you have a challenge you won't turn to these people because they have already said out loud "you are not going to get compassion from me". All the other adults laughed too! Only I spoke out and they looked at me like I was crazy! Does that make any sense at all?

Hanne:
Yes… it doesn't make sense what they are saying… It doesn't sound right…

Anthony:
But in Norway it does?

Hanne:
Yes.

Anthony:
Would you ever say something like that in front of your future children?

Hanne:
No!

Anthony:
Why not?

Hanne:
Because, if they are my children I would like that they could trust me and tell me anything... I don't want them to struggle that they can't tell me because they think that I don't care... That I'm not going to give them sympathy.

Anthony:
Now, that you're looking at it slightly differently, don't you think? "Why, if I would never do that to my children, why are the adults doing it to me?"

Hanne:
I don't know (*laughs*).

Anthony:
How about you, Anita? I think that this is one of the major issues of Norway... How did you feel when you heard those words and how do you feel now?

Anita:
They were saying it as a joke and that is the Norwegian way... to say something serious as a "joke".

Anthony:
They were laughing when they said it but they meant it.

Anita:
Yes... that's the way that we Norwegians do it. If we have to say something to somebody and especially if we are not super close, then we "joke".

Anthony:
Oh, that's the way is it?

Anita:

There are a couple of people… not a lot of people… that I can be 100% honest with; where I don't need to make a joke to tell them something serious. That's how Norwegians do it. They just cover it up with a joke. When they want to actually tell you something serious, unless they are 100% comfortable with you.

Further discussion

Anita:

The people that we know, like family friends are much more stable than the typical Norwegian, but I know that they all know that this is going on.

Anthony:

That's a very interesting point. Why do you think so? You know that they know that all of this is going on? Do you think it's that they just don't care because they've got money and are sorted in their lives?

Anita:

No. I think that they don't care because they don't feel it in the same way. Basically… this is, OK, I don't think that anyone other than you guys will ever understand this but I really appreciate the family that I have grown up with and I really appreciate the way that I have been raised and I think that it's made me really smart and really reflective and all of this. But there are some things that I would obviously never tell my mum or tell my dad, even though, and I know that this is such a teenager thing to say, but they will never ever understand the situation, for example, teenage girls like us two are in right now. They will never ever know and I know it.

Anthony:

It is possible! You just need to have intelligence, an open heart, courage… You just have to care and you just have to listen to people. I think that many Norwegians are so conditioned to BS and pretend that everything is "OK" that they don't see it anymore. They don't see the obvious… so I think that so many actually need to relearn how to start empathising, seeing things and being emotional again… and not being like the Janteloven tells them to be… does anyone actually ever ask you what the problems are in your life? Do people ever come up to you and ask you what pain there is in your life?

Anita:
I don't think our parents will ever know what we are dealing with because I think that it's because they don't care enough. I don't say that to make them out to be bad people because they are very good people.

Anthony:
Absolutely, you can say how you feel and be truthful.

Anita:
That's the truth… For example, the reason that my parents wouldn't care… even though that they know… obviously, I think that if they really knew about how strong we feel about this, then they would probably care…

Anthony:
But if they're not aware and they don't understand they're never gonna get it are they?

Anita:
Yes… but I think that them and their group of friends… obviously they are still in it… but they don't have it as hard as we do at if that makes sense?

Anthony:
I understand.

Anita:
My *(AN – redacted)* literally doesn't give a s*** what anyone thinks about them… I know that even though *(AN – redacted)* pretends to be confident all the time… I know that *(AN – redacted)* makes *(AN – redacted)* insecure at times because, I notice that so easily… Like now, for example, I know that *(AN – redacted)* is insecure because *(AN – redacted)*…

Anthony:
Yes.

Anita:
(AN – redacted, examples of insecurity)… and I think that they and their friends are very comfortable with themselves and their group, so they don't care enough to engage in our (issues)… I don't think that they… obviously, I know that my parents care about me but they don't take

this as serious as I do because they don't know how strongly I feel about it.

Anthony:
I think that this is the most serious issue in Norway.

Anita:
Yes.

Anthony:
This has been a very tough project to do because when I even hint at one of these subjects all of the adults get very scared. Their faces go red and they become uncomfortable.

Anita:
Yes, they get very uncomfortable!

Anthony:
You should see them. They can't even speak about anything! They are so scared at that moment... they are scared of me.

Anita:
The thing is, is that our generation didn't turn out like this on our own.

Anthony:
That's a very good point.

Anita:
They coached us to be like this.

Anthony:
They caused this?

Anita:
Yes!

Anthony:
They are culpable?

Anita:
Yes, exactly!

Anthony:
They know that I am getting to the truth and they don't want me to expose them?

Anita:
Yes!

Hanne:
They made us this way.

Anthony:
What did you just say, Hanne?

Hanne:
They made us this way!

Anthony:
Do you think that because I'm gently pointing this out, they are getting uncomfortable because they don't want this to be revealed?

Anita:
Yes! That's what I said about that they know exactly what is going on because they started it and they raised us to do this! So basically they brought this on us… obviously they felt like… when they were teenagers… they had a somewhat similar situation and I think they are done! They don't care enough… they don't want to talk about it even!

Anthony:
Now, here is the thing… I talk to them gently about it… gently… and I see their faces go tight, I see their eyes go watery, I see their jaws lock up… I see their body language gets weird… and they start getting "ooh errrr, what exactly are your intentions and aims with this book?"… nearly every adult has done that… nearly everybody!

Anita:
Yes.

Anthony:
And then I think to myself "OK. How far do I want to go right now?"
But they are so scared because it's the first time that somebody is going to
tell the truth and they know it. What do you think about that?

Anita:
Yes! That is true obviously.

Anthony:
But I think that if they had any dignity then they would say "Anthony,
say the truth loud and help as many people as you can… say it!"… but
you are saying that they don't say that because they have culpability, they
are guilty? Is that true?

Anita:
Yep.

Anthony:
That's kind of crazy don't you think?

Anita:
Yep! Everybody knows what's going on but they don't care enough to talk
about it.

Anthony:
Hanne, do you think that there are a lot of taboos in Norway?

Hanne:
Yes! (*Laughs.*)

Anthony:
Is there anything that is NOT a taboo in Norway? (*AN – I say this as a
joke.*)

Hanne:
(*Starts laughing.*)

Anthony:
Do you know what… let's answer that question! Is there anything that is
not taboo to talk about in Norway? Maybe I'll give some suggestions…

Skiing? Hiking? The roads? They are the things that I noticed that are not taboo. People will talk openly about them. But what is not taboo in your opinion, that you can have a real public conversation about?

(AN – they are both silent.)

Anthony:
I know that this is a deep one... I can see that your faces are dumbstruck!

Anita:
We are already like that!

Anthony:
(Laughs.) Can I just point out, that you are both incapable of telling me one thing which is not taboo to talk about in Norway!? Hanne, please tell me something which is not taboo to talk about in Norway? Go ahead go ahead... you're taking a looong time!

(AN – we all start laughing.)

Hanne:
The only things that are not taboo are the things that you HAVE to talk about.

Anthony:
The weather? That's not taboo... they can speak about that for six weeks and they will then say "he's a good boy! He talks about the good Norwegian weather!" OK, so we have, weather, skiing, hiking... what else? What is not taboo? You are both being very quiet! And you haven't even giving me one thing yet! Go ahead!

Hanne:
I have no idea... *(AN – She looks like she is about to come up with just one subject that is not taboo in Norway and starts to speak but then stops.)* No... I have nothing...

Anthony:
(AN – I burst out laughing. We all burst out laughing.)
Anita, can you name *something* which is not a taboo to talk about in Norway?

Anita:
No!

Anthony:
So we said weather, hiking, skiing and toll roads. Oh toll roads – that's a new one! So they can say anything about those subjects... but what else?

Anita:
Basically... I think not even those!

Anthony:
What?! You can't even tell the truth about those?

Anita:
Nope! Basically I think that one of the biggest taboos in Norway and this kind of relates to the Janteloven thing, is that you cannot talk about yourself. Like, never!

Anthony:
So that means you can never say what you feel! You don't have freedom in Norway?! Is that true?

Hanne:
Yes.

Anthony:
You can't say what you think and feel because it's against the "Janteloven"!?

Anita:
Yes!

Anthony:
Guys, don't you see!? What the hell?!

Anita:
Yes! But this is my point! Because everything somehow relates to you... so if you talk about skiing, it's going to come up "oh are you a good skier?" so you can't talk about skiing. Or if you talk about mountains "Oh, do you like walking in mountains?", "no I don't", "Oh! You don't like walking in mountains? That

makes you a *really bad person.*" (AN – *she puts on a horrible person's voice in a Norwegian accent.)*

Anthony:
Wow.

Anita:
<u>You can't talk about anything without being like attacked!</u>

Anthony:
Exactly, because *everything* is from *your* perspective. Which means that if you give an opinion one way or the other they are still going to attack you, right? Because even if you say that you like mountains, "Oh, that person is so arrogant they think that they're such a good mountain climber!" And if you say that you "hate" mountains... "Oh they are so unfit! How can they not like our mountains!?" You are damned either way?

Anita:
Yes!

Anthony:
That means that you are doomed?

Anita:
Yes! And this ties back to the first thing that we talked about which is the fake friends... obviously I am not comfortable with 90% of my friends... 98% of my friends... There are only three people that I trust that are my age in my home town.

Anthony:
I just think that you've said such a great point Anita because what the Janteloven does is that it doesn't allow you to raise any opinion which does not subject you to ridicule... It subjects you to ridicule for any opinion. That is the craziest thing! By the way, have I got that right?

Anita:
Yes.

Anthony:
Is that right, Hanne?

Hanne:
Yes.

Anthony:
Please continue your previous point though Anita...

Anita:
Yes... basically the reason that I am not a nutter right now... not an idiot and crazy... is that I have a couple of people around me that I can be real with, I know won't judge me or talk s*** about me, if I say my opinion or what I mean and they can do the same to me and I know that they know that they can and I'm not going to judge or spread it or whatever because that's dangerous in our country, obviously *(Giggles)...*

Anthony:
Can you explain what you mean by that comment, "dangerous in our country" please?

Anita:
Well, that's basically what I just said about the Janteloven point. Even if Hanne said, for example, "I don't like climbing mountains."

Anthony:
Yes.

Anita:
Then she will probably be "judged" for that... but then if she told me and she was comfortable with telling me but I told other people, then it would still be as bad or even worse...

Anthony:
Because they would be like she didn't even have the courage to say?

Anita:
Yes...

Anthony:
This is evil. This is evil.

Anita:
That's why it's so important to at least have one person…

Anthony:
One person that you can be open and honest with otherwise you will go insane?

Anita:
Yes.

Anthony:
Hanne, when Anita mentioned the mountains you said "yes"…

Hanne:
Yes, because when Anita said that you can't speak about yourself… I thought… Norway is proud about our skiing… but you can't talk about yourself… "oh I am so good at skiing"… because then you are like…

Anthony:
A bad person?

Hanne:
Yes! Selfish and you just think about yourself and stuff like that.

Anthony:
But how about if you *are* a good skier?

Hanne:
Yes, but then you are just "bragging".

Anthony:
Who actually cares if you are "bragging"?

Hanne:
Everyone!

Anita:
Everyone!

Anthony:
OK, everyone cares, but can I ask you something? I want to know what is so bad about saying that you are good about something if you really are good at something?

Hanne:
When I was at a party, a guy asked me "are you good at dancing?" and I can say now… that I kind of am…

Anthony:
What do you mean "kind of am"? (AN – Hanne is an absolutely incredible dancer with an extremely high level of performance and talent.)

Hanne:
When I was going in the first team…

Anthony:
Wait, wait, wait… the answer is very simple is "hell yes!"… That's just two words, "hell" and "yes"! Hell yes! So what is all this analysis in your head? Go on…

(AN – we start laughing.)

Hanne:
Because that's like… because then I was like… "I don't know… Yeah I think…"… but that's like…

Anthony:
Just so you know, think about what you have just said logically… don't you think that's strange? You know, in fact everyone knows that you are an amazing dancer… everybody! It's so obvious! You actually had to think about that and you actually undermined yourself. Questioning yourself "Am I? Am I?" That's strange. Don't you see that that is peculiar?

Hanne:
Yes… but that is what I was saying… and he said "you can say if you are good at dancing or not"…

Anthony:
Oh, he said that?

Hanne:
Yes…

Anthony:
My goodness so you can't even say if you are good or not!?

Anita:
He said, "You are allowed to tell me." He was like "you know that you can say yes?" It's not bragging if I'm asking you… but I can't say that I'm good because that is bragging!

Anthony:
So that tells you everything right there… you cannot say what you think even when you know it is true… because of these "rules" that people impose on you. By the way what did you say in the end, Hanne?

Hanne:
I was like "OK then… I… I… I… *think* I'm good."

Anthony:
Oh, you only "think" you're good? When you know that you actually are good, right?

Hanne:
It was like an almost humble way to say like "yes".

Anthony:
Let's see this. You are an amazing dancer. Fact. True?

Hanne:
(Silence.)

Anthony:
Don't worry, you are speaking to me. Now tell the truth.

Hanne:
OK. Yes.

Anthony:
What do you mean "OK. Yes"? You are an amazing dancer! Is that true?

Hanne:
It's like... even now! I can't say "yes", because it's bragging!

Anthony:
Remember that you are speaking to me. So I am asking you, you are an amazing dancer, is that not correct?

Hanne:
Yes.

Anthony:
OK. How come it was so hard for us to talk about a simple fact?

Hanne:
Because this is the land of the Janteloven! *(AN – she laughs.)*

Anthony:
But you weren't even born when this thing was written! What has the Janteloven got to do with you now and why does it affect you today?

Hanne:
(Silence.)

Anthony:
Who taught you it? Who taught you to deny yourself?

Hanne:
The whole society teaches you that you can't brag because that is wrong and you are like... you are bragging.

Further discussion

Anita:
Because they're not our friends.

Anthony:
OK, let me sum up how this sounds. You are surrounded by people that aren't your real friends, that you don't really like, and you can't even talk about it because if you do then you are going to get into trouble in some kind of way?

Anita:
True!

Anthony:
Is that true or not Hanne?

Hanne:
Yes!

Anthony:
Are you joking or are you actually telling the truth?

Anita:
No... That's the truth.

Anthony:
How do you feel about that?

Anita:
Well, I am so used to it that I don't really feel anything special about it if you know what I mean?

Anthony:
Yes.

Anita:
This is just normal.

Anthony:
Hanne, tell me more about this crazy situation that you live in where you don't get support and you can't give your opinion?

Hanne:
It's just the way it is in Norway.

Anthony:
Random question. Do you know what the word 'conformist' means?

Hanne:
No.

Anthony:
Anita do you know what the word 'conformist' means?

Anita:
Conformist?

Anthony:
Yes… but you can say no, it's no problem at all.

(AN – Anita is silent.)

Anthony:
Conformity is when everybody acts the same way, does the same thing and can't say anything different… Norway came extremely high on a survey on conformity but hardly a soul seems to talk about it in Norway and 99% of the people I ask don't even know what the word conformity means it seems… maybe anything which exposes the truth seems to be ignored? You just said "yes" Anita, is that true?

Anita:
Yes! It is!

Anthony:
OK, is there anything else that we need to discuss or shall I wrap this up now?

Anita:
Well if you turn it off we're probably going to carry on talking and then you're going to probably have to turn it on again!

Anthony:
Alright, well let's pause it for now! Thank you!

THE VICTIMS OF JANTELOVEN: HANNE, 16 YEARS OLD, OSLO

IT'S WRONG TO SHOW EMOTIONS. THAT'S WHAT THEY'RE SAYING. I KIND OF WISH THAT IT WASN'T THAT WAY BUT I FEEL THAT I HAVE ACCEPTED THAT IT IS THAT WAY. THAT IS WRONG AND THAT IS HORRIBLE BUT IT'S JUST THE WAY IT IS IN NORWAY

THE VICTIMS OF JANTELOVEN: ANITA, 16 YEARS OLD, OSLO

I THINK THAT THE PEOPLE WHO ARE ABLE TO MAKE A CHANGE LIKE IT BECAUSE IT KEEPS EVERYONE IN CHECK. I DON'T THINK THEY WANT IT TO CHANGE AND I THINK THE PEOPLE WHO HAVE THE POWER TO CHANGE THEY LIKE IT THE WAY IT IS. I KNOW THAT THEY ALL KNOW THAT THIS IS GOING ON

A Conversation with a
Norwegian Museum Worker

Ragnhild is a forty-five-year-old Norwegian woman and works in a museum. She is married to a non-white non-Norwegian and suffers discrimination. She explains that it will take much more than ten years for Norway to change its ways. Here is that conversation.

Anthony:
This may take at least ten years?

Ragnhild:
(*Laughs.*) More like twenty years. I'm forty-five years old and it's been like this all of my life… maybe twenty years.

Anthony:
Say that one more time… what you just said a few moments ago?

Ragnhild:
I don't even remember what I said!

(*AN – Many of the respondents said that they don't remember what they just said. We will look at this closer later.*)

Anthony:
You said, "When you tell people the truth they don't hang around with people like me", is that what you just said?

Ragnhild:
Yes.

Anthony:
Is that what you just said? Please say it one more time for the recorder.

Ragnhild:
People don't like to hear the truth, so when you tell them it, they just don't hang around you too often.

Anthony:
Is that lonely?

Ragnhild:
Naa... you find people that are like minded.

Anthony:
But there are not that many around, so what do you do?

Ragnhild:
There isn't that many around!

(AN – We both burst out laughing.)

Anthony:
Then what do you do?

Ragnhild:
You stick to the few that is there... I'd rather stick with a few than with a lot of people that I just can't tolerate the viewpoint of everything...

(AN – I now make a note for the recorder.)

Anthony:
I am with Ragnhild who has lived fifteen years outside of Norway and she has come back to (AN – redacted – town in Norway), and her friends tell her to "lower her voice in the café", because she has a different dialect... and then I asked her why... Can you just summarise what you said to me please?

Ragnhild:
It's just because I have a different dialect... That my voice kind of stand out amongst the crowd.

Anthony:
But why do they tell you to be quiet?

Ragnhild:
Because this is such a small town that people are worried about gossiping...
That people can hear... People are like, "Arr but I know this and that person
sitting on the table over there and I don't hear what we are talking about."

Anthony:
So they tell you to be quiet?

Ragnhild:
Even if we talk about, "it's been raining for three days in a row"... I mean, I
don't know so many top secret things... It doesn't even matter if people hear
what I am saying or not!

Anthony:
But people tell you to be quiet?

Ragnhild:
Yeah yeah yeah yeah yeah!

Anthony:
And how does that make you feel? Can you see my face... I'm in shock!

Ragnhild:
For me it's, I'm not used to it I'm not from here... I grew up outside of
Oslo... like where it's much... like people don't care and stuff like that...

Anthony:
I'm going to make a guess... You living outside Norway has affected your
social interaction in Norway? I'm guessing that it had an impact because
fifteen years is long enough to be retrained, into speaking loudly and
talking to people that you don't know etc.?

Ragnhild:
Yes! Around Oslo it's what it is like that... It's OK because it's not that much
of a gossiping culture... But here it is a small town and everybody knows each
other and they are more inclined...

Anthony:
Can you just explain to me exactly what a "gossiping culture" means?

Ragnhild:
Like I have friends, if I meet them, and I have never gone to school here I didn't grow up here, I don't really know a lot of people here, and they are like "arr I need… Do you know this or that person?" and I am like "no I don't know who that is"… And they are like "yeah yeah yeah you know that person there"… And I am like "no, I don't know"… And then they are like, "well I have to tell you anyway!"… They are so desperate to tell some kind of gossip! Regardless if I know the person or have any connection! They just need to get it off! *(AN – Their chest.)* They are just gossiping… I don't know… For me it's very weird… Because I've never grown up in this kind of culture… around Oslo it is not like that… It's too big.

Anthony:
In a city, you bump into people that you don't know every day and I guess that you're not going to care about their life?

Ragnhild:
And here there is only a few cafes and one shopping mall and stuff like that… like places around Oslo there are so many malls and stuff like that… so many cafes that no one cares, who is sitting next to them but here they do.

Anthony:
OK you just described it as "weird". Can I describe that's in another way? For me I think that that would be so tough on mental health? How can anybody live like that?

Ragnhild:
(Laugh) I don't know. *(Laugh.)*

Anthony:
Do you find it tough?

Ragnhild:
Well… I don't care because I don't know anyone here! *(AN – she sounds upset.)*

Anthony:
OK... Imagine that? They tell you to be quiet!?

Ragnhild:
Oh, I talk even louder!

Anthony:
OK!

Ragnhild:
I am like I don't care if people don't like it if I shout!

Anthony:
And do your friends go red in the face? What do they do?

Ragnhild:
Yes they sink down and I'm like "I don't care if people hear that we talk about the weather!"

Anthony:
So your response is basically to raise up the level of your uniqueness?

Ragnhild:
Yes.

Anthony:
And then they "sink down" you said?

Ragnhild:
Yes... well... now they're getting used to it!

Anthony:
How long have they had to get used to it?

Ragnhild:
I don't know... Years? I don't know...

Anthony:
This sounds very tough Ragnhild?

Ragnhild:
Yes… I can't stand living here! *(AN – She laughs.)*

Anthony:
Thank you for sharing this and saying that to me.

Ragnhild:
It's very narrow-minded here.

Anthony:
I've been all over Norway, do you think it's just this latitude where the attitudes are like this?

Ragnhild:
I don't know but the places are even smaller so I guess that they would be even worse!

Anthony:
You said that you lived outside of Norway for fifteen years?

Ragnhild:
Yes, I lived in (redacted) for fifteen years.

Anthony:
OK, so you have a type of communication style there, which you experienced for fifteen years… How do you then come back to this? I don't understand… I don't understand how psychologically you can do it?

Ragnhild:
You can't. You can't.

Anthony:
But you have to do it? You are here? You are standing here?

Ragnhild:
For me… My family member is really ill… So that's why… So I am kind of half forced to be here, for the moment.

(AN – She laughs. It is very sad to see.)

Anthony:
Can I just say thank you for telling me that... I feel honoured that you have shared this with me.

Ragnhild:
I wouldn't be here...

Anthony:
If you had a choice?

Ragnhild:
No.

Anthony:
Where would you go if you had a choice, by the way?

Ragnhild:
(AN – redacted Major capital city in the world outside Scandinavia)

Anthony:
Really?

Ragnhild:
But my husband doesn't want to go back there...

Anthony:
Where is your husband from?

Ragnhild:
He is from *(AN – redacted)*.

Anthony:
And he wants to be here?

Ragnhild:
He doesn't want to be here but he wants to be somewhere else.

Anthony:
Away from *(AN – redacted)*?

Ragnhild:

Yes… we talked about Amsterdam… I need to be where it's more multicultural. It's not multicultural here… He is *(AN – redacted – ethnicity and race)* and he gets starred at all the time! It's very racist! Very racist… but it's not even down to colour… it's any kind of foreigner! So, Eastern Europeans… any kind of foreigner.

Anthony:

And that means that because you have married someone that is visually different to the majority of the Norwegian population, because you are close to him, you will see the racism a lot more?

Ragnhild:

Yes, but I have grown up with that my whole life because I have a foreign surname… from my ancestors. *(AN – she sounds upset now.)*

Anthony:

This is horrific! This is not right!

Ragnhild:

That's why I prefer *(AN – redacted – non-Scandinavian capital city.)* *(Laughs.)*

Anthony:

Can I ask you one more question. Do you think that most Norwegians can handle hearing what you have just said?

Ragnhild:

Oh no! But I tell them to their face all the time! I don't give a s***! And I'm Norwegian so I'm *allowed* to say it.

Anthony:

There seems to be a lot of denial in Norway about racism, and to be honest about anything which is perceived as a criticism often seems to be ignored or undermined? What would be your message to Norway and the world about racism in Norway? If you could say one thing… for example, does racism exist in Norway? The propaganda is that everything is fair, there's very little abuse, everything is equal, everything is transparent, very low racism… is that not all true?

Ragnhild:
Racism is *very* high in Norway... but like I said, it's not even just down to your skin colour or look... It could be your name, for example I have grown up for that my whole life... And it's tough!

Anthony:
Yes, don't you get upset?

Ragnhild:
It's tough to apply for a job, for example, when your name... so <u>foreigners in Norway often change their name to a Norwegian sounding name... just to get your foot in the door</u>... But then—

Anthony:
Can I just say, this literally sounds—

Ragnhild:
So it's not necessarily just down to colour... What people think of "normal" racists, that's why Norwegians themselves say, "No we're not racist" because we don't necessarily just discriminate... It's not just a colour discrimination... It's bigger...

Anthony:
I'm a normal person from London and I'm just going to try and translate what you have just said to me... "Discrimination is literally so widespread in Norway that many Norwegians don't even class racism as "racism" because it's just standard blanket discrimination to everybody and anybody who's different? That is what you just told me?

Ragnhild:
Towards everyone who is not Norwegian, yes.

Anthony:
So, it's so widespread that it's not even noticed any more in Norway? Is that true?

Ragnhild:
Well, in a way yes!

Anthony:
Does your husband speak to you about this?

Ragnhild:
Yes, we talk about it all the time... I talk to my colleagues about it!

Anthony:
What does your husband have to say about it?

Ragnhild:
And I challenge my colleagues, and I challenge my Norwegians as well.

Anthony:
How do they react?

Ragnhild:
They don't like it. (*Laughs.*)

Anthony:
They don't like it?

Ragnhild:
Of course not. (*Laughs.*)

Further discussion

Anthony:
I've just turned the tape recorder back on because you just said that "Norwegians need to be challenged"?

Ragnhild:
Yes!

Anthony:
And you said that you challenge Norwegians?

Ragnhild:
Yes. It's so ingrained here and people think, you know, *we are voted the best country in the world... And they are just sitting there riding their white horse...*

And just think that they are above everyone else… And that's the problem! That is so ingrained in the culture… That I think that for Norwegians to change that they need to live abroad for a while. Most of my friends that have lived abroad are not like that… And people from around Oslo and biggest cities…

(AN – We will be speaking to other Norwegians from various major cities and look at this in detail.)

Anthony:
Just so you know, it is still there.

Ragnhild:
Oh yeah yeah yeah yeah! But less.

Anthony:
Can you just say what you said again please?

Ragnhild:
I can't remember what I. (*Laughs.*)

Anthony:
You said that when you went into the job interview every time they mention to you "your name is not"?

Ragnhild:
Oh yeah… "Where is that name from? That's not Norwegian!"

Anthony:
Is that what they say to you every time?

Ragnhild:
Yeah, yeah… Yeah yeah.

Anthony:
Tell me what they say to you exactly?

Ragnhild:
And here… When I'm here, because I have a different dialect, they will say "Where are you from? What are you doing here? Are you going back?"

Anthony:
They assume that you are an "outsider"?

Ragnhild:
They don't assume because they can hear it! Because I speak such a different dialect.

Anthony:
And do they treat you in a different way?

Ragnhild:
Yeah yeah yeah… and some even say "Is there someone here that we can talk to about who you are?"… Like kind of…

Anthony:
Wait wait…

Ragnhild:
Like… It's not good enough…

Anthony:
Please explain that to me like I'm a young child. Are they trying to say that you are not good enough, to your face?

Ragnhild:
They just say, because I haven't got a local surname, they don't see any connections that they can ask… because I haven't gone to the schools here so they can't ask.

Anthony:
What has that got to do with applying for a job? I don't understand?

Ragnhild:
Because they, the locals, they always ask around… "Oh this person applied for a job in my place, do you know him?"

Anthony:
That is blatant discrimination though?

Ragnhild:
Yeah yeah yeah!

Anthony:
How does that make you feel?

Ragnhild:
Horrible.

Anthony:
Is it normal here?

Ragnhild:
Yes… every single time I've gone for a job interview here, I get these questions… every single time.

Anthony:
Haven't they got discrimination training and law here?

Ragnhild:
(Bursts out laughing)

A Conversation with Norwegian Teenagers (2)

Helene and Petr are sixteen years old and fifteen years old respectively. Both are students from different schools. They are girlfriend and boyfriend and kind and intelligent. We have been discussing the Norwegian 'stereotype' books that you will find in most, if not all, Norwegian bookshops. You join us as Helene is expressing that she would not tell somebody, that she did not know, if she liked their trainers (sneakers) but her boyfriend Petr is disagreeing.

Anthony:
I think that it's a tragedy that you can't tell somebody if you like their nice trainers, even if you want to. Now, you just told me Helene that "I don't want to speak to somebody that I don't know" but then Petr on the other hand said, "I do!" Petr, speak to me… what's going on in Norway?

(AN – A quick pre-discussion in Norwegian has just taken place before I said this… we note that although I asked Petr the question, it is Helene who answers… we will immediately see that Helene is attempting to convince Petr that he is wrong about his own point of view.)

Helene:
I can tell you what we said in Norwegian. I said "who?" and he said… the people that are one year older than us and I said, "well, that's not a stranger", 'cause you know them but you don't *personally* know them.

Petr:
I don't really know them.

Helene:
Yeah, but you follow them on Instagram, like, they know who you are, they know your name, so it's not like…

Petr:
Yeah, but I've never spoke to them.

Helene:
Yeah, but then it's a way to get to know them. He's talking about if you walk in to the shopping mall and see a random person that you've never seen them before and you like their shoes then you would just think to yourself that "you like their shoes"… you wouldn't say it!

Petr:
Well, if, I'm with my friends and they had some friends, I will speak to them, if they were strangers I would say it to them.

Helene:
No, you wouldn't!

Petr:
Yes! I would say that they had nice trainers!

Helene:
No, no… I promise you would not!

Anthony:
Now, let me ask you something, Petr, straight out…

Helene:
It's bull***t, that's the…

(AN – Helene is now angry. She is agitated, uncomfortable and interrupting Petr for sharing a point of view that she doesn't agree with.)

Petr:
How's it bull***t?!

Anthony:
Petr, now let me ask you a question, OK…many people are telling me in Norway… I understand that; if you say that you want to talk to somebody that you don't know well, you will probably be attacked and people will say you're "crazy" if you want to talk to that person… "you don't know them!" they will say, "why are you speaking to them?"

Petr:
Yes. It's not normal.

Anthony:
It's not normal in Norway? In this country?

Petr:
It's not normal… in this country.

Anthony:
Tell me more about that?

Petr:
If you speak to people you don't really know they think you're "crazy" or completely out of your mind.

Anthony:
Let me tell you something, Petr. It feels like they pressure you, even if you want to speak, you can't? So, this is sad isn't it?

Petr:
Yeah, instead of being a nice person you become like a weird person.

Helene:
But I don't think that always applies… because sometimes… I've done that before and told them "that's nice whatever" and people have done it to me and then I don't think, "they're so weird!" I don't know but with girls then "oh my God that's so sweet".

(AN – Helene sounds unsure.)

Petr:
Already, ladies, they like to talk!

Helene:
Nooo!

Petr:
Yeah! *(Laughs.)* Everywhere.

Helene:
If you see another teen… I don't know… I don't know if that applies to boys though.

Anthony:
Now, It feels like, it does feel like there are expectations? So, let's just say that you like this person's bike, they've got a very nice bike, or they've got very nice shoes, and you don't know them at all and let's say you were in a happy mood and you just want to give them a compliment, "Oh, nice bike, girl!" or "Nice shoes, man!", then it seems that that is not normal in Norway? It's kind of punished then? People might look at you like that person might be a bit "weird", do you know what I mean?

Petr:
Yeah.

Anthony:
What do you have to say about that?

Petr:
Sometimes, it applies but when I, for example, play football and I see a guy off the training ground, it's like a community… we talk to each other.

Anthony:
But, this is a network that you've already created within the community but I'm talking about inter communities… if you don't know the person and you're not associated with them then I think that it appears that it's more "risky" to say something to them? Do you agree with that?

Petr:
Yes.

Anthony:
Now, this is the question which I want to get to which these books don't, what is the effect on the psychology of the people, these expectations, these pressures, I think that they might have a bad effect? I think that they probably cause anxiety because the bottom line is this: if you want to say "hi" to somebody or you want to say that somebody has nice shoes, then you should be FREE, with no pressure, no nothing, free to say that with no one judging you… that's my opinion. What do you have to say about that?

Petr:

It's true. Like erm, if you want to be, if you just see a guy on the street and you think, "oh, he's cool", I want to be his friend, you don't go up to him and say "hey, let's talk". *You just walk in the other direction…*

Anthony:

Do you pretend?

Petr:

Yes, you *pretend* that you didn't see them…

(AN – He is stating categorically that he is forced to act in a way that he doesn't agree with.)

Helene:

But, that <u>wouldn't be normal!</u> You wouldn't see… like… you don't look at a person and think "oh, I want to be their friend!"

Petr:

You see like, "they look cool… he seems nice!"

(AN – Helene is becoming angry and is combative… she seems triggered by Petr expressing his own opinion and view. She immediately tells him the way he "should" act and tells him directly that his actions are abnormal.)

Helene:

No, you can't… I don't think, now, I think that… this is kind of too much now! *(AN – Helene looks about to cry.)* I don't agree with that at all because I don't think that any, I don't think that that applies to Norway, I don't think that <u>anyone</u> would see a random person in the street and be like, "I want to be their friend!" **because you don't know anything about them and maybe they're a serial killer and you wouldn't know!** I don't think that anyone would see like "oh, they look cool and I want to be their friend"… <u>it's just not right!</u>

(AN – She is seemingly exhibiting signs of fear at the mere <u>thought</u> of this scenario. Her boyfriend's words seem to have elicited a traumatic response which is now translating to real emotional distress.)

Anthony:
OK, so now, do you think that that has never happened and doesn't happen in Norway?

Helene:
Yeah.

Anthony:
Petr?

Petr:
(Petr turning to his girlfriend), So when you saw me for the first time?

Helene:
Yeah, I knew who you were, we have all the same friends, and that does not apply and that is not the same situation.

Petr:
But, you didn't know me.

Helene:
No, not personally, but my best friend and best friend…

Petr:
But I seemed cool?

Helene:
Yeah, but you're not a stranger that's my point!

(AN – Helene claps her hands hard and has raised her voice.)

Petr:
For you, I was.

Helene:
No!

Petr:
Yes.

Helene:

Nooo… you weren't a complete stranger. If I saw you on the street then I would have known your name was Petr. You would know me… but… I…

(AN – She rejects Petr's completely logical explanation. She now starts to alter the definition of words to suit her own interpretation of reality, i.e.… he wasn't a "complete" stranger. We will observe many others do the same thing throughout this book series and take a closer look into this later.)

Anthony:

So, you're saying that it's more of a safety question because maybe they're a threat?

Helene:

No. not… errmm… for example… they might just be weird. I am just saying, nobody would look at a person and think "they're pretty I want to be their friend", that's <u>JUST NOT RIGHT!</u>

Anthony:

I'll tell you something really interesting, this might shock you. In our country that actually is pretty normal. What do you think of that?

Helene:

Yeah, but that's <u>WRONG!</u> I mean if it's like, for your example now, when I saw him, then I'm like, I trusted to talk to him and obviously be his friend because we literally, like, it's the same group of people, you know?

Anthony:

So you felt safe?

Helene:

Yeah!

Anthony:

But if you saw the person that you thought was nice and they weren't in the group and you didn't know them, would you never say to yourself, "I want to be their friend?" If you didn't know them already?

Helene:
The thing is that if you see somebody on the street once then you won't feel connected at all!

Anthony:
Or in the café or in the shop? Basically, anywhere in public...

Helene:
Yeah, 'cause, then you just see them for just a couple of seconds and you will never see them again so they won't make a... maybe you will think... "Oh... there was this handsome guy" but it wouldn't be anything more!

(AN – She explains what many of the respondents will state explicitly; you simply don't connect with people you don't know well and this "rule" is apparently strict, rigid and inflexible for many in Norway?)

Anthony:
So here's the thing, this is what it feels like, the way you "enter" somebody's life, it has to be by protocols? It has to be very "safe" routes into their life? You cannot randomly meet somebody on the street, because they might be perceived as a threat? Have I got that right?

Helene:
Well, not as a *threat*...

(AN – Helene stresses her disagreement with the word "threat" but has obviously indicated that at least some "strangers" are potential threats, even potentially a "serial killer".)

Anthony:
So does that mean that the only friends that the young people have are mainly school friends from their "gang"?

Helene:
Yes, but like, for example, there's kind of like... there are three types of people; popular people, the people that are just weird and then just like the middle class...

(AN – Multiple young people all over Norway have explained the hierarchy which is very clear in schools and is instilled young. They will explain themselves that

school people are divided into groups of importance, including labels such as: "losers", "r*tards", "middle class" and the "alphas". At the same time we are told repeatedly that Norway is an "equalitarian society" and that "hierarchy doesn't exist in Norway".)

Anthony:
Yes.

Helene:
Everybody knows their place. So now everyone, there is kind of a mix, for example, like our friends, are like, some from this school, some from, like, from another school… and it's kind of like mixed.

Anthony:
So, that means that, in a way, even though there are like three "levels", you still know each other? You see each other, you still talk sometimes?

Helene:
What do you mean?

Anthony:
Do you know you said that there are those three classes of "weird", "middle" and "popular"… those groups?

Helene:
Yes.

Anthony:
Do the different social groups interact?

Helene:
Yes. The "middle class" and the "popular", yes, but *not* the bottom.

Petr:
But you still go in the same class as some of the "weird" ones, like, and then you *have* to talk to them.

Helene:
But you *don't* hang out with them.

Anthony:
Can I ask you a question about this "popular" level? What were the names of the groups again? Popular...? Tell me the groups?

Helene
(*Laughing.*) Popular, middle class (*laughing*), weirdos. That's what I know...

Anthony:
Now, can I ask you guy's a personal question?

Helene:
Yeah.

Anthony:
What group are you guys in? I think you guys are in the popular cool group! What group are you in? You're in the top group?

Helene:
Yeah.

Anthony:
Petr?

Helene:
(*Helene answers for him*). Yeah...

Anthony:
Petr, you're in the top group aren't you? OK, well let me ask you a question. When you read those books about Norwegian culture, they tell you that there's no hierarchy in Norway. Like in the UK, we have hierarchy; do you know what that means?

Petr:
Yeah!

Helene:
Yeah.

Anthony:
I believe that they are complete nonsense!

Petr:
Yeah!

Helene:
Yeah.

Anthony:
I have seen Norway and there is hierarchy. Even you have just described that to me, so that means that there is something that's not adding up here? Tell me?

Petr:
In high school, you can't sit on the table of older people and the popular kids on one table and the other kids on the other guys have another table and if you come and sit on the table with an older person, you're like, weird...

Helene:
Then you're like, "What the ****?"

Petr:
Like, "what are you doing here?"

Anthony:
Would you just say that to them verbally or would you just stare at them?

Petr:
Look weird at them...

Anthony:
OK, *(turning to Helene)* and how about you?

(AN – They are both now describing their own non verbal passive aggressive behaviour and normalisation of it.)

Helene:
Yeah, you would just like, B*TCH them basically.

Anthony:
(AN – I react with a cry of shock at what she said!) Now, this is the curious thing. The stereotype and even what so many Norwegians repeat; "we

don't like hierarchy" and "everybody is equal here, we don't have hierarchy in this country"... this is not true? You've just described some?

Helene:
We teens do...

Anthony:
Alright, I have another question. If you were in the "bottom" group. What's that called?

Helene:
Just weirdos.

Anthony:
The "weirdos", how do you feel, or... how do you think... now this is imagination... how would you feel to live life in the "bottom" group?

Petr:
When I was in the seventh grade.

Anthony:
How old is that?

Petr:
Twelve, thirteen... I was in the bottom group.

Anthony:
Tell me about that?

Petr:
I was a weirdo. Like all the people who are good at school and just sit at home and play video games and do homework all day... I was THAT person.

Anthony:
Yes, OK. How did it feel?

Petr:
I think it was, like, great. At the time...

(AN – Helene strongly interjects.)

Helene:
I think that it *works* in a way. The weirdos are so far out anyway!

Anthony:
That they enjoy it?

Helene:
That they don't care. So they don't care and they don't need to have loads of friends, they don't care… *if everything was morally correct,* everybody should strive to like those people, because, they don't care for how people see them and they just have a good time any way and then the *middle class of people* (laughing), it's either that they are very happy with their group of friends, and in our case, as in for the girls, the people that are "middle class" are actually really good friends, so either they are, they don't care because they love each other la la la… but it's like one or two people who want to be very popular… so then, they're like pressuring to be popular basically but then… I think…

(AN – Stated simply, she is stating that the "weirdo" group are so weird that they enjoy their position because they "don't care"… ("let them eat cake"?) Her next statement, "if everything was morally correct", implies that things are NOT currently morally correct, which is evidently the case?)

Anthony:
Do you ever feel pressure too? Do you know what the word "conform" means? Like to behave in a certain way because you're in the "top group", like is there any time when you just say, "oh my goodness, I wish I could just be myself and not worry about these silly groups"… does that ever happen?

(AN – They both exhale big breaths and take their time… this is incredible. They are under so much pressure which they will explain right now…)

Petr:
Yeah, yeah.

Anthony:
Feel free to speak honestly…

Petr:
Because like, the people in the middle group feel so connected to each other, they're like good friends, they accept each other, like, much more.

Anthony:
So peer pressure is in the top group a little bit?

Petr:
Yeah.

Helene:
Yes, a lot!

Petr:
You have to be a certain person, you have to have big muscles and the girls
need to have like certain big ass.

Helene:
(*Laughs.*)

Petr:
You have to be like "handsome" or "cute".

Anthony:
You know what, that sounds quite tough, because some days you
might feel, "Oh my God, let me just go to the shop…" and you might
feel like you have to dress up and impress them or something, is it like
that maybe?

Petr:
Yeah. You *always* think about what you're going to wear and how other
people are going to see you.

Helene:
Yeah.

Anthony:
Now, let me ask you something. From my perspective, that sounds tough.
As in, that's a lot of pressure to put on a person, I mean, do you ever
think about that?

Helene:
YES!

Anthony:
Tell me Helene, speak…

Helene:
Yes! Every day! (*Laughs.*) I literally feel like I have no friends or that I literally have like three friends because people care so much more about how they appeal to others, than their actual friendships and stuff and I don't think that some of them realise and it's just people pick their friends.

Petr:
That's more girly, the guys are more connected like, we do sh*t together.

Helene:
They're more like brothers.

Petr:
We're more like brothers. *They're* striving to be the "best".

Anthony:
Striving to be the best, you say?

Petr:
They're trying to get on top of the like, in the like cool of the cool gang.

Anthony:
Let me ask you a question. Who teaches you these things? Who is the person who invented this whole system? Where did it come from?

Petr:
It's an unspoken rule.

Anthony:
Say that again? In Norway?

Petr:
It's more like an unspoken rule.

Anthony:
Now, let me ask you, do you think that that "unspoken rule" is a positive thing or a negative thing? But really think about the answer to this one

because this is quite a deep one… do you think it's good for you or bad for you in the end?

Petr:
It's both positive and negative.

Anthony:
Tell me why?

Petr:
Like when you think about more about how people observe/perceive(?) you as a person, trying to be the nice person… errr… helpful person.

Anthony:
OK.

Petr:
But in the same way, you always have to dress up… it's like pressure.

Anthony:
How about you, Helene?

Helene:
I think, it's more bad in the end because it's all pressure but then at the same time it **makes the world work. Without this I think it would all be chaos… so it's good to keep order** (laugh)… But mentally, I don't think it's good in the end.

Anthony:
Mentally, you don't think it's "good" in the end, did you say?

Helene:
Yeah, yeah.

Anthony:
So, my message, has always been, 'you are free to break out of it if you want to break out of it'… but it's quite funny, that I am realising now, that after living in Norway for a time… let's just say that you woke up one day and wanted to break out of this "system" and live differently, I think it would be so hard to do?

Helene:

You wouldn't be able to. Because, I think, personally, if I could have I would have definitely because it's like so much fake sh*t, basically, and when I look at the middle class girls for example, I'm actually jealous of them because they're actually friends.

(AN – The pressure that is forced upon them is unacceptable. This book's aim is to help those who wish to break free of this concealed suppression in Norway.)

Anthony:

Did Petr just... Petr, you just said the same thing didn't you?

Petr:

Yes.

Helene:

So I wish I had that many real friends (laugh), erm but then, when you (sigh), kind of when you're at the top everybody wants to be there, so it takes a lot to give it up.

Anthony:

I totally get it and I totally understand that.

Petr:

It's not like the top class girls don't want to talk, the top class girls choose their friends, if the middle class girls were their friends, middle class girls, then they would have been in the popular.

Helene:

Yeah, so basically, there is one person, just one person, just one girl...

Anthony:

What's her name by the way?

Helene:

(AN – redacted name.) She's like **alpha**.

(AN – Note that they have such an understanding of hierarchy and labels like "alpha" at their young age.)

Anthony:
OK.

Helene:
If she like switched.

Anthony:
I'm very impressed that you know what "alpha" means by the way.

Helene:
(Laughter.) Yeah! Basically, you have the middle class girls and all of my friends,
our group, except for (named "alpha"), if she just switched us out with them, let's
just say that it's always been like that, if they were your friends, they would be the
popular.

Anthony:
Wow, that's incredible. So, by association to one person they would now
be "top" too?

Petr:
Yes.

Helene:
Yes.

Anthony:
Who's the "alpha" boy? You?

Petr:
No, the boys are more like spread out. They're like, multiple alphas… like *all*
alphas.

Anthony:
So, it seems to me like there might be a little bit of pressure to be an
"alpha" male?

Petr:
Yes, but then it clashes. Two alpha makes in the same room… is bad.

Anthony:
Give us the gossip Petr!

(AN – we all start laughing.)

Petr:
Like, if one alpha wants one thing and another alpha wants another thing,
they make like groups and they're arguing, rivals gets very personal for the
boys. Yep.

Anthony:
What you guys have described to me… it sounds TOUGH! It seems like
you can't just make a friendship with them alone. You make a friend then
you get the whole group?

Helene:
You make your friends through your friends.

Anthony:
So, the friend comes through the group not through the friend?

Helene:
Yep.

Petr:
Yeah, you don't decide who your friend is.

Anthony:
Oh… guys… this is painful to hear!

Petr:
It's more for the girls then the boys. The boys are like, as I said, more
"connected".

Anthony:
So listen to this, now that you've verbalised this to me right now, talked
this through, I don't know if you've ever talked about this ever? I don't
know, but what I will say is this, do you think that if you could describe
everything you've just described in one word, is it "good" or "bad", just
from your heart, what would say? Good or bad?

(AN – They are struggling to answer this question.)

Anthony:
One word only. What would you say?

(AN – They look scared to answer truthfully.)

Anthony:
Don't be scared! Good or bad?
Shout it out! There is no wrong answer! Is it good or bad?

(AN – They are like struck silent… the question has elicited fear… they are scared to answer it.)

Petr:
I think it's good.

Anthony:
Really? Brilliant. Helene?

Helene:
Bad.

Anthony:
(AN – to Petr) Now, can I ask you something… you have just described very logically things which are—

Helene:
Wait, I want to say something…

Anthony:
Helene, please, speak.

Helene:
Hmm… I think that if you ask the… because obviously, you know your place in the popular group as well… everybody knows who are the most popular, so the people that are the most popular will say it's good. He (Petr) would say it's good.

Anthony:
Because he gets the benefits of being at the "top"?

Helene:
Yeah.

Anthony:
I understand.

Helene:
Because he doesn't have anything bad.

Anthony:
Petr, would you say that's fair enough?

Petr:
Yes.

Anthony:
So, you're getting the glory of being the "alpha" male?

Petr:
Yeah, but I think that several of my friends would say that it's good. Ermm, I think it's bad anyway, I don't think it's good but overall it has benefits…

Helene:
But overall it benefits him, but for me, I'm not very popular…

Anthony:
Now, Helene you just said something very important, if you can imagine, if you are not on the top then it can be extremely tough. That's what it seems like? Like, pressure… pain… emotional pain?

Helene:
Everybody looks at it, as the best thing is to be in the popular group kind of and it gets worse to be in the like, the middle class, but I would say that its worse to be at the bottom of the popular group, like I am.

Anthony:
Now, what's this system based on, is it based on looks? What's this based

Petr:
No, it's somewhat appearance, but erm who you are.

Anthony:
Like status?

Helene:
Yeah.

Petr:
Like up on the top all the time, like…

Anthony:
But Helene, you've got so much talent, you're popular, you're brainy…
do the people not see this?

Helene:
I get judged so much because I'm smart! *(Laughter.)* Everybody's, like, OK,
I'm kind of like just a nerd.

Anthony:
But you're cool and smart too!

Helene:
Noooo… because I'm too scared to be myself. These people, because I don't
trust them 100%.

*(AN – She describes living in fear which prevents her being herself. Are they are
inadvertently whistle-blowing on Norwegian society?)*

Anthony:
Yes, yes.

Helene:
I'm too scared to like… like… show myself…

Anthony:
I can understand that. Can I give you guys a confession? I understand
exactly why you would be scared, because I really see this as a tough
situation, from a mental health point, it's not "safe", it's quite risky, if

you... you're nodding, do you know what I mean?

Helene:
Yes. The thing like *(sigh)*, if I like had a choice now, I would way like to be friends with the popular girls, because I love them and I really appreciate them and if I could then I would have known them better and stuff but I'm like, I don't have that choice. They have that choice and since they have the right to pick and choose... and I'm not picked or chosen. So, I'm like, I can't do anything about it.

Petr:
For the boys it's like... all say they benefit from being... but they actually don't mean that because it's more "girly" to think you're not good enough, not brave enough, not strong enough, you don't look as good as the others, and if you SAY that then you're more like a "girly"...

Anthony:
Are you saying that in the boy group that if you show vulnerability and emotion like that then that's bad?

Petr:
Yeah.

Anthony:
Or it's not safe to do that?

Petr:
It's safe, in a certain way, if you're a certain person...

Anthony:
Ah... so if you're the "top", you have maybe your group, like a secret group where you can tell them?

Petr:
Yeah!

Anthony:
But the others will never know the truth?

Petr:
Yeah, no, it's like, erm, you can be like heartbroken and the boys would like understand it's like not that type of girly but if you don't like yourself or don't have strong muscles.

Helene:
You're not confident in your appearance, basically…

Petr:
You have to be confident.

Anthony:
So you have to pretend?

Petr:
To be confident.

Anthony:
Even if you are not? Inside you pretend?

Petr:
Yep.

Helene:
Yep.

Petr:
You don't be "you".

(AN – He is stating in plain English that you have to "disassociate" to function in their "system". They will now describe themselves as being like clones. They are very intelligent and articulate. I am very impressed, considering the environment they are in and what they have been taught is "normal" behaviour.)

Anthony:
Yep.

Petr
"You" are like all the other guys. All the guys dress the same… all the guys speak the same… all the guys are like "cocky".

Anthony:
What you've just described sounds like a clone army!

Petr:
Yeah! It's like clones! Yeah! If you like, have seen us on the street you will have thought like, "they're clones". They're all like the same person! (Laugh)

Anthony:
Helene, what do you have to say about this clone stuff?

Helene:
Yeah, that's true actually.

Anthony:
Helene, what you've just described to me… it affects me… it's not something which I think is normal and it's not good for the mental health, in my opinion… you have just described when you guys are alone, maybe you feel pain, maybe you feel pressure, and maybe you feel that you can't share your fears and after a while, after years of that, even when you're a teenager and there are enough issues, that can really hurt you and make you feel depressed or maybe suicidal and maybe you don't have anybody to turn to tell these things? What do you have to say about that?

Petr:
Yes, I think that's very true.

Helene:
I think that, yes, I agree with you, it's very true because you can't tell anyone because your friends are the ones you're trying to escape, if you get that?

(AN –I have heard this from the <u>majority</u> of respondents up to eighty years old.)

Anthony:
That makes amazing sense.

Helene:
I tried to tell him this on like Sunday. And he was like, "Oh you're so stupid!"

Anthony:
Tell me what you think about this. I feel so honoured that you have just

shared what you have just shared, with me. Because, sometimes I have found that many of the Norwegian people are a little bit fearful, they have expectations of how they think and what they should say, and sometimes that doesn't match what they feel in their heart and you know what, they're scared. So many seem scared to say what they really think, that they're going to be judged or even like it's going to be bad, so it's like you need to know for <u>sure</u> that you're going to be safe revealing how you really feel and those vulnerabilities... Now, can I ask you a question? The things that we have spoken about today, have you ever spoken to anybody about them before, truthfully? Have you ever, like, spoke out about these things to anybody? Petr, you first...

Petr:
Yeah, I talk to my close friends, like er, people I trust the most.

Anthony:
And what do you conclude? Do you just say that that is the way it is and we just have to keep marching on?

Petr:
No, like when I'm with these friends we talk about things like that. We can say that we don't think we're good enough. I think that I'm fat, for example. One of my friends, think they're too fat and he can say that to us but in the same way, I'm not very smart, me, like in school, so he's like more smart in school, so he thinks he can say "Oh, you're so dumb" in school, to me...

Anthony:
What! He says it to you?

Petr:
Like to joke, but it's not a joke.

Anthony:
Sometimes people say things as a "joke" because they can get away with it but sometimes it's serious?

Petr:
Yep and we like joke about him being fat...

Further discussion

Anthony:
Imagine if the "lower" groups knew that the "upper" groups thought like this, don't you think that it would be so cool that they knew that they also have insecurities?

Helene:
But then, we wouldn't be as popular, you know…

Petr:
We would show, like weakness, when we say we don't like ourself.

(AN – If there is anything which I have observed all over Norway it is simply this: expressions of vulnerably are too often perceived as "weakness" by both the victim and the community, so it is often just covered up, as Petr is stating now.)

Anthony:
Can I just say that I am so honoured to have this conversation today with you. Let me ask you a question. I have had many of these conversations in Norway, where people have told me the truth, like what we just discussed today… you will never see that in the usual books about Norway… are you comfortable about me speaking about these things and why do you think people have been open with me?

Petr:
I trust you. I feel like, I think you're a very smart person, you know people and have a bunch of stories to tell me about people, like you've been to the north people and people in other places, you have been too, I think you can help if I talk to you.

Anthony:
How about you, Helene? Why am I getting this like real stuff… because it's not in any of the Norwegian "social guide" books, newspapers or on YouTube or on TV, so why am I getting it? I'm curious about what you think?

Helene:
Do you mean why people trust you?

Anthony:
Yes, to tell me the things that they don't tell other people?

Helene:
Because they have nobody else to tell, basically, my case… my case… my opinion 100% (is) I feel way smarter than 99% of my friends and I don't feel comfortable because I don't think I would, I know I would just feel judged and I think a lot of people can relate to that, that they can't even show their weakness or opinion to their…

Anthony:
It's about authenticity… people know that when they speak to me they know they can be real with me and I think because I'm real with them, they'll be real with me and I have to say I don't think that there is a lot of "real" communication in Norwegian society that I can see. You often can't be authentic it seems? You can't reveal your real self… if you do, you will be smashed? What do you have to say about that?

Petr:
Yes! Like my father. If I ask my father something then he won't tell me the 100% the truth, every time. For the better and for the worse, so if I look strange, if I look strange, like if you don't like what I'm wearing… still say that and if I have something very personal to talk to you about, it will say that, I would I hear you, will say that… what he thinks is best, and I appreciate that… it's where I talk to my father much more than I talk to my mother, because my mother is like "Oh, it's OK it's fine, everything will be OK, don't worry about it"… earlier my father thinks the real, the best things, so they must be not that many people in the world. The older generation, like, tells the truth but my mother is a bit younger and from the city, and my father is from the country and they tell each other the truth… are there is just like Helene and her friends like they all strive to be the best… everyone wants to be alpha…

(AN – Petr has communicated mixed messages so I am going to explain, as I understood it in the room. His father doesn't tell him the truth on every occasion but he will at least try and listen and will at least try to give a reasonable answer, even if it's not completely truthful. His mother is from the city and just like Helene and her friends … her priorities are being better than the rest, materialism etc. When Petr approaches his mother with an issue, she dismisses it with the usual, "OK, everything will be fine… don't worry about it… etc." Petr is fully aware of

this dynamic and understands that it is a waste of time speaking with his mum. He states that the "older generation… tells the truth" but has stated earlier that his father won't tell the complete truth. (Note that, Petr has already learned that there are "percentages" of truthfulness, from his parents, evidently? We will meet a Norwegian academic who will explain how it works, in detail shortly). He implies, that his mother does not tell the truth because she's from the city and wants to be an "alpha" and he explains that he believes that people in the countryside tell the truth.)

Anthony:
The things that you told me today… sounds like the effect of all this… could possibly get people feeling very down about themselves, at certain points, because there's so much pressure to deal with and you know that you don't deserve to deal with this… it is not right. Can I ask you, what I just said… that the things you describe today, in my personal opinion, might potentially result in mental health challenges… you know what I'm talking about… do you have any view on what I'm saying?

Petr:
Yes. Like my mother, when I say something very hard to her she takes it very personal… She reacts very hard on it… I think it goes in her mind and she thinks about it a lot when me and my brother, like say s***, that we don't mean, but we say it, she like, reacts in a certain way, she gets quiet… she holds it in her.

(AN – To hear a child have this understanding of his parents is both incredible but also horrifying. Even at this young age he has learned to equate being honest with being "hard" because she, in his words, "reacts hard on it". This is without looking at the answer as a whole… he is clearly communicating that his mother's behaviour is unstable. He also references obvious passive aggressive behaviour, "she holds it in her…" which is often described as "standard" behaviour in Norway, according to almost every respondent I interviewed.)

Anthony:
Hold it in?

Petr:
Yes, I think my mother thinks about it a lot and it's not healthy for her or for me or my brother… or my father.

(AN – Petr is analysing the adult's irrational and unhealthy behaviour and concluding that it is unhealthy for him and everyone around.)

Anthony:
Tell me about your dad. How does he react to that?

Petr:
My father like, talks about things, he gets it out, he wants to talk instead of waiting… he doesn't want to wait on the person… just like he goes right at it.

Anthony:
So he doesn't let it build up and then explode, he just gets it out every day?

Petr:
Yes. They are like the opposite of each other.

Helene:
I think that it will eventually affect your mental health I can actually relate to it because I was like the biggest weirdo ever like below the lowest class even it was bad… because I go to a brainy class… I didn't know anybody before I started my hobby, like I didn't kind of have any friends outside of school, outside of the activities like skiing and stuff… but then I didn't care… I didn't care about anyone… I was just being myself and life was more fun I was like, happier. **Now… there is literally just pressure like everywhere and especially this year, I'm literally like crying all the time.**

(AN – This is clearly not "just a normal teenage problem". It's not her fault but she <u>thinks</u> it is her fault. Her behaviour and response has been mirrored by people of all ages. She thinks she is alone but does not know that her response is wide spread.)

Anthony:
Do you feel like crying is not OK? Do you feel like you can't show this side to society? For example, know that you can tell me anything and cry right now if you want to, and you know I will be cool. Is that not the case in your society?

Helene:
Well, you can't cry to your friends when you're crying *about* your friends!

Anthony:
I totally understand.

Helene:
So, I cry to him all the time but I feel like I can't because I cry all the time and I feel like I'm annoying.

Further conversation

Helene:
You can't cry to your problems!

Anthony:
So, guys, how do you feel now that we have talked about this today? How do you feel now? We've just had a really interesting conversation, we've shared things, you gave me your view, how do you feel after this conversation?

Petr:
It's like kind of a **relief to talk about it** because I don't talk about it as much. I just can't like, talk about it every time when I'm just with my close friends…and it gets annoying for them and I can't always talk about it with Helene because then it gets annoying for her.

(AN – They have both now described "expressing their emotions", as not only being perceived as "annoying" to others but as BEING annoying. This is exposing the main issue now, which we can view in the respondents all over Norway. This behaviour is taught young and normalised by their teenage years. Even though Petr knows that it is "unhealthy", as he said. Where did they learn it? From their parents? Janteloven?)

Helene:
No *(laugh.)*

Anthony:
Helene, how about you? How do you feel after our discussion today because… we started off funny when we started talking and then we started talking about these deeper things?

Petr:
Yes, it starts light and then it gets heavy.

Anthony:
Yes! Helene, how do you feel?

Helene:
I'm happy that we talked, because now I know how you (Petr) feel about things and *(AN – turning to Anthony)*... I already knew how you feel about things, but basically I don't know...

Anthony:
Let me ask you one more thing, the suicide of teenagers last year, on the other side of Oslo in one town? Or the year before, there was like six or something deaths?

Petr:
Yes, six friends.

Helene:
Yes.

Anthony:
Do you think it has anything to do with this, with anything we have talked about today?

Helene:
<u>It has everything to do with this!</u>

(AN – This problem, the subject of this very book... is making children kill themselves... five or six in one town, in one year. They are taught that it is THEIR FAULT... read on...)

Petr:
But at the same time the group that took suicide they dealt with smoking weed and harder drugs.

(AN – Note the minimisation and victim blaming that he's probably been taught and exposed to?)

Helene:
I think that that probably came out of this!

(AN – A young person is expressing in plain language that what I am saying is true and causing young people to commit suicide… this is a message I have heard all over Norway from the youth. Unfortunately, too many adults in Norway are in denial to such an extent that they don't see reality or the pain of others any more.)

Petr:
Yes they probably turned to the drugs to relieve themselves from this pressure. *I think that they handled it very poorly.*

Anthony:
Maybe, not "poorly" maybe it was just that they couldn't handle the pressure? To be honest with you, it's hard.

Petr:
But then suicide is like a *selfish* thing. It gets harder for people around you when you're gone after you do that.

Anthony:
Now, let me ask you this… now do you know… the really interesting thing about that… they felt alone… who could they turn to?

Petr:
Hmmm… nobody.

Anthony:
And because they felt like they couldn't turn to anybody and they felt alone…

Helene:
Because the thing is that *(turning to Petr)*, I see your point with the thing about selfishness but I don't think it always applies because obviously if you committed suicide you thought that you couldn't trust anybody… I can't trust anybody, and that means that you don't have anybody to talk to, and that means that literally you don't have a good friend, you don't have a family member and then you don't even have one person that you trust 100%, and then I get that it's hard. Then if everybody is going to cry about you then

they don't have the right to do that! Because then like after somebody has died they are going to pretend that they cared! And I was like their "best friend" *(AN – sarcastic tone)*. Bullsh*t! Obviously like a couple of people like the closest friends, the parents… I would get that, but then like the whole town, like EVERYONE was "sad" because these people committed suicide and I was like…

Anthony:
Like, "You weren't sad when they were sad", is that what you mean?

Helene:
Yeah!

Petr:
Well, it's like a train when one person jumps off…

Helene:
It's like a domino effect.

Anthony:
Do you know what, guys, I think that there is a lot of trauma linked to those things. It's like almost you guys need to hear that it's OK to feel insecure, it's OK not to be perfect. It's OK… and it is OK! But you don't feel that because nobody tells you that?

Petr:
People think after they take suicide, they don't think before, the actions come after the suicide. Then they think like all I could have done things differently I could have like saved the person.

Anthony:
Yes.

Helene:
Basically I think. I'm not trying to say that I'm suicidal because I'm not, I'm just like using me as an example, like my friends now if we look at our group. Then I think that I would be closest to commit suicide than (the "alpha"), for example who is like the top, who's alpha. I don't think that they would even realise…

(AN – Who will take action to help Helene or all the other "Helenes"? Her school teachers? Her parents? Her friends? Who can help her if nobody listens or cares or even notices there is a problem? I asked her and she said, "You are the only person I speak to about this and when you go it will be bad." What you read in this book, truly, is the tip of the proverbial iceberg.)

Anthony:
Like, if you were at that level of pain, they wouldn't even notice?

Helene:
Yes.

Anthony:
That's so bad… can you imagine, Petr? You can be upset in front of somebody and too many would probably ignore you, just smile and say, "Hi! Hi!", if they noticed at all?

(AN – A sixty-year-old Norwegian man told me near Drammen: "I visited Africa and there are things there which are better than here. They said that I was in paradise (Norway) and I said that "yes, in a way, I have won the lottery by being born in Norway". However, in Gambia if your neighbour is hungry they will find a 1kg bag of rice outside their house. I envy that. In Norway, your neighbour could be dead and they'd just complain about the smell!")

Helene:
Yes.

Anthony:
And they'd literally go around the corner and cry in your heart because no one gives a s*** about them… this is what I see. Now, what do you have to say about that?

Helene:
I agree.

Petr:
I agree.

Anthony:
Another thing is, this is where it gets really deep… when that person sees

and hears the other person with their fake smile and superficial "Hi Hi!"… totally ignoring that you are obviously hurting inside… and the sad person sees that they are so "happy"… that will make them feel like there is something wrong with *them*, no?

Petr:
Yes, because they are "happy".

Anthony:
They make you feel like there is something wrong with YOU? What do you have to say about that?

Petr:
Yes, I think that is very true. And you can notice it in people, like, when they are sad… you see that they are sad… but then they act like they're "cool".

Helene:
I don't think that people notice when you're sad. I think that this is also a problem related to the suicide. Because only your closest friends or like your partner would notice if you're sad. And I don't think that anyone else would and I think that if you're at that point where you don't have anyone that's close enough then they won't notice.

(AN – She is describing an extremely uncaring and unsympathetic environment. Something which almost every respondent echoed, either directly though their words and experiences or by their demeanour and behaviour during their interviews.)

Anthony:
Do you know what's funny; I feel that I notice these things.

Helene:
Yes, you would… but you're on another level.

Anthony:
Do you understand now why I'm going to write my book? I want you guys to feel strong and happy and know that it's OK not to be "perfect".

Petr:
I think that people need to notice what are happening. This happened and

they brush it off their shoulder and go along with their lives. But we really need to think about what really happens.

(AN – Incredible... what a message...)

Next conversation

Anthony:
Pause, pause... I turned off the recorder and then we got gold... *(AN: The "alpha" named)* is the alpha and what would happen if the "lowest" girl on the rung said "come and sit down come and have a sandwich"... would the universe explode?... and then Petr went on to say...

Petr:
I think that (the "alpha") would think that the world would explode collapsed...

Anthony:
And you said?

Petr:
It's cool not to restrict yourself to a certain group or people.

Anthony:
This is so true!

Petr:
I think that when you speak to the "weirdos" when you are "cool" that's cool!

Anthony:
I agree that it's cool to speak.

Petr:
That's cool, not just for you, but for them and everybody sees that she's like "talking with her". They might think that that's weird but that if she does it then it's cool.

Anthony:
So in a way it kind of paves the way for others to see that it's OK?

Petr:
Yeah!

Anthony:
Can you imagine that? Then it might even change the whole of society!

Petr:
When people that don't usually talk to each other, talk to each, that's cool.

Anthony:
I agree. Now let me ask you something, you said something about restricting and I think that this brings us back to the beginning of the conversation nicely, sometimes in life you never know who you might meet… someone just on the bus. It's *possible* obviously *(AN – turning to Helene)*, that a person might murder you (laugh)… That could be, but there might be some special people… and I think it's important to think about that because outside of your social circle might be where some happiness lies?

Petr:
My mother used to say that you never know what the person next to you has in their mind. Maybe they become your boss in the future maybe they become a whole other person and if you as a good person talks to them maybe you have saved their life.

Anthony:
That's so true… your mum has said a very wise thing.

Petr:
When my father… I was in school, he had a boy in his class and he was like weird and he wouldn't shower after the gym and he settled down on the bus and my father started to talk with him on the bus one day… and some weeks later… he was talking and told him he was going to take his own life that very day but because of that talk… he saved his life. He didn't shower because his father beat him and just having one person to talk to… one person for half an hour was cool for him…

Anthony:
This is amazing.

Petr:
He thought that it was so cool to have a friend and now he would not live without that experience.

Anthony:
I just think that that is so beautiful.

Petr:
And now he is a whole other person.

Anthony:
Have they kept in contact?

Petr:
He knows him but he has moved to a whole different place. He is like a normal person.

Anthony:
And he would have been dead?

Petr:
He would not be alive today if it wasn't for him.

Anthony:
Now, let me ask you a question, do you think that your father describing that situation to you… maybe that's had an effect on your view of speaking to people. Do you think so?

Petr:
Yes, I think that and he told me a story that he had heard from a place… there was a boy where there is a boy who had so many books in his backpack… He said, I know you're alone as he walked all alone half an hour home every day, and there was a group of like, the cool kids, who walk the same way every day and they saw that he had so many books in his backpack…and they saw that he had so many books in his backpack and asked him… can I give you some help with the books? The person with all of the books said "yes" and really enjoyed that somebody was talking with him… do you know the reason why he had so many books in his backpack?

Anthony:
Tell me?

Petr:
Because he was going to clean his cabin so other people didn't have to when he was gone. He was going to take suicide later that day. So he was taking all of his books home so nobody had to go into his closet to find them.

Anthony:
And your dad told you this story?

Petr:
Yep my dad told me the story when I was like thirteen. He told me to be kind and nice to people because you, like, never know.

Anthony:
This is brilliant, do you try and live like this?

Petr:
Yes, I think that this is a good statement.

Anthony:
This is a good statement to end as well... I'm very honoured today.
Thank you.

OPINION: Norwegian generalisations and myths

Every one of the 350 respondents (Norwegians and non-Norwegians) that I spoke to for this project generalised about Norwegians and Norway. In fact, the majority were so confident in their assertions, when challenged or questioned they'd often become so upset and sensitive it negated any rational discussion.

Here is a rough overview of what the 350 respondents themselves told me about "Norway and Norwegians":

Number 1: Norwegians are honest

Number 2: Norwegians are trustworthy

Number 3: Norwegians are fair

Number 4: Norway is an equalitarian society

Number 5: Norwegians treat everybody equally

Number 6: Norwegians are straightforward and direct

Number 7: Norwegians are antisocial

Number 8: Norwegians like skiing, mountains, hiking and nature

Number 9: Norway is the best country in the world

Number 10: Norway is the happiest country in the world

Number 11: Norwegians are rich

Number 12: Norway is a tolerant society

Number 13: Norwegians don't sit next to other people on buses

Number 14: Norwegians are polite and respectful

Number 15: Norwegians are very hard-working

Number 16: Norway is a very environmentally friendly country

Number 17: Norwegians don't talk to strangers

Number 18: Norwegians do not brag or boast

When repeatedly asked, "Who taught you about these things?" most, including the Norwegian academics and medical professionals, would usually answer the same way: "They are kind of true", "Society. Everybody is taught them" or "I don't know". When the question became: "Who specifically taught YOU these things?" they usually said, "Everybody in Norway just knows these things" or "That's just the way it is in Norway".

I spoke to a forty-year-old Norwegian woman in Longyearbyen who works for the University of Svalbard (let's call her "Martha") who explained it this way:

"Being a Norwegian, you are brought up with this set of traits of a typical Norwegian which you bring with you when you are introduced to somebody new… that is something common for all Norwegians. It's something that you need to have or that you inherently have… we Norwegians, we come with this identity of what Norway is."

What Martha described is something that I encountered many times across Norway. It felt like a pre-programmed response or a well-rehearsed script. It was fascinating to observe because so few seemed conscious of it. Even when some attempt was made to articulate it, as Martha did, it didn't stop them repeating the same generalisations.

Generalisation and Norwegian stereotypes are promoted heavily within Norway

A *faulty generalisation* by definition is illogical so we can disregard these, as they are based on logical fallacy. However, these stereotypes and generalisations are still promoted heavily in Norway. Here is a typical example of the type of thing you will see:

THE 'TYPICAL' NORWEGIAN AS PROMOTED IN NORWAY

OVERJOYED

UPSET

ENRAGED

DRUNK

The above stereotype was heavily promoted in sixty-six of the sixty-seven bookshops that I visited in Norway. Often these are given big display stands and prominently placed. When visitors arrive in Norway this is what you'll find in many airports. The displays in Oslo Airport's bookshop include imagery such as this as well as messaging but in multiple languages – in gigantic displays.

Additionally, almost every member of staff that I met across Norway in these bookshops *actively* promoted them, confirmed these stereotypes and argued for them. What's really interesting is that these generalisations and stereotypes were the only real option offered when I enquired about books on the Norwegian people and Norwegian culture. Beyond the usual superficial travelogues, they could offer me nothing else *except* stereotype and "comedy" books about Norway and Norwegians. There is no significant alternative. This happened in every bookshop with the exception of one in the far north, whose manager told me, "We try to avoid that as a matter of our philosophy. We don't want to be like them."

The same type of stereotypes are heavily promoted in the Norwegian media and entertainment industry. They are construed as "humour" and "comedy" but are certainly interpreted as truthful or at the very least "based on truth" by many in Norway. Take the talented Norwegian group, "Ylvis" and their song, "The Cabin" and take a look at the comments by Norwegians below the video online, which has been viewed millions of times. I put this to many bookshop managers. One of them in Oslo said, "You are right. It is sad. People only want books about trolls and the vikings. We would love to have some real books but nobody is interested and the publishers aren't either." This was the same person who had, moment earlier insisted that the same stereotypes were in fact true. This was almost unanimous but the question for me is, are they actually believed or just repeated? I think it's also noteworthy to remember what sixteen-year-old Anita told us earlier about "jokes" and "comedy" and how she perceives them in Norway: "Yes... that's the way that we Norwegians do it. If we have to say something to somebody and especially if we are not super close, then we "joke". That's how Norwegians do it. They just cover it up with a joke."

Could the promotion of these stereotypes affect the Norwegian self-image, behaviour and mental health in a negative way? Could it even be a case that it's actually less painful to have to accept damaging stereotypes about yourself then to hear the truth to such an extent that so many Norwegians, marketers, publishers and companies will promote the former? I put this question to many experts in and outside of Norway, including renowned doctors and other experts who we will meet throughout this series.

Authors Note and Important Trigger Warning:

To any reader in a Nordic country and particularly in Norway or for those it may concern;

Serious discussion of this subject may be triggering. I encourage you, that if you have been affected by Janteloven unconsciously or consciously at any time in your life, either directly or indirectly, then to seriously consider the emotional impact of continuing to read on. I also extend this to those who may have a vested interest in perpetuating an idealistic view due to personal relationships or visits to a Nordic country etc.

It may be the case that everything in your being will tell you to close this book because you are upset by what you read. If this is to be the case, it is best that you do so now and not continue any further. If you close the book now then at least you can avoid facing something you are not ready to face at this time.

If you do continue past this point, then I ask you to force yourself through regardless of how you feel for the sake of those young Norwegians and others who shared their stories and experiences. Fight the compulsion to deny and to reject automatically because ultimately, if Janteloven has been imposed on you, in any way, shape or form... it was not your fault. Much of this may be unconscious. Please take this seriously and remember that you are not alone. Contact a professional medical practitioner for help if you need it. We will now continue.

An artificially imposed blind spot?

At the beginning of this journey I was in the Norwegian capital, Oslo, and I was with three highly respected Norwegian friends. They're intelligent, successful and well-established pillars of the community. We were engaged in a long conversation and I noticed that when they spoke about Norway, these three individuals with usually variant opinions now shared a common view. It was if they spoke in unison. As an observer this was disconcerting to hear.

I continued speaking with them but observed and listened intently.

One of them went on to discuss something that was highly illogical; a fallacy in fact, but interestingly the group *all* seemed to agree. I thought about it and I instinctively knew not to raise the issue. Their sense of identity and their strong beliefs about being "Norwegian" was clearly of utmost importance. I would suggest such sensitivity relates to their sense of self-belief and personal identity. So I didn't point it out and continued to observe them, collectively and individually.

I noticed something very interesting though – a collective lack of social regulation.

We have three very intelligent people and one of them has said something irrational that the other two people didn't pick up on. In actual fact they actually confirmed what was said, supported and enabled each other.

However, I know how intelligent they are and I respect them as honest people. I don't believe they would try and convince me of something about Norway and Norwegians that they didn't believe to be true and rational. So there was something happening. **It seemed as if there was a blind spot in how they viewed their own country.**

Any kind of questioning (or mere suggestion) of the *collective identity* was taken as a *personal* insult whereas a positive affirmation of Norway was taken as a *personal* compliment. I've seen this before in Norway. I once pointed to a mountain and said that it was "beautiful" and my Norwegian friend, standing next to me said, "Thank you."

I also realised that because the group were seemingly unaware of this, all that was needed to demonstrate the phenomenon was to record the dialogue. If unaware, there would be no blatant attempts to hide it. They could however deny it in *retrospection,* in embarrassment or shame if pointed out. All I had to do was ask, "Can I record this fascinating conversation, please?" All but one person across the whole of Norway agreed to being recorded. This suggests they were comfortable and not consciously hiding anything. To the contrary, they seemed confident and in no doubt about their beliefs. So much so they were willing to share them with any "outsider" who would listen.

As long as the exchange is recorded, a rational logical individual will be able to see the irrationality in the responses and dialogue and identify any blind spots. In fact it gets a little scary to observe because it resembles someone speaking on autopilot totally unaware of their words. It's something which the Norwegian woman in Longyearbyen explained very clearly:

"Being a Norwegian, you are brought up with this set of traits of a typical Norwegian **which you bring with you when you are introduced to somebody new**"

Martha even tells us that it is brought out when a Norwegian is "introduced to somebody new" but if this is the case then who writes this "script" and who teaches this set of beliefs? What exactly is going on here? How can it even be possible that every Norwegian has the same traits? Why isn't it questioned by the respondents? Who teaches these things? Are these beliefs enforced or imposed? Are they genuinely held beliefs like they appear to be? Why does there appear to be so little dissent or disagreement? Why did 100% of the respondents generalise about Norwegians and Norway in the first place? How can so many different people of different ages from different walks of life, from different parts of Norway, think and say almost the same things when they haven't met before? Why isn't this discussed in Norway? Where are the people that disagree? Are there any people that disagree? Could it be that sixteen-year-old Hanne gave us a possible plausible answer in the previous chapter when asked "How come it was so hard for us to speak about a simple fact?" She simply answered, "Because this is the land of the Janteloven!"

Martha has a point. The "script" is indeed often brought out in the first few moments in a first meeting. To me it felt like a **test** – a way to gauge a response and determine where to "put" you? So for example you're asked: "How do you find *Norway*?" Often it seemed like a challenge or a dare had been issued, *not* to say anything bad about Norway or to disagree with their beliefs about their country.

This was explicitly stated by a Norwegian millionaire in his seventies called "Magnus" that I interviewed in Alesund. He said that if a non-Norwegian even *dares* to say something even remotely negative about Norway when asked for their opinion, then a **"Norwegian will give you the *sour face*"** and **"will never talk to you again"**. He raised this point during a discussion we were having about why he thought that Ibsen's "Peer Gynt" who was a character that (according to Brokett and Hildy, 2003, P.391 and Meyer, 1974, P.284 – *Wikipedia*) lived a life based on *"procrastination and avoidance"*. Magnus explained that he believed that this fictional lying fantasist actually represented the Norwegian "soul":

Anthony:
Of the people of Norway? Tell me why though?
Why does he represent the soul of Norway?

Magnus:
He started lying to his mother on his deathbed and starting telling her fantasist stories, and then he goes out into the world and makes a fortune, and then he comes back to the true world and finds his true love from before.

Anthony:
Now, do you feel that though?

Magnus:
Yes, to a certain extent.

Anthony:
Do you know why?

Magnus:
Because he lives in a fantasy all his life! Because he is a loudmouth and we are the "best in the world" and the "best" of everything, you know?

Anthony:
So there's a little bit of… arrogance?

Magnus:
Yes. Anybody that comes to Norway. They ask him "what do you think of Norway?", and when they answer, "Oh, I think that Norway is fine!" then they get happy and say "haaaaaa"… **THEN** you are welcome to Norway! That is why we have this abnormal celebration national day. It gets more and more abnormal for each year. Now "The Scream" has taken over us!

We will hear more from "Magnus" later in this series.

As pointed out, "Norway is great! Norwegians are the best!" seems to be the preferred response because then once it's confirmed that you aren't going to "burst their bubble" by disputing their beliefs, myths and generalisations about themselves they could then feel secure, relax and settle down? A simple response to avoid trauma?

So the next question is "Why *Norway*?" often delivered in a faux "shocked" tone of voice. If it's a script – then the cast know their lines well. And your "part", as the "outsider/stranger" seems to be simply to smile and not say a "bad" word about Norway or the conversation will typically end *very* quickly. This makes perfect sense if these are sensitive sacrosanct beliefs that are not to be questioned or disputed. Much better to avoid and block out reality than to accept that Janteloven and faulty generalisations have been imposed on you for your whole life and most importantly, that you have been *forced* to believe and accept them as true, to such an extent that you really do now believe and accept them as true?

Let's briefly take a look at just one of these often repeated "myths and generalisations" that we so often hear in Norway. One that seems to be extremely sensitive and taboo, as young Hanne previously explained; "*Number 18: Norwegians do not brag or boast*".

"Norwegians do not brag or boast"

Contrary to this assertion, the evidence suggests otherwise. For example, an article was published entitled "Norwegians urged to stop bragging", 23rd January, 2013 (**www.newsinenglish.no** – Views and News from Norway/Aasa Christine Stolt"). It was subtitled; "So much for Norwegian modesty: New research shows that Norwegians are now seen as bragging about their affluence, strong currency and lifestyle so much that their Nordic neighbours want them to shut up and calm down". It was based on research by Gillian Warner-Søderholm, from the Norwegian Business School BI. The anthropologist was interviewed by the newspaper *Dagens Næringsliv* (DN) and interviewed 700 managers from all over the Nordic countries. The article also quotes Professor Thomas Hylland-Eriksen of the University of Oslo who suggests that Norwegians should "show some manners".

We will take a closer look at this and others later but this is repeated in Norway elsewhere: The Nordic Page (**www.tnp.no**) published an article entitled "Norwegians Believe Norwegian Culture Is Better Than Other Cultures":

"Norway is the only western European country where the majority believe their own culture is better than other cultures… A new survey done by the US Pew Research Center revealed that "Our people are not perfect, but we have a superior culture than others" is a common perception among many Norwegians." Even *TIME MAGAZINE* reported; "Oslo, Norway ranked 12th out of 459 cities worldwide: Selfies". Norway's capital city Oslo makes it into the top 3% of "selfie cities" out of 459 cities worldwide. Oslo has 89 "selfie-takers" per 100,000 people, according to world respected *Time Magazine* (**time.com**, Chris Wilson, 10th March, 2014).

Even as I write this today, if I click on the Norwegian news website, "Norway's News in English" (**www.newsinenglish.no** 2020/05/29) then we can read in plain language in the top article about Covid-19, in the opening words and I quote, "NORWAY CAN BOAST among the world's largest declines in Covid-19". It literally states it in BOLD CAPITALS and starts off the article with **"NORWAY CAN BOAST"**. What mental gymnastics would be required to even deny this when it's written in plain language and the evidence is everywhere to be seen?

You boys took a hell of a beating!

One of the most exciting and historic Norwegian moments was actually a Norwegian boasting and bragging when the Norwegian football team beat the English football team in 1981. It was an incredible moment for Norway and the commentator Bjørge Lillelien couldn't control his excitement and launched into the greatest boast and brag of all time. This included gleeful screaming and yelling. It's on YouTube and I encourage you to go and have a listen right now. It's brilliant! Here is what he said to the whole of Norway on its national broadcaster live:

"We are the best in the world! We are the best in the world! We have beaten England 2-1 in football! It is completely unbelievable! We have beaten England! England, birthplace of giants. Lord Nelson, Lord Beaverbrook, Sir Winston Churchill, Sir Anthony Eden, Clement Attlee, Henry Cooper, Lady Diana – we have beaten them all. We have beaten them all. Maggie Thatcher can you hear me? Maggie Thatcher, I have a message for you in the middle of the election campaign. I have a message for you: We have knocked England out of the football World Cup. Maggie Thatcher, as they say in your language in the boxing bars around Madison Square Garden in New York: You boys took a hell of a beating! You boys took a hell of a beating!"

(Translation Source: https://en.wikipedia.org/wiki/Bjørge_Lillelien*)*

There is no doubting this is an authentic expression of pure joy on the achievement and good for him and good for them. The question is, how does all of this reconcile with the generalisations propagated by so many Norwegians themselves? Let's take a closer look.

Could plausible deniability and denial be used as tools to covertly circumvent the pressure of Janteloven?

There is a bridge in a place called Atlantic Road and it is truly beautiful and magnificent. I have driven the road many times with several different people. Almost every *initial* trip I've taken with a Norwegian person on that road, I was told, "This is the *best* road in the world" or some kind of variation of that line. I was fascinated each and every time it was delivered and listened closely to the exact variation in words used. I think that my friends mistook my smile and keen attention as agreement which often encouraged them to ramp up the "promo" further. Inside a travel brochure for the area, for "Averoy, Eide, Fraena" is a beautiful photograph of the same road. If you open it and look at the bottom left corner, you will read:

"Voted the world's most beautiful road trip in the British Guardian. The road between Bud and Karvag is one of the National Tourist Routes in Norway and winds its way over the rocks and reefs right out of the ocean."

There is no doubt that it genuinely is one of the most beautiful views in the world… I love it… but what's evident is that this opinion is not expressed *directly* in writing. Of course, that would contradict the social "rules" of Janteloven. A way to circumvent this is to express the opinion of *someone else*, e.g. The *Guardian* newspaper in Britain. It's a legitimate 'non-brag' because it's *someone else's* opinion. Another way might be to, as shown previously above, make a statement with words like "can"; "Norway *can* boast", so the statements' unambiguous meaning can be later disputed on a technicality? I put these points to a Norwegian linguistic expert directly who will help us shed some light on this shortly, from a Norwegian perspective.

If you go to the Norwegian embassy in the United Kingdom, you will find exactly the same technique used on their website. Click on the "Norwegian values and society page" (**www.norway.no/en/uk/values-priorities/norway-today**) and read it very carefully:

"Norway has on a number of occasions been ranked the best country to live in, for example by the UN Human Development Index. It is one of the countries in the world with the highest life expectancy, 80.6 years for men and 84.2 years for women. According to the World Bank and the IMF, Norway has one of the highest levels of income per capita in the world. In Norwegian society, there is close cooperation between the authorities, employers, employees, and civil society. This is often referred to as the 'Nordic model'."

The Norwegian embassy in the UK has *indirectly* "messaged" several things, including:

1) Norway is the best country to live in
2) Norway has one of the highest levels of income per capita in the world
3) Close cooperation between Norwegians in Norway is often referred to as the 'Nordic model'

I hardly spoke with a Norwegian respondent who did not imply, suggest or state the same things, directly or indirectly: "Norway is the best country in the world" or some variant thereof. When this point is raised it is often denied. What's worse, is many of those Norwegians who say these things and then deny them, truly believe their own denials. It's the denial part that's interesting because the question is: *why?*

In my opinion, plausible deniability could be one of the main foundations of Norwegian life and used as an attempt to covertly circumvent the pressure of Janteloven.

The problem isn't, of course, the act of "bragging" itself – being proud of something – what's the harm in that? Who would actually care if you are proud of your country and like to brag about it? Even if you were slightly obsessed with your nation… who would actually care? I believe that the harm is not in the constant "bragging" but in its seemingly widespread compulsive delivery, defensiveness when it's raised and the act of later *denying* it, individually and collectively.

Medical experts categorise Norwegian approved stereotypes

I took the "humour" books and copies of the stereotypes and generalisations that promote Norwegians as unemotional/anti-social/cold people that are promoted in almost *every* Norwegian bookshop and endorsed by so many Norwegians as "true", to several doctors and medical practitioners. I asked them directly, "If this was a real person how would you diagnose them?" Here is what the doctors and medical professionals said:

THE 'TYPICAL' NORWEGIAN AS PROMOTED IN NORWAY

OVERJOYED   UPSET   ENRAGED   DRUNK

Doctor (GP): *"Depressive and maybe addicted to alcohol."*

Pharmacist: *"If I saw this I would assume that this person doesn't really experience true/real happiness unless he or she is intoxicated… this would generally indicate a deep underlying state of psychological disturbance that would result in his/her apparent masking of emotion/ unhappiness."*

Norwegian Psychologist: *"You are right. These are not helpful."*

Norwegian Doctor: *"Anthony, if there is any way you can communicate in a book what you have communicated to me today, it will be very successful in Norway."*

However, the Norwegian doctor (and indeed the psychologist) *first* tried to convince *me* that the stereotypes were TRUE (*"had some truth to them"*, she said) and it was me who convinced the doctor that she had this one wrong and I explained why. While she agreed with me, she seemed in shock at *herself* after I explained the potential negative mental health consequences of "confirming" these stereotypes to Norwegians and non-Norwegians alike as "true".

These national myths and stereotypes are propagated officially too, as we have seen. Take the commonly repeated assertion: "Norway is one of the happiest countries in the world". This is technically taken from a UN report. So it can be legitimately said, that "We did not say it... the UN did!" However, the UN is basing it on questions answered by *Norwegians*. So, the source is Norwegians *themselves*, which is then repeated and reported and then *that* is then used to legitimise the generalisation which is then too often weaponised as shown in the transcripts of this book; disagree and you'll be excluded. Point it out and you'll be ostracised... unless you add the obligatory "only joking" label on it which enables a tentative plausible deniability and an opportunity to "back track".

It's now time for us to move away from opinion and look at some official sources, news articles and stories from within Norway itself... but first...

What Are the Chances?

It is most certainly worth discussing how Norway was interpreted by English actor, Michael Palin. He is one of the world's most discerning and respected adventurer travellers, known for how he exposes the heart of a place and its people in his travel documentaries. It's no surprise then that he did the same with Norway in his BBC documentary series *Pole to Pole* in Episode One. This first aired on the BBC on 21st October 1992. Part of Palin's ingenuity is being able to 'laser focus' on any pretence. And that's what he did so eloquently in this episode.

What are the chances that he specifically used the words "façade" and "conformity" when talking about the Norway? Well… he asked: what was behind the façade of respectable conformity? What are the chances of Palin meeting Norwegians who on camera state that something Norwegian is the *best* like their beer, for example: "The best, the best… it's the best in Norway… that's why it's so famous"? What are the chances of Palin asking a Norwegian man if he *liked being with people* and the man replying on camera, "No, only me and my friends"? What are the chances of a Norwegian implying something which, Palin challenges with the most elegant, friendly intelligence, which turns out to be slightly different to what was originally being implied… see for yourself in the following example.

Palin had already seen so much drunkard and crazy behaviour by the time he arrived in Hammerfest, Norway, that when he met Troels Muller, his Norwegian "fixer" and asked him if there was anything he ought to know about driving in Norway, he knew to probe what was implied immediately. In reply to his question he was asked by the Norwegian, "You haven't been drinking have you?" to which he said that that was a serious problem in Norway, where people can even be imprisoned for three weeks, with no appeal, fined and have their license suspended. Palin then looked at him and said, so politely, *"But I mean not being rude or anything, because the beer's very good here, but I've seen a lot of people in Norway drink quite a lot so presumably, either the roads are empty or everyone's in prison!"*

Once challenged though, things took a different turn. The Norwegian's facial expression changed and he laughed as he then revealed, "Well, yes, in fact, for this offence there is a line up (a waiting time)… people are waiting one or two years to do their three weeks."

Michael Palin's *Pole to Pole* book (Publisher: Phoenix – an Imprint of the Orion Publishing Group; UK ed. edition, March 5, 2009) gives us even more incredible insight into this exchange, where the Norwegian confesses:

"People are waiting one or two years to get in prison. And then when you go off to prison you don't want your friends to know obviously, so you tell them that you're going to travel… There is a prison near Oslo they call Costa del Ilseng, because everyone… you know, goes to Spain… and, well, they're not in Spain at all…"

Rather than accepting what he was told, Palin knew to ask the right questions to get at the truth. It's interesting that Michael Palin's Monty Python 1979 film, *The Life of Brian* was actually banned in Norway for a number of years. In fact, the Swedish, who didn't ban the film advertised it there as, "a film so funny they had to ban it in Norway."

101 Stories from an Upside-Down Society

Did you know that in Norway if a tourist publishes a letter calling Norwegians "impolite" you will soon see, with no shame or embarrassment, an article in a newspaper or online (or both) disputing it and quoting "experts" to explain why Norwegians are not "impolite", are in fact polite in their own "special" way and that you should "forget" what you have heard? Yes, they will actually instruct the reader, in writing, to "forget" what they have heard.

It is not hidden. Many are proud and exhibit no shame whatsoever in supporting their nation when they feel that it is criticised or an inconvenient Norwegian "truth" is revealed.

When *The Guardian* published an article by Sindre Bangstad, "Norway is in denial about the threat of far-right violence" (16th September 2019) we quickly saw an article of rebuttal published within the week entitled *"Does Norway have a far-right problem?"* (*Spectator*, 23rd September 2019 by Kathrine Jebsen Moore) where the author ends the article with the line; "So is Norway in denial about its far-right problem? **Don't believe it.**" You will often see readers around the world instructed not to believe what they have read or hear or see with their own eyes within Norway.

Another technique is to question or undermine credible research outright and "sow doubt" when Norway or Norwegians are criticised, like in this *Norway Today* article entitled, "Racism in Norway: Bad FAFO research?" (26th May 2019), which popped up to rebuff a (in their words) "controversial" report which, of course, was actually credible, well researched and respected but *inconveniently* shone a light on and revealed the high levels of racist views in Norway. The article begins, with no shame or embarrassment:

"Graham Dyson sows doubt about the quality of both the report and journalism on this matter."

By now, any reasonable person will realise that there are major problems hidden underneath the surface of Norwegian society. Below are 101 media stories, articles and other items from Norway...

1. "Norwegians impolite? Forget it!"

<u>Sciencenorway.com</u> published an article (11th March 2017) from the Norwegian School of Economics (NHH), written by Sigrid Folkestad, who interviewed Kristin Rygg who *"found a letter to the editor published in a Norwegian newspaper a few years ago very interesting. The descriptions of Norwegians as unsociable and unfriendly also hit a nerve among many of the newspaper's readers"*. The letter stated: *"Will I end up becoming like most Norwegians? Unfriendly and impolite? I don't want to insult Norwegians in any way, and I don't believe that all Norwegians are unfriendly... But whatever happened to normal politeness?"*

Of course, this was refuted by expert Kristin Rygg from NHH's Department of Professional and Intercultural Communication who, according to the article, has written several research articles on 'politeness theory'. She was clear in her dismissal of the letter saying, "No, Norwegians are polite..." and was asked by Folkestad if she dismissed the claims to which she replied, "Yes, I do, definitely."

Articles like "Norwegians impolite? Forget it!" are widespread in the Norwegian media, especially when the observations or criticisms "hit a nerve".

2. "Norwegians are polite – in their own special way: Researcher"

The Local Norway (**www.thelocal.no**) published an article *"Norwegians are polite – in their own special way: Researcher"* on 27th March 2017, which described Norwegians as being "polite" but *"in their own special way"*.

3. "Why international students should not come to Norway"

Curt Rice, the President of the Oslo and Akershus University College of Applied Sciences (Høgskolen i Oslo og Akershus) wrote an article entitled, *"Why international students should not come to Norway"* which was published in the *Huffington Post* (26th October 2015) where he outlined the challenges that international students face in Norway. I applaud the article, however, we must note the "usual" when he talks about the reactions, which international students trigger in his Norwegian colleagues, he refers to "well-meaning colleagues":

"This also triggered reactions, also from well-meaning colleagues. We should be careful that we don't get too many non-Norwegians, they would say."

4. "Survey indicates underlying racism"

www.newsinenglish.no published an article, May 20th, 2019 entitled, *"Survey indicates underlying racism"*. It starts out with the usual "positive" angle but finally gets to the point; *"Around 25 percent of all those questioned, however, said they fully or partially agreed that some human races are more intelligent than others"*.

5. "Racism on our vacation a reminder people see us as 'The Others'"

Canadian born Dr. Davidicus Wong wrote an article about racism in Norway entitled, *"Racism on our vacation a reminder people see us as 'The Others'"* for "Burnaby Now" (4th February 2019). He wrote:

> "We had a different experience travelling with cousins last August in Norway. In a public square of shops in the seaside town of Alesund, we saw a teacher talking to a group of high school students. For a moment, I thought they were talking about us. Later it felt that they were all watching us. Finally, we learned that their assignment was to take photos of tourists… and those of us who looked Chinese or half-Chinese stood out. An hour later, while walking around the harbour, we were approached by a motorboat with two elementary school boys. They pointed at us, laughed and mockingly made the gesture of bowing in the stereotypical Asian fashion. The next day, in Bergen Norway, we ascended Mount Floyen, and on the peak was a sign proudly announcing nine recently born goats. Each had been given a name, and the black goat was named Obama."

What an incredible doctor to actually take the time to write the article. How many people would just leave and never return without raising the issue? He raised another issue too:

"We didn't stay long enough in the country to find out if racist attitudes are endemic or if people just don't realise what demeaning public signs say about them."

6. "Care but no caring… lack of respect and empathy from nurses"

Science Norway (sciencenordic.com) published an article entitled *"Care but no caring"*, 24th May 2014. The article looks at a new study by researcher Aud

Moe from Nord-Trøndelag University College, which finds that elderly residents in "care" homes in Norway (120 patients), "frequently encounter a lack of respect and empathy from nurses."

7. "Pupils with low grades feel less supported by teachers"

One of the main observations is this book series is that the weak/victims in Norway are too often undermined and the strong/perpetrators/bullies elevated. norwegianscitechnews.com published an article by Veronika Søum (26th February 2019) about research carried out by Associate Professor Per Egil Mjaavatn, senior lecturer Lena Haller Buseth and Professor Per Frostad at NTNU's Department of Education and Lifelong Learning into upper secondary school students and it is very clear: "A recent study of upper secondary students shows that strong students experience more support from teachers than do students who have lower grades." It also quotes the response; "researcher surprised" by the results, which we will often hear.

8. "Being Norwegian means never having to say you're sorry"

J Russell Mikkelsen (editor/curator of *Estimated Time of Arrival*) wrote an article called *"What's Weird About Norway: A touchy-feely guy's view of a touchless, feel-less nation"* on 19th September 2013 on **medium.com**. He wrote, *"Norwegians are weird. I say this out of affection. I'm half-Norwegian. I've lived in Norway for years at a time"* and points out that a recent visit reminded him of *"all the bizarre habits and peculiarities of the Norwegian people."* His article outlined many of his views on the Norwegian people and Norwegian interaction and behaviour, including: *"There is no word for sorry. There's "excuse me" and "I feel bad for you." No sorry. Nothing you can say in Norwegian that implies both guilt and regret simultaneously. Consequently, Norwegians rarely feel either one".* What's also interesting is that the Norwegian language already includes many English words and the vast majority of Norwegians that I met spoke great English… which begs the question, why not simply use the word "sorry"?

9. "How Norwegians avoid saying *please*"

Yngvil Vatn Guttu wrote an article published on 28th March, 2017 by **www.norskbloggen.no** entitled, *"How Norwegians avoid saying "please"*. She wrote:

"Norwegians are neither known for being particularly polite or particularly rude. But it often puzzles newcomers that we never say "please"… or do we? In this blog article you'll learn how to politely and respectfully ask for something in Norwegian. Without saying please…"

What's interesting is that the author acknowledges that "newcomers" are puzzled that "we never say please…" and also raises that Norwegians are not "known for being particularly polite…" It's also noteworthy that the articles title suggests an active avoidance of using the word "please". As stated previously, why not simply use the word "please"? The Norwegian language commonly uses many other English words which are used in day-to-day life in Norway, so why particularly *avoid* using words like "please" and "sorry"?

10. "Norwegians urged to stop bragging"

An article was published entitled *"Norwegians urged to stop bragging"*, 23rd January, 2013 (**www.newsinenglish.no** – Views and News from Norway/Aasa Christine Stolt"). It was subtitled; *"So much for Norwegian modesty: New research shows that Norwegians are now seen as bragging about their affluence, strong currency and lifestyle so much that their Nordic neighbours want them to shut up and calm down"*. It was based on research by Gillian Warner-Søderholm, from the Norwegian Business School BI. The anthropologist was interviewed by the newspaper *Dagens Næringsliv* (DN) and interviewed 700 managers from all over the Nordic countries. The article also quotes Professor Thomas Hylland-Eriksen of the University of Oslo who suggests that Norwegians should *"show some manners"*. It's noteworthy that the article ends, after giving some "good advice" for those doing business in Norway, with this ominously toned "friendly" warning for those coming to Norway:

*"Oh, and be prepared for Janteloven, which Warner-Søderholm **apparently believes** still rules in Norway: Don't assume you're better than another…"*

11. "Norwegians believe Norwegian culture is better than other cultures"

The Nordic Page (**www.tnp.no**) published an article entitled *"Norwegians Believe Norwegian Culture Is Better Than Other Cultures"*: *"Norway is the only western European country where majority believe their own culture is better than other cultures… A new survey done by the US Pew Research Center revealed that "Our people are not perfect, but we have a superior culture than others" is a common perception among many Norwegians."*

The Pew Research Center (**www.pewforum.org**) survey is unambiguous and clear. It surveyed 24,599 adults across fifteen countries across Western Europe.

12. "The Norwegian Personality Disorder"

Writer John Olav Ytreland published an article online entitled *"The Norwegian Personality Disorder"* on 21st February 2018 where he highlighted the "narcissistic traits" of his country: *"We tend to believe that we are better and smarter than anyone else, and that we deserve special treatment."* He asked *"What if an entire society has this disorder, what if society actually encourages this behaviour?"* and then goes on to nominate his own country as highly collectively narcissistic and explains his reasons why in a very simple and logical way.

13. "Oslo, Norway ranked 12th out of 459 cities worldwide: *Selfies*"

TIME MAGAZINE: Norway's capital city Oslo makes it into the top 3% of "selfie cities" out of 459 cities worldwide. Oslo has 89 "selfie-takers" per 100,000 people, according to world respected *Time Magazine* (**time.com**, Chris Wilson, 10th March, 2014).

14. The Norwegian referendum: "It is one of the most lopsided referenda in history"

I can find no record of a legitimate referendum or vote more lopsided in world history as the Norwegian *"Dissolution of the union between Norway and Sweden"* on 13th August 1905. Almost 100% of the Norwegians who voted, voted for independence from Sweden. In fact, only 184 Norwegians voted against the proposal. 99.95% voted "yes" against just 184 voting "no". Sweden and Norway, with all of their shared history, were previously joined in a union from 1814 with a common monarch and common foreign policy. In fact the two countries had been linked for over 500 years since the Kalmar Union in 1397. There is no question as to whether this was a fair referendum. It was 100% free, fair and legitimate. Interestingly, the most shameful dictators in the most rigged elections could only dream for 99.95% of the vote! For comparison we note that, for example, Raul Castro received a lesser percentage at, 99.4%, of the votes cast in the 2008 Cuban election. Even Turkmenistan's Saparmurat Niyazov "only" secured 99.5% of the vote in 1992. In that vote the only candidate was incumbent President Saparmurat Niyazov himself and he received *less* than 99.95% of the vote. There are many examples of extreme lopsided votes through Norwegian history. It's noteworthy because they ARE free and fair, not because they're not.

15. "Migrants not particularly prone to depression"

This is one of those bizarre articles and headlines which could be a parody when you examine the results of the research. The full title and subtitle of the <u>sciencenorway.no</u> article by Steinar Brandslet (15th July 2019) which was produced and financed by NTNU Norwegian University of Science and Technology is: *"Migrants not particularly prone to depression: Migrants are doing well generally, but experience higher rates of depressive symptoms than the population at large in some European countries. One country stands out as an exception."*

So, we immediately read that the headline of the Norwegian article and see that migrants are *"not particularly prone to depression"*… sounds positive, obviously. We then click and see a subtitle where we immediately read that *"migrants are doing well generally…"* which also sounds good. We even end the subtitle with *"one country stands out as an exception"*… this is all sounding very positive! However, when you look into the results, once you get past the headline, you notice that the picture is actually quite different. I decided to go and find the original study myself. The actual study was called: ***"Depressive symptoms among migrants and non-migrants in Europe: documenting and explaining inequalities in times of socio-economic instability"***

Author details:
Gkiouleka A1, Avrami L2, Kostaki A3, Huijts T1, Eikemo TA4, Stathopoulou T2.

1. Department of Sociology, University of York, York, UK.
2. National Centre for Social Research, Athens, Greece.
3. Department of Statistics, Athens University of Economics & Business, Athens, Greece.
4. Department of Sociology and Political Science, Centre for Global Health Inequalities Research (CHAIN), Norwegian University of Science and Technology (NTNU), Trondheim, Norway".

I found the report and read it in full. Here are the actual results, and I quote:

*"RESULTS: Our findings show that **migrants report significantly higher levels of depressive symptoms in seven of the examined countries**, while in Greece and in the UK, they report significantly lower levels compared with non-migrant populations."*

What were the worst seven countries for migrant depression compared to the local populations? Obviously, not Norway right? Wrong. Of course, ALL of the Scandinavian countries were included in the seven "worst", including Norway. So a more accurate headline might have read something like this: *"Migrants more at risk to depression in Norway, Denmark and Sweden, compared to native population, than in the majority of the other twenty-one European countries surveyed."*?

How many people would actually go and find the report or even read past the headline of *"Migrants not particularly prone to depression"* by Sciencenorway? In fact it's much worse for Norway than even that, because deep within the report we read:

*"Still, the differences in the means of depressive symptoms between the two groups across countries are significant only in Greece, Switzerland, Germany, France, UK, the Netherlands, Norway, Poland, and Sweden (table 1). The largest differences between the two groups appear in Poland, followed by the Netherlands, **Norway**, and Switzerland."*

So, in actual fact, Norway was actually the third "worse" out of twenty-one countries surveyed… conveniently not reported, of course. Much better to report a headline of *"Migrants not particularly prone to depression"* instead?

16. "Living in Denial in Norway"

Andy Skuce of **www.skepticalscience.com** posted an article entitled *"Living in Denial in Norway"* (28th February 2013) where he outlines the "shades of denial" in Norway before revealing a more accurate picture and a country "in denial". The article looks at the work of Kari Norgaard who's a sociology professor at the University of Oregon and author of *Living in Denial: Climate Change, Emotions and Everyday Life* (MIT Press, 2011) which is based on her sociological research that she carried out in Norway. The article points out that "after taking Kari Norgaard's guided tour through the society of rural Norway, upon your return you may never look at your own circle of friends, colleagues and neighbours… in quite the same way again" because you will encounter "attitudes that are surprisingly familiar" on "almost every page".

17. "Why I love Norway but Hate Norwegians"

Norwegian Gram Franck published an article entitled *"Why I love Norway but*

Hate Norwegians" where he encourages fellow Norwegians to *"Dare to be different. Dare to be you. Dare to be real, and if need be, controversial. Have some unpopular opinions. **Have some damn opinions**".* The Norwegian writer, only twenty-two years old at the time of publishing wrote, *"Norway has receded into a beautiful country occupied by five million cowards"* and talks about the state of his country in detail.

18. "New Book Leaves Norway's 'Heroic Role' in the Holocaust in Tatters"

"New Book Leaves Norway's 'Heroic Role' in the Holocaust in Tatters. The Norwegian resistance didn't warn the Jews about their deportation to Auschwitz and smuggled Jews to Sweden for money, according to a journalist's research" by Ofer Aderet, Published 22nd December 2018 in Haaretz (www.haaretz.com). The article outlines Norwegian journalist and Holocaust researcher Marte Michelet book (*What Did the Resistance Know?*) which they say "threatens to shatter Norway's greatest myth: the heroism of the resistance that fought the Nazis and saved half the country's Jews during World War II". The article describes "Norway's perceived version of events" and then the reality, revealed by journalist Marte Michelet, which of course, paints a different picture. It goes on to outline how she has been criticised by Oslo "establishment historians... who have **cast doubt on her findings and attacked her professional integrity**". We must note the words of famed Norwegian resistance fighter Ragnar Ulstein who also criticised Michelet in an interview with the Dagsavisen newspaper saying, "Michelet doesn't understand the nature of the war". Doesn't understand... complicated... look out for these phrases throughout this book series.

19. "Norwegians Use the Word 'Texas' as Slang to Mean 'Crazy'"

Dan Solomon of *Texas Monthly* www.texasmonthly.com published (20th October 2015) an article entitled *"Y'all, Norwegians Use the Word "Texas" as Slang to Mean "Crazy""* which describes Norwegians who instead of saying something is "wild" or "crazy" say that it is "Texas!" ... as in Texas, United States. This type of language is portrayed as something "funny" and a "joke".

20. "Norwegians perceived as arrogant abroad, by Norwegian team"

An article by *Export Credit Norway* (www.eksportkreditt.no) published an article entitled, *"Norwegians perceived as arrogant abroad, by Norwegian team".* Export Credit Norway "helps Norwegian exporters to succeed abroad..."

according to their website and referenced a report by Innovation Norway. The article is very clear: "According to a report by Innovation Norway, **Norwegians appear conceited and arrogant to business partners in many countries**". The article states that Innovation Norway "surveyed and received input from 227 persons working in seventeen of the world's most important export markets. While much of the feedback was positive, Norwegians were described as arrogant and distant". Note the insertion of "… much of the feedback was positive" immediately before, "Norwegians were described as arrogant and distant".

21. "So much better than everyone else because of their nationality."

The culture website **www.theculturetrip.com** published an article (22nd November 2017 by Danei Christopoulou) entitled *"The eight Types of Norwegians You'll Meet on Tinder"*. The author refers to "proud Norwegians" and that "Most Norwegians are proud Norwegians" and many other observations, including "aloof personalities" etc. The author also adds: *"Don't be surprised when every conversation ultimately revolves around how they're so much better than everyone else because of their nationality."*

22. "Norwegian Death Diving as amateurs risk lives to belly flop from a 10-metre board into a pool"

According to Norway's official tourism website **visitnorway.com** Norwegians created a "sport" called "death diving" and reported that the "world champion", Truls Torp said, *"It's just how Norwegians are. We're all totally insane."*

The article also states that it *"could only have been invented in Norway"*. In fact "Death general" Paul Rigault of the International Dødsing Association told **visitnorway.com** under the sub title "National identity", that he believes that there are two reasons why Norwegians are fascinated by "death diving":

"It is a low-threshold test of manhood open to anyone. All you need is a 10-metre high dive and water. The other reason is perhaps that Norway lacks its own identity abroad. The Finns have the sauna, but what does Norway have?"

23. "Norway's reputation as a leader in tackling fake news is in tatters"

Forbes.com's senior contributor, David Nikel, reported in an article entitled, "Norway's 'Time-Free' Island Was Just An Elaborate P.R. Stunt" that:

"Norway's reputation as a leader in tackling fake news is in tatters after a government agency admitted to making up a story and fabricating photos that went viral around the world."

In an article exposing a fake P.R stunt story promoted by **visitnorway.com**. In fact, the Forbes' article reported Norwegian media reports that the state owned enterprise "knowingly" promoted the story with "false information and staged photos".

24. "Is life in Norway as happy as it's cracked up to be?"

www.theconversation.com published an article entitled *"Is life in Norway as happy as it's cracked up to be?"* on 24th July 2017 by Nathan John Albury, research fellow at the Center for Multilingualism in Society across the Lifespan at the University of Oslo and assistant professor, Hong Kong Polytechnic University. The website's tagline is "The conversation. Academic rigour, journalistic flair". In the article he describes that Norway, contrary to the projected image, is a place where you can enjoy certain freedoms "only if you are Norwegian", as a country with a "history of exclusion" as well as stories of widespread discrimination and racism in Norway.

25. "Told that Norway is the West's most anti-Semitic country, diplomat lashes out at Israel"

Writer Raphael Ahren wrote an incredible article for the *Times of Israel* where he reports on historian of religion Hanne Nabintu Herland who accused Norway of being "the most anti-Semitic country in the West". Raphael Ahren reported Herland's comments which were spoken on a panel organised by the Jerusalem Center for Public Affairs: *"The degree of anti-Israelism in Norway today on the state level, in the media, in the trade unions and at the universities, colleges and schools is unprecedented in modern Norwegian history."*

During the panel discussion many topics and reports were raised. The article reported: "Herland quoted several surveys and anti-Semitism reports that showed, among other worrying trends, that "Jew" is the most often used curse word in Oslo schools and that a third of Jewish children feel continuously bullied". The article also noted the official response from the Norwegian deputy head of mission, who of course, responded "in part by questioning the accuracy of some of the statistics she quoted". The article also added that "The Foreign Ministry noticed the unfriendliness of the diplomat's remarks but said it was used to such statements from Oslo."

26. "One then wonders why no historian had ever investigated this issue in almost seventy years…"

Dr Manfred Gerstenfeld interviewed Norwegian journalist Eirik Veum from the Norwegian Broadcasting Corporation, NRK, author of *The Fallen* about Norwegians in the SS and other Nazi units, in an "OpEd" for www.israelnationalnews.com published 21st January 2014. Eirik Veum's ground breaking and painstaking new research revealed Nazi collaboration and crimes, never before discussed in Norway by historians. He outlined the, quite predictable response: *"Reactions were mixed however. Several historians claimed that my topics should be dealt with by historians and not by a journalist. One then wonders why no historian had ever investigated this issue in almost seventy years."*

He also stated that although some family members had no problem with the truth coming out others "said that we had dishonoured their families by identifying relatives by name(s)". It is not surprising that several historians claimed that such matters should only be "dealt with by historians and not by a journalist", of course, none of this is surprising, except towards the end of the article we note this line: *"It is interesting to note that more energy was devoted to discussing the issue of the [public] identification of these people, than to their actions."*

I think that tells us all we need to know. Eirik Veum ended with these words: *"There were probably more Norwegian collaborators than resistance fighters. Much more remains to be researched. I believe that there may be Norwegian criminals from that period who are still alive and who have never been prosecuted for war crimes they were involved in."*

27. "Book lists 16,000 Nazi collaborator suspects"

We're going to delve into fact stranger than fiction now. I had to read this article several times because I couldn't believe what I was reading. A Norwegian article actually chose to extensively quote the *son of a soldier for Nazi Germany* who then undermined and criticised the release of a book which revealed the names of 16,000 suspected Norwegian Nazi collaborators. Fact surely is stranger than fiction in Norway… to, with no shame, quote the son of *"a Nazi supporter and a Waffen-SS volunteer"*, as described by the "The Ukrainian Center for Holocaust Studies" *to undermine the revelation of the names*. In fact, here is the "The Ukrainian Center for Holocaust Studies" (holocaustkievua.knopka.chost.com.ua) description of the Nazi from their own website:

"During the Second World War a young Norwegian Petter Westlie was a Nazi supporter and a Waffen-SS volunteer to fight for Germany on the Eastern Front."

The article, entitled, *"Book lists 16,000 Nazi collaborator suspects"* published by thelocal.no, 13 March 2014, describes a new book which lists 16,000 Norwegians who are suspected of collaborating with the Nazis. We immediately note that the tone is set by the article describing the publisher as *"maverick"*. The newspaper then extensively quotes Bjørn Westlie, the *son* of the Nazi, who then unsurprisingly undermines the whole project. We note the usual techniques: questioning the publisher's "expertise" with their handling and editing of the suspected collaboration list: *"But I ask, 'with what expertise do they do this?'* We also note the usual expected attack, with the article reporting that he *"attacked the move as irresponsible"* in Norway's *VG* newspaper.

Authors note:

I travelled to Warsaw and interviewed an expert of World War Two history at a prominent World War Two museum in the city who spoke to me about the Waffen-SS destructive impact on Warsaw and specifically the SS Norwegian Nazi volunteers. You will read his interview later in this series.

28. "Norway to restage human zoo that exhibited Africans as inmates"

To celebrate the 200th anniversary of the Norwegian constitution two artists decided to build and a recreate a "human zoo" which exhibited Africans in Norway. Yes, you did just read that correctly. This actually happened in 2014… *it was sponsored by the Norwegian Government.*

The Congo village: "It's wonderful that we are white!"

However, let's firstly take a look at the 1914 human zoo called "The Congo village" which was set up in Frogner Park, Oslo displaying which "showcased African men, women and children housed in palm-roof cabins, surrounded by "indigenous" artefacts" (*Huffington Post*, Katherine Brooks, 18th April 2014) and was opened by the King of Norway, which, over the course of five months about half of the population of Norway visited. The newspapers at the time reported that the Norwegian attendees said that the "Kongoslandsbyen" was: "exceedingly funny". Another visitor proudly told the Norwegian magazine *Urd*: "It's wonderful that we are white!" (*The Guardian* – "Norway to restage

1914 'human zoo' that exhibited Africans as inmates" by Bwesigye bwa Mwesigire, 29th Apr 2014.)

Recreating the human zoo in 2014 – sponsored by the Norwegian Government

The Norwegian Government decided to sponsor a full recreation of the "Human zoo" in 2014 to the tune of approximately £99,000, reported *The Guardian* newspaper. Of course, the complete recreation and re-staging of the "human zoo" was widely defended and argued to be in fact, *anti-racist.*

29. "Six out of ten Norwegians are negative about having a Muslim in the family"

An article by Andreas Slettholm (**aftenposten.no**, 27th May 2015) reported *that "6 out of ten are negative about having a Muslim in the family",* however, the next day **thelocal.no** published an article with a little more information. They were referring to the annual survey by Norway's "Directorate of Integration and Diversity" (IMDI) which revealed, that "58 percent of Norwegians surveyed said they would be unhappy about gaining a Muslim son-in-law or daughter-in-law" but also that they would be unhappy with Hindus (32%), Buddhists (27%) and Jewish (24%). I also noted the tags on the article of **thelocal.no** article on the matter: "Somalis, Muslims, integration, immigration, imdi". It's incredible that the figures are this high from a survey where it must be expected that many people will lie to make themselves seem "nicer"… can you imagine what the *real* numbers are?

30. "Norway unwilling to confront war crimes"

The Jerusalem Post (**jpost.com**, 21st November 2013) published an article by Sam Sokol entitled *"Norway unwilling to confront war crimes".* He spoke with world respected Nazi hunter Efraim Zuroff who said, "Oslo won't admit to its part in war crimes in Ukraine during World War II".

31. "Raise a monument over the graves of the Nordic country's Nazi soldiers"

Norway's *VG* newspaper reported (By Jon. H. Rydne – updated 16th November 2017) and asked: *"Should the Norwegian state give descendants of fallen front fighters during World War II a memorial to visit in Norway?"* The Norwegian

Red Cross argued "yes" and got on the case. For avoidance of doubt, the fighters referred to are Norwegian Nazi soldiers... who fought for the axis powers against the allies. 800 Norwegians served Hitler in the "Waffen-SS Division" murdering and carrying out countless Nazi atrocities across Europe. The Norwegian Red Cross argued that these Norwegian Nazi SS men should have a monument in Norway. An article by **sputniknews.com/europe** reported it this way: "Red Cross Norway has come up with a polarizing initiative to raise a monument over the graves of the Nordic country's Nazi soldiers, as a place of remembrance for their descendants". Let's take a closer look at those Norwegian Nazi soldiers. Did you know that the German Nazis were shocked by their brutality? The Nazis in Germany were shocked by the brutality of the Norwegian Nazis, who tortured prisoners and shot them for "sport" to such an extent that some were even jailed. They killed so many prisoners that they had to be removed. The prisoners said that their lives improved when the German Nazis took over as they were more "humane" because they weren't treated like animals any more. Yes, this is real... let's take a closer look...

32. "Norwegian camp guards shocked SS with brutality"

Richard Orange wrote an article for **local.no** (6th November 2013) entitled, *"Norwegian camp guards shocked SS with brutality"*. He interviewed author, Norwegian Eirik Veum, about his book, *Unforgiven Norwegians – Hird 1933– 1945*, who tells the story of 400 Norwegians who guarded Serbian prisoners. Just to be clear, these were Norwegian *Nazi* soldiers. Before we get to what the author revealed in his book, I want to point out what he said about the Norwegian reaction to the revelations.

The author of the article points out that the "biggest controversy" was not in response to the horrific actions by the Norwegian Nazis but by the *revealing* of the acts and names. He specifically said that many were more angry at him for revealing the crimes than the acts themselves; "interesting that we are discussing my decision to identify more than what actually happened, that Norwegians also played a part in the war crimes committed during World War II, and on a larger scale that we had been aware of".

I think that's it's certainly not surprising as it's obviously the standard response to any revelation of bad acts which have been ignored or suppressed? It's just the usual modus operandi and it's completely predicable? "Most criticism comes from historians in Norway, who don't like this kind of identifying, because it's not how we do it in Norway", he is quoted to have said. The author then goes on to point out that this information is not part of Norwegian war history, even though many people know about it, including Norwegian historians.

This correlates exactly with a Norwegian historian, who works for a major Norwegian museum and told me point blank: "Norway doesn't include real history that it doesn't like" and focuses purely on "positive things that make it look good". This was from a Norwegian historian's own mouth. We will soon hear from a group of teenagers in the north about what their *history teacher* told them about just finding out from *them* that there was a war in northern Norway at all!

Eirik Veum also revealed:

– *The SS soldiers told the Norwegians to "calm down" because they were too brutal for the Germans.*

– *After ten months the Norwegian Nazis were removed from active duty because they were involved in too much killing and torture of the prisoners and their behaviour "unnerved" the German officers.*

– *Some of the Norwegian Nazi's were even jailed by the German's Nazis for their behaviour.*

– *When the Germans took over they said that they got medicine and their conditions improved. The Yugoslavian prisoners said that they were then "**treated like humans not animals**".*

– *The German SS guards were more humane then many Norwegian guards, he said.*

– *Some Norwegian guards, as young as fifteen years old would sadistically tie rats to the prisoners so that they would eat the prisoners' flesh.*

– *Norwegians get very "emotional" about these truths because they like to talk about how "brave the Norwegians were in fighting the Germans" but that the other part and the hundreds of Norwegian Nazi volunteers themselves are "never talked about".*

The title is actually "Merciless/Ruthless Norwegians" – minimisation?

Something which is really interesting is that the <u>local.no</u> article reports the books title as being *Unforgiven Norwegians – Hird 1933—1945* when the name is actually **"Merciless Norwegians"** or **"Ruthless Norwegians"**… in fact that's the name of the whole series that Eirik Veum authored, which you can see on the publishers own website here: tanum.no. Why was the word "unforgiven" used at all? Could it be that a Norwegian newspaper/news website actually got the translation of "Nådeløse Nordmenn" wrong? Could it be a coincidence or an honest mistake? Could it be minimisation and intentional? I will let the reader decide for themselves.

33. "Proud Nazi honoured in Norway with his own stamp and coin"

Fact is often stranger than fiction in Norway. We have already seen that the indefensible is often proudly defended, victims undermined and perpetrators elevated. However, you haven't seen anything yet…

"Adolf Hitler,

I'm not worthy to speak up for Adolf Hitler, and to any sentimental rousing his life and deeds do not invite.

Hitler was a warrior, a warrior for humankind and a preacher of the gospel of justice for all nations. He was a reforming character of the highest order, and his historical fate was that he functioned in a time of example less (unequalled) brutality, which in the end failed him.

Thus may the ordinary Western European look at Adolf Hitler. And we, his close followers, bow our heads at his death.

Knut Hamsun"

Knut Hamsum Honoured Norwegian

You have just read the words of honoured and famed Norwegian Nobel laureate Knut Hamsun's obituary for the German Führer Adolf Hitler, which was printed in the Norwegian newspaper *Aftenposten* in 1945.

762 Jews murdered (minimum) in Norway alone

You will find a document on the United Nations website

(https://www.un.org/en/) which references the *Encyclopaedia of the Holocaust*, based on research at Yad Vashem. It documents that the MINIMUM number of Jewish people murdered in each country. If you go to Norway you will see that the minimum number of Jews murdered is "**762**", in Norway alone.

5,596,000 Jews murdered (minimum) by the Nazis and Adolf Hitler

If you go down to the total you will see that the MINIMUM number of Jews murdered by Adolf Hitler and the Nazi's was **5,596,000**.

5,000,000 non-Jewish victims (minimum) murdered.

Ina R. Friedman, author of *The Other Victims: First Person Stories of Non-Jews Persecuted by the Nazis* (Boston, Houghton Mifflin, 1990) wrote (**www.socialstudies.org/**) that an additional **5,000,000** people were murdered under the Nazi regime including the disabled, mentally ill, alcoholics, blind, deaf, homosexuals, blacks, Jehovah's Witnesses, travellers, artists, resistance fighters, Slavic people, to name just a few. The justification for that murder was, and I quote her words: *"The Nazis' justification for genocide was the ancient claim, passed down through Nordic legends, that Germans were superior to all other groups and constituted a "master race". Who constituted this "master race?" Blue-eyed, blond-haired people of Nordic stock, or "Aryans." As such, they had the right to declare who was worthy of life and who was not, who was to be maimed by sterilization or experimented upon in the interest of attaining racial purity, and who was to be used as slave labour to further the Nazi empire."*

Knut Hamsum the unrepentant Nazi collaborator

In an article entitled *"In From the Cold"* for *The New Yorker* (18th December 2005) Jeffrey Frank wrote that, "during the German occupation of Norway in the Second World War, Hamsun had been a collaborator; he had met Goebbels and Hitler, and was unrepentant to the end." Knut Hamsun's Wikipedia page (**en.wikipedia.org/wiki/Knut_Hamsun**) provides us with some additional information in the entries *source notes*, referencing Nazi Minister of Propaganda Joseph Goebbels personal diaries where he claimed that "from childhood on he (Hamsun) has keenly disliked the English" *The Goebbels Diaries, 1942—1943*, translated, edited, and introduced by Louis P. Lochner, 1948, pp. 303–304. The Nazi Propaganda Minister wrote a "long and enthusiastic" entry concerning his private meeting with the Norwegian and wrote that his "faith in German victory is unshakable". Hamsun wrote several newspaper articles defending the Nazi's in Norway and proudly asserted, in 1940; "the Germans are fighting for us, and now are crushing England's tyranny over us and all neutrals".

Yes, but he was a "great author" and won the Nobel Prize in Literature.

There are many in Norway who prefer to focus on his books and especially point to his Nobel Prize for literature. He did indeed win the Nobel Prize for literature and his books were very popular in Norway and worldwide, especially in Germany, since he had also supported Germany during World War One and viewed them as a superior people with a common shared culture and heritage with the Norwegian people. With regards to his Nobel Prize… the one that weighed 196 grams and made of eighteen carat gold? Knut Hamsun donated it to the Reichsminister of Propaganda, Dr. Joseph Goebbels as an act of solidarity with the Nazis.

His son was a Waffen-SS volunteer who received the honoured Iron Cross

Knut Hamsun's son, Arild Hamsun, was a decorated Nazi Waffen-SS soldier served and fought for the Nazi's. He even received the Iron Cross (second class).

Knut Hamsun actively solicited volunteers for the Waffen-SS

Fortunately, we can read about it quite easily if you know where to look. One book, gives us a great insight into the Norwegian SS Viking Nazi Division and Hamsun's role in soliciting soldiers, his son's service to the cause and also details about the Norwegians who swore oaths to Adolf Hitler, personally; "Frontfighters: The Norwegian Volunteer Legion of the Waffen-SS 1941-1943" by Richard Landwehr (based on the book *Legionsminner-Trekk Av Den Norske Legions Historie*, assembled by E. Jul Christiansen Furum in 1943 and originally published by Viking Vorlag, Oslo, 1943 and an English language translation published by Roger Hunt in 1986):

"On 29 June, 1941 the Legion Norwegian was officially launched at a massive recruiting rally held on the university Square in Oslo. A number of prominent citizens and celebrities including the opera singer Kirsten flagstad and the Nobel Prize winning author Knut Hamsun actively solicited volunteers for the legion… A former Norwegian Royal Army officer, Col Kjellstrup, placed in charge of the Legion recruiting efforts which initially were very successful."

11,902 Norwegian victims of the Nazis

We already know that at least 800 Norwegians volunteered for the Nazis but Norwegian magazine *vg.no* reports the total number of Norwegian dead, in an article entitled, "Where did the Norwegians perish during WW2?" was 11,902, including soldiers and Jews sent to concentration camps, *"These are 11, 902 Norwegian victims of the second World War"*. Many of them were Norwegian heroes betrayed by Nazi traitors like Knut Hamsun.

Treason charges unsurprisingly dropped

Considering his blatant and shameless treachery it would have been hard for him not be brought to court on treason charges. However, of course, the treason charges were later dropped because he was, conveniently, some may say, found to have "permanently impaired mental faculties" by the court and cleared of any direct Nazi affiliation. Interestingly, those adjudged "impaired faculties" were not impaired enough for him not to later write his 1949 Norwegian classic and bestseller *Paa gjengrodde Stier (On Overgrown Paths)*.

A rehabilitated Norwegian hero – the Norwegian Nazi honoured with stamps, statues and coins

You would think that this candidate wouldn't be anywhere near the top of the list for his face on a stamp or his own coin or statues in Norway, right? Couldn't be that insensitive?

Wrong. Norway chose to honour him with his own stamp, his own coin, statues and much more.

The UK's *Independent* published an article, by Andy McSmith (7th August 2009) entitled, *"Rehabilitated: Nobel Prize winner who fell for Hitler"* where he outlines the Norwegians choice to put his face on a stamp and celebrations, like the one in Hamarøy, where they had been: "…celebrating six consecutive "Hamsundagene" (Hamsun Days), with seminars, meetings and exhibitions dedicated to the writer, to mark the 150th anniversary of his birth", with a Knut Hamsun museum actually opened by Crown Princess Mette-Marit. We have also seen a seven-foot statue in his birthplace Hamsund and special coins too! *The Guardian* newspaper published an article entitled, "Knut Hamsun commemorated on Norwegian coin" by Alison Flood who interviewed Leif Veggum, a director of the Norwegian bank, "Norges Bank", who is quoted to have said that the new coin was, "in honour of Hamsun's works, which have had a strong influence on both Norwegian and international literature."

34. "Al Pacino pulls out of 'Nazi' Knut Hamsun play"

The Daily Telegraph reported that Al Pacino decided to wisely pull out of a Knut Hamsun play because he couldn't reconcile with his blatant support of Adolf Hitler and Nazism. Ironically, the article by Richard Orange (www.telegraph.co.uk: 27th May 2015) interviewed a Norwegian called Hege Faust who said that it was "strange": "… *that people today could not separate the "literary brilliance" of Hamsun's early years with the politics of his old age".* The sad thing is that these are genuinely held and proud beliefs by many in Norway, which explains why she genuinely would find it all very strange that there is an issue at all.

35. "The Norwegian hero condemned for fighting the Nazi invaders"

"Either I will be decorated, or I will be court-martialled. Fire!"

Colonel Birger Kristian Eriksen

If any Norwegian deserves to be put on a stamp, coin and to be honoured it is surely Colonel Birger Kristian Eriksen, who fought against the Nazi's initial invasion of Oslo and sunk the ships of the Nazi invaders on 9th April 1940. He sunk a 16,000 ton German cruiser called "Blücher" and his actions changed the course of Norwegian history. I can find a statue to the man but no special coin or postage stamp.

Of course, it cannot be surprising that this true hero was actually questioned, bullied and undermined.

He defended Oslo when invaded but had to make a choice because there was no time to call for final advice, since Norway was neutral. He acted in the defence of his country with the words; "Either I will be decorated, or I will be court-martialled. Fire!" Not only did he save lives but he gave the King, members of the Royal family and government thirty hours more time to escape. Although he did receive certain honour I was shocked to see that not only was he also criticised but that his actions were investigated by government investigators who questioned him. He died a "bitter man" according to some reports… of course, he was honoured more appropriately *after* his death. In his book: *9 April 1940 – a historical deception*, historian Aage G.

Sivertsen wrote: *"He was treated unfairly after the war. The perennial colonel was* **regularly bullied**. *Admittedly, he was decorated with the War Cross with swords, the highest military distinction one can get. Besides this, it was a small honour to obtain."*

So we have a situation where the prolific Nazi is supported and put on stamps and coins but a true Norwegian hero dies, bullied and feeling unappreciated.

36. "Norwegian industry complied with German war efforts"

Science Norway (**sciencenorway.no**) published an article entitled *"Norwegian industry complied with German war efforts"* by Hanne Jakobsen (11th April 2013) stating, *"Seventy-three years ago, on 9 April 1940, Nazi Germany attacked and occupied Norway. The Germans needed aluminium to win the war. But rather than resist their German occupiers, Norwegian industry leaders chose to cooperate instead."* The article then quotes a Norwegian historian who condemns the companies who profited from working with the Nazis…

… I'm kidding… of course it didn't!

The article quotes a Norwegian historian called Hans Otto Frøland, a history professor from the Norwegian University of Science and Technology (NTNU) who explained to us that it's a case where the companies *merely worked* with the Nazis, "but without ideologically having a Nazi orientation" and stated that they only did it for the money… "this was pure economic strategy". We are then told that many people have "simplistic perceptions" that the war had "good guys" and "bad guys". Enlightened historians like him want to change this view apparently; "those of us who study the war want to change this simplistic perception".

37. "Group Psychosis" and Norwegian traitors being "more scary than the Gestapo"

James Sorg (SGT U.S Marine Corps) spent his adolescent years in Oslo. He was featured in a Walter Cronkite TV special (CBS News) which broadcast footage of him, as a young man, escaping Oslo when the Germans invaded. The American TV special stated that the Norwegians described the day as *"our day of panic"* and used a phrase to describe the behaviour of the Norwegian people which was fascinating: *"a group psychosis gripped the Norwegian people"*.

In 2006, James Sorg made a speech to the "Robert H. Jackson Center" and he spoke about remembering the exact day and the events of the day (news footage of which had just been played for him and the audience). In his speech, made just two years before his death, he described the German paratroopers dropping down on Oslo, in detail. He also said something which I don't think has ever been committed to text before. James Sorg stated that the "Norwegians traitors" who numbered "an awful lot of them" were "more scary than the Gestapo". This is what he said verbatim:

"When we returned to the city (Oslo) there were Germans all over and one thing I forgot to tell you, the site of the German paratroopers coming out of the sky and the trucks on the road and the jeeps they had and what have you, it was scary! I mean we had parachutes up on houses... middle of the street... On lawns... they were all over! I don't know how many paratroopers they dropped on Oslo but it seems to me that they said 6000 on the film and I think that it was 5 or 6 times that but I was a little guy. When we returned the soldiers were all over, they were patrolling the streets and most of the time they were patrolling two and two and they were going up and down the street and they had their vehicles and they're driving alongside the roads, and the majority of these German soldiers, I want to be quick to say, they all didn't have horns and tails, there were a lot of good Germans, but the guys that you had to be afraid of were the ones in the brown shirts, Swastika on their arm, black pants and we called them the SS or the Gestapo... **but there was one element that was more scary than the Gestapo and that was the Norwegian traitors. We were scared to death of those people. You didn't dare to talk to them or tell them you're thinking, the way you were brought up, you didn't dare to say anything to them because if they didn't like you, they'd turn you in, whether you said it or not. You were on your way to someplace else which you never knew... whether you knew you're going to come back or not, but those traitors, there was an awful lot of them!** *And they were basically led by, you just saw him, Vidkun Quisling. He was the head of the minority government in Norway, when the Germans came in and he helped them organise and take over the city and the country. He was a fat guy like me! But I'm a lot cuter than he was. We had a lot of respect for the Germans... and the Norwegian traitors. Keep in mind that an American citizen and 7-year-old when I came to Norway... I was fourteen when I came back to this country."*

He then went on to say that he had to report to the Gestapo every Friday for "five years". Let's take a look at one of the most notorious traitor of all time, which he referenced in his speech: Vidkun Quisling.

38. "Quisling – the dictionary definition of traitor"

Vidkun Quisling's name was actually added to the dictionary to describe treachery:

Quisling
noun:
a traitor who collaborates with an enemy force occupying their country.

He founded the Norwegian fascist party, the National Front and went to his death as a coward saying:*"I know that the Norwegian people have sentenced me to death, and that the easiest course for me would be to take my own life. But I want to let history reach its own verdict. Believe me, in ten years' time I will have become another Saint Olav."*

(Quisling to Bjørn Foss, 8 May 1945, Dahl 1999, p. 367, Dahl, Hans Fredrik (1999). Quisling: A Study in Treachery. Stanton-Ife, Anne-Marie)

His final words were without remorse or shame: *"I'm convicted unfairly and I die innocent."*

(Bratteli & Myhre 1992, p. 198, Bratteli, Tone; Myhre, Hans B. (1992). Quislings siste dager)

Kept quiet in Norway?

I was speaking to a self-proclaimed Norwegian history World War Two expert, whose grandfather fought for the Nazis, who could not name Vidkun Quisling. It got me thinking… the English language literally has this Norwegians name in it as a synonym for treachery and all of a sudden he is unknown by many Norwegians? I started to ask people and you would be shocked that hardly anybody I spoke to seemed to know anything about him at all… some of the older ones knew of him but none of the younger ones (under forty-five years old) could name him. It's as if he wasn't taught in history lessons at all in Norway. If you go to YouTube's "Vidkun Quisling: The Man Who Sold his Country to the Third Reich" (Biographics Video Hosted by Simon Whistler and currently well over 260,000 views) and you will see some of Norwegian youtuber comments underneath it:

L**s:

"I'm Norwegian, never heard this but OK…"

H****t:
"It's true, but I've never actually heard anyone use the term. Probably more common among older generations."

L*****:
*"I haven't watched it yet, but **OMG I'm so excited that you made a video about him (I'm Norwegian)!**"*

Jan **********:
*"**I am so happy you did a Norwegian person, even though this is a national traitor.** I would like to see a more beloved Norwegian like Henrik Ibsen one of the most known Norwegians of all time"*

Håkon ********:
"He was a hero… betrayed by his own people"

… and this comment has 100 likes:

H*****:
"It's so Scandinavian to fight an occupying enemy force by being passive aggressive and giving the cold shoulder."

39. "What is typically Norwegian?"

"Easy Languages" posted a YouTube video, hosted by Sindre Garcia where they went around Oslo asking Norwegians: *"What is typically Norwegian?"* They are a non-profit video project aiming at supporting people worldwide to learn languages through authentic street interviews. The video currently has 500,000 views and over 1,124 comments. The video is horrifying. Norwegian after Norwegian after Norwegian gives the same robotic answer: "Brown cheese (giggle)". The people asked often look scared to give the "wrong" answer.

He interviews old people, young people, male and female and almost every one giggles and gives "brown cheese" as an answer… or names a cheese cutting utensil. A few even criticise Norwegians themselves as "cold" people. This video is real and the Norwegians in it are real… it's not a comedy show. That's why it's horrifying… they are telling their truth. Please, go and watch the video for yourself and come back… take a quick look at the comments too. Did you notice that the comments are almost entirely positive? You will see the majority, the overwhelming majority say that the Norwegians in the video are "good looking" or "Norwegians are so good looking" or something commenting on the aesthetics of Norwegians or Norway. These comments are from almost entirely non-Norwegian people. You then have a high number of comments from Norwegians commenting on their own country and about how great it is and "how proud we are to be Norwegian" etc. However, there are (although in the extreme minority) a few other comments which are interesting, especially the ones from Norwegians themselves or people that have lived in Norway:

The top comment with 1110 likes:

"Me: hello nice to me…

Norwegians: BRUNOST"

The second comment, also with 1100 likes:

"So, Norway is 50% cheese 50% cheese accessories. Good to know."

Additional comments from Norwegians and more…

Comment: *"**I think a lot of us Norwegians are obsessed with our own culture,** if there is a video about our country, there will most likely exclusively be Norwegians in the comment sections."*

Comment in reply: *"So truee, everytime i click on a video about norway theres just a bunch of us Norwegians there wondering what foreigners think of our country and us lmao."*

Comment: *"They say a lot of critical things about themselves, but they actually seem very nice and down to earth."*

Comment in reply: *"I live in Norway. I have my entire life. But im not Norwegian by blood. Trust me. They're not nice."*

Comment: *"SO NICE PEOPLE!"*

Comment in reply: *"me a norwegian – sure about that?"*

Comment: *"I know the compliments aren't directed at me and directed at norway but they make me happy and makes all bubbly and giddy."*

Comment: *"Brown Cheese." Very informative."*

Comment: *"Lol, this is accurate. Especially the smug part and just accepting things."*

Comment: *"This convinced me not to go to Norway at any time in life."*

Comment: *"I love my country so much, it almost hurts!"*

Comment in reply (from Norway): *"What is typically Norwegian? Typical Norwegian are self-obsessed. They love to brag on comment sections online they are "From Norway." Norwegians like to consider their country as a very important one in peace/war-issues and world politics, that if it wasn't for Norway's efforts, the world would collapse very soon. Couldn't be more misleading, and so far away from the truth. A typical Norwegian have to say "They are from Norway" if any article or anything that for fills their narrow-minded ego. It's rather embarrassing how they got to show their ass kissing ego. "They are from Norway" Norwegians love to act, like Norway is a superior country in this world. Norwegians, COME ON! GET YOUR ACTS TOGETHER!!! One thing is being proud, this is just embarrassing. WHY do you HAVE to tell you are from Norway? Who cares. Only the world get to see is how disgusting self-obsessed narrow-minded egocentric behaviour you are showing to rest of the world. Shut up!! Learn how to be humbler. Remember. Norway wouldn't be the country it is today without its rich oil-resources. People in Norway show their narrow-minded and some get the feeling of superiority, and they think they are better than other people. They don't want the truth. They rather being told lies about how "great Norway is" and having their ass kissed with lies. Rather than told true words on how their realistic their world really is. That's why Norwegians can't show any humbleness to this comment... Watch..."*

Comment in reply: *(blank – no comment in reply)*

Comment: *"In my opinion the **most typical Norwegian thing** is The **Beauty**!! Yes the **beautiful** face and body, the **beautiful** personality, the **beautiful** society, the **beautiful** nature, the **beautiful** weather and the **beautiful** buildings and infrastructures. Norwegians have the **best** quality of life in the world, the **best** prison, the **most** productive, the **best** weather (I love cold and snow)."*

Comment from a Norwegian ten-year resident: *"Norwegians are very nice people. but as the girl said, they have a coldness about them. yes, if you break the ice with them. then everything is great. but that's the thing… breaking the ice with a Norwegian is the most complicated thing in the world. No way is the right way – unless BEER is involved. but even so… the next day; don't talk to them like you 'know' them. unless you talk to then like you DON'T know them. Like that great party last night never happened. The Norwegian, and Norwegian culture is the first one I've seen a BOOK written for to understand. And… it gives an idea of how to understand them, but, Stll no idea of how to 'interact' with them. Norwegians themselves don't understand Norwegians, THAT'S the problem. He asked "what's typical Norwegian" and 95% of them say brunost (A type of cheese). NOTHING about their 'character'. The one girl that DID say something about their 'character', first said "brunost is surely used up" Showing, that they are all aware of the 'jerk response' answer. THEN she makes her statement that actually came from THINKING AND OBSERVATION. Which is exactly what I've experienced after living here for almost 10 years now. But… as I began… Norwegians are great peoole. just… weird"*

Comment in reply: *"Yeah I agree, I am not ethnic Norwegian but born and raised here and even us "utlendinger" always complain that Norwegians are cold people. But Norwegians like me with different ethnic backgrounds are usually very open to everyone. That's one of the reason most of my friends here are not ethnic Norwegians too, because it's hard to interact with majority of them (and like you said, except when it comes to drinking involved)"*

40. "Many people share Breivik's conspiracy theory"

During the sentencing of Norwegian terrorist Anders Breivik, one of the world's most evil murderers and mass killers, the Norwegian court said: *"Many people share Breivik's conspiracy theory, including the Eurabia theory."*

Eurabia is a conspiracy theory described by Wikipedia as: *"Eurabia is a political neologism, a portmanteau of Europe and Arabia, used to describe an Islamophobic conspiracy theory, involving globalist entities allegedly led by French and Arab powers, to Islamise and Arabise Europe, thereby weakening its existing culture and undermining a previous alignment with the U.S. and Israel."*

During my discussions with many Norwegians across Norway I found myself doing something which shocked me, when I thought about it later. When I started to discuss Anders Breivik with people I often prefaced with this quick question, "Just to make sure we're on the same page... you are against Anders Breivik, right?" They would always reply, "Yes!" It was unconscious but I actually felt the need to ask, because when you start to talk to people, you find that many people do, to some extent, support some of his views in Norway. I have personally sat down with many of them, including one man near Trondheim who explained that he believed that the Notre Dame cathedral fire in Paris, France was carried out by Muslims "who burned it down" and that the media kept it quiet for the sake of "political correctness". Obviously, this should not be surprising as the court in Oslo itself stated unequivocally that "many people share Breivik's conspiracy theory, including the Eurabia theory". I also found a reluctance of many people to condemn him unequivocally but on the other hand, people like Greta Thunberg often condemned quickly, harshly and unequivocally.

41. "Winning Fair and Square? Norwegian Ski Supremacy Driven by Doping"

I can say with certainty that I have never spoken with a single Norwegian that accepts that Norwegian skiing legend, Therese Johaug, doped... even though she is guilty of doping and has been banned, for doping. Every single person I asked refused to accept that she doped. They do, however, often recount conspiracy theories as to why she tested positive for illegal substances, blaming her doctor and blaming everybody but her. Some of the interview recordings are quite comedic because I asked questions like, *"Do you think that convicted doper, Therese Johaug, who was found guilty of doping and was banned for doping actually doped?"* The reply, always was, *"No!"* No exceptions. We will speak to a ski expert later in this book in detail. Now, we have already seen that perceived criticism, even if true, is so often rejected or excused in Norway, but could it also be something to do with media bias? Interestingly, a researcher looked into the media coverage of the Therese Johaug doping case. *Sciencenorway* published an article entitled *"Doping scandal covered very differently by Swedish and Norwegian media"* by Nancy Bazilchuk (22nd May 2019). You don't have to be a clairvoyant to anticipate what is to come next but let's go there anyway.

The Norwegian media "avoided" calling the case a "doping scandal" unlike the media in other countries, found researchers Elsa Kristiansen of University of South-Eastern Norway and Ulrik Wagner at the University of Southern Denmark. Whilst abroad they said that they found it "interesting" that the reporting was so different from the Norwegian reporting and decided to study hundreds of articles worldwide and to log those articles. We note that the adjective "interesting" is often used, just as the journalist did when he revealed the Norwegian Nazi atrocities and described how the media were more concerned with the revelation of the names than the actual acts themselves. I find it "interesting" that certain people don't simply state the obvious but seemingly only feel comfortable using euphemistic language. However, let's get back to the article, which of course, wouldn't be a Norwegian article if it didn't refer to the situation as being "not quite black and white", and it surely doesn't disappoint us as those are the exact words the article goes on to use in its sub heading.

Of course, we must also expect the usual defence from the usual enlightened expert to educate us and make sure we are seeing things from the "correct" perspective and on this occasion that comes in the form of Egeberg Honorary Committee leader Børre Rognlien, who was also former Sports President. The Egeberg Award is a big deal in Norway and he said, as reported by **aftenposten.no** (article by Petter Fløttum,Bernt Harald Burnevann, 5th August 2019) that he doesn't feel that, and I quote, "the doping case will be crucial" with regards to Therese Johaug being considered for the prestigious award. He also stressed that he believed that there is a big difference between a doper who acted "intentionally" and that this wasn't the case with Therese Johaug.

You don't have to be Sigmund Freud to deduce that any criticism of a Norwegian popular skier would be perceived as a direct threat on the Norwegian sense of identity and thus, by many, a direct attack on Norwegians, and probably be rejected and denied fiercely as a matter of reflex. Many Norwegians are religiously brought up with the saying that "Norwegians are born with skis on their feet" and if they are not, then they are taught that they should be… it is repeated like a mantra in Norway. Just like any religion or strong identifying association, any participant will go on the attack and refuse to accept any criticism or undermining of that identity, regardless of logic or reality. An academic in Norway called Ingvild Tennøe Haugen, who, in her introduction to her study "Chapter 9, A Nation Betrayed – The Dramatic Coverage of a Doping Case, Ingvild Tennøe Haugen, MA student, Department of Journalism and Media Studies Doping in Norway" from the book *Putting a Face on It: Individual Exposure and Subjectivity in Journalism*, states:

"… the journalist's positioning of himself as part of a victimised unity: the Norwegian people. I discuss how the coverage elevates cross-country skiing as an expression (and creation) of national identity. Thus, a crisis for one of Norway's cross-country skiers is portrayed as a crisis for all Norwegians."

Ingvild Tennøe Haugen intelligently states that the coverage by the Norwegian media "actively create allusions to emotions on a religious level in terms of belief and faith. This, and the assertion that the Norwegian people are affected by the case, serve to establish cross-country skiing as a kind of secular religion for the whole nation". What doesn't seem to be addressed is why would that kind of manipulation/tone be tolerated as a normal means of communication from so-called "reputable" journalists?

I was in Norway when Therese Johaug gave her famous press conference. She was weeping and came out with chapped lips (her excuse was that she needed a special lip balm, which had the illegal substance in it) and dishevelled. As I watched this performance I started laughing and said to my Norwegians friends, "Every time I come to Norway this skier is crying on TV… what has she done this time and what's wrong with her lips?" They explained that she has a lip condition which caused her doctor to "mistakenly" give her "lip balm" which contained banned substances. I told them, "She doesn't have a lip issue during this press conference though does she? Her lips were fine the last time she was on TV the other day? Why is she weeping and looking dishevelled at THIS press conference? You don't actually believe this performance do you?" They laughed and said that she was innocent and that it was the doctor's fault. Not a single one even questioned her illogical narrative. I actually laughed and then I realised… they weren't joking and that they 100% believed her narrative and this weird press conference. It was one of the most preposterous displays I have ever seen… that's when I realised… it's obvious when you think about it.

Certain cultural aspects, and possibly *all* aspects of Norwegian culture, are sacrosanct to a great many Norwegians, which is why any perceived criticism is automatically dismissed, rejected and shut down. It just can't be accepted or computed by a great many people. Skiing is too much a part of the identity and culture that it's beyond any kind of reproach or criticism even if a skier is found guilty of doping… it just won't be accepted by many within Norway.

We note that in Ingvild Tennøe Haugen's analysis of the Norwegian reporting of the saga she uses the words; "emotions", "religious level", "belief and faith". Norwegian journalists positioning themselves as part of a "victimised unity: The Norwegian people" and as skiing being a "secular religion" for Norway.

The Norwegian people being a "victimised unity"?

If skiing is a secular cultural "religion", what other aspects of Norwegian culture are perceived by Norwegians in this so-called "religious" way? There are many seemingly sacrosanct aspects of Norwegian culture that are venerated just like skiing, if not more so. If you think about it logically, it obviously makes sense because when you look at how those who dissent from the standard Norwegian "narrative" on any cultural matter related to Norwegian "identity" we see that they are often shut down, shunned or at best, undermined, as a seeming auto-response? However, is the word "religious" really accurate and appropriate? I actually don't think it is because if we look at the definition of "religion", we see that it is:

religion:
(noun) "the belief in and worship of a superhuman controlling power, especially a personal God or gods."

I don't see how that definition has any link to this particular situation at all. However, there is another word which seems to more accurately describe this type of behaviour and situation. I will not name the word at this time but will give its definition;

1. a system of religious veneration and devotion directed towards a particular figure or object.
2. a person or thing that is popular or fashionable among a particular group or section of society.

That's a more accurate definition of the previous behaviour described... certainly more accurate than the word "religion", in any context, in my opinion. Carolyn Steber wrote an article for www.bustle.com, published 21st June 2018 where she listed the traits of people who would be susceptible to the kind of manipulation described above, which might be of interest to the reader:

1. Those Who Want To Feel Validated
2. Those Who Are Seeking An Identity
3. Those Who Are Followers, Not Leaders
4. Those Who Are Seeking Meaning
5. Those Who Have Schizotypal Thinking
6. Those Who Are Highly Suggestible
7. Those Who Constantly Blame Others
8. Those Who Are Always Angry
9. Those Who Have Very Low Self-Worth

Immediate defence of Johaug

Although, The Norwegian Ski Federation immediately came to the defence of Johaug, the international media weren't as "understanding" as the Norwegian media: "Winning Fair and Square? Norwegian Ski Supremacy Driven by Doping", reported <u>sputniknews.com</u> (14th October 2016) and listed the responses of various international sports commentators, including from Sweden. Expressen's sports (**www.expressen.se**) commentator Lasse Anrell, wrote: *"Norwegian cross-country skiing stinks. There is a certain arrogance in Norwegian skiing, as their skiers' dominance allows them to do as they please. That's why they don't give a damn about the rules."*

Sports journalist Johan Esk *(***www.dn.se***)*, of Dagens Nyheter's wrote: *"First, Martin Johnsrud Sundby and now Therese Johaug. Now it's definitely time to put Norway in the same bunch of cheater states."*

Martin Johnsrud Sundby was another famous Norwegian skier who was stripped of titles for alleged doping, the same year.

Twitter user @**orde*orttila (Twitter: 20th July 2016) wrote:

"Norway skiers finally caught of cheating. Sundby doping just tip of the iceberg. All Norwegians use doping. Ugly secret no more a secret!"

The question is, why would so many Norwegian people genuinely believe that their skier was innocent in the face of overwhelming evidence? How can other reputable international media outlets report exactly the same story but in a totally different way and get it so "wrong"? However, let's move on for now…

42. Norway… the greatest most beautiful most amazing place on earth!

If you type "Norway" into *any* social media platform or into YouTube and simply look at the tags and the titles, you will notice something. You'll see these words mentioned constantly in the titles and comments:

Norway is…

"perfect!"

"paradise!"

"heaven!"

"miracle!"

"best!"

"beautiful!"

"rich!"

"amazing!"

Titles from the first page of YouTube when you search "Norway":

Title: "Norway – Is It The **Perfect** Economy?" (800,376 views)

Title: "Norway: A Socialist **Paradise?**" (106,221 views)

(Top comment: *"So COOL!!!! An interview with a Norwegian Economist!!! .. . who says hard facts… we need more internet like this… so freaking awesome!!"*– 538 likes)

Title: "American REACTS to Norwegian Lifestyle | Norway Is **Amazing**" (35,245 views)

Title: "Why you should visit Norway – Unspoken **paradise**" (255,245 views)

Title: "VLOG, travelling to Norway, Norway day one, **most beautiful country**" (14,069 views)

(Top comment: *"I am from Bergen in Norway, lik vis du er norsk, i am so proud to be from Norway"*– 16 likes)

Title: "Why Norway Has The **Best** Educational System In The World" (39,771 views)

Title: "Why is NORWAY **so RICH?** – VisualPolitik EN" (990,264 views)

(Top comment: (3.9K likes) *"So… who from Norway came here just to boost their ego?? I certanily did"*)

Title: "Norway's tips for **achieving happiness** | DW English" (62,563 views)

Top comment: (100 likes) *"Do you know why we are so happy? Because religion have NO power here, men and woman are equal, people are educated and believe in science and reason. That's what makes a good life… the more you know the better you do. And we want equal rights for all, not just for the benefit of the richest, but for ALL. Americans call it communism, we call it being civilized. And by the way, we are not communist, communism is when the people fear the government and the state have ALL the power. That is NOT Norway."*

Title: "Norway's **Stolen Children**?" (406,417 views)

Title: "**Typical** things about NORWAY | PART 1" (308,238 views)

Title: "Norwegians are **racist**? Life is difficult in Norway!" (506,095 views)

Title: "Norway – The **Happiest** Country of the World" (207,076 views)

(Top comment: (153 likes) *"i'm not a norwegian but i believe if you want to migrate to another country, you must obey their culture,their rules and not yours and live peacefully with the citizen of that country.don't act that you're some kind of special,instead be grateful that this nation accept you to be the citizen of their homeland. regards and respect from the Philippines!"*)

Title: "Norwegian men make the **best** husbands" (22,496 views)

(Note: This Associated Press video includes interviews… vacant, fake, slightly scared look… it has it all.)

Exaggeration and use of evangelical language and imagery

If you search "Norway" you will see for yourself an extremely high number of videos and social media posts that have some kind of evangelical use of exaggerated language or imagery and very often extreme over the top enthusiastic smiles and laughter with public displays of affection. They are seemingly sincere too and the *overwhelming majority* are made by tourists and foreigners… but not all. Search any Norwegian city on Youtube; "Kristiansand" or "Stavanger" or "Alesund" … it doesn't make a difference, take your pick. You will regularly read exaggerated evangelical language like, "The Norwegian miracle!", "The happiest place on earth", "Norwegian paradise". If you search on Instagram you will constantly see comments and tags like, "I came to Norway and found happiness!", "I came to Norway and found heaven" etc. In addition to this you will often hear emotional ethereal, euphoric or new age music (always in a major key it would seem) dubbed to cliché sweeping superficial drone and aerial shots. Have a look at the videos and how many images and thumbnails you will see of very smiley happy people with their arms outstretched. Take a look at the start of the video above entitled; "Norway's tips for achieving happiness", it's a DW documentary and opens with the smiley person arms outstretched in nature and happy, as an example. Look at the proportion compared to other countries. Type in "France" or "Germany" and take a closer look and it will become very clear. When you search for nearly any major Scandinavian city or location but especially Norway or a place in Norway, note that the overwhelming majority appear like completely one-sided promotions or closer to adverts rather than a reflection of the reality of the location and it's people. In the official domestic videos, note the constant references to being the "best" and words like "highest standard" and "top". Note that you will usually find an implication of teaching the world something, being a "world leader" or being "cutting edge". Note the constant use of the word "typical" ("Typical Norwegian" or "Typical Swede") and almost without exception promotion of stereotype and generalisation as fact. In many foreign made videos, you may also notice that you are often told what you "must do" or what you "must not do" explaining the "rules" regarding the Nordic way of life.

Materialism and superficiality

Note the constant references to money, wealth, riches and materialism and a general high level of narcissistic themes.

As a Norwegian…

If you take a look at the comments underneath these videos you will notice that the main weight of comments including a high number of comments on the looks and aesthetics of Norwegians or/and Norway. You will notice an extremely high number of "smileys" and emojis. You will notice a high proportion of back-handed "jokes" and subtle passive aggression. You will also notice a high number commenting on the pronunciation of Norwegian words and adjudging their delivery, with a hint of condescension. However, most interesting is a comment that you will see extremely regularly which goes something like this:

"As a Norwegian…"

The commenters regularly put their country, or the collective identity first before their personal expression of their opinion. The opinion is nearly always the same comment in a variety of forms. They tend to never state, "I really enjoyed this video, I love my country"… it's usually stated in the third person, "As a Norwegian…" especially on YouTube. This is even the case with almost any subject, as long as it links to Norway and Norwegians, like for example the ABC News "Witness to terror" YouTube video below:

"Oslo, Norway Terrorist Attack: Video Footage of Explosion and Camp Shooting Aftermath (07.23.2011)"

If you look at the third comment down, you will see a Norwegian commenter called "E***a" who's comment has 204 "likes" and starts off with:

"As a Norwegian…"

She then expresses the pain. Note, projection of Norwegian identity *first*. Expression of pain *second*. This is extremely regular and typical under any video linked to anything Norwegian. It can be any subject matter linked to Norway. If we take a look at "The Norwegian Butter Crisis and the Ark of Taste: Citation Needed 8x02" by YouTube celebrity Tom Scott, which has over 324,819 views, and if we take a look at the top comment, below the video authors comments we see that the top comment is by Norwegian "LJ" and has 482 likes:

"As one coming from NORWAY here…"

The commenter even capitalised the word "NORWAY" so that we are not mistaken. Take a look for yourself… you can't miss them. Many residents from countries do this kind of thing, especially on the Danish themed videos, but it is to a very high degree on the Norwegian themed videos.

43. "Tail Fin Heroes, Norwegian Air"

Norwegian Airline created a series called "Tail Fin Heroes", where they placed a famous Norwegian or somebody who has had an impact on Norwegian culture and honours them with their portrait on their aeroplanes. Aksel Sandemose, creator of the "Janteloven", of course, is a Norwegian Air, "Tail fin hero". I personally flew on this aircraft on my repeated journeys across Norway, on the Tromso to Oslo route.

44: "How Norway turns criminals into good neighbours"

BBC news published an article entitled *"How Norway turns criminals into good neighbours"* on 7th July 2019. A BBC reporter visited a Norwegian prison where the prison guards describe that they eat and play games together with the prisoners. They call it "dynamic security". The guards insist that they are not "guards", they are prison "officers" and role models to the prisoners, which include murderers. The inmates also receive flat screen TVs and have en suite rooms.

45. "Bully-free school"

I interviewed a Norwegian family whose son was bullied at school. However, they described that the same school had actually proclaimed itself to be a completely "bully-free" school in the local media.

46. "Norway top two coffee consumption in the world"

According to **worldatlas.com** Norway has the second highest coffee consumption in the world based on per capita consumption: 9.9KG per capita. If you look at the list you may notice a theme:

1. Finland
2. Norway
3. Iceland
4. Denmark

I've looked into the reasons and the most obvious reason seems to be conveniently ignored. Type in "why do Norwegians drink so much coffee?" and you're going to hear every reason under the sun except the most obvious one. You'll see articles about Norwegian "coffee culture", you'll see the usual suspects exclaim that it's because coffee is "good" for you, you'll hear a lot of the usual "What Makes Norway's Coffee Culture Unique?" articles trotted out… however… there is one reason that seems to be, well, conveniently ignored:

"Caffeine is a central nervous system stimulant of the methylxanthine class. It is the world's most widely consumed psychoactive drug."

It's interesting that the countries that are usually voted the "happiest" in the UN's World Happiness Report are in the top 4, don't you think? Why would the happiest people on earth have to consume so much of the psychoactive drug caffeine via the highest coffee consumption in the world?

47. "Bergen Police whistle blower"

Bergen police whistle blower Per Terje Engedal revealed massive failures which caused him to leave his job, as reported by vg.no. "Alerted about system failure and conflicts in Bergen police: There was pure war at the house". He exposed the number of officers who needed counselling and to speak to a psychologist due to stress and problems with their superiors and managers. He told *VG*, that: "I was directly opposed and had no confidence, neither with the police management nor in the Police Directorate". He said that he did not want to pursue the case because he was *afraid of future repercussions with regards to promotion* etc.

48. "Are 72 % of all Norwegian doctors depressed?"

Tidsskriftet.no, the *Journal of the Norwegian Medical Association*, published an article, 7th May 2013 entitled: *"Are 72 % of all Norwegian doctors depressed?"* What can I add to that? These are the types of articles that you will regularly read in Norway. Regardless of the validity, the fact that these questions are regularly asked as a matter of routine are a big enough red flag to indicate that Norwegian society has serious problems.

49. "Racial discrimination in seven out of eleven Oslo Bars"

The Local (thelocal.no) published an article entitled *"Norway celebs slam 'racist' nightclubs in Oslo"*, 29th December 2015. Norwegian non-white celebrities teamed up with an anti-racism agency and were turned away and suffered racial discrimination from seven out of eleven bars.

50. "Making friends with Norwegians takes too much time"

Mari Bore Øverland wrote her Master's thesis and it's entitled; *"Making friends with Norwegians takes too much time: the role of social capital in highly skilled temporary migrants' aspirations and opportunities for citizenship enactment"*. She said; "…a significant lack of social capital between Norwegians and highly skilled temporary migrants pushed the migrants' citizenship enactment away from the Norwegian society".

51. "Expats say it's not just Norway's weather that's cold"

The Local (**www.thelocal.no**) published an article 29th August 2016 entitled, *"Expats say it's not just Norway's weather that's cold"*. It's about the InterNations Expat Insider 2016 survey which is disgraceful reading from a Norwegian and Danish perspective. It basically surveys expats who describe "ease" of settling in and making friends etc.... it truly is shameful for both Norway and Denmark but a clear indicator that there are major issues in Norwegian society, as described in this book series. Again, the fact that news titles like "Expats say it's not just Norway's weather that's cold", are normal and typical in Norway proves the point... however, what's really interesting is that Norway comes nowhere near the top on any of the sections on "quality of life". So, when many Norwegians themselves are asked they often express that they have a great quality of life and are the "happiest" people on earth and all the rest of it, but when expats in Norway are asked, they don't describe a positive experience or a particularly high "quality of life" at all according this survey? The survey places Norway, not stone cold bottom... but close, for "friendliness" and "feeling welcome" Norway ranks 63rd out of 67, for both. For the "finding friends" category Norway ranks even lower. Stone cold bottom with Denmark. Denmark has the "honour" of the bottom spot kept company by Norway who place 66th worse out of 67 countries. In the 2018 Survey Norway came 57th out of 64 for "personal happiness".

52. "Lawsuit against Utøya memorial by locals"

The Guardian published an article, 21st June 2017, where they describe a lawsuit by twenty locals on Utøya Island against the building of a memorial to the seventy-seven victims of Anders Breivik. The article states that the government backed down after the outcry from the residents against the memorial to the victims.

53. "Twisted killer Anders Breivik receives thousands of letters a month from fans"

The UK's *Daily Mirror* newspaper published a story entitled, "*Sick supporters: Twisted killer Anders Breivik receives thousands of letters a month from fans*" by Nick Owens and Ben Griffiths (26th August 2012) and explain that the prison chief in Norway had to assign five guards to handle "fan mail" sent to the neo Nazi.

54. "Utøya memorial defaced with Swastika on anniversary of attack"

A memorial on the island of Utøya (not the one mentioned before which did not go ahead) was attacked and vandalised with a Nazi Swastika on the anniversary of the killing of seventy-seven people by neo Nazi Anders Breivik. It has been desecrated on numerous occasions, I understand. The Prime Minister responded, "If this is just a prank, it's extremely insensitive to do it on a day like this," according to **thelocal.com** (23th July 2019). I think the fact that this act can be even potentially described as a "prank" is shocking and telling in itself.

55. "Norway: Anti-refugee Soldiers of Odin patrol in Stavanger"

In Stavanger, Norway the "Soldiers of Odin", a far-right group patrolled, as reported by Ruptly, 30th April 2016. If you type in the name; "Norway: Anti-refugee Soldiers of Odin patrol in Stavanger to help the police" into YouTube you can see the gleeful comments beneath the video for yourself, describing them as "heroes" and "defenders"… almost 100% actually.

56. "Farmed Norwegian Salmon World's Most Toxic Food"

Marcus Guiliano researched Norwegian salmon farms and uploaded, with 4,382,588 views "Farmed Norwegian Salmon World's Most Toxic Food" (25th March 2017) on to YouTube which tells the story of Norwegian fish farms. It's a shameful exposé and incredible journalism which exposes Norwegian practices outright. Stephen Castle of the *New York Times* published a piece called "As Wild Salmon Decline, Norway Pressures Its Giant Fish Farms" (6th November 2017) researching the impact of the Norwegian famed fish.

57. "We do not respect human rights the way we should – MEP"

Ruptly Press report from a child support protest Norwegian parliament (14,580 views, uploaded, 30th May 2015): "This is a Nazi system" – MEP on Norwegian foster care system": "Member of the European Parliament Tomas Zdechovsky called the Norwegian foster care system a "Nazi system" as he joined a demonstration in Oslo together with several hundred other demonstrators, supporters and parents on Saturday." An unidentified individual, possibly a Norwegian member of parliament also said:

"One thing that I am very concerned about is that when people are addressing their CPS cases on social media they are being threatened by the authorities to drop that."

A sign at the parliament protest said: "Children are abducted by armed officers, brought to secret locations at Barnevernet EVERY DAY – NORWAY"

58. "A Harsh Climate Calls for Banishment of the Needy"

The *New York Times* published an article, 9th July 2014, by Andrew Higgins entitled: *"A Harsh Climate Calls for Banishment of the Needy"* about Svalbard. The then Governor described it as a "special place" and the reporter states, "homelessness, like unemployment, is banned" in Svalbard. The Governor states categorically that if you can't work and support yourself then you can't stay in Svalbard. I have personally visited Svalbard and can confirm that the treatment of many foreigners is appalling. We will speak to a Norwegian who spoke to me, to blow the whistle. The *New York Time*s article ends with a quote from a local American who states that if you want to live in Svalbard then there is something "warped" about you.

59. "The Norway town that forgave and forgot its child killers"

On 20th March 2010 *The Guardian* newspaper published an article entitled: *"The Norway town that forgave and forgot its child killers"* by Erwin James and Ian MacDougall. The article compares the UK's reaction to child killers in the Bulger case to Norway's reaction to a similar case their where a five-year-old was beaten to death by two boys. The UK reacted with fury and anger… this Norwegian town, "forgave and forgot its child killers". The article described that one of the perpetrators is in trouble again and that the victim's family still suffers. The article asks, "So why has the public reaction in Norway been so startlingly different?"

60. "A ban on beggars in Norwegian cities is not the answer to homelessness"

"Norway's dirty little secret is out: how did one of the world's richest nations grow so mean as to consider banning begging on its streets? We must use this controversy to tackle deeper issues facing our cities", wrote Professor Harald N Røstvik in his article for *The Guardian* newspaper (12th February 2015). Multiple Norwegians have told be point blank that "Norway does not have homeless people". We will be talking to some of them in this book series.

61. "Open Racism in Scandinavia"

www.stuff.co.nz published an article *"The truth about living in the so-called utopia of Scandinavia according to Kiwis who live there"* by Lorna Thornber (January 22nd 2018) about open racism in Scandinavia, on this occasion, towards a person from New Zealand and others around Scandinavia. If you take a look at this article, make sure you look at the passive aggressive comments below it. The New Zealander involved chose to hide her identity, for obvious reasons. The individual from the Norwegian section of the article describes that one will never be accepted as a local due to "foreigner" status, even after years of living in Norway and also explains that "**Norway is sceptical toward foreigners** and, especially in the government and local councils, they **do not like to be challenged.**"

62. "Norway: not such a social democratic model society"

Professor Harald N Røstvik, Stavanger, Norway wrote in the *Financial Times* (www.ft.com) 29th May 2015); "Norway: not such a social democratic model society."

He stated: *"In my book,* Corruption the Nobel Way *(2015), I demonstrate how foreigners' perceptions of Norway are totally wrong. Norway is not at all what it appears to be, a social democratic model society. On the contrary, it is a shockingly egotistical and self-serving nation where some of the most predatory businesses are state owned. Around them corruption flourishes, as arms and oil are spewed into the world, making the state rich. But poverty is growing in Norway because the cost of living is high. Inequality is growing too."*

63. "The lack of ability to make quick decisions can be frustrating…"

The "Ukrainian Norwegian chamber of commerce" (nucc.no) in their article, "Working with Norwegians" by Karin Ellis (30th January 2018) states:

1) Norwegians are among the "most trusting people in the world", according to their research.

2) "Lack of clarity": Most Norwegians will give negative feedback in an "indirect" way.

3) Consensus driven: "The lack of ability to make quick decisions can be frustrating for Ukrainians."

4) "Negative feedback from Norwegians is a bit like a bitter pill in a sugar coating."

Karin Ellis, has a website where Norwegians can learn about "working with Indians" (**ellisculture.com**) and a section which decodes "working with Norwegians". It states categorically: "The Norwegian way of doing business may therefore often cause confusion and frustration for people from other cultures".

The Canadian "Global affairs" website is very informative: **www.international.gc.ca**. It poses questions and then answers them from both a Norwegian "local" perspective and a "Canadian" perspective. It's an OFFICIAL CANADIAN GOVERNMENT WEBSITE.

For example:

"Ethnicity: Norway is struggling with multiculturalism, and what this will mean for "the Norwegian way". Ethnicity – more so than gender – is cause for concern in terms of workplace discrimination."

"Weather and sports are always good topics; Norwegians are obsessed with both."

It also warns Canadians in Norway to be prepared for anti-Americanism:

"One should be prepared for a significant degree of anti-Americanism (though often combined with some hints of admiration towards Americans)."

"Very public or overt displays of emotion (of any kind) are not very common."

"Your staff will almost certainly not tell you if they are not happy until it's too late… because of the fear of confrontation. You won't know how your staff views you until you are in a very casual social setting and they've had some wine… seriously."

64. "Dark lands: the grim truth behind the 'Scandinavian miracle'"

Author Michael Booth wrote an article for *The Guardian* newspaper, published, 27th January 2014 entitled, *"Dark lands: the grim truth behind the 'Scandinavian miracle'"*. He quotes Norwegian anthropologist Thomas Hylland-Eriksen who said that, with regards to oil, that "most people are really in denial". If people are in denial about Norwegian oil, could they be in denial about other things too?

65. "Norway's Silent Scandal" (BBC – Our World, 2018)

BBC Norway's Silent Scandal: *"In April this year, a highly respected Norwegian child psychiatrist was convicted of downloading thousands of images of child pornography. The psychiatrist had been used as an expert, until his arrest, by Norway's controversial child protection system and was involved in decisions about whether children should be removed from their parents. Campaigners in Norway have long accused the system of removing children from their parents without justification and now, despite the serious nature of this man's offence, the authorities are refusing to review the child protection cases he gave evidence in. For Our World, Tim Whewell has been to Norway to try to discover why child protection in one of the world's wealthiest countries appears to be in crisis. This programme contains adult themes"* BBC World News, BBC Worldwide 2018.

This BBC documentary is horrific on many levels. If you watch the interviews with the "experts" you will notice many of the things pointed out in this book happen in front of your eyes.

66. "Norway's Stolen Children?" SBS Dateline

SBS Dateline (**www.sbs.com.au/news/dateline**) reports, in their 2016 documentary "Norway's Stolen Children?": *"Why are so many parents in Norway claiming that the state is kidnapping their children? With a spike in cases in recent years and accusations of racial intolerance, Dateline asks whether these children are being saved, or stolen."*

67. "The Bjugn abuse in 1992 in Bjugn, Norway"

According to "Collaborating Against Child Abuse: Exploring the Nordic Children's Home Model" (by Susanna Johansson, Kari Stefansen, Elisiv Bakketeig, Anna Kaldal) the "Bjugn" abuse case involved the arrest of seven people in the Norwegian town of Bjugn in 1992 accused of child abuse and child rape. 550 interviews of 220 witness, 61 "judicial hearings" of 40 children. Out of the seven people, six had their charges dropped. I understand that the last of the accused was also acquitted two years later. In the end, nobody was punished or held to account, it appears. In fact, the investigation *itself* has been criticised by some in Norway.

68. "Boasted of abuse and not arrested"

Norwegian newspaper *VG* (**vg.no**) published a report, "Boasted of abuse, not arrested" (13th October 2017 by Håkon F Hoydaleinar, Otto Stangviknatalie, Remoe Hansen): "A Norwegian man bragged about abuse he had committed to members of a child sexual abuse website run by the Australian police for almost a year. Only when *VG* identified the man was he arrested". They reported that "several" of the child abuse forum members were Norwegian.

69. "Norway's hidden scandal (BBC News)"

BBC News website published a report entitled "Norway's hidden scandal" by Tim Whewell: *"The UN rates Norway one of the best countries for a child to grow up in. And yet too many children, according to a large number of Norwegian experts, are taken into care without good reason. The conviction of a top psychiatrist in the child protection system for downloading child abuse images is now raising further serious questions."*

We note the words "hidden" and the fact that the **Norwegian expert, the top psychiatrist involved in removing children from parents was himself convicted for downloading child porn.** In Norway, he wasn't named to "protect" his identity, so he maintains anonymity.

70. "Nazi Swastikas and magazines in Norway"

Many airports and shops in Norway prominently display magazines with Hitler, the Swastika and other World War Two imagery in the form of historical magazines. These are prominently placed, like at Oslo Airport where the stand is next to the hot dog table. The Swastika itself was on the cover on that occasion. On other occasions, the Swastika is removed and replaced with a generic cross. However, these World War Two magazines are often prominently placed displaying this iconography all over Norway and its stores, especially at airports and magazine shops. In some countries in Europe it is illegal to display the Swastika in such form and I have never seen such magazines displayed in such a prominent way in such a number of stores than in Norway, from Molde to Oslo and made it a habit to film and take photos where I found them.

71. "Norway child abuse: Man held over assaults on 300 boys" (BBC)

BBC News (bbc.com) published an article (21st November 2018) entitled: "Norway child abuse: Man held over assaults on 300 boys". The article describes one of Norway's biggest abuse cases of all time... currently known, at least. It's appalling on every level and we note that the article states that the victims felt unable to tell their parents what happened: *"The alleged victims varied in age from 9 to 21 and all but one had felt unable to reveal what had happened to their parents, police told Norwegian media."*

"All but one" translates as 299 child abuse victims out of 300 child abuse victims did not feel that they could tell their parents about the abuse that they suffered/were suffering.

72. "Norwegians and anti-depressants"

All of the Nordic and Scandinavian countries (Iceland, Denmark, Sweden, Finland and Norway) are in the top nine of the list anti-depressant consumption in Europe according to OECD as reported by Amanda Taub for vox.com (24th February 2015):

"Is Scandinavia all fun and reindeer games until winter comes and throws everyone into deep depression?"

Iceland and Denmark are at the top for anti-depressant consumption, according to that report.

"Depression and Anti-depressants: A Nordic Perspective" – NCBI (www.ncbi.nlm.nih.gov) by A Vilhelmsson, 26th August 2013, stated:

"Almost 300,000 Norwegians were prescribed an anti-depressant in 2011 (6.3% of the population) and estimated sales were almost €50 million."

73. "Mental health website... helpful information?"

If you type in "mental health help Norway" into a search engine, one of the top search results you will find is the official mental health website of Norway: www.fhi.no

You will note that the FIRST thing it chooses to state, at the top of the webpage

("Health Status in Norway 2018 – FHI") is this: *"Norway has, together with the other Nordic countries, the highest quality of life and happiness in the world. This applies to both adults and adolescents…"*

Note: *I note that this paragraph was previous more prominently at the top of one of the main web pages but has subsequently been moved, it appears.*

74. "Norway's Green Delusions"

Lars Petter Teigen wrote an article for **foreignpolicy.com** (19th September 2018) entitled, "Norway's Green Delusions", where he states, "The country may seem a haven for clean energy, but that's because it exports its pollution". When it comes to Norway do you often notice the constant use of words like "hidden", "delusion" and "secret"?

75. "Fifty churches burned down and Satanic murder"

Did you know that Norway had a problem with people burning down churches? Wikipedia tells us: *"In 1992, members of the Norwegian black metal scene began a wave of arson attacks on Christian churches. By 1996, there had been at least 50 attacks in Norway; in every case that was solved, those responsible were black metal fans."*

The Guardian newspaper's Alex Godfrey wrote about this in his article: 'Before you know it, it's not a big deal to kill a man': Norwegian black metal's murderous past (22nd March 2019): *"In the early 90s, Norway's black metal scene turned into a satanic cult as musicians burned churches, self-harmed and killed."*

If you want to know any more let me leave you with this… the story of forty-five-year-old Norwegian drummer "Faust" who currently tours with the Norwegian band "Blood Tsunami". In 1992 he decided to stab Magne Andreassen thirty-seven times and kicked him in the head to his death. He described feeling no remorse and his band member said that he: *"Had been very fascinated by serial killers for a long time, and I guess he wanted to know what it's like to kill a person."*

He didn't serve his full sentence and was released by the authorities early.

76. "The community of 2,000 people with 151 cases of sex crime"

The BBC World Service published an article by Linda Pressly (22nd March 2018) about the Norwegian community of Tysfjord entitled: *"The community of 2,000 people with 151 cases of sex crime."* The BBC reporter asked: *"Norwegian police have documented 151 cases of sexual abuse, including child rape, in one small community of 2,000 people, north of the Arctic circle. The offences occurred over decades – between the 1950s and 2017 – but were only recently uncovered.* **How could such serious sex crimes go unchecked for so long?"**

77. "Norway's rules about everything"

One of Norway's most popular blogs is by a French author: afroginthefjord.com. On 16th December 2018 she published an article and interview entitled: *"Norway's rules about everything – Interview of the authors of 'Norske standarder'"*… it's about a book called *The 100 Unwritten Norwegian Social Laws*… all described as "hilarious" and "funny" of course.

78. "Seven years after Utøya Survivors Receive Hatred and Death Threats"

The same author published an article entitled, *"When the Roses turned Black. Seven years after Utøya Survivors Receive Hatred and Death Threats"* afroginthefjord.com – 30th July 2018). She states that after seven years survivors of Norway's biggest ever terrorist attack which killed seventy-seven people "are threatened and bullied". If we take a look at the comments below the article then we are not surprised by the "usual" and the expected denial… there are some beauties pointing to Donald Trump too! I have no idea what the President of the United States of America has to do with Norwegian people in Norway threatening and bullying the victims of Norway's biggest ever terrorist attack, by a neo Nazi and mass murder.

79. "Soccer: Hegerberg 'mentally broken' by Norway national team experience"

Norwegian football player Ada Hegerberg said that she was "mentally broken" by her Norwegian national team experience, according to **www.reuters.com**. The bullying and attacks that she received from fellow Norwegians for standing up against bullying and mistreatment tells you all you need to know… members of her own team attacked her and many stood by silent as she was attacked. Norwegian footballer Martin Odegaard did his duty and publicly said: "Maybe you can find something better to do than destroy the national team's preparations for the World Cup?" Fortunately, whilst those inside Norway attacked her, those outside of Norway *elevated* her. In 2016 she was awarded the UEFA Best Women's Player in Europe Award and in 2017 and 2019 was named BBC Women's Footballer of the Year in the United Kingdom. The best Norwegian footballer of all time was not included in the Norwegian football team for the World Cup 2019.

80. "Gender issues are ridiculed and sabotaged in the military"

"Women and girls are affected particularly hard in armed conflicts. They sometimes become targets themselves, and are exposed to sexualised violence and abuse" wrote Elida Høeg, Kilden Kjonnsforskning, Cathinka Dahl Hambro for sciencenorway.no published 30th October 2019. The article describes that although the issue was raised years ago, that it still unresolved and abuses still happen. In fact, the article states that gender issues are "ridiculed and sabotaged in the military". The Norwegian Ministry of Defence published a response to the report which was a beauty, including some of the "usual" classics.

81. "Academics hide, play dumb, don't care or over-perform"

In an article that can't come as a shock to anybody reading this book, by sciencenorway.no by Georg Mathisen/Nancy Bazilchuk, 25th October 2019, we note that the "narrative" vs reality dynamic is also real in the academic community according to research into twenty-five academics at a major Norwegian university... it is admitted outright: **"A culture of secrecy... It turned out that many people started the interview by answering the questions with "the official version"** — or the way they would be expected to describe reality under an internal audit... "It's clear that there is a culture of silence at university colleges and universities and that people are uncomfortable criticising the system". Culture of silence, uncomfortable criticising the system, academics hide and play dumb, "official version". You can read it in black and white... this is Norway and these are its *academics*!

82. "Norway Justice Minister's Partner Arrested With Accusation of Setting Their Own Car on Fire"

"Norway Justice Minister's Partner Arrested With Accusation of Setting Their Own Car on Fire", reported www.tnp.no. Laila Anita Bertheussen, the partner of the

Norwegian Minister of Justice and Public Security was charged with faking an attack on their family car… this was the NORWEGIAN JUSTICE MINISTER'S partner engaging in such nonsense… before the usual excuses about isolated incidents and all the rest of it are trotted out… let's move straight onto the case of Norway ex-minister and Parliamentarian Svein Ludvigsen who was "convicted of abusing his position to gain sexual favours from three vulnerable male persons."

83. "Norway ex-minister Svein Ludvigsen guilty of sexually abusing asylum seekers"

On 5th July 2019, BBC News reported the news that Norway ex-minister and Parliamentarian Svein Ludvigsen was convicted of sexual abuse and given five years in jail. He abused his position to get "sexual favours" from asylum seekers. The BBC reported: "The men, now aged 25, 26 and 34, told the court that they first met Ludvigsen when he was Trom's Governor and that he offered them housing and jobs in exchange for sexual favours. The abuse took place in Ludvigsen's home and country house, in hotel rooms and in his office".

84. "Why is the suicide rate not declining in Norway?"

An article was published entitled, *"Why is the suicide rate not declining in Norway?"* by Øivind Ekeberg, Erlend Hem for **tidsskriftet.no** (16 August 2019). What's really interesting is that although almost every person I have spoken to in Norway knows somebody that has committed suicide… at least one… the statistics do not reflect an above average suicide rate. However, if the official numbers are to be believed then, even they suggest that suicide is not declining at the same rates as the other Scandinavian countries. I will state for the record that a scientist in Norway told me outright that suicide is not reported accurately in Norway and is often covered up. Although, I cannot verify this, it certainly wouldn't surprise me.

85. "Norway hit by biggest welfare scandal in its history"

The Norwegian Labour and Welfare Administration ("NAV") incorrectly interpreted EU rules and convicted innocent persons and sent them to prison. It accused hundreds of innocent people and issued fines and punishments. **dailysabah.com** (6th November 2019) described the scandal as "the biggest legal scandal in Norway's history".

86. "Use of painkillers in Norway has multiplied in 15 years"

"Use of painkillers in Norway has multiplied in 15 years" was the title of an article published by <u>norwaytoday.info</u> by Tamara Lopes, 25th November 2019: "The use of the analgesic drug Oksykodon has doubled in Norway over the past 15 years. The same drug is linked to the epidemic of overdose deaths in the United States."

87. Norwegian Princess's boyfriend, "Norwegian media, you are bullies"

Durek Verrett, Norwegian Princess Märtha Louise's boyfriend said: *"I will not let the bullies prevail any more. Norwegian media, you are bullies. You bully my girlfriend for selling newspapers. It is a pity. You don't want people to know the truth."*

His book was "pulled" by its Norwegian publisher and Verrett is reported to have stated that it was banned. However, he was (forced?) to apologise and retract that statement. Durek Verrett is black and I can attest to the fact that he receives almost constant discrimination and racism from many of the people that I have personally encountered in Norway. Not a single nice word was said about him by any person I interviewed.

Princess Märtha's ex-boyfriend's suicide on Christmas Day 2019

Princess Märtha's ex-partner and the father of her children committed suicide in Norway on 25th December 2019. Her current partner Durek Verrett (who is often labelled as "controversial", which some would consider a racist "dog whistle"), received extreme racist abuse immediately. I personally captured many incidents online under Norwegian newspaper articles and social media, blaming him for her ex's suicide and calling him a "scoundrel!" I also captured individuals with the Norwegian flag as their profile who said: "Having Durek f**k your children's mother is not a good thing."

In fact, Oskar Aanmoen, historian, author and lecturer as well as the senior Europe correspondent for "Royal Central" tweeted:

"Most Norwegian newspapers have now closed the opportunity to comment below articles about Ari Behn's death. This is done after hundreds of negative messages are published about Princess Märtha's current controversial boyfriend, the American Shamen Durek Verek."

88. "Who is the greatest and known Norwegian philosopher?"

Who is the greatest and known Norwegian philosopher? That was a question posed on **www.quora.com**. I have personally asked countless Norwegians to name just one Norwegian philosopher or original thinker, psychotherapist or somebody that has had an impact on Norwegian thought or philosopher or somebody that asks Norwegians questions or tries to examine society and its people's attitudes and behaviour… I am still waiting for some names, beyond Ibsen… a fictional author from over 100 years ago. To say that the list is threadbare is an understatement. I asked a bookseller on Oslo's main central street who gave me this very representative answer: *"There is one! There is this guy that they bring out to comment every time something happens. He's always on NRK. Ermmm… he has a beard! What's his name!!? He is the philosopher guy. Other than that, I don't know."*

89. "The Law of the Jante"

Author Michael Booth penned a great article for the Paris Review entitled, "The Law of Jante" (11th February 2015) where he wrote about Aksel Sandemose's "Law of the Jante" also known as "Janteloven" and its Danish founder. He wrote that "Knowing even just a little of their author's biography, one would think it easy to dismiss these rules as the products of a somewhat unbalanced mind, an irrelevance…" The author exposes the hypocrisy across Scandinavia and the disparity between reality and the attempted projection of reality through the imposition of the warped lens of the "Janta Law".

90. "Norwegians give each other little room to manoeuvre"

Norway is one of the most conformist countries and cultures on the face of the earth. When a study entitled: *"Differences Between Tight and Loose Cultures A 33-Nation Study"*, the Norwegian professor said that it was "a surprising result". **NHH.no** reported that "Norwegians give each other little room to manoeuvre." Associate Professor Vidar Schei is reported to have said to **nhh.no** "The researchers cannot find a simple explanation of why the social norms in Norway are so strong"… The answer to this question is on every page of this book series.

91. "The lawyer defending the indefensible"

100% of the Norwegians that I asked described Norway's number one terrorist and murderer Anders Breveik's *lawyer* as, "respected" and in glowing terms…

zero exceptions. When I asked them why he was so respected, they'd often go into monologues which went around in circles but didn't communicate much. Here are some reported news stories about Norway's Nazi terrorists' lawyer. According to *The Independent* newspaper (**independent.co.uk** "The lawyer defending the indefensible" by Tony Paterson, 15th April 2012), the lawyer for the murderer was actually a "long-standing member" of the Norwegian Labour Party whose youth members were actually murdered by his client:

"He is a long-standing member of the Norwegian Labour Party, whose young members Breivik gunned down in cold blood as they were attending a political summer camp on the fjord island of Utøya last summer."

He was personally requested to defend Breveik…by Breviek himself. Afterwards Lippestad told the French newspaper *Le Monde*: *"I feel I have lost my soul in this case… I hope to get it back once it's over – and that it will be in the same condition as before."* After the Breivik case, Lippestad experienced a "significant increase in financial revenue". www.vg.no: "Geir Lippestad's law firm has grown strongly following the July 22 case" and he was nominated for Norwegian honours, especially from charities and organisations… with articles in the media about him being seriously considered for the Mayor of Oslo.

92. Norwegian Police Federation sign contract with number one Norwegian terrorists lawyer/law firm.

Wikipedia section "After Brevik" quotes an article published by www.vg.no (30th Janaury 2014) by Jarle Grivi and Morten S Hopperstad entitled "Lippestad becomes a police officer": *"In January 2014, the law firm Lippestad signed a contract with the Norwegian Police Federation, the trade union organising all employees in the police sector in Norway. The agreement included assisting with all types of legal issues that members would have. It also included legal representation in cases where police officers are accused of criminal offences, as well as Lippestad holding lectures and speaking at events organised by the Police Federation."*

The **Norwegian Police Federation** have signed a contract with the countries number one mass murderers' chosen law firm to defend "police officers accused of criminal offences"?

93. "It is very puzzling that the Norwegians so often voted with the group" by Stanley Milgram 1962

American social psychologist Stanley Milgram noticed Norwegian conformity back in 1962. What's really interesting is that this has been ignored by most in Norway. I can find zero mention of his experiment in Norway or by the Norwegian media or by a single person. It's very "interesting" that, considering he was one of the most famous, if not the most famous psychologists of all time, how his Norwegian experiments can be ignored by Norway but his other experiment "The Milgram experiment on obedience to authority figures", is more widely known. The Stanford prison experiment film was even broadcast on Norway's national broadcaster in early December 2019… they seem to have missed his other experiment though. The psychologist actually wrote that he was "puzzled" by the Norwegian conformity and behaviour. I believe that this book answers the puzzle once and for all. Here is an excerpt of what he wrote:

"It is very puzzling that the Norwegians so often voted with the group, even when given a secret ballot. One possible interpretation is that the average Norwegian, for whatever reason, believes that his private action will ultimately become known to others. Interviews conducted among the Norwegians offer some indirect evidence for this conjecture. In spite of the assurances that the responses would be privately analysed, one subject said he feared that because he had disagreed too often the experimenter would assemble the group and discuss the disagreements with them."

By Stanley Milgram, Volume 205, Number 6 of Scientific American in December 1961 (republished scientificamerican.com 1st December 2011: "Which Nations Conform Most?").

94. "Utøya survivors experienced that the treatment programme disappeared too quickly and that the support system was not proactive enough"

After the Utøya terrorist murders we saw that hundreds of thousands of people expressed their grief publicly in Oslo. However, survivors later reported that they felt betrayed and let down. NRK.NO reported that the National Knowledge Center on Violence and Traumatic Stress found that, "Utøya survivors experienced that the treatment program disappeared too quickly and that the support system was not proactive enough…"

What's not so known is that at least one innocent victim was arrested and detained by police ("Survivor-held-for-17-hours-after-attacks", news24.com).

The arrests were actually defended by the usual "experts":

"Psychologist: Understand why the police arrested Utøya victim – Sorry, but understandable that the police did what they did, says psychologist Atle Dyregrov."

Source: https://www.vg.no/nyheter/innenriks/i/51Bv1/psykolog-forstaar-hvorfor-politiet-paagrep-utoeya-offer

95. "Norwegian tradition of the 'Russ'"

Graduating Norwegian high school students traditionally celebrate "russefeiring" (or the "russ celebration"). They get drunk and go crazy from around the 20th April up until the 17th May, which is the Norwegian constitution day. They wear a red outfit and many even get arrested for engaging in drunk and disorderly behaviour. Kate Taylor of businessinsider.com (18th April 2018) published an article about the Russ entitled: "Norwegian teens celebrate a bizarre, month-long holiday full of drinking, sex, and wild dares". She describes the cost involved for the teenagers who often spend hundreds of thousands of pounds on their "Russ party buses": "… can cost up to $350,000… the average Russbuss is used by 15 to 25 students and costs around $116,000". The UK's *Sun* newspaper in their "THE KIDS ARE ALRIGHT inside the debauched world of 'Russ', when Norwegian school leavers get drunk, naked and very rowdy Russ is a national tradition involving outdoor sex, pimped-out party buses and insane quantities of booze" by Benedict Brook (**news.com.au** George Harrison, 27th November 2016) article, reported: *"As the weeks of debauchery go on, students are set increasingly difficult challenges, which could include drinking 24 beers in 24 hours, kissing a police officer or having sex outdoors."*

96. "Norwegian murderer front page in the UK… no mention in the Norwegian media?"

Norwegian killer Roger Bullman appeared as the *Daily Mail's* top story in the United Kingdom at the end of August 2019. **www.thaiexaminer.com** reported: *"Norwegian killer accepts he's going to Thai prison after violent killing of UK man at Phuket hotel"* by James Morris and Son Nguyenin, Thailand (31st August 2019):

"Roger Bullman, the Norwegian killer who took the life of UK IT engineer 34 year-old Amitpal Singh Bajaj at a 5 star hotel in Phuket on August 21st… after he broke

into the adjacent hotel bedroom of a UK family naked and violently took the younger man's life with his bare hands. It followed complaints from the UK man about the Norwegian man's opera singing from the balcony of his room."

I monitored the Norwegian media to see when they would report that he had absconded from court. To the best of my knowledge it was not reported in any meaningful way or in any way that I can see or find, even when headline news around the world, including the *Daily Mail's* top story. Months later, I still cannot find a Norwegian press article about the Norwegian murderer. A big internationally reported story about a Norwegian abroad is usually headline news in Norway, so this is very strange indeed.

97. "Norway apologises to its World War Two 'German girls'"

The BBC reported, 17th October 2018, that Norway's Prime Minister Erna Solberg issued an official government apology to the Norwegian "German girls" who had relationships with German soldiers during the war. It's thought that 50,000 women did and that they were later bullied and mistreated. The article reports that "10 – 12,000 children" were born to the Norwegian/Nazi soldiers and that "Some of the children were also targeted for acts of revenge, given up to foster families or placed in institutions".

98. "Inclusion and delusion"

Malin Donoso Martnes (Microsoft Business Applications MVP) published a blog on <u>linkedin.com</u> (1st October 2019) entitled *"Inclusion and delusion"* where she discusses behaviour of certain big tech companies in Norway: *"One of the big companies tells how they, to get more females to the interview stage, lower their standards and qualifications for female applicants! If I worked there I would quit my job today and find a place of work that doesn't implicate that women aren't as good as the men and thus need an easier way in! This isn't being inclusive, this is discrimination and telling women that they need an easier way in to be able to get to the interview, like saying their resume isn't as good as their male counterparts".*

Note her use of the word "delusion".

99. "Pensioner Frode Berg pressured by Norwegian intelligence services to spy is imprisoned and convicted in Russia and 'hung out to dry'"

BBC NEWS: "Home for Christmas: Jailed Norwegian spy released from

Russia" (2nd December 2019) reported: *"A Norwegian pensioner convicted of spying in Moscow says he was wrong to trust an intelligence officer who recruited him to pass on payment for secrets about Russia's atomic submarine fleet."* He was pressured by the Norwegian intelligence services to take envelopes to Russia… fortunately he was realised in a "spy swap". After his release he talks about how he was manipulated and pressured by the authorities in Norway. In fact he says that he was "hung out to dry": "Norwegian Spy Jailed by Russia Is Free. He's Angry, Too, but Not at Moscow… Frode Berg, a trusting pensioner, willingly worked for Norwegian intelligence. Then, he says, they hung him out to dry" wrote Anton Troianovski, *New York Times*, 28th December 2019.

100. "Instagrammers love this iconic spot, but there's something they don't want you to see"

CNBC published an article by Monica Buchanan Pitrelli (1st December 2019) entitled, *"Instagrammers love this iconic spot, but there's something they don't want you to see"* about Norway's "social media hotspots". She exposes the truth behind the "perfect" images and describes it as what "they don't want you to see"… including the massive queues and overcrowding at these tourists sites that you won't see in the airbrushed perfect images unless you turn the camera around.

101. "Yes Norway, that's racist"

"Yes Norway, that's racist" is the title of an article published by <u>universitas.no</u> (by Indigo Trigg-Hauger, 23rd February 2018) which states: *"The world's happiest country isn't so perfect when it comes to race. But no one wants to talk about it."*

The author raises blatant examples of Norwegian racism in the media and states what I have seen and heard repeatedly in Norway, "Racism is not racism":

"But what exactly is the problem? I can hear the Norwegians asking. On a purely academic level, the video is indeed a parody. The responses I've received from NRK have been insistent on that point — it's seemingly their only argument. It's satirical they say, and making fun of another race isn't racist."

A Conversation with Five Youth Activists

Seline (nineteen years old), Mathias (eighteen years old), Nina (fifteen years old), Emma (nineteen years old) and Ole (eighteen years old) are political activists. You will now see bullying. You will see repeated passive aggression in the form of attacks against three teenage girls *at their most vulnerable*. You will then see the bullying justified. You will see the whole group, tell us that bullying and enabling of abuse is *completely normal in Norway*. But you will also see something incredible happen near the end of the conversation.

This is a story that I have heard *all over Norway*, it's not an isolated case… this is going to be hard to read. We start not at the beginning but at the conversation's "turning point".

Ole:
But I have been indoctrinated as probably every Norwegian, so that is my first reaction.

Anthony:
What you have just said is absolutely incredible! You just basically said, after we logically talked about it, "Maybe I was wrong."

Ole:
Well, I just think that this has been an amazing conversation because you have helped me think that way. You know you should start a podcast or something!

(AN – we all burst out laughing.)

Matthias:
You should!

218

Ole:
We've recorded several episodes already!

Nina:
Just upload this!

(AN – we all burst out laughing again!)

Anthony:
Ole, we are in a safe space right now. We all make mistakes… It's OK…
This is going to sound weird but I would even say that it's OK to say
something "bad" as long as you can understand it, then you can change…
And that's an incredible thing.

Nina:
Yes, it's like we were talking about earlier… The thing about that woman that
posted about Isis *(AN – Norwegian politician?)*…she didn't apologise…

Anthony:
She didn't acknowledge?

Nina:
Yes, she didn't. She didn't change, and it doesn't matter that she says, "Sorry
that you are offended"… she's not going to change! Because she doesn't say,
"This was my fault… I am sorry I did wrong"… like you have to
acknowledge that what you did was wrong… Because she makes it seem like
we are drama queens… like, "I'm sorry that you were offended but this is my
opinion."

Anthony:
Yes, it's very passive aggressive.

Nina:
Yes, it's very passive aggressive!

Anthony:
Here's the thing though. This is when the magic happens. It has to be
open. Open dialogue. And then something magic happens. When you are
not judged and you open up about how you feel. And it's logical. It has to
be logical. If we hadn't have analysed like we have just done today then

we probably wouldn't have thought of these things in these ways. In the end you get through it and I promise you that is the way you grow. And it's a really cool thing! And that's how we learn.

Nina:
It's very grown up to be able to say "I was wrong."

Anthony:
Yes. It's always a good thing to analyse and really think about the way we think. Ole, what you just did is incredible and it takes a lot of strength... And you did it "live"... I guarantee you that many people would just stick to what they initially said, end the conversation or they would just keep on going against logic.

Ole:
And that's cognitive dissonance.

Anthony
Wow!

(AN – The whole group burst out laughing.)

Anthony:
You have intellectual integrity.

(AN – The group burst out laughing again!)

Anthony:
Do you know that everybody doesn't have that?

Ole:
Well, thank you because I think that's one of the best compliments I've ever heard in my life!

Anthony:
Many people can't do that "against" themselves, because if they say something earlier... they will remain firm regardless of new evidence to the contrary... anyway! So everybody *(AN – speaking to the group)*... I think that that is what you call a good discussion! It was fluid... and everything in life is fluid in the end... but I'm very impressed, Ole especially... thank you!

Nina:
(AN – Nina is reading about "intellectual integrity" on her phone)
"Can conclude with their own thoughts…"

(AN – Now, Ole feels the group collective warmth and feels included and now he participates in looking up this word which he didn't do for the others, earlier.)

Ole:
(AN – Reads from his phone.) "When someone's thoughts and conclusions within himself or a group of people is logically cohesive… and free of resistance…"

Anthony:
"Free of resistance". That's what it is because it's that resistance which prevents development but you are pretty free about where your logic goes and that is a very big strength. Thank you everyone! I think that we have just killed it! I think that that was something special!

(AN – The whole group burst out laughing. They are very pleased and happy… in fact, they are euphoric.)

Ole:
I love this! I love this!

Nina:
The topics that we spoke about today are the ones that people step over and I think that the collection of people you have spoken to will tell you what you need to know to tell the truth in the book.

Anthony:
And to the people that are going to say that this is not "representative"?

Seline:
What I think is interesting about this is that you have been all around Norway… I think that people around the world think that, Norway is "perfect", it's a democracy. You have got to see the different side!

Anthony:
The biggest respect that you can give people is to actually listen to them, and I feel that on too many occasions the people of Norway are rarely

listened to. It's kind of just like "How are you?"… "Good"… "OK, good" and that's the end of it.

Unanimous:
Yeah!

Nina:
What we were talking about earlier the Sami *(AN – The indigenous people of Norway)* "problem" I think that a lot of Norwegians see it as something that *has* happened but not something that *does* happen and I think that it needs to be brought up again. It's still an issue and it needs to be still talked about… not as something that has happened but something that is happening… and we need to talk about it.

(AN – I am sitting next to an incredibly talented Sami young man called Mathias.)

Anthony:
Nina, I hope you understand how amazing it is what you just said considering who I'm sitting next to and he just listened to what you said *(AN – I turn to Mathias)*… How does it feel hearing that Mathias?

Mathias:
It feels very good!

Anthony:
I don't know but maybe you've never heard that before Mathias? But to hear that from your friend… I'm quite emotional just hearing that!

Mathias:
Well, I usually haven't ever heard that before, kind of.

Anthony:
What you just said, Nina… for a Sami person to hear that… that's incredible.

Anthony:
Mathias, you can tell her directly… she's just sitting there…

(AN – I am alluding to something very interesting. In group discussion the

respondents often tended to talk about each other like they were not there. Respondents often looked away from each other and talked like they were in separate isolated pods… even when in close proximity.)

Mathias:
(AN – Looks her straight in the eye and says, "Thank you.")

Anthony:
Do you realise what he just said, Nina? He just said that he's never heard that before in his life… how does that make you feel?

Nina:
Yes, but that really hurts me.

Anthony
Why? You just verbalised it so he heard it with his ears right now?

Nina:
Yes, but it hurts me that he's never heard it before.

Anthony:
You've just done it. You need to be proud… and just let him hear it… You have just started the chain.

Ole:
You are fixing it Nina!

(AN – Ole, is now elevating and encouraging Nina. I can see that Nina appreciates it too. It's apparent that he might not have ever experienced positive reinforcement before as his previous interjections and interruptions were to undermine his friends.)

Anthony:
Ole, you are exactly right! *(AN – Turning to the group.)* Guys, listen to me, always be proud when you do the right thing.

Nina:
But that just shows that things need to change if he hasn't heard it before.

Anthony:
And that change started because he's just heard it right now.

Mathias:
Yes! Amazing!

Anthony:
Guys, it's been an honour speaking with you today.

Seline:
I think I'm going to remember this for my whole life!

Mathias:
I think I will too actually!

Anthony:
Really?

Mathias:
Yes, this is pretty big!

Nina:
It's a big impact!

Ole:
It's one of the more enhancing days of my life!

Mathias:
This is the best day of my life! This is the weirdest thing that ever happened to me…

Seline:
Can I tell you something, Anthony?

Anthony:
Go ahead, please!

Seline:
I have been very ill this summer. It's been very boring just being in bed doing nothing… So this is like the best thing that has ever happened to me! This has made my summer.

Ole:
You are doing some good work.

Anthony:
It's been very tough but when I meet people like you it reminds me that I am doing the right thing.

Mathias:
Well you are! You're definitely doing the right thing! You awaken things in people! You awaken things they haven't thought of before!

Ole:
I can actually say that you have changed the way that I think about things – permanently!

Mathias:
Yes, I think so too!

Seline:
Same!

Nina:
It feels like I've been to a therapist! Because I think that so many of us have let go of so many feelings about everything about Norway!

Ole:
Like there are so many things that I identify like a "northerner"… That I didn't even know were an issue.

(AN – We talked earlier about the bullying they receive, that they perceive as a "joke" but now realise that they don't deserve to be bullied for being born in the north).

Seline:
This summer many people have talked about the issue that many people in the south don't care about the people in the north in Norway… and that's the main reason for example why we don't get the train… They say that it is about the money but the main reason is that this is the north… They don't care that much about the north and because of that everything that we have talked about I really think that it makes sense!

Nina:

You have showed us to think about the way that things are because we have just accepted that these things are the way they are and that is it… like we were talking earlier about the dialect thing and you were like "I understand but what exactly is funny about what they are saying?"… We didn't even think that it shouldn't be like that!

(AN – Many people were saying derogatory things about their accents and they were happy to accept that as normal "jokey" behaviour.)

Anthony:

That's really interesting because I was asking you, "What's funny about what they are saying?" and you guys couldn't give me an answer.

Mathias:

Yes, because then I thought… "Wait a minute… It's not actually funny!"… and this shouldn't be a reality… we should think about things. It's something that we should think about!

Anthony:

In the end it's about positivity and being able to say that something is not right… and simply being able to say it… I think that a lot of times you just need someone to encourage you and to be enthusiastic about it.

Seline:

One of the main things we want for mental health is a psychologist in every school… because people need to talk with someone! Just like you are talking to us now!

Mathias:

Feels like you are one!

Nina:

We feel SEEN!

(AN – Seline approached me afterwards separately.)

Seline:

I care a lot about mental health… it upsets me… they just talk about things that they are doing but I don't think that they are doing enough!

Anthony:
You know this because of personal experience, you said?

Seline:
Yes… in my family we had a member that died of cancer… and the family member of his who also took his own life… I know that he should have gotten better help… In two weeks' time is the anniversary where the person lost their brother. The help that I got afterwards in school was not good enough… So I was suffering with that and still do… I can't handle the dark… In that period I really suffer from it because, all of this happened in the dark months. When it gets dark I just feel that all of the feelings are coming back… And I have been going to a therapist for this but… but the reason that I went there.

Anthony:
You did it for yourself? No one helped you to go there?

Seline:
Yes… because I am strong enough to know that I need this but I don't think that many people are just tough enough to do like I do it. It should be much easier! It should be easier to get help.

Anthony:
Thank you very much for sharing that. Thank you very much.

(AN – The group are on a high and return to say goodbye as I leave.)

Nina:
You have changed our lives! Yes, because we think about things totally differently… and I think that when I speak to my friends in the future… we're going to know how to communicate in the right way to like not undermine everything we say.

Ole:
No bull***t.

Nina:
Like a typical Norwegian. Where we are just like "No, it's OK."

Ole:
Considering that we have just met each other… I have probably just had one
of the most important conversations of my life… imagine if everybody was so
efficient!

Nina:
These are the conversations which (give) you the most out of your
friendships. When you can sit down and actually talk about things… and I
wish that we could do that more instead of just saying "How are you?",
"Fine"… I wish we could be like honest with each other. I just want you to
know, I know that you said that the book will be anonymous… In the book
it's not so important that our names are in it, because still _at least we have been
heard!_

Anthony:
I have heard! And just know that I am proud of you guys…

Ole:
Without identifying us… you have identified us!

So you have heard the turning point and the results of this important discussion
so now let's hear how we got there and more importantly the resistance to
reaching such a positive end point.

Anthony:
Your job is to speak out about what you perceive as injustice… is that
right?

Unanimous:
Yes.

Anthony:
And you have said that because of that there are "consequences", and you
Seline, describe losing your boyfriend because of that activity, is that
right?

Seline:
Yes.

Anthony:
I'm sorry to hear that... would you like to tell us what happened?

Seline:
Of course, it was one of the reasons, but he felt that we were kind of different, because I'm like... loud... I'm going on demonstrations and screaming in the towns and stuff.

Anthony:
He thought that you should shut up and be quiet?

Seline:
Yes, maybe... he thought that...

(AN – Seline becomes emotional. I have noticed that many of the Norwegian respondents (regardless of age, location or demographic) would undermine themselves and their own viewpoint when faced with any kind of (internal) emotional resistance. It appears that for many respondents altering the description of reality is a way to try and attempt to escape the "pain" of that reality. This is seemingly achieved by changing the definition of words and using euphemisms, equivocation or a kind of doublespeak to dampen the description of their experiences as a way of changing how they process it. You will see that, in one way or another, many of the Norwegian respondents interviewed will do this repeatedly, through this book series. Another indication of this, as you will see, is that she starts "arguing" with herself. She actually verbalises the inner conflict. On this occasion she begins to equate the processing of pain in relation to her ex-boyfriend and starts talking about her view of Norway and how "good" it is. This confused response is elicited by a very simple question which had no direct link to her views of her country whatsoever.)

Seline:
Because Norway is a good country to live in! It is!

(AN – I sat completely impassive and she re-confirmed what she said but in a different tone of voice, first time emotionally and second time much more forcefully, like she was arguing with herself in the way that she said "It is!" like she was trying to convince herself. She answered a question twice, which wasn't asked.)

Seline:
Yeah… maybe people are like…

(Extended silence.)

(AN – I did not interrupt the silence and could see that she appeared to be talking on autopilot now… like she was disassociated from the words she was speaking. However, she realised what she was doing and naturally let her voice fade out to silence. She did not finish the words… she essentially just mumbled to nothing and sat silently until her friend interjected to try and "help" her. I have regularly noticed the same type of demeanour, tone of voice and mannerisms when the respondents would often start talking and characterising what it's like to live in Norway and also noticed that it's often raised for no rational reason and used as an answer to a question which hasn't been asked.)

Ole:
(AN – Interrupts and start to finish the answer for her.) I think what you're *trying* to say Seline, is that Norwegians, we like to think of ourselves as very well off, you know… We live in a good part of the world… We're doing pretty OK… and some people think that we shouldn't complain about the injustice and stuff, because we're doing so good.

Anthony:
Do you agree with that? Do you feel that you shouldn't complain about injustice because you have got money?

Unanimous:
No

Anthony:
This doesn't sound like a cool thing?

Ole:
Or stand up for what is right… but *some* people… *(AN – implying some people don't.)*

Seline:
A lot of young people suffer because of their *mental health* and climate change… the government doesn't do enough to stop it and everything in society is politics.

Anthony:
Tell me if I am wrong or am I right... I have not observed so many people standing up against injustice?

Unanimous:
Yes, you're right! Yes!

Emma:
But some things are changing...

Anthony:
Does that mean that you guys are making a difference, personally?

Unanimous:
Yes.

Ole:
We hope so! I think it's becoming more and more common for young people to do stuff like this... It's more socially acceptable.

Seline:
Yes I think that they are *scared*...

Anthony:
Would you say that you are separate from the older people? Do they support you?

Ole:
No.

Seline:
There are people that care about the planet...

Ole:
Or they want people to *think* that they do!

Unanimous:
Yes, yes!

Anthony:
Are you supported in your activities? Do your parents support you?

Seline:
Yes.

Anthony:
Do your friends support you?

Nina:
My friends don't support me… but my parents do.

(AN – Her voice filled with emotion and the room went silent when she said this.)

Nina:
People in school are very judgemental of like what I do… I am here…

Anthony:
Do they bully you?

(AN – As soon as I said the word "bully" she reacted and became visibly uncomfortable. She reacted with obvious fear… she was scared to characterise her treatment as "bullying"… it is obvious that she is or has been bullied.)

Anthony:
You can say it if they do, please don't worry…

Nina:
No… no, no, no… It's not *bad*!

(AN – Nina will soon go on to talk about not only bullying but sexual harassment that she suffers at school. When she said "bad" ("It's not bad!") her voice broke with emotion. A clear indicator is to listen carefully when respondents speak and see if their words line up with the emotion they are attempting to communicate. It's very easy to see whether it has any relation to what they actually feel and think. I have noticed a verbal pattern of responses and very often: disconnect. Interestingly, this has happened repeatedly in my conversations but is not limited to only Norwegian respondents. The non-Norwegians respondents and immigrants also regularly did this repeatedly in describing their experiences in Norway. You can usually determine with an extreme degree of certainty by listening to the

secondary key words used and then inverting the "feeling" or emotion behind it. For example, you can almost always disregard the equivocation/auto-response, if the words don't match the impression they are attempting to communicate. For example, "Did you have a nice time at the lake?" The respondent might smile and reply, "Yes, yes, yes... I didn't have a disgusting time." The emotion of the word doesn't match the (untrue) impression they are trying to communicate. The word "disgusting" is out of context but it was volunteered by the respondent themselves. I believe that this could be a subconscious attempt to communicate truth, even when a respondent is saying something untrue that they don't fully believe themselves? An appropriate response which aligns with both the feeling and the words might be, "Yes, yes, yes, I had a great time." I also see it as an indicator that they want to tell the truth about how they really feel but are conflicted. Finally, another indication is to observe the respondents' reaction when an untruth is gently challenged... it will almost always elicits a "snigger" or "burst of laughing", i.e. "I have been caught out." Finally, and this is one of the reasons why many of the Norwegians respondents, in my opinion, eventually opened up completely to these questions... by listening to them and responding to what they are ACTUALLY communicating, not just the words they say, they seemed to realise that you really do listen to them and understand them. That elicits almost immediate trust and respect and consequently, openness. In plain language... the respondent sees that I don't accept their untruths and can see through them very easily. I have seen this reaction to exposure of an untruth in almost 100% of my sit down interviews in Norway.)

Anthony:
Just judging by what you've just said to me I would say that that is bullying.

Nina:
(AN – She bursts out laughing.) I think it's like... if I was sitting and having a conversation with like a girlfriend... the boys would come up to them and say, *"Don't talk to her!"* because I get angry because I am motivated... like I get angry at the person...

(AN – She now realises that she can trust me not to fall for her untruths which is obviously a relief for her... now she can increase the "honesty level" because she can now trust that I listen to her. She immediately burst out laughing, as predicted, and she immediately changed direction to describing the bullying, which only moments ago "didn't" happen. As previously pointed out, she has already started the "usual" undermining of herself and blaming herself, "I get

angry because…". Most of the Norwegian respondents interviewed undermined their accounts with equivocations, often pre-emptively, even when they were the innocent victims.)

Anthony:
You mean that you are passionate?

Nina:
Yes, passionate! I use my hands! I'm like… *(AN – she is just gesticulating.)*

Anthony:
You're alive!

Nina:
Yes! *(Laugh.)*

Anthony:
I would say that that is clearly bullying because they literally say, "Don't talk to her because she…"… isn't that the definition of bullying?

(AN – Nina begins to open her mouth to reply when Ole interrupts her abruptly with a sarcastic tone of voice.)

Ole:
Well, yeahhhhhh…

(AN – 100% of the group discussions have had at least one of the respondents exhibiting clear passive aggressive behaviour and bullying. Passive aggression is a real problem all over Norway, for a great number of people. Ole interrupted Nina in her moment of vulnerability with a sarcastic attack on her, which was completely inappropriate and insensitive. The tone was completely juxtaposed to what Nina expressed which just ruined her moment at a point of vulnerability… especially after she had to push through a resistance point of untruth to reveal a truth. This is why she tested me by the lie… she can gauge my response. I believe that this is too often "required" in Norway due to, quite possibly, the prevalence of passive aggressiveness and unempathetic responses? This will be a feature of today's conversation, repeatedly… make a note of how many incidents of passive aggressiveness you see from the respondents in this book series and see for yourself.)

Anthony:
In my opinion.

Ole:
As an *outsider*, I can understand it…

(AN – Let's take a closer look at those seven simple words, delivered with a condescending tone of voice. I was passive aggressively labelled as an "outsider", which was a clear attempt to undermine and demean me. The subtext is: "You are an outsider, so you cannot know the reality of this situation, as an outsider your view of reality is wrong, this wasn't bullying". Warping of reality is also a method of passive aggression which is used by bullies. It's a method of manipulation to try and discombobulate. It's a tactic used to make you question your sanity and perception of the situation. Let's look at this situation logically. Nina described an experience of bullying. I characterised that description as "bullying" accurately based on the Oxford dictionary definition of the word, consequently I don't need any other information or location-based context at all… It is simply a description of a reality. It is unambiguous. Action "a" = definition "a". I completely hear what Nina is saying, I believe her and I have characterised her treatment correctly based on the treatment she described. You could be an "outsider" but if somebody describes something, then it doesn't matter where you are from, you can understand what is being described with a simple understanding of plain language. She describes bullying clearly both verbally and with her non-verbal communication. However, even she emotionally reacted to the original use of the word and now, so has Ole. The question is, why? This is something which we will encounter repeatedly during this conversation and repeatedly all over Norway. I even met with a Norwegian Linguistics expert to see if it's a linguistic or language issue. These very simple words used to describe reality, even when they are the appropriate words to describe that reality, often seem to trigger an emotional response related possibly to guilt and shame in the respondents? i.e. A bully doesn't like a victim talking about bullying in front of their face because it makes them upset and they actually perceive the word (just having to hear the word) as a personal aggressive attack on them?… a victim of bullying doesn't like to hear the word either because it elicits a trauma response? An enabler doesn't want to hear it because it elicits shame in them too? So there seems to be a reluctance to use an accurate word and is probably actually simply a method of avoidance. You will see it repeatedly during our journey across Norway. All of the girls have become completely passive, they look upset and they are all in silence now.)

Ole:

But I think it's *like I said earlier*… it's just normal for us. It's just normal for us… we're just more *honest*… It's also just normal for us…

(AN – Norwegian society, from his perspective at least, equates bullying behaviour with being "honest" i.e. "It's just normal for us… we're just more honest." I have observed this repeatedly throughout the country and through the conversations I have had with hundreds of Norwegians. Passive aggressive bullying and attacks are very often mischaracterised as "just being honest" and "straightforwardness" or "we're just brutally honest" or "No nonsense Norwegians"… it's often carried out with no embarrassment or guilt. Which is not surprising, because the act itself is carried out without self-reflection or shame too, often with a tape recorder recording it. He has just passive aggressively undermined Nina at her point of vulnerability, sharing such a sensitive story and he attempted to crush her and then undermine me. She is sitting silently and upset. He achieved this with a very few number of words, tone of voice and timing… I can see that he probably gets away with it regularly.)

Ole:

Well, it's not like we don't accept it… It's just normal for us.

Seline:

But we shouldn't accept it! We do… but we shouldn't! If people don't want to talk to us because we are engaged *(in social issues)*… They don't want to hang out with us! People break up with us, because we care about our society, and we want to change things!

Anthony:

Let me ask you… why don't people just say "No! This is not normal" and change it? That's what I don't understand?

Nina:

That's kind of the problem that I work with… what I am doing here is working against injustice. At the same time, I have to be friends with the people that tell me it's stupid… Because… I don't know… It's just normal!

Seline:

I think it's got something to do with people *not liking politics*…

(AN – She immediately starts blaming and undermining herself and her

treatment, for working in politics. This is interesting and I will tell you what I think she is doing, even though she doesn't consciously know it. She is pre-emptively undermining herself... she is undermining what she is ABOUT to say, which will obviously be to describe mistreatment and bullying. She undermines her own experience, blaming herself, before she even speaks it. It's an auto-response and it's obvious and predictable. I have seen hundreds of Norwegians do it and recognise it straight away. It's an indication of a potential disclosure of mistreatment... however, if I would have been insensitive she would have shut down, so it's a kind of test. Many respondents don't fully seem to believe what they are saying... she knows that she is not bullied because of "people not liking politics"... if I would have agreed with that assertion then I would have failed the "test" and she would have closed up for sure, I suspect? You will often encounter these "tests" in Norway, like when you are so often probed for your view of Norway within moments of meeting a new person, as we have discussed earlier. Your answer will indicate your treatment, categorization and the nature of your forthcoming interaction?)

Anthony:
Yes?

Seline:
I think it's some of that... because when I went to school before... people were like *"Oh we can try to say something to Seline that she won't like!"*

Nina:
Yes, they try to annoy us!

Seline:
They try to like, test...

Anthony:
Provoke you?

Nina and Seline:
Yes yes... and provoke!

Anthony:
So wait a minute. They use your sensitivity for your society as a means to provoke you and to just cause you trouble?

Seline:
Yes!

Ole:
We *(Seline and himself)* went to Junior High together and we were always the two people that were always engaged… and… to be honest… *I like it…*

(AN – He is admitting to liking the confrontations.)

Ole:
People will provoke me because, like, like… this is what I love to talk about… and it was also fun… because we wanted to speak the most…

(AN – Seline is expressing her pain at her bullying and Ole has now undermined her too by categorising that same experience as "fun", whilst she is sitting next to him… it's an incredible lack of empathy. Her interpretation of reality is now being challenged by his own imposition and passive aggressiveness… she reacts with a kind of scared laugh.)

Seline:
(Giggles – embarrassed.)

Ole:
We like it! So when you say it's "mean"… and "accepted"… I just don't think about it too much… some people are just like that…

Emma:
But sometimes!

Anthony:
We are thinking about it right now, Ole. What do we think about it?

Nina:
Those people you won't get anywhere with… you can never change their minds… they're just there to provoke! That's the difference between the people that ask me questions because they genuinely care… There are a lot of people that just asked us to provoke and I have learnt to see the difference between those people, because I should be like, "Do you know what, I don't want to talk… Because I know that you don't really care."

Nina:
But I have learnt to see the difference... and when people actually care, I will
be like, "Yes... we can talk about the topic."

Nina:
And like... don't... I think it's... it can be mean but sometimes used as a
joke.

(*AN – she is unconvincing when saying this part of the sentence... but suddenly
changes and forcefully says the next part.*)

Nina:
But when you, hear it every day! It can kind of get like...

Mathias:
It's kind of like a stir up...

Anthony:
A stir up?

Mathias:
Yeah kind of just like bad conversation.

Anthony:
What's interesting is, you guys are passionate about something and you
are stigmatised for it... It's stone cold bullying... Some people might call
it "comedy"... You can call it whatever you want to call it... but it's
simply mistreatment for being different. What I am trying to get at is...
that kind of behaviour and acceptance of that behaviour as "normal" is
not normal in any way shape or form. It can't be described, as normal,
but you have said that it is "normal" in Norway, right here today. You
have said it a few times Ole... so I am trying to ask you... do you think
that it is right?

(*AN – All of the girls tentatively but unanimously and emotionally replied with
"No no no no" but Ole is silent and does not answer the question.*)

Anthony:
But does it hurt you ever?

Nina:
It's draining…

Anthony:
It's fatiguing?

Unanimous:
(The girls all say, yes.)

Emma:
If you get bullied or little comments… It's draining!

Anthony:
Yes.

Emma:
It's draining… like in the long run… like when I went to high school… We have this *weird* tradition… like when you are in your last year of high school…

Anthony:
You mean the Russ?

Emma:
Yes! Yeah, yeah, yeah, yeah, yeah!

Anthony:
You know I've done my research.

Unanimous:
(Burst out laughing.)

Emma:
And some guys in my class had a rap group called *"ridiculing rape victims."*

(AN – This is not the original "name" of the rap group, but it was a "joke" ridiculing rape victims. Ole, giggles at her when she said the name, even though he is fully aware that this is a rape "joke" about her and it has caused her a lot of pain and distress, and still does.)

Ole:
(Giggles.)

Emma:
They made a song where they made fun of rape and they said that they were going to kill their organiser, just because she was a woman and I and some of my friends went *"This is not OK"*… because of this we spoke up that this. We spoke up because it is not right, they gave me the Russ "name" as "Emma loves rape". Just because I cared so much…

Anthony:
That is targeted harassment against you.

Emma:
Yeah, yes… Yes because I said that this is not OK.

Anthony:
Who supported you? Did the majority support you or did the majority support them?

(AN – Emma goes on to describe that some did but then goes on to describe how the group made another song saying that they "don't f*** with curvier women"… "They were like hating on us"… because we were feminists".)

Anthony:
I am trying to understand something… did people around you just say, "Oh, they're just joking… just get over it?" or did the majority of people support you? Do you feel that you were supported or not supported?

Emma:
The girls supported us… The girls did… The guys didn't. The guys thought it was funny too…

Nina:
(Interjects)… this was before the "me too" movement.

Emma:
It was before the "me too" campaign, but still… The guys thought it was funny to like singing songs about rape and raping the organiser… and the girls didn't think it was cool.

Anthony:
What was the official line and response from the official organisation about this, like the school?

Emma:
They said that the group needed to apologise… and they had this YouTube video… And they had to mute out the part of the video where they said that they wanted to "nail" the organiser…

Anthony:
Nail? Like, crucify?

Emma:
No no no… the box you lay in when you're dead.

Anthony:
A coffin?

Emma:
Yes! Yeah yeah yeah… They want to nail the coffin with the organiser in it! So that line in the song was blurred out…

(AN – Just to be clear: the bullies were only instructed by the school to merely "mute that part" of the rap whilst being allowed to keep it up.)

Emma
That part was blurred out… they needed to say sorry which I don't even think they did!

Anthony:
Did the school actually support you?

Emma:
They didn't say anything about all of the hate we got by talking about it! They didn't care about that!

Anthony:
You are talking about the school now?

Emma:
Yeah yeah yeah… yes, the school.

Anthony:
You got attacked and vilified for speaking out at school which has obviously affected your life?

Emma:
Yeah yeah yeah!

Seline:
(Interjects.) The same has happened to me too!

Anthony:
Please go ahead, Seline… Emma, we will come back to what you said, please don't worry.

Seline:
I was at a school training sports camp and the boys were sitting in the sauna, and the boys, when the girls were going in there, were "blotting"…

Anthony:
Do you mean they were exposing themselves?

Seline:
And the girls were like (I wasn't there), "We don't want to see your penis!" … "Can you have some clothes on you?" And they were like, "Yeah yeah yeah just go out and we will fix it"… And then they were like "Come in!" … Then the girls came in… And then the boys did it once again! And then some girls came to me and told me the story about what happened… And I was like "This is not OK!" because I am a feminist and I have learnt a lot about these situations.

(AN – Very interesting that she states that she has learnt about these situations because she is a "feminist" and not from normal everyday society or her school.)

Seline:
So I was going to my trainer… my coach… and told her, what happened and they were like, "oh they were just joking!"

(AN – Virtually all young people described that they would never tell a teacher because they never do anything about abuse or bullying or they'd dismiss it as a "joke"… or on many occasions that the teacher themselves is a bully and a sexual harasser.)

Anthony:
They minimised it and just dismissed your concerns?

Seline:
Yes… they said, "You don't have to do something about this" and I said… "No! This is not OK!" It was right after the "me too" campaign… I was like screaming to the boys… "You have to stop doing these things! It's not OK!"

Anthony:
The people in charge… they didn't care?

Seline:
Yes… So what happened was… Everyone at that training camp said, "Oh she's such a drama queen… She is making drama out of nothing!" *(AN – she now gets visibly upset.)* And it was just my best friend that said, "No, you are right."

Anthony:
How many people were against you and saying that you were causing drama? Can you give me a number?

Seline:
Thirty! *(AN – she said this very forcefully.)*

Anthony:
And only one person supported you, even though it was overt blatant sexual harassment?

Seline:
Yes!

Anthony:
That's crazy.

Seline:
It is! And they were like "You're a feminist!" as if that was something bad.

Anthony:
Were there any other consequences to that? Did they exclude you or anything like that?

Seline:
Some of the other girls at the camp, were like, "Don't listen to Seline! She's a drama queen! She's always making drama!"

Anthony:
One out of thirty… almost no one… one out of thirty people… no one else supported you?

Seline:
Just my best friend, who is a girl.

Anthony:
Did she have any trouble as well because she supported you?

Seline:
Yes, maybe they thought "She is on Seline's team so we do not have to talk to her either…"

Nina:
(Interjects.) That's pretty normal! It's pretty normal calling a girl "dramatic", because she like cares about it… This has happened to me too.

(AN – You have three young girls who have explained that abusers were defended, enabled and that the community enabled the abuse, who say that this is "normal". In this group you have five young people. 100% percent describe that they have been bullied, 60% describe sexual abuse and out of that 60%, 100% say that they were victimised by the people who had a duty of care to protect them and complaints were dismissed. Almost 100% of victims interviewed minimised their abuse/treatment as something other than abuse and often even got upset when their abuse was characterised as "abuse".)

Anthony:
Would you like to talk about it?

Nina:
Well… when I was younger… there was like a gang of boys and they were

like… not very… errrr… nice to us. *(AN – she appears very upset and scared.)* They would have competitions to see how many butts they could touch in a school day… and stuff like that… and we told our teachers and our teachers would just say, "Oh they are just flirting with you!" That's like the common.

Unanimous:
(Girls.) Yes yes yes yeah yeah yeah!

Nina:
And even a lot of the girls… were like "Oh they're just joking!"… and I was like "This is not OK!" … and the boys are like still bothering us… *(AN – the boys are still continuing their harassment, she said… years later)* This was like many years ago… but they are still like bothering us… when we moved to another school. And I was like "This is not OK they are still bothering us… this is sexual harassment." And when I went and said that it got "too serious", for the girls and they were like "No no no no no no no"… "We don't… we don't want to talk about it now…" and I was like, "But we have to talk about it because this is a big deal!"… "If we just dismiss then the boys will just keep on going"… and then I was like… well the teachers don't really care! And now I'm like (labelled) as the drama queen and the feminist… The term "feminist" is used in a lot of schools to describe bathing *(AN – as an insult.)*

Anthony:
As an insult?

Nina:
Yes.

Anthony:
I would say that you are the strongest person in the group! And I say that you are too, Seline! Because you pointed it out, against what everybody else said. Emma, you were agreeing with them and nodding… Have you had any experience where you've had to face anything because you spoke out?

Emma:
I was made fun of… it was my own classmates *(AN – Group enabling.)* who gave me the "Emma loves rape" label…

Anthony:
And they did that to intentionally hurt you?

Emma:
Yeah yeah, of course! It was only because of them that what they had said was not right! That I was like praised with that name.

Anthony:
And I say, Seline... You said that the authorities in your camp did nothing... The teachers didn't care, that's what you said to her, and you said that the teachers were a little bit ambiguous, they didn't enforce the apology... and they didn't really help you afterwards?

Emma:
Yes!

Anthony:
What you have just described is the fact that you don't get help. That the victim... is labelled as a "troublemaker". That is exactly what you have just described to me?

Unanimous:
(Girls.) Yes, yes, yes...

Emma:
If a boy sexually harasses you... The teacher will almost always say, "That's just the way they are."

Nina:
"Boys will be boys."

Unanimous:
Yes yes!

Emma:
When my sister was younger... two boys ran after her with a knife and a lighter... My sister and her friend told the teacher, what the teacher said was, "It's only because you are so cute."

Anthony:
That is shocking!

Emma:
Yeah yeah yeah, like… assuming that the boys were going after them to "eat" them like because they were so "cute"!

Anthony:
That's not mature. That's not even a logical response!

Emma:
No!

Anthony:
And what did you guys say to the teachers?

Emma:
I don't know… My sister was like six years old… and she still remembers this!

(AN – Her sister is around seventeen now.)

Anthony:
So your sister remembers this to this day?

Emma:
Yes! She thinks… Yes yeah yeah yeah… I actually talked about this with her like two days ago.

Anthony:
So something that this teacher said, something that happened over ten years ago, you still talk about and think about the impact of that teacher's inappropriate response?

Emma:
Yes yes! Yeah, yeah, yeah, yes.

Anthony:
Would you say that it has affected her?

Emma:

Yes! She told me that she even remembers thinking "this answer that the teacher has given me doesn't make any sense"… I came here with big issues! These guys ran after me with a knife, a fork and a lighter… And you said, "It's only because you are so cute." She still remembers that strange response.

Anthony:

That's inappropriate and crazy. It's almost a psychopathic answer.

Unanimously:

(Girls.) Yeah, yeah, yeah!

(AN – Ole has been silence and has not uttered a word of encouragement to the girls. As you can read the respondents describe; vulnerability and pain are too often not treated with sensitivity in Norway.)

Nina:

You like remember when you get like minimised! That was a really big problem and you were like freaking out and you are thinking "I really need to get help for this"… So you go to talk to like a teacher or something… And you get minimised!

Anthony:

It sounds like you don't have anyone in authority you can turn to because you know, they're not going to help you and they're going to minimise it?

Unanimous:

(Girls.) Yes! Yes, big problem, it's a really big problem…

Emma:

It is a problem because girls are told from their childhood if a boy does something… It's because he's in "love" with you.

Anthony:
Really?

Unanimous:

Yeah! Yeah! Yeah!

(AN – They are conditioned from childhood?)

Emma:
We are told that our whole childhood!

Anthony:
So essentially, if I rephrase it: "It's your fault!"

Seline:
Yes! Yeah…

Anthony:
They are basically saying, it's the "scenarios" fault or it's *your* fault but it's never the perpetrators fault?

Unanimous:
(Girls.) Yes, yes, yes, Yeah!

Seline:
They say that our short skirts are raping!

Anthony:
Is that what they say?

Emma:
Yes!

Anthony:
The teachers?

Emma:
The whole society! If you get raped, they will instantly say, "What was she wearing?"

Anthony:
Wow!

Unanimous:
Yeah, yeah, yeah!

Anthony:
I've noticed something, tell me what you think about this… I've spoken

to so many people across Norway and they are saying the same thing... notice a pattern... The wronged or the victim is often undermined... And the incident minimised... And the perpetrator is too often excused and elevated... It doesn't matter the age, it doesn't matter the scenario, it doesn't matter at all... That is the theme that I am seeing in so many situations across Norway and you have just described it now... Is there any truth to my observation?

Unanimous:
(Girls.) Yes, yes, yes!

Nina:
They use very often that they don't want to "ruin it for the boy"... like if a girl has been sexually assaulted... or something like that... It's always "but he has a future... we can't do anything."

Anthony:
So you are blamed again? Basically you are victimised and then you are victimised again even though you've been abused? They are saying that if you say anything then you are going to "destroy" the perpetrator who was being abused you... So they are victimising you twice?

Unanimous:
(Girls.) Yes, yes!

Anthony:
In fact they're victimising you three times because they don't even support you afterwards?

Nina:
Yes! So a girl being raped and harassed I would *never come out and say it*... Because they are afraid that they won't believe them... Or they will believe them but they will say "Oh but are you sure?"

Anthony:
They will support your rapist?

Emma:
Yeah, yeah, yeah!

Anthony:
Rather than support you? With regards to all of the scenarios you have described, not just rape... let's talk about the scenario that you have just described... that's the victim is not supported... the event being minimised... this is not normal. Why is it, as you say, "normal" in Norway?

Nina:
I think that in my scenario the girls were afraid that it kind of got "too serious"... like actually using the word "sexual assault"...

(AN – Another confirmation... using the appropriate words to describe abusive situations would probably shake up Norwegian society... because people would be empowered to describe the sexual abuse, abuse rape, bullying, unempathetic behaviour which is now being described as being so prevalent. So instead of labelling it as it is, I have observed that many of the respondents get very upset or even scared when you use the correct word/label for the corresponding behaviour. I have often observed the victimised, also, become uncomfortable with these words because they are scared of reprisal and exclusion by the perpetrators? It appears that the perpetrator must use doublespeak or would obviously have to address their issues immediately called out. Many of the respondents are "drowning" in abuse so label that abuse as "comedy" or "normal behaviour" to make sense of it?)

Anthony:
But was it not sexual assault? It was, wasn't it?

Nina:
Yeah, it was! I was like "This is what it is!"... Oh no... "But are you sure that you didn't like misread the moment?" and even the girls that it happened to! They were like, "Oh I don't know...". They were making excuses because they didn't want to be the girl that talks out.

(AN – This is a technique has featured in a many of sit down conversations that I've had in Norway; A passive aggressive undermining and warping of reality to undermine the victim/victim blame.)

Anthony:
Because they would then be targeted?

Nina:
And they would want to be friends with the boys! Because they think that

they owe the boys, to not talk about it and say that! Yes... they feel like... because they have been told... That they will like ruin the boy's life!

Anthony:
They are blackmailing you?

Nina:
Yes, but we are like taught since we are children that is what boys do! And even very often when the girls in my class when it would happen to them they themselves would minimise it, themselves because they didn't want to ruin... Then they would be friends with the boys... Then it would happen again! And when I like it was so <u>absurd</u>. When I said it to them they were like, "Well I don't know... I don't want to talk about it or speak out."

Anthony:
So you had that insight to realise that the abused would go back to the abuser because they had no other options?

Nina:
Yes!

Anthony:
Wow!

Nina:
We are just taught this from a very young age.

Anthony:
This is not very cool.

Nina:
It's not.

Anthony:
Just know that you girls are in the right, well done, well done for fighting against it.

A later discussion

Anthony:
So guys, we were discussing about the north being "ignored". Can you tell me what you said?

Emma:
I had a history teacher who was from Bergen say to me "Only learnt just now that the major war was in the north of Norway... I didn't know this before now." And she was the history teacher!

Anthony:
That's crazy.

Emma:
Yes, that's crazy... The real war happened in Narvik people fought against the Germans! Just a few moments from here.

Anthony:
It is, all of these things that you say, are not taught?

Emma:
We are taught because we live in the north of Norway but in the south they don't know anything about this!

Seline:
Not everybody here even learns about it... I learn about it because of my grandmother... during the war the Nazis burned the town.

Anthony:
Is this the Nazis "Scorched Earth" policy as they left?

Seline:
Yes.

Anthony:
You are saying that this is not known?

Nina:
Not by many!

Seline:
I only found out about it a few years ago because of my grandmother!

Anthony:
You were saying earlier that these things are just "jokes"… but I am saying; isn't it a serious thing if the history of your area is not taught?

Emma:
They don't care about the north in the south of Norway. They had a policy in Oslo that you could rent an apartment but not if you were a northerner.

Nina:
Yes, it would say it! It would actually say this on the papers that no "northerners" should even apply for this.

Anthony:
How long ago was this? A couple of decades ago?

Emma:
They said that when the people from Pakistan came to Norway. Then they started caring about the people in the north… yes, yes… So when the dark people came then they started caring.

Anthony:
To me that sounds like the projection of discrimination and rage transferred over to somebody else?

Emma:
Yes, yes!

(AN – Ole has not uttered a word of support of the girls… but now decides to speak.)

Ole:
But there is kind of a history of like… *not* racism…

(AN – He has again passive aggressively undermined the girls at the moment of their vulnerability. Have you noticed? He has not once responded with a word of support, kindness or encouragement to anything they have said or expressed today, so far.)

Emma:
(Interjects forcefully.) Yes, its racism!

Ole:
If you have a—

(AN – Ole immediately begins to argue with Emma.)

Anthony:
Whoa, whoa, whoa.

Emma:
It is!

(AN – Emma looks towards Ole and is angry at him now.)

Anthony:
Let's look at this. Emma, you just described the history of racism… you said that it was racism… and straight away (Ole, you quickly came in)… So let's clarify what it is?

(AN – the moment I say that he starts pulling back because he knows he is wrong.)

Ole:
But I'm not.

Nina:
It is racism!

Emma:
Yeah! *(AN – is now upset too.)*

(AN – Ole responds with a condescendingly tone of voice.)

Ole:
Well… *(A long exhalation of breath.)*

Anthony:
Ole?

(AN – Often, when emotional distress is displayed or expressed it will be met with a reflex reaction. It will usually be undermined and dismissed, in a variety of ways; I have regularly observed technical analysis/undermining based on faulty logic as a passive aggressive technique by many of the respondents. Another way is to make the victim appear stupid by undermining their description of an event; another way is to make a "joke" about it. It's like if somebody is struck by a "hammer" and is injured, panicked and upset, somebody might completely ignore their pain and argue with them and say "No! You were not struck by a hammer like you have just said"... because they were in actual fact struck by a mallet. Or chastise the victim of a crocodile attack for misstating that they, just moments earlier, had their arm bitten off by an "alligator"... when in fact it was "technically" a crocodile.)

Ole:
I don't know what words…

(AN – Feigning ignorance is a typical passive aggressive tactic of bullies, especially after an attack and especially when they have got a reaction from the victim, which he has, all of the girls are very upset now.)

Anthony:
OK, but here's the thing though…

(AN – Ole attempts to overpower the conversation and interrupt… I raise my finger as if to say, "Pause for moment.")

Ole:
Oh, but I was going to tell a story though…

(AN – Attempt at a diversion and manipulation.)

Anthony:
But let's talk about the characterisation of what is, because this is important. We use words.

Nina:
They treat us differently because of where we from! That's racism!

(AN – They are having a meltdown because Ole has angered them intentionally. I have noticed that many fully expect that their victim will be silent… or the victim

will react and then the instigator will sit seemingly calmly and imply that the victim, that they have provoked and abused, is emotionally unstable (gas lighting). The girls are so used this behaviour, it is clear. This is why any society with high levels of suppression and bullying would fear exposure from accurately defined and understood words as well as people with courage to speak with intelligent communication. This is why a society based on fear and bullying would need to bring a) critical thinking levels down b) discourage use of effective accurate language and c) discourage and disable the ability to communicate true emotions (by fear, exclusion and intimidation, for example) to have a situation where bullying is normalised on a societal level. We will analyse this in depth with specific examples later.)

Anthony:
Nina and Emma have just described... to me... the Oxford dictionary definition of racism and discrimination.

Nina:
Yes! *(AN – she sounds exasperated.)*

Anthony:
And you seem *(Nina)* very passionate about that... And you obviously agree?

Nina:
Yes! And it's undermining it not saying what it is!

Anthony:
Where are we now? Are we wrong or are we right?

Ole:
Well what I was going to say... well... is that... hmmmm... if you... if you, what in school and you were going to look at all the footage... of any historical footage of anything important happening... You're never going to hear anybody speak the northern dialect... Because in all of the official broadcasting people didn't dare... To speak their own dialect.

Emma:
No! They weren't allowed!

Nina:
They weren't allowed!

Ole:
Kind of the same thing with the Sami language and it's the same thing with a lot of people who have moved from the north to the south they have completely changed their dialect…

(AN – I regularly encountered this on my journey also, respondents often started talking about sensitive subjects (Holocaust, Slave trade, Sami discrimination etc.) as if they believed that they were going to get some kind of reflected victimhood status from merely referencing names of abused people(s), like they really care. Ole actually referred to this technique himself earlier in the conversation when he said that "people like to make people think that they care about climate change". It's chilling to watch somebody engaged in bullying refer to the Sami people, whilst sitting next to a Sami person, so nonchalantly as a means of passive aggressive attack on a vulnerable and visibly upset young lady. Note that he will also elicit the American "Slave Trade" as means to try and "win" his passive aggressive arguments too, shortly, reinforcing my point.)

Nina:
There were a lot of haters…

Emma:
My grandpa! He had to move to Oslo and he had to change his dialect to get a job!

Ole:
That's what I'm saying, like it was not law!

Emma:
I know it was not law! But you couldn't get a job!

Anthony:
OK guys… From my perspective this sounds like blatant discrimination… and blatant racism… and Ole… I think that you would agree that that is what they have just described?

Ole:
Well!

Anthony:
Or would you not?

(AN – I say that with a smile… because I see that he's actually going to continue to argue against them.)

Ole:
Well… yes… but…

Anthony:
What is this "but"? But what?

Ole:
The thing is… saying "racism"… We're not like a different race.

(AN – He's arguing about the technicality of the word, arguing over semantics… you will see this technique many times through this book series.)

Anthony:
Right, I understand… So let's talk about technical language now.

(AN – Ole, tries to interrupt.)

Anthony:
So you are basically saying, it's not "racism" but it is "discrimination"?

Ole:
(Long silence.)

Anthony:
OK, what word would you use? How would you characterise it?

Ole:
Well that depends on the… errrrrr…

Anthony:
Depends on what specifically? How do you define it? You tell us how you would define it?

Ole:

Errrrr… It's complicated because… that depends on how you define racism.

(AN – This is a phrase that I have heard over and over and over again. Many respondents pull out this line when they are confronted with a clear "right or wrong" situation and instead of just saying that something is "wrong", it all suddenly gets very "complicated". It's a typical minimisation technique and it is a clear indicator of a "cut and dry" wrong situation, I find. We have a great story coming later about a racist attack of vandalism with multiple shotgun blasts which was not condemned but described to me as "complicated", by a museum curator. Whenever I hear those words you know that something is almost certainly not going to be "complicated" but on the contrary… very clear. Simply ask them to explain logically why it's "complicated"… it falls down in ten seconds flat… it's just a simple technique of avoidance and minimisation. He intentionally also tries to confuse the definition of "racism" as portraying the meaning as fluid and "dependent", which we will see repeatedly on our journey too.)

Unanimous:
(Girls raise their voices.)

Anthony:
How would you describe what they have just said to you?

Ole:
I would say discrimination because that's (what they just described) against another race.

Emma:
Yeah, but what is a race!?

Ole:
Well, that's a very philosophical question.

(AN – Ole uses a very condescending tone now. Subtext: you are all too stupid to understand reality; it's too "philosophical" and "complicated" for you to understand. A technique we saw repeatedly in the previous Norwegian media articles.)

Emma:
We *(Norwegians)* don't talk about race!

Nina:
Yes!

(AN – Ole is doing what something which I have seen many times on my journey. He is now trying to manipulate them to perceive themselves as wrong, unintelligent and "crazy" and when they get upset by that then tries to say to them all it's "philosophical" and it's "complicated". This is why it's very important that strict definition of words be avoided in day-to-day life, because then a victim could immediately identify and expose illogical behaviour, arguments and behaviour. This is why racism can't be defined as the dictionary definition of racism… it must be "dependent" or it must be understood and interpreted to be, say a "joke". This is why bullying can't be defined as the dictionary definition of "bullying", as it must be portrayed as the victim just being "confused" or "dramatic" because then the victim can just say "No, this is what it is! STOP!" and it could then be exposed. If bullying and abuse is normalised, it would need to be disguised and you would need to confuse the victim by use of doublespeak… and it truly works, because I have witnessed victims undermine themselves regularly. You will see it through these books and the message is clear as day; "No you did not experience bullying, abuse or racism, you do not even know what bullying, abuse or racism is, it's much too complicated for you to understand, it's philosophical, very complicated… you're such a stupid person… too stupid to understand these complicated philosophical concepts… you're so emotional, weak and unstable for even getting upset about it".)

Emma:
What is race?

Ole:
(Condescendingly)… when you identify yourself as a different race…

Emma:
No!

Nina:
It's about where you come from!

Ole:
Well I don't know the answer!

Nina:
(Giggles and speaks softly.) No.

Anthony:
Ole, this is where it gets interesting… I'll tell you why *(turning to the girls)*… You guys have just expressed pain and that family members of yours have experienced what you describe as racism and discrimination, I would agree with completely. Now Ole… I'm sure that you can recognise that on a human level, right?

Ole:
I have stories too!

Anthony:
But you know what I'm saying? I'm sure that you acknowledge… What they are saying? And intellectually speaking… the word racism does actually cover it… is related to race, ethnicity and location… you know exactly what they mean?

Ole:
Yes.

(AN – The room is now still and silent.)

Anthony:
So… maybe we got there in the end… we got to the understanding of exactly what it is?

Ole:
Yes, I agree, but I think that I don't want to use the word "racism".

Anthony:
Why?

Ole:
Because I don't want to put this issue with… It's, it's, it's, it's a serious issue… was, was at the time but it was <u>not as bad as other cases of racism at the time</u>…

(AN – This is shocking. He reverts to the technique of comparison as a means to undermine the victim.)

Anthony:
With regards to? Wait wait wait…

Ole:
Like slavery and stuff.

(AN – This is chilling to observe and listen to.)

Emma:
Yeah but we didn't have that in Norway.

Ole:
Well… That's what I'm saying… The word "racism" puts it up on that pedestal.

(AN – You can now see how much mental gymnastics simple words trigger and elicit within the mind. We observe a warped subjective interpretation of words with arbitrary thresholds which need to be reached to use that word "legitimately". If that totally manufactured and created "pedestal" is not reached then it does not deserve to be defined as the word, according to the respondent. The respondent disqualifies the official dictionary definition and replaces it with their own warped definition, which will be argued and imposed on those around the respondent. This is subjective from person to person and changes according on their emotional state. This is incredible and completely unhealthy. So a mentally distressed person may refuse to see pain in others because they do not observe a high enough level of pain that they judge to be "worthy" of the word. This actually explains the frustration and anger often expressed when these words are often used in our discussions, by the respondents. The pain and discomfort is often real for the respondent and they genuinely can't understand why you are using the dictionary definition of a word and not their warped interpretation of what they think the word should be. The respondent will do anything to avoid the legitimate definition of words because then they will have to face the reality of possibly having to SEE the behaviour and action that that word describes… that will "burst the bubble of delusion and fantasy", so is rejected. Subtext: "Only a lynching in Alabama (which I have put on a pedestal/altar of special reverence) is worthy of being called "racism" and that means, obviously, that your racism is "impossible" as it's impossible to experience TRUE racism in a small village in

Norway… it doesn't exist in Norway… and you'd be insensitive for even implying that you'd experienced racism… be grateful that you weren't lynched like they were in Alabama! You are emotionally unstable and rude for even saying it!" Very simply, if it's not defined as "racism"… how can it be racist? Obviously it can't be and this all perpetuates a kind of widespread delusion? It's potentially an education issue; Low travel and life experience, low levels of interactions with different races and cultures and a nationalistic mindset combined with a culture of normal passive aggressiveness would naturally create an unhealthy environment and behaviour, would it not?)

Girls:
(AN – The girls explode with rage.)

Anthony:
Just from my perspective as an "outsider", they (the girls) are describing the archetype dictionary definition of racism. Why don't you want to call it what it is? And what has another story got to do with their experience?

Ole:
Well, no… That's… er… no… it doesn't… but… errr… wer…

(AN – This is a very typical respondent response when confronted with logic. You will see exactly the same answers and behaviour from a professional linguistic expert when confronted with his illogical arguments too, in a few pages time.)

Anthony:
You said that it does though? You said it just now…

Emma:
I think that that is typical in Norway!

Anthony:
Yes… It sounds to me like your experience… Do you feel that your experiences are being undermined right now?

Emma:
Yes! Kind of! But I think that that is common in Norway… But not just about racism. We say all the time in Norway… "Norway is the most eco country in the world"… So if we talk about say a feminist case we are told that that is not important, "Why don't you talk about the winning in Saudi

Arabia!?"… "You have it so great here in Norway!" I think, they always say that our problem is not important, because someone else is having it worse!

Anthony:
And do you think that that is an intentional device to undermine what you are saying?

Emma:
Yes!

Nina:
Yes!

Anthony:
What do you think about that, Nina?

Nina:
Yes… I really agree!

Anthony:
What do you think about that, Seline?

Seline:
I really agree!

Anthony:
An intentional device to undermine your position?

Emma:
Yes!

Anthony:
And also to dismiss what you're saying?

Emma:
Yes, it's like… if you don't want to change something you can just say, "You have it good don't complain!"

Anthony:
Yes… I've already been thinking about a section of the book that I'm

going to write. I am already pre-empting the excuses that people are going to come up with. For example, when I talk about bullying and I talk about racism *(AN – The girls start laughing)*... and I know what's coming... So one of the first things I'm going to say is... "This book is not the secret Australian, it's not the secret American, it's not the secret Italian... It's the secret Norwegian"... Just because something happens on the other side of the world, it does not negate what is happening in your country! In fact... the fallacy is weak. It removes your responsibility "Oh but but but!" ... It's like a child stealing biscuits and then jumping up and down and when caught, "Oh Mum! But he (my sibling) stole the sweets!"

Unanimous:
(Girls.) Yeah, yeah!

Anthony:
It's weak. And it's dismissive... Let's be honest about what it is... It's just a technique to dismiss?

Unanimous:
(Girls). Yes, yes!

Anthony:
Just trying to evade responsibility?

Nina:
It's because you don't want to deal with it now saying that it isn't as urgent, I guess... I think it is kind of like they don't want to deal with it right now... So they just dismiss it. We should do something about that... even if they don't do something about it the bigger issues.

Anthony:
Do you think that Janteloven has had an effect on people's expression of empathy? I'll tell you why... You just described an experience... And it was characterised at this table... In a way which I imagine hurt you?

Emma and Nina:
Yes!

Anthony:
Do you know what I'm saying?

Emma:
Yes.

Anthony:
But do you think that this could be related to Janteloven as a kind of conditioning which creates a kind of reflex response... rather than thinking "Wait a minute... they have just described pain... maybe I should think about that?" rather than immediately just jumping to characterising what they have said in a "logical" framework or undermining it. Maybe try to emotionally relate to what they are saying instead? It appears to me that very often the emotional response to expressions of pain is not there in Norway... It is too often just dismissed for semantics, irrational examination and interrogation of the technicals, I am observing repeatedly. Do you understand what I have just said?

Emma:
Yes... yeah, yeah, yeah.

Anthony:
That's what I am observing all over Norway... For example if you say something heartfelt, for example like you have just now said, "I have also experienced that..." something which makes me stop in shock... I would then never dream of undermining your experience or saying "What experience!?" ... Or minimise it, or undermine you or, to be honest, even characterise it in a different way, to what you did... I have observed that in front of my own eyes repeatedly in Norway though?

Unanimous:
(Girls.) Yes, yes, yes.

Anthony:
Because for me... you are describing your experience and I can see that you are intelligent and I can trust your intellect to be able to determine what something is characterised as.

Nina:
And it can hurt just as much!

Anthony:
I've noticed this so much in Norway during my conversations... that too

very often the emotional response is just not there. More about technicality... a colder response. But with that said... if that is "normal"... then the only way to solve it is to talk about it... That people understand, because obviously we understand your pain (looking at the girls)... All of us at this table *(AN – opening my body language to include Ole too)* understand your pain that you have just described to us... I'm guessing?

Ole:
(Mumbles.)

Anthony:
Do you not understand?

Ole:
Of course... *(Giggles.)*

Anthony:
Let's say that you are crying... It's almost like a refusal to see that she is crying... It's almost like... There is an emotional disconnect which I often see... And I think that the only way to get through it is to discuss issues... But here's the thing... As you just said... People don't do what you three (the girls) just did... You said "no"! And you stood your ground... Do you know that this is not something which I have seen done many times? So it appears that what you ordinarily do (if I wasn't here)... Would be to keep it inside... But now it has turned into an open discussion where we can all learn... But is that rare in Norway? You said "no! This is how we feel!" But is it usually very hard to do that in Norway?

Nina:
I was having a conversation with someone... And we were both like in a bad place... And we were talking about like what has happened... the person was immediately like, "I don't have to tell mine because yours is so much worse!" But like that's so wrong! Because their situation can hurt just as mine.

Anthony:
Yes.

Nina:

They don't know how I reacted to my situation… And we can never feel like what's the other person is feeling… like never… It can be described but we will never… Like I will never know the person was hurt just as much as me even though it didn't sound bad… so I think that Norwegians are pretty good at if something is in the media like… like the subject of catcalling in the street… Then they will say, "So you should think about the girls in Libya!" because we hear it so often!

Anthony:
To me that sounds like deflection?

Nina:

Yes… We hear that like in the media… or like in school… or like from our teachers… and I think we kind of take that into our own lives… Like "you have a much bigger problem… Let's talk about yours and not mine because… you are much more hurt then I." But you deserve to say your thing too!

Anthony:
So do you think that could be self-minimisation as well?

Nina:
Yes!

Anthony:
Through a kind of indoctrination?

Nina:
Yes!

Anthony:
That's incredible.

(AN – Ole, interrupts again in her vulnerable moment to undermine her.)

Ole:
You're using such an aggressive word indoctrination!

Anthony:
Do you know what's interesting though? Have any of you got a phone
that works?

Ole:
Yes.

Anthony:
Can you just type in the word... look at the dictionary definition of the
word "indoctrination" and then we can determine together as a group if
it's "aggressive" or actually quite appropriate?

Ole:
But you can describe any cultural...

*(AN – This is a standard "tu quoque fallacy" argument. Used as a technique to
discredit. Look out for it regularly on our journey. It's completely irrelevant and
used as a tactic of avoidance.)*

Anthony:
Well, let's decide it together right now. Please go to the word
"indoctrinate" in the dictionary. We will look at the definition in the
dictionary together and we will see if it relates to the description of her
experience of what she just said and then we will decide together?

*(AN – Ole, realises that he can't misdirect the group so puts his phone away. Nina
grabs hers and enthusiastically starts typing.)*

Nina:
(AN – takes over and quickly start typing in the word.)

Ole:
It probably does though!

Anthony:
So if it does then it's not "aggressive", it's accurate?

Ole:
You could call it that but *(mumbling)* it's a cultural thing.

(AN – Previously Ole suggested that bullying was a "normal Norwegian thing" and now, incredibly, he is arguing that this behaviour is just a normal "cultural thing" in Norway. He has demonstrated twice before that he likes to impose restrictions on use of words and use of language to prevent analysis, to avoid blame and facing reality. It's a standard form of suppression and it happens frequently on our journey, as you will see. If there is any form of solution to this problem it is simply to produce a dictionary. It never fails to end any nonsense or intentional misdirection tactics.)

Nina:
(AN – reads the definition of "indoctrination".) Yes! Yes!

Anthony:
Please read it out Nina…

(AN – All of the people in the room except Ole start translating the word, including Mathias, who have been very quiet… They all take turns in translating a word…. Ole interrupts them.)

Ole:
Well, that's like saying "British" people are indoctrinated to say…

(AN – The group ignore him and speak over him to accurately translate the word exactly… They are getting excited as they read and every time they see a word in the description that they relate to, they say it out loud.)

Nina:
(Nina reads.) "Systemically making somebody change their opinion… or a way of thinking".

Anthony:
Nina, what you have just told me is the definition of what you just described?

Ole:
(AN – Ole interrupts Nina) Yes!

Anthony:
OK, let's take a look at this. I have just used a word which you have just given me the definition of, which we agree sums up what you have described, is that right or wrong?

Nina:
Yes! Yeah, yeah, yeah!

Anthony:
OK. Is the word a good word to describe what you have just described?

Nina:
Yes. If it's the right.

Anthony:
But is it the right word?

Nina:
I guess yeah!

Anthony:
OK, Ole, *(turning to him),* you described the word which she has described as accurately representing her experiences as "aggressive" and just a "cultural thing"… now you have got to justify it Sir! Go ahead…

Ole:
I don't disagree with what you just said! But errrr… That's like saying, that "British people are in indoctrinated" to say sorry all the time.

(AN – Again, this is very simply an irrelevant "tu quoque" argument, simply a diversion tactic. Ironically, I didn't mention a culture or country at all. I just characterised a set of behaviours that Nina said she experienced and I used an accurate word to describe them, based on her own words. It's very easy to deal with tu quoque… you just keep focussed and call it out directly, which is what I will now do. I have noted that a many of the respondents do not like to be challenged but doing so directly nearly always signalled a backtrack, reversal or retreat.)

Anthony:
What has Britain got to do with her accurate description of her experience? What has Britain got to do with anything that we are discussing right now?

Ole:
Nothing! It was just… that… a similar thing…

Anthony:
You said that the word was "aggressive". Please explain that for us?

Ole:
It's not…

And then the conversation changed, which takes us back to the beginning of this chapter.

A few days later I received a message from Ole;

"Thank YOU for challenging our way of thinking on so many levels and the amazing work you're doing. I can only imagine how many other people you've challenged in the same way, and how many people are now questioning everything we view as "normal" because of what you're doing… we might make an impact with our political activism but you're the one travelling around impacting and changing people every day!"

What an incredible group of young people. With that, I said, "Good bye" and continue my journey south… over 1500 km south. We will return to the north later on my journey… in fact, my journey will take me to the most northern settlement on earth… but for now, to the south we go… it's time to address these strange linguistic issues with a professional Norwegian linguist.

A Conversation with a Linguist (and Others)

It was becoming clear to me that the definition of words in Norway possibly wasn't as clear-cut as it is elsewhere. Strange as this may seem, it often appeared to be dependent on the Norwegian I was speaking to, and how *they felt* at the time. Consequently, I decided to take my evidence to a linguist. I searched online for 'Norwegian linguist' and that's how I eventually found "Aksel" who is a teacher with a Master's degree in Linguistics (in Norwegian – Mastergrad i lingvistikk). I travelled a considerable distance to interview him given his qualifications.

Aksel was very enthusiastic, smiled a lot and a little brash in his manner. His whole demeanour and dress sense exuded his confidence. While immersed in a group of people he was instantly keen to get started. I asked him if it might not be better if we talked alone but he insisted. While I had not anticipated an audience with his wife and other Norwegians, it did actually prove fruitful as the conversation progressed. I hoped to put some of my observations to him and I anticipated that an academic would handle them fairly easily but that maybe a non-academic might not be so receptive – it turned into a long and *edgy* conversation as you will see. Certainly not one full of academic clean factual answers to simple questions as I might have expected.

You will now have an opportunity to see what this normal group do when they are **challenged with basic logic.** You will see dishonesty, enabling, bullying, passive aggression, collective bullying and logical fallacy. You will also see how this group of average Norwegians treat and perceive a non-Norwegian and the effect on them.

I strongly advise you to take breaks during this chapter and warn you that just reading what they say is potentially upsetting and disconcerting. Understand that these people are almost certainly **typical people with widely held views.** I am honoured that I captured this because it gives us an insight into a completely normal group of Norwegians, including a very intelligent academic and the way they think and perceive and view their country, society, Norwegians, non-Norwegians and the world.

The participants: Aksel (twenty-eight) (Master's degree in Linguistics), Amanda (twenty-seven, non-Norwegian), Jakob (fifty), Benji (twenty-four) and Nora (fifty).

Anthony:

I was thinking about asking you for some opinions on specific words and giving you some of my observations and then asking you for your expert opinion on those observations. And then maybe we can talk about some other stuff and your views?

Aksel:

OK.

Anthony:

Do you have any explanation for a thing that I have been encountering repeatedly in Norway? If I ask somebody "Do you like chocolate cake?" I've been encountering, something which goes like this:

Anthony:
Do you like chocolate cake?

Respondent: I like almond cake.

Anthony:
OK, thank you for telling me that you like almond cake but I'm asking you whether you like chocolate cake?

Respondent:
Well you know… hmmmm… I also prefer orange cake.

Anthony:
Thank you for telling me what you prefer, but without comparison, can you just tell me directly whether you like chocolate cake?

Respondent:
Well, hmmmm… errrr… I don't prefer chocolate cake.

Anthony:
I'm not asking you what you prefer… I'm asking you a direct question, "Do you or do you not like chocolate cake?"

Respondent:
Hmmm... well... I don't like chocolate cake.

Anthony:
Then after travelling through those resistance points and finally getting an answer, they will then tell me a million things they hate about chocolate cake!

Aksel:
(Laughing.)

Anthony:
Now here's the thing OK, that scenario which I've just described to you, is this something which you understand? Is this something which is usual in Norway? What am I encountering and why am I encountering it?

Aksel:
Well, I don't really know... err... I think...

Anthony:
Do you relate to what I've said? Is it valid? Is it something that you would understand or would expect?

Aksel:
Errrrrrrrrrrrrrrr... yeah... errrrrrrrr.

Anthony:
So, comparison?

Aksel:
It doesn't sound too unexpected... But errr... Because they don't want to be... hmmm...

Anthony:
Impolite?

Aksel:
They don't want to be dissing chocolate cake, you know?

(AN – Note that he equates expressing a personal opinion with insulting a thing. He has just stated a concern of "insulting" an inanimate object. He is being completely serious.)

Anthony:

OK, so let's talk about that. What you just said: "They don't want to be dissing…" explain to me how stating how you feel about chocolate cake could be offensive to anybody, if it's somebody's personal opinion?

Aksel:

So I, think that it's because they feel that people who do like chocolate cake would be offended… I don't know, yeah.

Anthony:

These conversations are frequently one-on-one conversations, so why would they be concerned about potentially offending anybody in the world, when there is nobody else witnessing the conversation?

Aksel:

Well, maybe *you* like chocolate cake! *(Laughs.)*

(AN – Note that he cannot explain in a logical way why any reasonable person would be concerned by the "feelings" of an inanimate object or offended by somebody's personal preference for various types of cake consumption. Obviously, it is illogical and abnormal. The actual reason is very simple but also peculiar: many Norwegians prioritise the opinion of the collective and the "other" over their own opinion and often do not feel comfortable giving an opinion (public or private) which differs, from the collective. Many genuinely don't feel that they have a personal opinion or that if they do, it is relegated in importance in relation to that of the collective view. Many exhibit a fear expressing a different view, so would never dream of expressing a different view to anybody else because they could perceive that as an "insult" or "offensive". We have just read a Norwegian respondent tell us that just expressing a personal preference can be perceived as insult or a "diss" in Norway… even expressing your dislike of certain flavours of cake. This is exactly what the American social psychologist Stanley Milgram encountered during his 1960's conformity experiments with Norwegians, in which the responses "puzzled" him. It's actually quite simple in my opinion; Alternative views are often passively aggressively punished in Norway, which explains the fear. More peculiarly, the linguist is describing this as if it is completely reasonable and logical behaviour.)

Anthony:
So you think they basically conceal their true feelings in the name of "politeness"?

Aksel:
Yeah… I think so.

Anthony:
OK. That's clearly pretence?

Aksel:
Yeah, yes.

Anthony:
Now pretence is also dishonesty, in a way?

Aksel:
Yes… in a way.

Anthony:
So now I want to talk about that. There is a reasoning which happens; "I'm not going to say directly how I feel because I don't want to offend this person." Is that what you were saying before?

Aksel:
Yes I think so… errr… because I think that it's not technically lying… you know? *(Laughter.)*

Anthony:
This is exactly what I wanted to come to so I'm very glad that you have brought it up. Now, I looked up the word "honesty" because I actually thought that there might be a language or linguistic issue talking to nearly all of the Norwegian respondents I have interviewed because almost all of them concealed and said things which were *obviously* knowingly untrue… and then I would say, "Oh, you've just demonstrated concealment and dishonesty" and they could not comprehend that being untruthful is also being dishonest. They literally could not link the two. So I was actually going to ask you, what does the word "honesty" actually mean in Norway? I understand that numerous respondents might "lie" in the name of politeness to avoid hurting "feelings" but then when you point out that

the respondent is being uncandid then they don't understand or look mortified and confused. Do you know what I mean?

Aksel:
Yeah, but in your example before, they weren't really lying, they were just not answering the question.

Anthony:
Now, we're talking about the difference between concealing, lying, pretence... ultimately, they are all, at their base: Dishonest.

Aksel:
Yeah but... err... but not... errr... I mean... but, they weren't lying... that's err... that's the point because, They weren't telling the truth... they weren't, they weren't... but you know... but they weren't saying something that was untrue.

Anthony:
Now, here is the thing. We're now talking about the difference not telling the truth and lying. There are obviously big distinctions between the two?

Aksel:
Yeah, yeah.

Anthony:
But here's the thing though, I've often noticed in Norway, the distinction is not there so much?

Aksel:
Really?

(AN – He sounds shocked... even though he will demonstrate exactly the same behaviours in this very conversation that he is now expressing shock about.)

Anthony:
Well, you just said, you said, "Oh they're not really...".... because in a different culture, if you didn't tell the full truth, you would be perceived as a liar. Like for example, in many cultures... I steal the chocolate cake from the fridge... and then Mum comes home, and says, "Who stole the chocolate cake?" and then I say, "Oh... hmmm... the cake that was in the

fridge, wasn't it? I did see it before…" Now, I didn't reveal to her that I stole it but I also didn't lie, but that act is dishonest, because, I know exactly what happened to the cake – I ate it! So I am being dishonest. So me not revealing that truth is being "dishonest" and could be perceived as lying. But here is the thing though, according to the Norwegian respondents that I have interviewed, "politeness" seems to supersede the revelation of truth, I find. If that's true, why?

(AN – "Lying by omission" is when an individual intentionally omits important relevant information or intentionally chooses not to correct a pre-existing misconception… this is done to mislead and hide the truth. You will shortly see repeated "lies of omission" through this discussion and throughout many conversations in this book. Please look out for them and consider these questions for yourself, when you see them during this conversation; how could somebody with a Masters in Linguistics and supposed high intelligence not understand what the concept of "lying by omission" is and also think that repeated "lies of omission" would go unnoticed? Is this feasible? Could it possibly be an unconscious "auto-response" of avoidance to attempt not to think about uncomfortable concepts, observations and truths about himself and others? Could it simply be that he thinks I am stupid? Could it be that he is simply dishonest? Could it simply be an unconscious normalised behaviour that he is accustomed to? Will the other four interviewees interject and offer any alternative helpful information when a "lie of omission" is told, or will they collude and sit silently? Will the other four members of the group actually endorse "lies of omission"?)

Aksel:
Errr… I guess it's to protect relations and stuff?

Anthony:
Yes, I've noticed that. Going back to the chocolate cake… who cares whether somebody is "offended" that you don't like chocolate cake? Why would you even care if I care or if anyone else cares? Why?

Aksel:
Hmmmm. That was a good question! I guess… errrrrr… I guess if you have things in common, then you have… errr… better relations and then in a town where everybody knows everybody, you want to get on everybody's good side.

Anthony:
OK, so do you think that it's probably linked to geography, population numbers, distribution of small communities across the country... so in a way Norway's geography and demographic has an actual impact, on social interaction? Would you say that that is the case?

Aksel:
That could be, yeah... yeah... I imagine that this would be less of an issue in a big city.

Anthony:
So basically you have to see the person, you "disagree" with every day if you live in a small place... but in a city you never have to see them again... so you don't have to worry about "offending" them? That kind of thing?

Aksel:
Yes, that's kind of what I'm thinking, yeah.

Anthony:
Now, back to not "revealing the truth" as opposed to "lying". Of course, they are technically different but underlying... there is dishonesty at a core level and I've noticed that according to the Norwegian respondents that I have interviewed there is often a big difference, between a "lie" and not "revealing the truth"... and I don't think that distinction is there, at such an extreme level, in other places. I would like to know what the word "honesty" actually means in Norwegian? The actual word.

Aksel:
Yaaaaaa... hmmm...

Anthony:
Because I think, that the word "honesty" seems to be defined and understood in a different way as it is defined in the dictionary. Can we look into this further?

Aksel:
Okayyyyy... that's a good question! (*Laughs.*)

Anthony:
Have you got your phone?

Aksel:
Yeah.

Anthony:
Would you mind looking up the definition of the word "honesty", so we can see how it is defined in Norway?

(AN – The question is asked at 9.22 minutes on the tape… please note the time. It should take no more than ten seconds. The internet is working perfectly… we will now see the expert linguist resist defining the word "honesty".)

Aksel:
OK, let's see!

(AN – after forty seconds of waiting… he seemed to be having trouble… I ask again…)

Anthony:
What's the definition?

Aksel:
Hmmm… This one doesn't give me a definition! *(Laughs.)*

(AN – It is now 10.22 minutes on the tape and he has been searching since I asked, so I interject.)

Anthony:
What dictionary are you reading?

Unanimous group:
(Burst out laughing.)

Aksel:
Well, I went to the University of Bergen dictionary

Anthony:
Bergen? *(AN – everybody laughs at my tone of voice.)*

Aksel:

Yes! Do you have anything against Bergen? (*AN – laughing, as he his joking.*)

Anthony:

Ha Ha, No. I'm not asking you to go to the Oxford English Dictionary but I thought that there might be a national dictionary in Norway?

(*AN – Amanda, his wife, interjects because she senses that this is becoming embarrassing. Amanda is not a linguist, she is an American lawyer.*)

Amanda:

(Turning to Aksel.) Maybe the University of Oslo?

Aksel:

(Turning to his wife.) The University of Bergen took over that one.

Anthony:

Whoa whoa whoa whoa! This is a very important point. Do you have a dictionary?

Aksel:

Errrrrrrr… what do you mean?

Anthony:

Do you have a dictionary in Norway? A national dictionary?

Aksel:

I mean… err… I mean… errr… kind of… sort of… we have like two big ones.

Anthony:

Wait wait wait wait wait!

Amanda:

(Laughing.)

Anthony:

In England we have the Oxford English Dictionary and we have other dictionaries like the Cambridge English Dictionary but we have standard language which the whole country uses, and if there is a definition of a word, then we go to the dictionary and there it is defined and that is the end of it. But I have just asked you to do that and you are having an issue finding the definition of the word?

(AN – It's 11.15 minutes in and he still hasn't managed to find the definition of the word "honesty", he claims.)

Aksel:
Well, yeah.

Anthony:
Well. Why is that?

Aksel:
Well, it's because, because a dictionary is a, well most of them anyway, are not prescriptive… although people perceive them in that way.

(AN – This is turning into a parody now… although, he is being absolutely serious.)

Anthony:
Yes, but there must be an understood standard reputable, which everybody agrees, dictionary in Norway, I guess… or is there not?

Aksel:
No, no.

(AN – The expert linguist just claimed that Norway doesn't have a dictionary?)

Anthony:
That is incredible. I am so glad that I have spoken to you!

Aksel:
(Starts to laugh.)

(AN – It's now 11.43 minutes on the tape and I still haven't got the Norwegian definition for the word "honesty".)

Anthony:
Do you know why? This is just what I was thinking because I observe that

words often seem to change definition in Norway depending on who I speak to. Language and interpretation appears arbitrarily subjective...

Aksel:
Yes.

Anthony:
I find that I often literally have to describe what a word means. Which is why if you say to me, if I ask you, "Do you like chocolate cake?"... if you conceal the real answer, then in the Oxford English Dictionary that is simply "dishonest" but here is the thing in Norway, it appears it is not necessarily dishonest because the word "honesty" isn't understood in the same way as it is understood in the Oxford English Dictionary? So there is no standard definition... unless, of course... can you give me a standard Norwegian definition?

Aksel:
Yeah, well, I mean... I can... err... I can look up "honest" here.

(AN – 12.36mins and no definition of the word "honesty"... it's of utmost importance that we stay very far away from the technical definition and keep it all loose and confusing. This is exactly the technique that Ole used too... it's simple transparent obfuscation and it's a tactic... he will need to stay away from the dictionary definition of the word, sow confusion, and keep dragging it out... I am not sure if he realises that I am fully aware of what he is doing. I find that the respondents don't appear to be used to direct polite exposure of their obfuscation and react in very strange ways, as you will see.)

Anthony:
And where would we look it up in Norway?

Aksel:
Well... there are two dictionaries that I usually use, one is the University of Bergen.

Anthony:
So the "University of Bergen" dictionary, is that like a big one in Norway?

Aksel:
Yeah, it's used to be under the University of Oslo but they decided that they

didn't want to work with it any more so they gave it to Bergen.

Anthony:
So would the University of Oslo actually use the same dictionary now as the University of Bergen?

Aksel:
Yeah, I mean, they do use it still. It's just that it's on the Bergen servers now.

Anthony:
And what's the second one?

Aksel:
The second one is "Ordbok" *(AN – inaudible)* book, is the bigger one.

Anthony:
Oh, so would that one be like the number one in the country?

Aksel:
No no, the other one is. It's for the two written languages.

Anthony:
Oh OK, is that for old Norwegian and new Norwegian?

Aksel:
No no... literally "book language" and "new Norwegian".

Anthony:
Ah... OK, so just, so I understand this clearly. Would you say that there is not one dictionary which everybody refers to in Norway?

Aksel:
I wouldn't say that no.

Anthony:
OK, so where are we looking right now to find out where the word "honesty" is defined? Where are we looking exactly?

Aksel:
Well, I have looked at the Bergen dictionary

Anthony:
OK.

Aksel:
And I couldn't find "honesty" there.

(AN – This is simply disingenuous now. An expert linguist is telling us that he couldn't find the word "honesty" in the dictionary, and he actually expects me to accept this answer. I often encountered this type of behaviour regularly on my journey; this is not untypical or isolated. This normalisation can be seen by observing the reaction of group: the other participants are watching, listening but choosing to keep silent. They offer no assistance or help whatsoever… in fact, it was only his American wife, Amanda, who attempted to assist, even though she doesn't actually speak Norwegian, like the rest of the group.)

Anthony:
What!?

Aksel:
But errr… errr… I mean they probably do have the adjective "honest".

Anthony:
Well, that in itself is incredible!

Aksel:
Well, no, it's not so incredible because "honesty" is a very common word in English but the noun "honesty", is not as common in Norwegian.

(AN – This is misleading.)

Anthony:
Thank you, this is great to know!

Aksel:
The adjective "honest" should be in there… I mean, I did find it there but without the definitions…

Anthony:
Oh, OK. So how is "honest" defined?

Aksel:
Now let's see…

Let's take a time out…

It's now 14.31 minutes into the tape and the linguist has still have not given us a definition of the word "honesty". Let's take a logical look at this now:

1) Contrary to what the expert linguist implied, Norwegians do have a word for "honesty". It is called, "ærlighet".

2) It is:

a) a normal Norwegian word and…

b) it is a commonly used Norwegian word.

3) As a confirmation, I messaged my friend's daughter. It took her eleven seconds to answer the question.

4) It's very important to note that this is a group discussion. Three other Norwegians, who were fluent in the Norwegian language and have a good grasp of English, were all completely passive. They did not correct him; they did not inform me… they just sat silently complicit. You will now read something very peculiar. It's has taken the linguist five minutes to give us a non-answer. It took a sixteen-year-old girl eleven seconds to tell us the truth. I then contacted a member of the same group (not the linguist) two months after our conversation. This is one of the individuals of the group who heard every word of the discussion and sat silently.

Here is our message thread:

Anthony: One more thing, could you tell me what this word means in English? "ærlighet"

Jakob: (Sent me a screen capture of an online translator from English to Norwegian)

Anthony: I have been told that it means "honesty" and that it's a normal Norwegian word and is used in everyday language in Norway? Is this true?

Jakob: (Emojis) I use the translator.

Anthony: But the Norwegian word itself… is it as I say above? I'm just asking whether it is a normal Norwegian word. I'd just like to confirm that it isn't a rare dialect or a rarely used word on an island in the middle of nowhere or something?

Jakob: (after several minutes of writing): Regard to: ærlighet or in personal: ærlig. It is common used word… but if it use in the "right way" as you say to dictionary it's another thing.

Anthony: Right way? All I need to know is if the word itself is a "normal" Norwegian word that is used in Norway in everyday life? I have asked someone else and they answered straight; "Yes, it's a normal Norwegian word and it's used in Norway and it means honesty". However, I need another confirmation, which is why I'm asking you. I am understanding your answer to be "yes"… but just to confirm, is the answer "yes" or no"?

Jakob: I was not so good in school on the term of words /language so best if Aksel or other confirm your question.

Anthony: I'll put it in the most simple way: "Have you ever used that word?"

Jakob: The answer is yes and I have used it many times (emoji).

Anthony: Very good. That is the info that I needed! Thank you!

Jakob: It took some time (emoji) You're welcome (emoji).

The above exchange took a solid ten minutes. Many of the adult respondents seemed to be genuinely scared to answer simple questions in case they gave the "wrong" answer or to "offend", by sharing their opinion which might be different to somebody else's. They often seemed to use mental gymnastics to confuse the questions and definitions to such an extent where they block up and can't answer or communicate in a simple logical way. However, this was often not the case in children sixteen years old and under. Did you also notice that he obviously knew the answer to the question but he relegated his own point of view in deference of Aksel, the linguist, asking me to ask him? This is simply a method of undermining and minimising one's own point of view and perspective. Often, even if a respondent knows the answer to a very simple question, even experientially, they will still undermine themselves, doubt themselves, question themselves and fearfully refer you to what they perceive as someone more qualified than them, to an "expert" or "higher authority", even though they know that they know the answer. The question could be as simple as "Do you like chocolate cake?" Can you imagine how preposterous it would be to answer, "Let me ask a cook for their opinion on this question?"

Look out for how many times you will hear and read the words "possibly", "maybe", "could be" "maybe so", "if", "yes, but not necessarily", "it depends", "probably"… look out for hesitation and very neutral responses to even the most mundane questions, even when asked for their *own point of view*. It's could potentially be a combination of insecurity and fear which could be the underlying reason for this apparent widespread behaviour… the group themselves will explain exactly that, later in the conversation but it will take me a very long time to get to the bottom of this… but we do get there eventually and we do have the "turning point" moment in this conversation, too.

One more thing to consider… could it be feasible that Jakob was colluding with Aksel? Could it be that Jakob intentionally obfuscated to help Aksel save face? Could it be that the group, collectively colluded by keeping quiet, even though they knew that Aksel wasn't being candid? Could they be doing it unconsciously because that is "normal" behaviour to the group? Could they be scared to confront Aksel or embarrass him by revealing the truth? Let's get back to the transcript…

Aksel:
Now let's see…

Anthony:
By the way, I do have a reason as to why I brought this up and will come to that in a moment…

Aksel:
Yes… there is a reason why they wouldn't have a definition here too because it's mainly for spelling… but it does have definitions usually… here we have "honest".

(AN – It's 14.53 minutes into the recording and he is now, finally, going to give us the definition of the word "honest", however, It's technically not the word I

*asked to be originally defined but it will do for the sake of our enquires... we
continue...)*

Aksel:
There is some other ways of saying honest...

Anthony:
OK.

Aksel:
Hmmmm... and it has some examples... errrrrm... And let me see, this one,
it means... errrrrr... *"which you can rely upon"*... hmmmm.

Anthony:
OK, let's stop there.

Aksel:
OK.

Anthony:
In that way, when I ask somebody a question and they don't tell me the
truth, because (in their mind) they are being "polite", that means, literally
by the definition...

Aksel:
(Bursts out laughing.)

Anthony:
According to what you have just given me, I can't rely on the information
that was given to me as being truthful. Would you agree with that?

Aksel:
Not necessarily because they did tell you that they prefer another cake.
(Laughs.)

Anthony:
But I can't rely, on the answer that they have given me to be reliable,
because they are actually being "polite" which means they are not telling
me the *full* truth?

Aksel:
Yeah, they won't be telling you the *full* truth.

Anthony:
So I can't "rely"?

Aksel:
Yeah... they're just telling you what they think they need to tell you, yeah...

Anthony:
And I can't rely on that because they are filtering the answer through a filter of "politeness", so I can't rely on that as the actual truth, because inside they actually have something else which they are concealing, in a way?

Aksel:
Yes, they may well be concealing.

Anthony:
OK, well now that comes down to, by dictionary definition, they are not being honest because you have just said, that it needs to be something that can be "relied" upon?

Aksel:
(*Starts laughing.*)

Anthony:
I can't rely on something if they're being "polite" to me and they don't tell me how they really feel... I can't rely on that answer because "politeness" has muddied the water.

Aksel:
Yeah well... errrrrrr... we looked at the first two meanings of honest.

Anthony:
Yes.

Aksel:
Errmmmmm... the first one was "truthful" which is also the most important one... the most frequent meaning.

Anthony:
OK, just so I understand you, what you are saying is that technically speaking if your words are *technically not lying* then you perceive that as being *honest?*

Aksel:
Errrrrr… Well it is one meaning of "honest", yeah! *(Bursts out laughing.)*

Anthony:
Now I'm asking, you. You're saying that if your words, technically speaking, are not a "lie", then they are "honest". Is that what you're saying?

Aksel:
Errr… errr… errrrr… yeahhhhhhh… yeah! Yeah, I would say that.

(AN – His American wife begins to laugh uncomfortably. The other members of the group are sitting impassively.)

Anthony:
Do you know what, what you have just said… I think it's a really interesting thing to say… Because you're saying, "Well, I didn't technically lie."

Aksel:
Yeah.

Anthony:
But when we went deeper, to the dictionary definition, it was something which could be "relied upon"?

Aksel:
Yeah but that is the second meaning.

Anthony:
OK, well let's go with the second meaning then. If somebody gives me an answer which is technically not a "lie" but it doesn't reveal the full truth it's something that cannot be relied upon… In my mind, that is a dishonest answer, isn't it?

(AN – Many respondents feigned that they didn't understand very simple concepts, when they were confronted directly with logic that contradicted them. We are just seeing a repeat of the behaviour that we saw earlier. It's not unusual but I am still shocked that he is willing to play this game on tape and in front of an audience… that implies, just like Ole previously, that this behaviour is, at least in these situations, normal and accepted… the other Norwegians in the room are passive and all look very comfortable and at ease.)

Aksel:
OK.

Anthony:
Because it's contrary to what honesty is… in a technical sense and in a moral way, isn't it?

Aksel:
OK.

Anthony:
And it seems to me that that is not the case here… am I wrong or am I right, tell me?

Aksel:
Well, I think you're putting too much weight on to the dictionary definition… because the dictionaries job is to capture the ways, words are used.

Anthony:
OK.

Aksel:
So, OK you're going to investigate what does "honesty" mean, what do people use it… OK, well it definitely means "truthful", that's one meaning… And OK "honesty" means, for example, keeping the law and stuff like that… doing your job… Yeah, you can be relied upon… Stuff like that…

Anthony:
OK.

Aksel:
And you try to capture these different meanings.

Anthony:
OK.

Aksel:
And put them into different items in the dictionary there... But er... But yeah... other than that... err... I think... having errr... err... yeah yeah... erm...

(AN – He is talking literal gibberish now and stumbling... he is lost. This is the same thing that Ole did, and for exactly the same reason... too many of the respondents do everything to avoid defining words accurately because then they can be held accountable for their behaviour... so they must confuse and avoid. However, after a few logical challenges it all falls apart and they can't logically continue so then nearly always revert to gibberish. It doesn't matter if you are a master linguist... or a professor... if your argument is illogical it will fall very quickly and you won't be able to justify it under intelligent questioning. He is drowning and it's getting embarrassing so I decided to jump in at this point.)

Anthony:
You seem to be struggling now?

Aksel:
(Bursts out laughing.)

Anthony:
Let's drop the pretence now: do you understand what I mean? If I'm your best friend and I'm going on a date and I say to you, "Listen, do I look good?" And you know that I *don't* look good... and then imagine you say, "Oh, you don't look bad." Let me tell you, even in the name of "politeness", you are being dishonest.

Aksel:
Yeah.

Anthony:
And it's an answer that, when I walk out of that door, the word, the dictionary definition that you gave... I can't "rely" on that answer to

really help me in my day-to-day life because it's not honest. Here is the thing though, the way that I am understanding it, is that you are saying that it is actually honest because it's not a "lie"?

Aksel:
Yeah, would you say, that's the answer was truthful?

Anthony:
Can you read the actual definition again please? Let's go back to the actual meaning.

Aksel:
Yes, OK, Let's look at this… they have listed for meanings… the first one is "truthful"… The second one is "reliable".

Anthony:
OK.

Aksel:
This one is as an adverb… "Properly."

Anthony:
OK.

Aksel:
Hmmm… and this one is a historical use.

Anthony:
Can you do me a favour can you just read the first two again… you said that it was "truthful"?

Aksel:
Truthful.

Anthony:
And then the second one was "reliable"?

Aksel:
Yes.

Anthony:

OK, well, let's base this only on those two definitions. It feels to me that in a lot of the "polite" Norwegian respondents' interviewees' answers probably only 50% is technically "truthful", but not necessarily reliable though.

Aksel:

Yes, but you are still making the common fallacy that, every use of the word has to contain all of the meanings, which is not the case. Say in Norwegian this word has both of these meanings; in another language you may have one word for the first one and another word for the second one. And so "was it honest?" in the sense of "truthful", yes… not necessarily in the sense of reliable.

(AN – Subtext: "I don't lie, it's simply that you are misunderstanding and it's actually a common fallacy that you are making too…". It's exactly the same tactic that Ole used previously.)

Anthony:

Now, let me ask you, with regards to technical definitions, you said that technically speaking it was truthful?

Aksel:

Yeah, which is the most important one.

Anthony:

Now tell me about that technically. Why are the "technical" words being "truthful" more important than the actual answer being reliable? Why is that?

Aksel:

So, for one thing, it is a secondary meaning. Errrrr… and… errrrr… well… why is it so important? Errrr… I don't know… errr… I… I feel that it is more important to be truthful… than to be… errrrrr… helpful. *(Aksel bursts out laughing.)*

Anthony:

OK, let me ask you this question… talking about human relationships now…

Aksel:
Yeah.

Anthony:
Would you want your friend to be "honest" or "truthful"?

Aksel:
Well, I expect him to be truthful… *(Laughing.)*

Anthony:
But that's technically "truthful"… What would your relationship be like with somebody, for example, a girlfriend or your wife or your mother, if you were only "technically" truthful… but didn't reveal the full truth? Is that something that you would be OK with people doing?

Aksel:
Errrrrrrr… hmmmm…

Anthony:
Wouldn't you feel hurt if they only "technically" told you things?

Aksel:
I would prefer it if they were, well *more* honest… *(burst out laughing)*… well… so.

(AN – This is an example of what I have seen repeatedly on my journey. Numerous respondents describe having a range of "truth" which is dependent on a number of factors, for example, how well they know you, whether they consider you a friend or an "outsider" or a "stranger". In their minds a lie can legitimately be considered and described as "honest", especially when the lie is considered as "just being polite" and they will argue that with no embarrassment. It is the public unashamed arguing of this that suggests to me that it could be relatively accepted and normalised behaviour. He knows that he will not be called out by the group… they are sitting completely nonchalantly and passive… they are not reacting or telling him to stop or "calling him out". It's just normal to them? It is obviously normal behaviour for Aksel. There is a tape recorder on and I am a guest in his country. Ironically, it's only his wife, who again, is not Norwegian, who is visibly uncomfortable hearing her husband talk and answer the questions in this way.)

Anthony:
So coming back to politeness and pretence. If you live in a society where,
people value the technical words over the reliability of what's said...

Aksel:
(*Laughs.*) Yes

(*AN – Every time he bursts out laughing or says something nonsensical I remain
impassive and continue talking to him maturely and respectfully.*)

Anthony:
That sounds to me like a very hard place to know where you stand with
people, it also puts you at a disadvantage, for example if you are going on
a date and somebody tells you something but actually, it doesn't really
help you, on a core level, then that seems very unhelpful and quite tough
actually?

Aksel:
Yeah, but with your best friend, I don't think you would care so much about
politeness.

Anthony:
Do you think that the definition for "honesty" would cover a relationship
with somebody that you know well, more than with somebody that you
don't know?

Aksel:
No... I don't think the definition is so important.

(*AN – He will say the complete opposite thing in couple of questions time.*)

Anthony:
The technical "truthfulness" with somebody that you don't know, might
well be there but the reliability might not be there with somebody that
you don't know, because you don't want to "offend" them?

Aksel:
You can say that, I think that with people that you don't know you might
lean to the side of polite and people that you do know so well you don't need
to be so polite.

Anthony:
I think that what you're saying is fascinating... being more "honest" with the people that you know... Would you say that that is the case in Norway?

Aksel:
Yes for sure!

Anthony:
Now would you say that it's really the case in Norway? Because there seems to be this thing where if I ask you whether you like chocolate cake you wouldn't want to say "no" because you don't want to "offend" me in case I like chocolate cake? Now, that same worry or consideration is not worldwide. Somebody, say in France or the UK would just say straight, "I hate chocolate cake" and they would just say that with no consideration to offending anybody. So I'm trying to work out why the consideration to offending somebody over something so trivial and inconsequential exists in Norway at all?

Aksel:
Hmm... well I guess it's a social protection mechanism.

Anthony:
Can you tell me more?

Aksel:
Well... errrr... if you don't diss things people like, they are less likely to not like you back, you know?

(AN – We have finally got some responses that are beginning to sound logical, however, he still can't answer the initial question, which is simply, "Why is an expression of a personal opinion considered a "diss" in Norway at all, by anybody at all?".)

Anthony:
Coming back to geography, do you think that that is something to do with communities and the lay of the land, as opposed to somewhere like London?

Aksel:
Yeah I would say that.

Anthony:
So, in a way, these are kind of devices to make life run smoother because if not there would be a lot of aggression?

(AN – Unambiguous words like "aggression" appears to be trigger words for many respondents, I observe… note his immediate rejection of the word. I replaced the word with "friction", which has a less "negative" connotation (for him) and he is more receptive to that.)

Aksel:
Not necessarily "aggression"…

Anthony:
Friction?

Aksel:
Yeah, you don't get along with people… if you don't like the same things… necessarily… not that that might be a big thing, necessarily… but I mean… all the small things add up.

(AN – This is incredible! He is now explaining why he thinks Norwegians don't like to express preferences and opinions outside of what the collective says.)

Anthony:
Now, the reason why I said all of this is because I have noticed that among the respondents "politeness" is regularly given as a reason for not being 100% honest… and that is a big thing in Norway, where it appears, according to what the respondents tell me, I observe that "politeness" seems to trump "honesty"… and when I say "honesty", I mean honesty in the sense of full reliability… full truthfulness and something which reveals the full truth. It is clear that "politeness" is probably equal to or more important to the hundreds of Norwegians, that I have spoken to… in that, if they were given the choice between being "polite" and being "perceived as being rude" by being honest… they will nearly always choose to be "polite"?

Aksel:
Yeah, probably I would say.

Anthony:
I want to know, how does that reconcile with the true meaning of honesty? That's what I am trying to get to... that seemingly common paradigm in Norway, that I observe so often, really does contradict with the true meaning of honesty... What are your thoughts on that?

Aksel:
Errr... well, errrr... I think... errr... words mean... errrr... errr... you know... the meaning of words is errrrrrrr... errrrrr... is errrrrr... is created by the way we use them and... errrrm...

(AN – You have just read an expert Norwegian linguist confirming exactly what I suspected, observed repeatedly all over Norway and have spoken about previously. This is why I wanted to speak with a linguist in the first place... to confirm my observation as being correct. When logically challenged many Norwegian respondents attempted to change the definition of words based on their personal subjective interpretation and when questioned about this felt and portrayed that as normal, rather than adjust their illogical argument, view or way of thinking. They repeatedly described that this was "normal" and so has the linguist now. If this is normal widespread behaviour then it would obviously completely inhibit effective communication because people would have their own unique narrative of the same experiences, warped through the "lens" of their own "mind", conditional on their emotional state, mental ability and intelligence level. This is the case with all human beings but would be significantly harder if people choose NOT to define words in a standard way but normalise subjective interpretation from individual to individual... which has clearly been described as the case by many of the Norwegian respondents.)

Anthony:
You're a linguist and this is why I wanted to talk to you because I have noticed that some definitions of words... the meaning is fluid, like for example the meanings in England, which have very strict meanings of words... but here, according to the respondents... it's a little bit more... fluid... with regards to, for example, different definitions... you might take part of the definition...

(AN – I was going to complete this with… "which suits you, only…" but he cut me off, probably anticipating my words.)

Aksel:

No, no, no, this is something that we see in all languages. Words have several meanings… because you can't have… well, maybe if you construct a language from the bottom you might have a single word for each meaning… and only that but in natural languages no, no, no… you have words that mean several things… you have words that sound the same… but mean different things because the meetings happen to be related… like, for example, you have words in English like "bank", which, yes, they might mean financial institution, but they could also mean like a "river bank" and those to have nothing to do with each other.

Anthony:
Yes.

(AN – I have directly challenged his logic of interpreting words subjectively and his normalisation of that. This is not a technical linguistic issue, it is a comprehension issue. Could it even be a conditioning issue?)

Aksel:

But the way which we used the words is what's important.

Anthony:
I think that some people… they can use the "technical" definition to conceal the truth, because, as we said before, "Technically, I'm being truthful!" … but actually they're not really being truthful?

Aksel:

Yeah… I'm not sure of everything… but I didn't lie.

(AN – Note that he is now feigning ignorance "I'm not sure of everything" and also speaking in the first person, "But I didn't lie.")

Anthony:
The fact that you didn't technically "lie", do you think that is good enough?

Aksel:
Yes! (*Very confident answer.*)

Anthony:
I've noticed that. Tell me what you think about this, because it feels a little bit dishonest?

(*AN – He starts laughing... and then after a period of silence, answers... I suspect that he is laughing because he is rarely challenged and has been caught out. The rest of the room is still watching and listening silently.*)

Aksel:
I think... well... as I said before you weigh up honesty and politeness and...

Anthony:
In relation to your relationships?

Aksel:
So, if you are close to someone then you prioritise honesty.

Anthony:
OK.

Aksel:
But if you are not close to them then politeness is more important.

(*AN – Note that "honesty" is conditional on the type of interaction. Which means that if one is considered an "outsider" then obviously, they might get "politeness" but not necessarily "honesty", according to Aksel's logic, however, that raises a very important point... who gets which? Who gets "politeness" and who gets the "honesty"? Who gets both? Your wife but not your cousin? Is he not close enough? What are the rules for this? Let's find out! But before we do... do you notice that he is speaking in doublespeak and euphemism? "prioritise honesty" simply means... in plain English... "less lying". These nonsensical word games are fatiguing, boring and tedious, but the group seem very happy and comfortable... let's continue!*)

Anthony:
A lot of the Norwegians that I have spoken to use the words "outsider" and "stranger" and there is a clear distinction between who you *know* and

who you *don't know*… and the stereotype is that a lot of Norwegian communities are quite closed. (obviously, that's a stereotype)… and obviously the implication is that it is only the people very close to you who get the real "truth"… and the people that don't know you get the politeness and pretence. Is there any truth to that?

(AN – The following exchange is incredible; "different roles", "public image" "mask" wearing etc.)

Aksel:
Yes, I guess so. Yes, you play different roles with different people.

Anthony:
Tell me more about that?

Aksel:
When you go to school, you like keep up your public image.

Anthony:
Yes.

Aksel:
Then when you start working you might have one mask on.

Anthony:
Yes.

Aksel:
When you start working your first job and then maybe when you start a new job later your mask changes with it. Yeah…

Anthony:
You have just brought up something amazing. Many of the Norwegians that I have spoken to have described experiencing a lot of anxiety and stress due to the fact that they have to be "amazing" or they feel that they have to constantly project the image of "strength" or they have to have the "cool" clothes in school etc.

Aksel:
Oh yeah!

Anthony:
And things like that…as you say, having these "masks" that they have to have… and it really stresses them out after a while!

Aksel:
Oh yes I, I can imagine, yeah.

Anthony:
I have heard this in almost every person that I have interviewed in Norway. This mask of… of essentially pretence.

Aksel:
Yes, yeah!

Anthony:
Why do you think everybody is telling me this? Do you think that this is an issue that's under the surface in Norway?

Aksel:
It is probably an issue and the cause of anxiety! Yes… yeah…

Anthony:
Going back to the "honesty issue", if we are best friends and say, I'm going on my date and I'm not looking so good… or… we're friends but not best friends and say, I look at you and I ask "Do I look terrible!?"… I *obviously* actually mean *"Do I look good?"*

Aksel:
Yeah.

Anthony:
Now, you say, "You don't look terrible."

Aksel:
Yeah, yeah. That's probably what I would say, yeah!

Anthony:
Now, we know that that's technically "truthful" but it's not helpful to your friend. Now, your friend then goes out on the date…

Aksel:
Yes.

Anthony:
And as they walk out of the door, in the back of their mind, they say "do you know what... I don't feel that I look good... but, on the other hand... my friend has just told me that I don't look terrible"... they would interpret it as being told... "I look good", on some level, would they not?

Aksel:
No, I think they would be aware of it.

Anthony:
Oh, so they're aware?

Aksel:
Yes, I think so.

Anthony:
Do you know what though, they would think, "My feeling is contradictory to what my friend just told me."

Aksel:
No, no, no, no.

(AN – Note that he explains that the "friend" (in this example) would automatically understand the pretence... which implies that these acts are even perceived as acts of pretence to be disregarded by the participants, and thus are unreliable. This totally aligns with the fact that so many Norwegians exclaimed that the people around them are "fake". Strangely, the same people don't correlate high levels of "pretence", which they themselves engage in regularly, accept as normal and defend and propagate, as being part of that "fakeness".)

Anthony:
No?

Aksel:
No, no.

Anthony:
So, they would believe your lie?

Aksel:
No, no, no, no, no! It's not a lie!... and I think they would be aware of it, I asked them whether they look "terrible"... and they say "no" but that doesn't mean that I look good!

Anthony:
Oh, so would that person understand?

Aksel:
Yes, I think so.

Anthony:
OK, how about... what would happen if they actually *believed* you?

Aksel:
No... but I mean... they did. It was true!

Anthony:
But don't you think it would be normal for that person, to think, "They didn't say that I look terrible but they also didn't say that I could improve or that I didn't look so good... they just let me go out"... don't you think it would be natural for them to think "They didn't mention anything... they didn't suggest to maybe, change my outfit, so that means it's reasonable for me to assume that I look good". Is that not...?

Aksel:
No... maybe you can assume that you look good enough... But not great...

Anthony:
Now, let me ask you something... why the hell wouldn't you just say, "Listen! Go upstairs and change, man... you've got much better outfits... this one doesn't look so good... go upstairs and change... you'll feel much better and you're probably have a good date." Why wouldn't you just say that?

Aksel:
Errrrrrrr... because you don't know him that well. So errrrr... maybe er...

Anthony:
Oh, back to the "offence" thing?

Aksel:
Yeah… you don't know how he will feel about being told what to do, you know?

Anthony:
But he has come to you and asking you for legitimate genuine advice?

Aksel:
Yeah.

Anthony:
He's basically saying "HELP ME!" That's the subtext to the question, isn't it?

Aksel:
But he didn't though! (*Laughs.*)

(*AN – His wife laughs too but looks very embarrassed.*)

Anthony:
So, would he explicitly have to say the words "I'm going on a date. I haven't got a clue if I look good or bad and I really need some help, please help me?" Would he have to say it in that way?

Aksel:
Well I mean… if he did… then I would *probably* help him. Yeah… (*Laughs.*)

Anthony:
But if they only said they were a little bit unsure or "Do I look terrible?" Then you'd just confirm?

Aksel:
Yeah, maybe… yeah… errr… cos…

(*AN – His wife laughs nervously again… She interjects… she's been wanting to explode and talk, the other three Norwegians look completely relaxed by his answers. They have not expressed any shock or surprise, yet, the American has and*

I am internally shocked… she has visually been shocked by hearing her husband speak today.)

Amanda:
That is exactly what I have experienced before! Because I don't know sometimes, he, *(AN – talking about her husband sitting next to her.)* I don't know whether he is, because, he's a Norwegian or because he is just straightforward because if I ask him, "Hey, do I look terrible?" He will say "No, you don't look terrible" and that's it… but I need some more concrete advice!

(AN – Let's look at a few phrases she said, she said; "just straightforward" and she also used the phrase "… but I need some more concrete advice!" The use of the word "concrete" implies that she needs a more STABLE foundation and means of communication, which aligns with my general view. Secondly, note her use of "straightforward". I believe that she is conflating, apathy or/and passive aggressiveness with "straightforwardness", which will become more evident later in our conversation. This is something which I have observed throughout nearly all of the interviews across Norway. She is acclimatizing to a different use of words and is now also speaking in euphemism… as you will hear her admit later, to avoid "offence"… she will soon be passive aggressively attacked for speaking… so in actuality, it made sense that she speak in that way. She will now speak about the anxiety that these interactions cause her… which is completely logical and expected by such unhelpful interactions.)

Anthony:
Now let me come to this… by the way this is why it's not so good to have a group conversation! *(AN – They all laughed nervously. I talk to Amanda directly now…)* Just so you know, I would suggest that that kind of interaction would elicit anxiety in you, because you don't know where you stand exactly? You technically have been given information… but it's not helpful to you?

Amanda:
Yes!

Anthony:
You want helpful information?

Amanda:
Yes!

Anthony:
So, the "technical" answer does not help you, when really... the subtext is, for example... you want possibly validation or encouragement?

Amanda:
Yes!

Anthony:
A bit of empathy or a kind word... but instead you just get a "technical", fulfilment of the question?

Amanda:
Yes!

Anthony:
And the subtext is totally missed?

Amanda:
Yes!

Anthony:
Which will elicit anxiety within you because, your needs are not being met by the given answer. So I would say that, obviously, that would elicit anxiety within you. Would you agree or not?

Amanda:
I agree! But the point is... I think, maybe... It's his personality... I can't really link it to culture...

Anthony:
OK well let's not link it to any culture, in fact, let's link it to nobody, let's just say that we're talking about a theoretical answer... So what happens is... you ask a question and you get a technical answer which doesn't help you?

(AN – She realises that she has gone too far. She is beginning to look uncomfortable, like she is scared of offending those around her... her husband will

soon start putting his arm around her and directly undermining her, when she starts to express what she really feels and thinks.)

Amanda:
Yeah…

Anthony:
In your core, emotionally and in actual fact that might leave you with residual anxiety because you didn't get the encouragement empathy, sensitivity warmth that you *really* wanted in the answer?

Amanda:
Yes!

Anthony:
Which means that if you would have wanted that, you would have had to ask a very specific question, you would basically have to give him the answer, to get the answer you want?

Amanda:
Yes! Yeah!

Anthony:
When really all you wanted was reciprocation… I want this person to see me and give me encouragement?

Amanda:
Yes!

Anthony:
But that encouragement is not forthcoming? You just get a "technical" answer. So really, that doesn't help you, as I said it also potentially causes you anxiety. Now, this is what I say; Multiple micro interactions… if a small minor thing like that causes anxiety… Imagine all of those micro interactions in your life and imagine the big things, like when you want to buy a house or when you're really angry and you don't show your emotion… imagine the anxiety that that's going to induce?

Amanda:
Yeah, you're right!

Anthony:
So those interactions regularly, in themselves, could probably cause psychological issues over time but the bottom line is this, you are not getting your feelings reciprocated?

Amanda:
Yes.

Anthony:
But you are getting a "technical" answer which on a human and psychological level is not helpful? So what do you think about that?

Amanda:
I agree! Because you can't just swallow your emotions... you have to express it, but I don't know how... I mean for myself... because, whenever I am sad or angry, I always voice it out... but I think it depends on your personality.

(AN – Note that she does not say, "My husband swallows his emotions" she says "You can't just swallow your emotions" she will only go so far before she feels the pressure of the group... it is tangible in the air and it is a feeling and experience that I have seen all over Norway when real topics and emotions are discussed. Could even the groups laughter be a form of indirect signalling? i.e. "Stop now, act like the group, or else!")

Anthony:
So let me ask you this then... we just had a discussion about honesty and the direction of the discussion... the "technical" definition... really, to hell with the "technical" definition because the implication is clear. Help is required. Give it to them! Why would you *not* give it to them?... and then we come back to the so-called "politeness" reasoning, so I am trying to work out... why is "politeness" more important than honesty?

Amanda:
Is it even politeness? Because...

Anthony:
Or fear of upsetting someone... Why?

Amanda:
If someone that you just met and they say "Oh, do I look good?"... I

wouldn't say, "Hmmm... because she's doesn't look bad... you look normal, alright"... So I would say "Yeah... quite good actually."

Anthony:
And if you didn't think that she looked good... you wouldn't say that?

Amanda:
If she doesn't look good... Or she looks really bad... I would be polite and say "Well, it's a nice dress but it may not suit you."

Anthony:
So you would *imply* that they don't look good?

Aksel:
She is saying that she would put it into soft words.

(AN – Note, the timing of his interjection and note the use of "soft words". Aksel seemingly only considers the <u>technical</u> definition of words as "legitimate" forms of communication and ignores subtext completely? Is this is what Amanda described earlier when she said she "needs more"? Aksel does not know that because he does not seem to comprehend it as important? You will see him, and the rest of the group actually articulate this later in the conversation. This is a major raised issue in Norway during my discussions. I call it, very simply a "lack of emotional reciprocation" i.e., lack of expressions of empathy... you will see it to the extreme shortly.)

Amanda:
Yes!

Anthony:
But here is the thing though, the "Norwegian way", which you just described, did not even put it into "soft words"... It didn't even go there?

Amanda:
Yeah yeah.

Anthony:
That's the difference?

Amanda:
Yes, yes, yes, that is what I have observed as well.

Anthony:
What you have just described is at least implied reciprocation. You at least
give *something*?

Amanda:
Yes, yeah.

Anthony:
But previously it was just the "technical" answer without any helpful
information, implied or real. So, now let me ask you again, if you didn't
give that additional information... that would be dishonest wouldn't it? If
you just told them something which didn't help them when they asked
you directly "do you think I look good"... You would at least say, "I
think you look better in another dress", that is at least more of a helpful
answer... It's still a technical answer but it still gives an additional piece
of information which is helpful, rather than "You don't look bad"...
which is not helpful.

Amanda:
But I think that's the word "dishonest" is so serious! It shouldn't be related to
morality. It's just being so polite... or...

*(AN – She too is now pulling back from the definitions of words as to avoid "offending". I
believe that the environment is not conducive to open honesty, so she is utilising the same
technique of avoiding these trigger words out of fear of offending the Norwegians in the room,
although... she will be informed passive aggressively that she has been offensive shortly... but
we will also address this later in detail when she is interviewed separately, away from the
group.)*

Anthony:
Is politeness synonymous with honesty?

Amanda:
It's not that he's not telling the truth, I think, that is related to "dishonest"...
because "dishonest" is really serious!

Anthony:
Are you saying that it *feels* serious? Like the word itself feels "strict"?

Amanda:
Yes, it's so "strict"! I think that in this situation it is saying what is true but is not giving anything helpful afterwards... *(laughs)*.

Anthony:
OK, this is what I mean about fluid, because we just read the dictionary definition of "honest", and it was something which was "truthful" and "reliable".

Amanda:
Hmmmm hmmm.

Anthony:
It's quite simple.

Aksel:
But those are two different meanings though!

Amanda:
Secondary meanings...

(AN – She is now just supporting her husband... however, you will see that she can't follow his "logic" for long and will end up in shock by what the rest of the group go on to say...)

Anthony:
Yes, secondary meanings but "truthful" and "reliable", I think we can all agree that that is a fair definition of "honesty", wouldn't you say?

Aksel:
Yeah.

Anthony:
I mean... that's what I read in the dictionary just now?

Aksel:
Yeah.

Anthony:
Can we agree now that's the word "honest" translates as "truthful" and "reliable" in our minds right now? Can us three agree on that?

Aksel:
OK! *(AN – sarcastic tone.)*

Anthony:
OK. So tell me how you feel Aksel?

Aksel:
For something to be "honest" it has to be either "truthful" or "reliable" or it can be something proper like, "Oh, it was an honest attempt".. that's another third meaning… but they don't have to be all of those at once.

Anthony:
Right. Can I just try and interpret what you're saying… Is it intention? If your "intention" is honest then that means that it's honest?

Aksel:
Yeah… yeah, that's a good way of putting it!

(AN – He was very receptive to that which suggests my other observation that many of the respondents prioritise "intentions" over affect/consequence/reality might be true.)

Anthony:
OK, so let me ask you… "the road to hell is paved with good intentions", so that is what comes to my mind when we have just discussed "intentions" right now. Just because your "intention" is to be "good" your "intention" is to be honest, in reality you might… now I'm going to use a "technical" phrase… be telling an "untruth". So why don't we agree from now on that we are going to say the word "untruth", rather than "dishonest" so something which you are saying which is not a "lie", but is also not the "truth"… is an "untruth"… and this is something which the British QCs do a lot in court… because they don't like to call anybody a "liar" or "dishonest" so they will say "I put it to you, that that is an untruth". So that takes away the personal blame… So going back to your friends or someone that you don't really know well who is dressed in a certain way… they come to you for help… But even then… there is still

wriggle room... because the bottom line is this: it's just not the whole truth. Do you know what I mean?

Amanda and Aksel:
Yes.

Anthony:
But you had just said, *(turning to Amanda)*... that you would need "more"?

Amanda:
Yes.

Anthony:
(Turning to Aksel) And then we just discussed it... saying that if you don't really know the person, as long as it's "technically" truthful, then that is good enough? And you were very clear about that?

Aksel:
Yeah, yeah, yeah.

Anthony:
(Turning to Amanda) But you have just told me that just being technically "truthful" is not good enough... you need more... is that true?

Amanda:
Yes! I need more!

Anthony:
Tell me about this "needing more"? In your experience do you need "more" often in your experiences in Norway?

(AN – Straight away you see fear come over her... this question scares her and she is obviously not comfortable to speak about her true feelings around the rest of the group... so I encourage her to say how she really feels... I will also raise this point to the whole group directly shortly.)

Amanda:
Errrrrrrr... hmmmmmmm...

Anthony:
You can just say "yes" or "no"...

Amanda:
Yes!

Anthony:
I noticed that there seemed to be a lot of resistance when you answered that question, is it because we're sitting among Norwegians?

Aksel:
(*Interrupts and answers instead of her.*) No, she is just being impolite.

(*AN – They all start laughing. Subtext? STOP NOW! DON'T GO FURTHER! YOU ARE EMBARRASSING US! The group's laughter enables it too... it's an endorsement... this passive aggressiveness is subtle.*)

Amanda:
When I first came here and experienced the culture and the people... they just gave you an answer to that sentence only.

Anthony:
And that doesn't help you?

Amanda:
Well... no, not really! I have to ask more!

Anthony:
When you meet someone, and they don't reciprocate or help you, does that not cause you a little bit of anxiety or resentment? So at the beginning, if you get treated like that, and you're accustomed to a more of an "emotive" response, would you feel a little bit of irritation?

Amanda:
Hmmmmmm... I don't think, it leads to anxiety... not that serious.

(*AN – She is now becoming inconsistent too, because she is forgetting her previous answers and is now adjusting her answers because she is reacting to group peer pressure. Just moments ago, she answered the total opposite to almost the same question. I believe that the "new" answer is inconsistent with what she truly thinks and feels. They both can't be correct at the same time, so which is it? The difference is that she has been COERCED, since the previous answer. The previous answer was before Aksel passive aggressively said that she was "just being impolite" which the group laughed at in response, endorsing him... nothing else changed, the question was almost exactly the same... but the answer was totally different, and that's exactly how it is done... it's very effective. It was all unconscious normalised behaviour. I've see it many many times on my journey... subtle manipulation with participation of the collective usually directed by a single bully who "orchestrates" it... I have almost never seen it fail to work.)*

Anthony:
Irritation? You know... like; "Just tell me how you bloody feel? Just tell me what I'm asking!"

Amanda:
Yeah, yes, yes! Sometimes in my heart I would say, "Hey! Just give me more answers don't make me ask you!"

Aksel:
Yeah... and sometimes in her mouth too.

(AN – The group burst out laughing. I remain impassive. Note, that as soon as she starts expressing her TRUE feelings (talking about her "heart") he passive aggressively undermines her and attacks her... we've seen it before and we will see it again. Note that nobody tells him to be quiet and to let her speak... they all encourage HIM by bursting out laughing, giving him their approval and intimidating Amanda.)

Anthony:
Now let me ask you something... If that happens a lot... That can be quite tough?

Amanda:
Yeah!

Anthony:
For example, let's say that that happened ten times a day... say at university?

Amanda:
Hmm hmm.

Anthony:
After a week, that's seventy times, in a week... that is going to affect you
psychologically, no?

Amanda:
Yes, I think... sometimes I think I have to... find a way... because there is a
cultural shock to me... because I have to find a way to get along, with how to get
along with some of the Norwegians because... it seems that if we don't ask them
something... they don't really reveal their real thinking... or real thoughts.

Anthony:
OK, now what you have just said, what you have just described, from my
perspective it is... concealment... or, it's not totally honest... it's not
helpful... probably the best way to describe it... it's not "helpful" to you.
So for example, if you need something... you're not getting the help that
you need in an answer. So the "answer" is actually damaging to you...
because you are not getting what you need. You're actually being misled
because technically... you're getting an "answer", but it doesn't get you to
where you need to be. It doesn't help you in any way?

Amanda:
Yes.

Anthony:
So would it not be better if they just said nothing? Because at least then
they are not misleading you... I would say that it is misleading. For
example, if there are two directions to go and two roads, the first road, on
the left, takes you to the destination and the second road, to the right,
also takes you to the same destination... but I don't know that and I
decide to ask, "Will the road on the right side get me to X destination?"
Now, if I am told "yes"... but they fail to also mention that there are
twenty-five hazardous mountains and valleys between me and the
destination if I take the right road and it's a simple twenty-minute ride if
I take the easy "left" road... So, yes, technically, I agree that the road on
the right does indeed take me to destination "X" but imagine as I go
through the twenty-five mountains and valleys I meet somebody who says,
"Why didn't you just take the left road?!"

(AN – Amanda bursts out laughing. The Norwegians in the group are simply listening and impassive. You are going to now see a split in the group between the Norwegians and the non-Norwegians, who will split into two camps… this comedic exaggerated hypothetical scenario will cause a lot of frustration and irritation to members of the group who only see it as a technical question and do not seem to comprehend the subtext from an emotional standpoint… it's going to get irrational now, if it wasn't irrational enough for you already… This will give Amanda an insight into how her husband and the others in the room REALLY think… and it will shock her.)

Anthony:
Because some idiot told me "yes" it was fine to take the right road!

Amanda:
But at least, in this example, I think that Norwegians are nice enough to tell you which way is faster. *(Bursts out laughing.)*

(AN – It's very interesting that Amanda, the American, is so sure of what the Norwegians in the group will do and say in that situation… it's also very interesting that it is she that pre-emptively jumps to their defence before any question has been asked… they are still listening. It's important to note that she defended "Norwegians" before she had a real understanding of what "they" might do or say… it was reflex. I had just laid out a scene and scenario… she laid out of value judgement of "Norwegians" being "nice enough to tell…" for some reason… let's continue…)

Anthony:
<u>Can I just ask you, why did you just say "nice"? Why did you use the word "nice" and say that they "are nice enough tell you" about the left road? Why did you use the word "nice"?</u>

Amanda:
Because I think, in this situation *they won't just let you…* Yeah… They won't just say… Yeah, you can go on the right! They might think "Oh, this girl is going up to the mountain."

(AN – She is so sure… why? She doesn't ask the Norwegians in the room, or wait for them to reply… she is judging this scenario by the way that SHE would react… which is wrong. It's irrelevant actually… how she would act has got no bearing on how the Norwegians in the group will respond… she is going to find out shortly… and it's going to frustrate and upset her very much.)

Anthony:
But by using the word "nice" that implies that on the other occasions when people don't give a full answer, that they are not being "nice"?

(AN – I am exposing their rational selectiveness now.)

Aksel:
I think it's about the intention.

(AN – Intentions are fluid and subjective… you can intend anything you want and you can use it as an excuse for anything. Subtext: I didn't mean to hurt you so it's totally fine that you were hurt because it's not my fault and I didn't mean it.)

Anthony:
We will come back to "intention" but, Amanda, you just implied, and basically said, if they didn't reveal that information to you then they would not be "nice"?

Amanda:
Yeah, yeah! Not nice… Yes.

Anthony:
But that happens a lot doesn't it? It happens in many situations when you don't know the person. You have just applied a judgement of morality i.e. "niceness" to the given answer. So what I'm trying to say is this, sometimes when you give a "technical" answer, when somebody wants or needs more information (that would be helpful to them) then withholding it is actually not nice, is it?

(AN – Amanda finished the sentence with me and said "not nice… yeah, right! ")

Anthony:
Would you agree with that?

Amanda:
Yes! I would agree with that!

Anthony:
Now, I'm going to come back to you, Aksel. It feels to me that it might be more appropriate for you to say, (in your mind) "my intention was just

not to offend you" or "not to hurt your feelings"… and "that is very important to me not to be impolite to you"… so that is "better" than the alternative "bad" thing for them?

Aksel:
Well, maybe he has some reason for wanting to go that way! Maybe he likes mountains!

(AN – Amanda burst out laughing in his face but he was being completely serious.)

Aksel:
I mean people in Norway tend to go to the mountains all the time!

Anthony:
OK, so can I ask you this, what you are saying is, maybe that the person likes the hardship of an additional journey across twenty-five mountains?

Aksel:
Yes! Maybe! Maybe he seeks it out on purpose. He just that, I mean, he's also going to that destination but it's not about getting their fast… maybe he wants to just enjoy the ride.

Anthony:
How would you know that?

Aksel:
Well… I wouldn't! But he asked me… "Is that way OK?" and I said "Yes."

(AN – Amanda bursts out laughing again… she is laughing because she knows what's coming but she is also laughing, I expect, with a little bit of embarrassment at the situation but she is going to be proved wrong by her own husband and the rest of the group AFTER she pre-emptively defended them.)

Anthony:
Would you not feel a little bit of guilt that, you know, that he has gone over twenty-five mountains, on the right road, even though you know that he could have got there within twenty minutes by taking the left road? Wouldn't you feel a little bit bad and say to yourself "maybe he

didn't know about those extra mountains on that particular road?"… or would you just say to yourself "it's his own fault!"?

Aksel:
Errrr… no… I mean… if I thought about it… I *might* suggest taking the other way but I mean…

Anthony:
But you probably wouldn't you said?

Aksel:
Well I… I don't know… but I… maybe he has some reason for wanting to go that way! I don't know!

Anthony:
But if you don't know that… you're not aware of that… would you not think to yourself, "Maybe, it's not such a great idea to send him over twenty-five mountains and valleys when actually there's a quick twenty-minute drive left road?"

(AN – Amanda bursts out laughing… before her husband answers the question…)

Aksel:
Well… if it's something like the way… then I guess I might tell them…

Anthony:
But probably not?

Aksel:
No, but… I don't know… It's an imagined example…

Anthony:
I'll give you an example, I would say, that the first thing that you should say, before anything else, the first thing out of your mouth: "Just so you know, there are twenty-five mountains and valleys over there (on the right) and a quick twenty minute route to the left"… That is really helpful information?

(AN – Amanda bursts out laughing again.)

Anthony:
That is the kind of answer I would want!

Amanda:
But from my observation… I think that's they (the Norwegians) are kind inside their hearts… but they are just so straightforward… and then… well, as you said… maybe they are not aware… I have encountered some of the problems which we have discussed in this conversation today with him (turns to her husband)… he sometimes says for example, "You didn't ask so I didn't tell you"… and then I say "What?!"

(AN – When she said "what?!" she put her hands on her head and opened her mouth wide, to mimic a "crazy" look. With regards to what she said though… "straightforward" is defined as "uncomplicated and easy to do or understand"…so that's obviously not what she actually means… in fact you can see the subtext of what she means very clearly by her use of the word "inside" and "heart": i.e. "not seen outside". She also states that, "maybe they are not aware"…she cannot say directly what she thinks or feels deep down because she is scared to offend and feeling pressure, although, she will state how she feels later when she is alone, more accurately. Also, why does she even feel the need to say that "Norwegians are kind inside their hearts" at all?)

Anthony:
Can I just say for the tape recorder… you just put your hands on your head and acted like you were going "crazy" when you said the word "what".

Amanda:
(*Laughs.*)

Anthony:
OK, Aksel, let me ask you a question, twice now she has just described anxiety… about not having the "full" information.

(AN – They both laugh nervously.)

Anthony:
So now, considering that she has just explained that, *now* would you maybe be more inclined to give more information?

Aksel:
Well… errrr… I guess so!

(AN – Amanda bursts out laughing again.)

Anthony:
OK, the "right" road… so with that said… you could communicate it in a different way and say "Oh, my God… you're crazy for taking the right road instead of the left!" but through your body language only… you show him, so your face might be shocked when they indicate that they are considering taking the right road, for example because they would then see in your face, immediately, that they should not go right or that something could be wrong, do you know what I mean?

Aksel:
Yeah.

Anthony:
Amanda, back to what you said, now, with regards to empathy and experience, it sounds like you're experience is different here (in Norway) to what you had anticipated? For example, you get "technical" answers which don't fulfil your emotional needs… you are saying that you have to explain what you need?

Amanda:
Yes.

Anthony:
So, why is that? Is it a different type of empathy or a different type of emotional understanding? Why? Have you got any idea why it's different here?

Amanda:
Do you mean why I need to explain more?

Anthony:
You said that when you came here you had challenges… for example, you would ask something and would not get helpful responses only the "technical" answers?

Amanda:
Yes, only technical answers.

Anthony:
And obviously, you put your hands on your head and demonstrated frustration and anxiety when you said it, right?

Amanda:
(*Burst out laughing.*)

Anthony:
Because then you would have to constantly explain what you need in full, verbally?

Amanda:
Yes.

Anthony:
Now here's the thing, in many places around the world you would not need to "explain". They would just understand…

Amanda:
Aha…

Anthony:
Empathetically… there would be a feeling that they know what you want and they would reciprocate… but you said that you were not getting that in Norway, there was a "culture shock" because of that, you said?

Amanda:
Yes!

Anthony:
Why? In your opinion?

Amanda:
Oh… hmmmm… I think that they… are not just aware of that.

Anthony:
Speaking empathetically, if you don't think about how the other person

feels then obviously you won't be aware of it?

Amanda:
Yes! Sometimes I complain to him, that he does not put himself in my shoes!

Anthony:
Empathy?

Amanda:
I also noticed, for example, we talked about the Norwegian bank thing (turning to Aksel), the other day and normally we ask for one thing, and then the bank will say, "You can't get it." They won't the offer you an alternative "Plan B" unless, you ask for more! (help).

Anthony:
Yes.

Amanda:
I think that that is really the culture here!

(AN – Amanda previously started off categorically stating that this was nothing to do with "culture"... yet now, she explicitly states that it is "really the culture here".)

Anthony:
Back to what you said about judgements of what's "nice"... Do you think that that is a bit mean?

Amanda:
Hmmmmmmmmmmmmm... yes, sometimes!

Anthony:
Yes?

Amanda:
Yes, sometimes.

Anthony:
Just so you know, for me... there is no ambiguity because I would ask myself "why didn't they just tell me?"... They could have saved me so much hassle!

Amanda:
Yeah!

Anthony:
But everything is different and everywhere is different and it feels to me that that initial feeling of hurt might not be considered (or considered in that way) in Norway culture, generally? Someone in Norway wouldn't feel "hurt" or "offended" because, as you said Aksel, the paradigm is that you don't want to get involved, maybe?

Aksel:
Yes.

Anthony:
Like Norwegians want you to just have your autonomy you said?

Aksel:
Yeah, Yeah, Yeah.

Anthony:
So, that "politeness" is so important that it supersedes even empathy and feeling? Is there anything to that, Sir?

Aksel:
Yes, because if you asked me, "Hey, is the right way OK?"… I would say "Yes", and if you wanted more information… Then you would ask me.

(AN – Amanda bursts out laughing and I laugh too… I then address the Norwegians in the group, only.)

Anthony:
So as you can see… us two are laughing… we are not Norwegians… because what we're trying to say after this discussion now… I'll tell you what I'm thinking inside… I know that that guy on the road is basically DOOMED! Twenty-five mountains will destroy him and I know how much hardship he is going to go through!

(AN – I am expressing empathy for the "traveller"… let's see what response this gets from the group. Amanda bursts out laughing AGAIN.)

Anthony:

Why, wouldn't I tell him?! Because I know that whatever risk there is to "hurting" his ego, feelings, or intruding on his so-called "independence" and "autonomy"… it's not worth him going through the pain of twenty-five mountains and valleys unwittingly!

(AN – Amanda starts laughing again!)

Anthony:

That is empathy. That is "me" putting myself in "his" shoes… but if you don't put yourself in his shoes, you will never know that?

Aksel:

Yeah, yeah… but yeah… you know… like the British say "I don't mean to intrude" and ask "Why are you going that way?"

(AN – Note that this is not what was suggested at all. It was not suggested that one should ask "why are you going that way?". However, Aksel is revealing that this is how he would warp the initial question and interpret it internally?)

Anthony:

Right! Is that interpreted as being impolite or disrespectful?

Aksel:

Well, not disrespectful… It's kind of just like none of your business what he's doing that way, you know?

(AN – Amanda is visibly shocked now and her mouth is literally wide open… she turns to her husband and speaks.)

Amanda:

I have a question to ask you *(Aksel)*. So if I am the traveller, for example and I asked you, "Can I go to the right?" You would just say "yes" to me?

Aksel:

Maybe!

(AN – This is genuine and the Norwegians in the group are in full agreement with Aksel.)

Amanda:
Or you would give me…

Aksel:
If I have to come along, maybe I would ask you, why you want to go that way…

Anthony:
Wait, wait, wait, wait, wait! What you have just said is incredible!

Aksel:
(*Laughs.*)

Anthony:
That is incredible, so because you will now personally have to go the hard route…

(*AN – Amanda starts laughing again.*)

Aksel:
Yeah.

Anthony:
Then you'd offer that information?

Aksel:
No, no, no.

Anthony:
Errr, yes yes, yes… that's what you just said! (*AN – by implication.*)

(*AN – Myself and Amanda start laughing together.*)

Aksel:
No, then I asked, why do you want to go there?

Anthony:
Yes, but you have just opened another layer, because you asked, "Why would you do that?" But only because YOU were personally going on the journey?

Aksel:
Yes, because now it's my business too! *(AN – big laughter.)*

(AN – Amanda bursts out laughing again.)

Anthony:
But isn't that selfish?

Aksel:
No! *(Laughing.)*

Anthony:
Tell me, why is that not selfish?

Aksel:
Because… I mean… If *you* want to go a hard way… you know some people like to do that, but it's none of my business what do they do!

Anthony:
But *you*…

Aksel:
Yes, if I have to come along… I want to know the reason why we are going this way!

(AN – Amanda is getting visibly angry now.)

Amanda:
I mean… my question is, you are just a stranger… I am just a traveller… I don't know… and I just ask you… really *you!* Aksel! *(AN – she raised her voice.)*

Aksel:
Yeah, yeah.

Anthony:
But he has already answered this for the last half an hour, Amanda…

Amanda:
(Turning to him)… You would just say "yes" and you wouldn't tell me?

Aksel:
Possibly, yeah…

Amanda:
Errrr… OK…

(AN – Amanda is visibly upset.)

Anthony:
Wait, wait, wait, stop, stop, stop… he has already answered this and he just told you that he would probably say, "Yes the right way is the right way"… you *(AN – Turning to Aksel)* just told you (Amanda) that he wouldn't tell you anything else.

Amanda:
I just wanted to clarify.

Anthony:
He has just said it repeatedly for half an hour.

(AN – Amanda has only now just realised that he is talking about HER… personally… that he would treat her in the same way he would treat everybody else and offer no helpful information unless he personally had to take the harder route. She literally couldn't comprehend what he was saying because she was CONVINCED that the group would certainly offer the information to the "traveller", and she stated that categorically… it has taken her quite a long time to work out, even when he has been very clear, that, no, she was wrong. Obviously, that will be shocking for a wife to hear… but now she will hear the others in the room say the same thing and she will become angry… but now she has to stick or retract with the original "nice" judgement… what will she do? Let's find out.)

Aksel:
I might add that you could go that way, its faster…

Anthony:
Amanda, can I ask you, why are you now shocked? Has it just dawned on you? I can see that you're sitting there with your mouth literally wide open with your hands on your head absolutely gob-smacked… He has just been saying this for half an hour… why are you now shocked?

Amanda:
Because I thought that when he answered before maybe he put himself into another person, in this situation. That's why I was curious so I asked him again!

Anthony:
Yes?

Amanda:
As a "stranger" and really him! That's why I asked… but… he really gave the answer! And it's just… (*laughs nervously*)… well… it's just…

(*AN – Amanda sounds really hurt and disappointed… the rest of the group are looking at her like she is crazy.*)

Anthony:
Do you understand now what I meant about interpretations of "dishonesty" and actions (or non-actions) which are potentially "mean"?

Amanda:
Yes!

Anthony:
It appears to me that that's what you're thinking now because you look absolutely shocked?

Amanda:
I'm thinking now… did you experience something like this that is making you ask this question?

(*AN – Amanda is in complete shock. She looks disgusted and isolated… her husband finds it all funny and the rest of group are impassive and completely non-reactive.*)

Anthony:
I will answer that question but first I want to ask you… you look absolutely shocked, why are you looking so shocked?

Amanda:
Because he is my husband! And if somebody really asked him he would

just say "Yeah you can go right" without giving any further suggestion or help!

(AN – Now she is angry and horrified. She heard the words before but she refused to connect them with reality. Now she has connected them and realised what her OWN husband has said. She has also seen the impassiveness of the group.)

Anthony:
Why would you be offended by that?

Amanda:
Because that's not helpful enough!

Anthony:
OK. That's what I've been trying to saying all along isn't it?

(AN – Her husband has just told her to her face, without any embarrassment or shame, that he would also do the same thing to her and now it has dawned on her what she is dealing with. It's actually horrifying to watch this behaviour and it's even more horrifying to watch the passive group response. It's also interesting that she was DEFENDING the same attitudes just minutes ago. She was defending a FANTASY in her head which was not based on reality... now she has seen and heard the reality and she is flabbergasted!)

Amanda:
But obviously some people would think that... but obviously he (Aksel) does not think that...

Anthony:
So, is that a problem?

Amanda:
Yes! *(She bursts out laughing.)*

(AN – Amanda adds in a furious tone. Aksel is completely oblivious, as is the rest of the room.)

Amanda:
Yes, it is a problem.

Anthony:
Why do you think it took us so long to get to that understanding? By the way... *(turning to Aksel)*, do you understand what she's saying?

Aksel:
Errrrrr... yeah... I guess so.

Anthony:
Is that a "yes" or "no"?

Aksel:
I mean, Yes... she er she she... erm, she was thinking... That I was just assuming the role of an average Norwegian and imagining... What they might do...

Amanda:
No no no no!

Aksel:
But now, it's like...

Amanda:
It's really you!

Aksel:
I mean now she knows that if it was also you... that you would also do it *(talking about himself)*.

(AN – Expressions of empathy are not something which I have regularly observed on my journey and we will later speak to a teacher who will tell us with no embarrassment that "Norwegians don't think from other people's perspectives and that they think of themselves", when I asked her why I am observing such a seemingly low level of empathy across the respondents... I will now put this to them directly and see if it elicits any kind of reasonable human response.)

Anthony:
This is what I think... if empathy is not a priority, over time the empathetic thoughts, feelings and ability will inevitably go down... and it will refer to the "technical" answers... I have encountered this so much in Norway, the empathy... seems to be suppressed... but the "technical" response seems to be elevated?

Amanda:
Do you mean here?

Anthony:
Yes! So, the whole point is though, which is why your mouth is open wide and shocked, is because now you have got the shock… just like I did at the beginning… because now you understand it… because for me it is shocking initially, too. To you… finally you've got that it's shocking… but obviously *(AN – turning to the Norwegians)* it's not shocking to the people that are sitting here… it's their normal way of life?

Aksel:
Yes.

Anthony:
For me, that is the most intriguing amazing thing! It's peculiar! Can I put this to the group? Is this the first time that you've ever thought about this?

(AN – Amanda has a confused look on her face… she still can't comprehend what she has heard her husband say.)

Anthony:
Amanda, why have you got a confused look on your face?

Amanda:
Hmmmmmm… because I am surprised! That, when it came to the two extreme ways, the Norwegian people will still say, "Yeah, you may go to the right"… and then you will have to go twenty-five mountains or something like that, because what I have encountered, which is daily life stuff, when it comes to the things like outfits and clothes, that's one thing… but when it's the big things…

Anthony:
Yes because this is now potentially a life or death situation?

Amanda:
Yes! And then they will still say something like that! I think, it's kind of a surprise to me…

(AN – she sounds very disappointed at seeing this side of her Norwegian husband and friends.)

Anthony:
And is it possibly, more than "surprising", that it is hurtful?

Amanda:
I'm shocked.

(AN – she is obviously hurt.)

Anthony:
Is it a little bit dishonest?

Amanda:
I can't say "dishonest".

Anthony:
Unhelpful?

Amanda:
Unhelpful, yes.

(AN – Aksel bursts out laughing!)

Anthony:
But can I just say something... if someone is so unhelpful... that is not cool?

(AN – Aksel bursts out laughing even louder.)

Amanda:
Not cool.

Anthony:
Here is the point. That pretence and "politeness", it's a barrier to truth, openness and helpfulness, isn't it?

Amanda:
Hmmm hmmm.

Anthony:
You have just explained it yourself, and so have I, and in my opinion, that would cause anxiety and confusion in day-to-day life in Norway, would it not?

Amanda:
But I think that Norwegians don't feel that way…

Anthony:
… Probably thinking "you oversensitive crazy foreigners!"

(AN – The group burst out laughing. Nora, who we haven't heard from yet, interjects. I am regularly asked by Norwegians, "What's your goal?" as many Norwegians describe themselves as very "goal orientated". However, what Nora will say, is obviously untrue; "To get a complete answer we need to know the goal of the question?" … to get a complete answer you just need to answer the question completely and honestly… you only need to know the "goal" if you want to adjust or orientate your answer around that "goal". However, if you don't know the "goal", then you can't easily adjust your answer, especially if you anticipate that you will not be answering candidly… I am presuming that a conversation like this is a scary place to be if you have a tendency to answer with half-truths too… let's continue though… I will now answer their original question directly, although it could cause them a little bit of embarrassed after our conversation today!)

Nora:
To get a complete answer we need to know the goal of the question?

Anthony:
OK, let me answer your question. Amanda asked the question, "Was this something that I have experienced in Norway?" and I am going to answer this question and it comes back to where we started which is the word "honesty". So I asked hundreds of Norwegians questions… kind of like a questionnaire… and I asked "What are the five traits of Norwegians?" … and one of the number one things that came up regularly was "honesty" and "honour".

Aksel:
Ahhhhhhh…

Anthony:
"Honesty" and "honour" also came up in conversations with the Norwegians that I spoke to. Can I ask whether this is what you would have expected?

Aksel:
Yeah, I would expect that.

(AN – Reader: would you say that you have witnessed "honesty" during this conversation? Do the members of this group seem honest to you?)

Anthony:
Because it's an important part of your identity and culture?

Aksel:
Yeah.

Anthony:
Honour? Morality?

Aksel:
Yeah... being morally correct and saying what people expect to hear.

(AN – Being "correct" and moral is equated with "telling people what they expect to hear". This is what I have regularly, observed on my journey. I am literally speechless and look shocked... I didn't hide my shock... they can see that... Aksel then adds, when he realises...)

Aksel:
As long as its technically correct, you know. *(AN – He bursts out laughing.)*

Anthony:
During my questioning of Norwegians the top traits which have been described by the Norwegians have been "honour", "truthfulness" and "integrity"... that's been one of the first things that people say. However, I have been speaking to them and there has not been a single example, not one, where somebody has given me a real life experience of "honour" or "truthfulness". Every story has been negative experiences, bad experiences of everyday life, and then I asked them specifically "You mentioned that truth and honour are important parts of your life, and a very big part of

your culture and society… can you please give me one example of one of those things from the last day, week, month, and year?" Because obviously, if it is such a big part of Norwegian culture you would be able to give me hundreds of examples, right? No… zero! Then, instead of telling me a single good thing… they will literally start recounting bad stories again. And I will say "Thank you, but I specifically pointed out to you that you haven't given me any examples of "honour"… you have literally been giving me the total opposite, and I'm asking you, why do you think that is?" And I always get the same answer: "I don't know."

Aksel:
Yeah… So there is an example of being truthful.

Anthony:
Exactly. That's what I'm saying…

(AN – Amanda starts laughing. I realise that they don't have the insight to be able to discuss these kinds of serious subjects without constantly giggling and being irrational, but I continue nevertheless.)

Anthony:
And I call it "the honesty paradox", because when you get past the pretence and bullsh*t, which you get a lot of, you then nearly always get to complete honesty and openness.

Aksel:
Yeah.

(AN – Note they don't react with anger to direct insinuation, only trigger words that THEY perceive as painful, which will usually be linked to ego. Specifically, if you don't use the TRIGGER word, then you can almost say anything with zero outward emotional reaction, especially if it is said indirectly and with a polite tone of voice.)

Anthony:
But you have to circumvent that nonsense to get to the truth.

Amanda:
Hmmm hmmmm… *(Giggles.)*

Anthony:

And that is something, which is a paradox in my opinion… Because guess what? It is not honest. It is concealing. In my opinion it is also dishonesty… But ironically when you get through that dishonesty then you get the most honesty ever. Like for example, the conversation that we are having now is incredibly deep… you won't get this in the UK… You wouldn't. So that's why I wanted to ask you… that's why I wanted to speak to an expert linguist and asked whether there was a word issue… with words like "honour" and "honesty"… because I thought that maybe the actual words themselves are different here… and it's really funny what you said about the dictionary… we had an issue just finding the definition of the word "honesty". So maybe there is something in that?

Aksel:

Yeah… I don't think so. I just think that the noun is derived from the adjective so you might as well just look up…

Anthony:

But here is the thing though. I still think that even now, speaking with you that you have a different definition to "honesty" than to me. Our definitions and understandings are completely different.

Aksel:

A little bit.

Anthony:

(I look at Amanda and ask her) Are our definitions of honesty different?

Amanda:

I think they are a little bit different.

(AN – I think that she is saying that just to help the Norwegians save face and is embarrassed to go against her husband anymore.)

Anthony:

But I think they became more aligned at the end when you said Amanda, that you were shocked if you would be sent over the twenty-five mountains? But Aksel wouldn't be shocked…

Nora:
I want to go the best way... then I will ask for it!

Aksel:
Yeah!

Nora:
It is my responsibility to ask for the best way!

Anthony:
So you don't...

Nora:
And then you can give me the right answer!

Anthony:
So you think that the onus is on *you* to ask the right question and there is no expectation that they should understand you?

Aksel:
Yeah, Yeah, Yeah.

Anthony:
It sounds to me like empathy is not something which comes naturally... You don't even think what the other person is thinking? You only give the technical answer... Because it sounds like, you think only for yourself?

(AN – Can you believe that this question/insinuation has elicited nothing except agreement?!)

Aksel:
Yeah.

Anthony:
You don't think about what someone else is thinking? Is there a barrier there?

Aksel:
Maybe.

Anthony:
You just said that didn't you?

Nora:
It's very annoying for me when I ask a question and somebody gives me an answer which I am not asking about… because they think they know what I am thinking!

Anthony:
Wow!

(AN – Looking towards Aksel.)

Anthony:
Do you relate to what she's saying?

Aksel:
Yes! I agree! *(AN – emphatically.)*

Anthony:
Now we're getting somewhere! Now we're getting to the reasons behind… but wait a minute… There is a contradiction there though!

Aksel:
No…

Amanda:
Anthony, can you clarify what Nora's saying for me?

Anthony:
Yes. She has just said that when, for example, when a question is asked by her, she requires only the "technical" answer and nothing more or they get annoyed… when they don't hear the exact answer *only*.

Aksel:
Yes.

Anthony:
I would say this though… There is a judgement call… a choice… there is answering the question and then also an option of answering the question

and giving helpful information. You can do both! Would that annoy you, Nora?

Nora:
I want to spend my time and effort achieving what I want to achieve… rather than listen to what other people think about it!

Anthony:
So that means what?

Nora:
I have a goal.

Anthony:
So expressing that information is not perceived as helpful by you but it is actually perceived as an *intrusion*?

Aksel:
Yes!

Anthony:
Did I get that right?

Aksel:
Yes, yes!

(AN – Amanda's mouth is, yet again, open wide…she is in shock… I turn to her.)

Anthony:
Does what they're saying make sense to you now, Amanda? What we would perceive as helpful advice they perceive as an imposition… as in… you are "imposing" on them, I believe you are all saying, right?

Amanda:
Yes, yes!

(AN – She finally understands and is in total shock, visibly.)

Nora:
It's the Janteloven!

Anthony:
How do you think that this links to the Janteloven?

Nora:
Because if I asked a simple question... and he is focussing on giving me lots of information... Then I will wonder about his motivations... or whether he just wants to show me that he knows his stuff! Or is he just saying it to show that he cares about me? Or something else?

(AN – Word meanings are warped, questions are warped, intentions are questioned... fear-based conditioning and trauma responses to mundane everyday events, obviously... Janteloven.)

Anthony:
OK, now... *(AN – turning to the Norwegians in the group, I tell them, "watch this." And then I address Amanda...)* Can I ask you something, Amanda? What they have just said... does it sound crazy? I'll tell you why, there is so much analysis over something so small and simple. Why would you not just say, "Yes, you can go to the right but be aware there are twenty-five mountains over there?" What's so bad about saying that? What are your thoughts?

Amanda:
Yes I agree! You shouldn't have so much analysis behind that!

(AN – Remember that myself and Amanda are only 33.3% of the room... we are in the MINORITY... we are the "crazy" ones in this room. The Norwegians in this room are cohesive and aligned... they consider us "crazy", emotional and illogical)

Anthony:
But I think that Nora has just pointed out that the Janteloven has been ingrained in their way of thinking, which we don't have, so that for me... It's so peculiar to hear all of this analysis for something so simple.

Amanda:
Yes.

(AN – starts laughing.)

Anthony:
It would just be a ten-second comment but it really does sound like it would be perceived as disrespectful and "imposing" if you just give that helpful piece of information?

Amanda:
Too much help! *(Laughs.)*

Anthony:
Help, yes… is it about too much help?

Nora:
No, I would think about their motivation to speak so much. I want them to only listen and hear what I am speaking about and then answer.

Amanda:
Oh… like just stick to the question?

Nora:
I want a simple exact answer!

(AN – Completely rigid thinking – zero flexibility.)

Anthony:
OK, let me ask you this. I'm going to give you a response to what you have just said… it sounds like a trauma response? It sounds like, for example, I can only get this much information and no more. Because if I get more, it might offend me or hurt me, cause me anxiety, make me question motivations and to me that sounds like a trauma response. Now let's look at the other side, let's say that somebody listened to you and they gave you the exact specific exact answer… exactly the answer what you asked for… But just for five seconds added on "by the way it's really tough on the right hand side because of the mountain range". What would be so…?

Nora:
If I need more information I can use the internet or books!

Anthony:
Now, I want to know. What is so bad about getting that information from somebody else? And also, would you not think that not everybody would have done that previous research on the internet or by reading books about the mountains and the directions? Especially if they weren't even aware?

Nora:
No, because I have another focus. I have a goal.

(AN – Living in an isolated bubble? Incredible!)

Anthony:
Oh, so are you saying that it's a time restraint issue?

Nora:
Maybe. If I had time… To ask you tell me about the mountains, tell me about this way…

Anthony:
But the communication would only take five or ten seconds? It might even take three seconds… just to give you that additional potentially lifesaving information?

Nora:
Too much information!

Anthony:
Too much information?

Nora:
Too much information… because I have a goal!

Anthony:
Is that "too much information" *stressful for you?*

Nora:
For me, it is!

Anthony:
Ah… right.

Nora:
I want it simple!

Anthony:
You just want the answer?

Nora:
I'm a structured person.

Anthony:
That sounds illogical though?

Amanda:
Hmmm.

(AN – I noticed that Amanda has reacted strangely to Nora.)

Anthony:
How does it sound to you, Amanda?

Amanda:
Yeah, it's… weird!

Anthony:
It sounds so ruthless. It sounds like if you fall off the cliff and die, it's your own fault and that's the end of it. I just don't see that if you can prevent pain and hardship, why would you not prevent pain and hardship? And if it only takes four seconds to do that why would you not alert them? I think that this comes down to simple empathy. As you said, Nora, your focus is your own goal only. For example, you could also say to yourself <u>"I am busy, I only want to know the answer, but for the sake of the other people that come down this road who may not be aware and may potentially go through hardship, I will listen to or share ten extra seconds to get that information because maybe someone else won't be as strong and informed as me."</u> So maybe it might be OK to get that information for like ten seconds… It's ten seconds out of my schedule, yes… even though I am busy… It's not so bad… Now, Amanda, you are

nodding enthusiastically... Why? Are you agreeing with me?

Amanda:
Yes, I agree with you! I want to clarify one more thing...

(AN – Amanda is now insecure about herself as she learns more about the thought processes of the people around her. She realises that her previous innocent comments and questions might be perceived as an insult or an inconvenience to other Norwegians in her life, and asks them if she is perceived as "rude" by the Norwegians... She now perceives herself as potentially rude after hearing how the Norwegians in the room actually think and wants clarity from them... she asked a question and it is ignored by the rest of group.)

Further discussion

Anthony:
No no... the obvious anticipation is that you give that information because you *assume* that they don't know.

Amanda:
Right!

Nora:
Why, why?!

Aksel:
Why would you assume such a thing?!

(AN – I explained in EXPLICIT detail the exact logic and reasoning as to "why?" less than sixty seconds ago. I will repeat it again for the reader:

"... I am busy, I only want to know the answer, but for the sake of the other people that come down this road who may potentially go through hardship, I will listen to ten extra seconds to get that information because... because maybe someone else won't be as strong and informed as me."

The group seemingly cannot comprehend this and have issues comprehending empathy? It's as if they can only think about themselves? This is strange because they obviously think of the "collective" (others) if it is a technical issue but seemingly only when emotions and empathy are not required. So this suggests that it's specifically avoidance of EMPATHY and emotions which causes a kind of "shut down"…and when I say shut down, I mean complete shutdown. They are genuinely confused… they are being serious when they ask "Why?!" They don't know the answer because the language of empathy that I just spoke is a language that they don't seem to understand… it's seemingly a completely different operating system… Amanda is exasperated and interjects.)

Amanda:

That is so Norwegian! That is so true! When I first met Aksel as a friend and then I told him that I am leaving for America… and my luggage was like 30 kg… 30 kg… and then he would just wait there! He said "goodbye" and just waited there… I am waiting too, because I am thinking that maybe he would be helpful enough to take my luggage downstairs… and then I just asked him hmmmm… I just waited a bit… and then I asked "Can you please take my luggage downstairs!?" … and then he said, "Oh yeah"… and I just wondered… at that moment, because you know in the UK, you have like the "gentleman" thing… you are helpful and some things like that but in Norway it is totally different!

Anthony:

It sounds to me like he did not think that you needed that help because you didn't "technically" ask for it?

Amanda:

Yes! Because he said in Norway, for example, if you're walking with a girlfriend and the boy offers to help then the girl would think, "Oh, you find me *stupid*! I can carry it myself!" Or something like that. So just now Nora said, "Why do you assume that I don't know about the left road!" Well, not if I ask you! Is there another way, so you answer me. So that is the same thing!

(AN – In addition to a strange warping of reality this is all sounding very neurotic: "Neuroticism is a long-term tendency to be in a negative or anxious emotional state.")

Anthony:

Can I just say that this sounds like the most inflexible, rigid and weird way of thinking about something. Would you agree with that, Amanda?

Amanda:
Yes. I think so! (*Laughs.*)

Anthony:
So here is the thing though… flexibility… now we're going to talk about flexibility.

Nora:
There is also the fact that we are taught to do things by ourselves and not rely on other people. We don't want to impose on people and we want to solve our own problems.

Anthony:
Do you believe that this "philosophy" that you are indoctrinated in is compatible with normal human nature?

(*AN – Aksel chuckled under his breath when I said the word "indoctrination".*)

Anthony:
Would you say that it's not normal human nature to inform a person enquiring about two roads, whilst you are aware that one of them is life-threatening, that you should tell them, even if they did not ask about potential "threats" explicitly and secondly, if you had 30 kg cases and you were not capable of carrying them, that they should help you if they are able without having to be explicitly instructed to? Would you not say that those things are just obvious natural human behaviours and common sense?

(*AN – Nora does not answer but Amanda does instead.*)

Amanda:
Yes! I think it's just natural but even, for example the 30 kg… some guy, some Norwegian would say, "So you should ask me first and then I will help you!" On the other hand I think "why can't they ask me and see that I need help!" (*Laugh.*)

Anthony:
So, you just heard now that those two situations *we* perceive as "normal" and no problem… but you (*AN – the rest of the group*) have told me you you may have been indoctrinated by the Janteloven? Now, you didn't

354

technically use the word "indoctrinated" as you used the word "taught"…
but it sounds like the Janteloven could have suppressed your normal
empathy levels to such an extent that you perceive being helped as a "bad"
thing… being assisted as a "bad" thing… or being given advice as a "bad"
thing… and not just a "bad" thing… you find it traumatic… like a
traumatic event… It sounds like the Janteloven has made being helped as
perceived as "bad" thing… being assisted as a "bad" thing… being given
advice as a "bad" thing… and for me, that is obviously a trauma response
because, obviously, if you can't just have a conversation, and mention for
just ten seconds "Oh, it's dangerous to the right", and it's only ten
seconds out of your life and that really causes you that much anxiety and
analysis… for me that is clearly a trauma response. It's not a normal
response, is it?

Amanda:
Yes, exactly!

Anthony:
Possibly due to this Janteloven? It really sounds to me that this is not
normal… this is a trauma response. Because I think that's most normal
people in the world that have not been taught the Janteloven… honestly,
they would have no problem in just saying "oh by the way…" It would be
a very quick conversation and it would be nothing. And somebody would
not feel "attacked" by that. Never! They wouldn't feel "undermined" or
"offended". They would actually be so grateful…

Amanda:
Yeah!

Anthony:
Even if they were busy, even if they knew… they would just say, "Oh
thanks, I'm aware I just wanted to climb the twenty-five mountains today,
thank you very much"… but they would understand, that he was just
potentially trying to save my life. They wouldn't feel "attacked", surely?
They wouldn't think "Oh! How dare he intrude on my independence and
my autonomy by offering information!?!" and become anxious… That's
an irrational abnormal response isn't it?

(AN – Benji has not said a single word… he interjects.)

Benji:

I would never think the thought that it would be dangerous... every Norwegian can do it, so... yeah... I don't know... *(AN – As stated, the THOUGHT doesn't even cross his mind.)* If I saw a tourist doing something dangerous, then maybe I would say something to stop being dangerous but not a Norwegian.

(AN – Myself and Amanda burst out laughing. The group can't comprehend what they are signalling: 1) I only think about myself 2) I cannot comprehend what you are saying 3) I have zero self-reflection, because even after this conversation I have no problem admitting that I don't even THINK about others at all. It's like they don't realise how they are perceived: no comprehension of subtlety and nuance at all?)

Further conversation

Anthony:

OK, so let's see... in this symbolic allegorical metaphorical theoretical story that the twenty-five mountains on the right are dangerous... with regards to this thought experiment we all agree that the valleys and mountains on the right hand side are dangerous.

Aksel:

If you don't know them, then they are probably a tourist.

Anthony:

Wow, this is great! "If you don't know them they are probably a tourist"... tell me about that?

Aksel:

Well, if you live in a small town then you probably know people and you can probably... you know if they speak if they have a local accent...

Anthony:

Or the colour of their skin maybe?

(AN – He is very uncomfortable with the question. I have often found that raising any kind of question which alludes to racism in Norway will usually see a very predicable response... uncomfortable, tight jaw, glazed eyes, red face... even at the mere mention of the single word; "racism".)

Aksel:
Yeah, yeah… well that's one way…

Anthony:
Now we have come down to the whole story of the book… which is… the "outsider"… the "tourist"… the "foreigner"… the "stranger" seem to have a TOTALLY different interaction with average Norwegian society than the a Norwegian citizen. They have a totally different set of rules *(AN – Amanda starts laughing at this word)* and expectations, with interactions… Benji just said categorically "If I knew it was a tourist… I would say… but if not I wouldn't…" and then Aksel just said "Oh, but I would know if they were tourists"… you both just said that you would differentiate between those people from outside the community and inside the community, correct?

Aksel:
Yeah.

TURNING POINT

Anthony:
I believe that many Norwegians are not really "allowed" to say how they feel to such an extent that it builds up, and it makes it more intense than it really is but I think it's counter-intuitive because keeping your views inside makes you rigid, it makes you more excluding of "outside" people but trust me if you feel understood and respected then usually things will be OK. But the Norwegians that I have spoken to feel so mistreated for so long, stereotypes are imposed onto them, for so long, that in a way I think that they start believing them about themselves… so that confusion is there… So they may just say to themselves, "Do you know what I'm just going to be quiet. I'm just going to speak to my family and to my best friend and I'm going to keep it all inside. If somebody asks me then I'm not going to tell them how I really feel, because it's not worth it!" … When I walk into Oslo Airport there is a bookshelf, which has multiples of about five or ten books… but loads of them have stereotypical derogatory pictures of so-called Norwegians… "emotionless", "sad", "drunk"… I asked the lady in the shop if she had any books on social interaction or Norwegian culture… She said "Yes, we've got these books," and I said, "But I don't want any stereotype books or comedy books, I

don't want any humour… I just want a real book which is serious." And the bottom line is that they didn't have a single book to give me… not a single anthropology book… not a serious single book on Norway or Norwegian culture, beyond cook books, WW2 and the usual travelogues… but then she said, "Oh, we do have this the social guide"… and I said, "No, they're offensive." She then laughed and said, "No… but it's true, there's a lot of truth to this!" And then I said, "Do you think that THIS is true?" And then she said, "Well there's a lot of truth in it!" And I said "OK, watch this" and I covered up the title to just show the pictures of the emotionless "Norwegians". And I said, "In my opinion if you took this to a doctor it would describe a clinical psychopath… I have met many Norwegians and I don't think that many of them were psychopaths… to be honest, I think that this is offensive and it doesn't help… and I think that it's bullying". She then had realisation on her face and said, "You know what? I've never really thought of it like that… I'm really sorry that these books are here because you know what? You are right… we don't even like these books!" And then I said, "But you laughed and you're the one who recommended them to me!?" She then said, "Yeah, yeah but I just thought that you were a normal tourist" Let me tell you about some of my dance students… the ones that turn up with their mums… the mums come up to me and tell me "My daughter, she's so shy!"… and then when the mum goes the daughters are not shy at all. They're just happy and outgoing. And then when the mother comes back after the class she'll say, "How's my little shy daughter?"

(AN – They all laugh.)

Nora:
This is Norwegian!

Anthony:
"How's my shy little one?" … and when she's twenty years old that daughter will explode and say, "I'm not shy you stupid m************!" and in Norway I think that so many Norwegians have been told repeatedly "You don't express emotions, you don't express emotion, you don't express emotion, you don't express emotion… you don't express emotion, you don't express emotion"… Do you know what happens after twenty, thirty, forty years of that? You'll probably start believing that you don't express emotion!

Nora:
Yes!

Anthony:
Obviously, you are emotional beings like every other human being so you do express emotion, but guess what... you believe that you shouldn't and that it is a "bad" thing... This includes the Janteloven as well, and then you go to Oslo Airport where straight in front of you you see a book that tells you that "as a Norwegian" you do not express emotion except when you are drunk... and you laugh at yourself being degraded and insulted and undermined. That is insanity! That is offensive.

Nora:
In Norway if you want to be something more, your family and the people around you will pull you back!

Anthony:
I am not from Norway. I am a complete "outsider". When I talk to Norwegians some of them have literally clenched their fists and said, "Yes! Yes! Write this book please... I don't have the strength to say it but you can say it for me!" Now all of these stereotypes and books, it's a number of factors, but I do think that these things do compound a negative self-view, individually and collectively... and it's also bullying... Janteloven indoctrination... I think that the Janteloven is bullying. It puts you down. Would you agree with that?

Nora:
Yes! It's alive!

Aksel:
We actually learnt in school that Janteloven is wrong...

Anthony:
Then why doesn't that align with how you think and act? I have seen many people break down talking about Janteloven and how it has affected them. So, even if you're school taught you that, you *obviously* don't seem to actually subscribe to Janteloven as being wrong?

Nora:
We learn it... But it's the moral. You learn one thing but you know inside

you that this is not right!

Anthony:
Aksel, how do you feel about that?

Aksel:
Aksel Sandemose said that and some of those rules I agree with... I think it was Aksel Sandemose that wrote down Janteloven...

Anthony:
The Danish author?

Aksel:
Yes, and he put it into writing some of those rules... I agree with some, yes yeah, some that's a stupid rule, but others, yeah, I agree with.

Anthony:
So tell me do you remember any of the ones that you disagree with?

Aksel:
For example, the one that says that you shouldn't think that you are anything. You shouldn't think that you are anything special... If you are something special then why not?!

Anthony:
Aksel, that is so refreshing to hear!

Nora:
But you mustn't tell anyone though... *(Sarcastically.)*

Anthony:
I love the fact that you have just told me that but what you have just said is actually quite revolutionary because there would be a lot of Norwegians who would be afraid to say that publicly and many others that totally disagree?

Nora:
When I grew up I was in a box. I had very strict... strong parents... they had rules, you should do this and not this... and I rebelled when I was fourteen or fifteen and when I had children I knew that I would not make rules because

they should grow up and be the person that they should meant to be.

Anthony:
Do you think that me writing a book about the subject that we have discussed today, do you think that that this can help Norway?

Nora:
Yes!

Anthony:
Aksel, can I ask you, I think that we have discussed some things today that have been a quite traumatic… things that people don't usually talk about?

Aksel:
Yes.

Anthony:
I know that it's tough to look at these things and to also look at the past but do you think that these things that we have discussed today should be discussed? Is it helpful to discuss these things? What do you think?

Aksel:
Yes I think it is.

Nora:
I think that people in Norway want to open up!

Anthony:
But you know what… It's really logical not to open up to people that treat you badly, is it not?

Nora:
In Norway they are so critical!

Anthony:
I have taught thousands of Scandinavians in Norway, Denmark and in London… all over… and at the end we have the usual feeling of exhilaration and I make sure that they hear "Well done!" And I have had to point individuals out. And when I do point them out they turn around

and look behind them… they often can't believe that I'm talking to *them*… And then I say "Well done… I'm talking to *you*! You did amazing!" And they are literally shocked. "Me?!" they say, "Yes *you*! You're amazing!"

Nora:
But do you say it if you don't mean it?

Anthony:
Never, never.

Nora:
I can experience sometimes… and you can see in their face… that's a lie.

(AN – Many Norwegians describe passive aggressiveness and "fakeness" around them in day-to-day life. However, if you accept dishonesty and lies, if you engage in dishonesty yourself too, how can you then complain that people lie to you and not see that contradiction? They spent most of this conversation promoting dishonesty as normal and now complain that people lie? It's bizarre. There is no concept of cause and effect, responsibility or consequence. It's all very juvenile and child-like… complete capitulation to the collective above themselves?)

Jakob:
Well I think that our behaviour comes from the manufacturers and the school system, where everybody should be "equal", and you shouldn't be anything "special"… Or maybe better than others…

Anthony:
So you are taught this in the school system?

Jakob:
Yes, yes! But in my opinion… there is a limit there.

Anthony:
Can you explain exactly what you mean by "limit"?

Jakob:
Yes, your grade system… maybe the sixth grade is the top… that is the limit and you can't… but of course they try to make everybody go as high as possible but there is a limit there! But you don't get anything special… Like if

you are better, come here and get an extra teacher... no! It makes no difference if you try to learn much or you need extra help they try to, get everybody standardised. I'm not an expert in this but I think the school system started in the 1800s... Maybe reading the bible and these kind of things...

Anthony:
What effect does what you have described have?

Jakob:
I think in the 30s and 40s when they had the communist revolutions they also had them in Scandinavia... Socialistic mindset. I think that's where you should be "equal" comes from... because previously in the 1800s and 1900s they had many big people...big differences.

Anthony:
You mean the disparity between the "haves" and the "have nots"?

Jakob:
Yes. In the society and then the reaction came which was this communism.

Anthony:
Against the people who had this wealth and had the money?

Jakob:
Yes, yeah yeah yeah.

Anthony:
So then it was a "bad" thing to have money so it switched?

Jakob:
Yes it's switched. Yes.

Anthony:
Do you think that there could be some kind of collective guilt complex related to that? Do you think there is some kind of crossover from the past which says wealth is "bad"?

Jakob:
Yes, yeah! I think that that was very common earlier, because of religious

puritan things. But now of course Norway is very socialistic... not so much as before... I think that we have this change to another direction again.

Anthony:
Are you referring to materialism?

Jakob:
Yes, materialism... it's going up and down and its counter reactions.

Anthony:
Yes.

Jakob:
Yes, but the Janteloven... where they tried to make everybody "equal"... so it's the theory... but it's not always that way in practice! (Laugh.)

Anthony:
As a human being... as human beings in that sense we are all equal... but I have never met an "equal" person... to the contrary... everybody is unique aren't they?

Aksel:
Some people are more equal than others...

Anthony:
You know your Animal Farm!

Jakob:
I think that this standardisation has gone too far! So they don't want it like old times when you had one big leader... and the workers... they try to maintain that everybody should be "equal"... at the work place you can talk to the boss, and he doesn't wear a suit... only ordinary clothes and you have this flat system.

Anthony:
But here's the thing though... you do know that in reality, there is no "flat" system? In reality...

Jakob:
Yeah, yeah.

Aksel:
Yes.

Anthony:
Aksel, you just referred to Napoleon's rules, from George Orwell's *Animal Farm*… that some people are "more equal than others"… and we all laughed at that… and that implies that all of you really know that this "egalitarian society" is not real, in practical terms?

Aksel:
Yes.

Jakob:
So then maybe, if we are in the school and everything, maybe we are a bit scared to say how you really… because then maybe you will be standardised! Probably…

(AN – Note the equivocations, "Probably"… "I think…"… "Maybe". With regards to Aksel's raising of George Orwell… it gives us a chance to ask the question straight out… Is this all brainwashing?)

Anthony:
Aksel, you just made light of a system which we know is not true… and you refer to that with a George Orwell quote. It's brilliant because it shows intelligence and it shows awareness and insight… but let me ask you straight out. Do you think that the system… the schooling and the Jante Law… is it brainwashing?

Aksel:
Errrrrrrrrrrrr…

Anthony:
I know that that's a loaded word… I know it is, but… is it a kind of indoctrination?

Aksel:
So I mean, school is a kind of indoctrination… let's be honest.

Anthony:
But with regards to what Jakob just said… everybody is "equal"… and if

you are rich it is "bad"… and he says that this is not reality and then you just made a joke about it yourself… so here is the thing… if somebody teaches you something which is not true then you will rebel against that but if you can't rebel against it publicly… that will cause an inner conflict, in your psyche… obviously… because you can't talk about it openly in school you can only talk about it among trusted friends… you can't talk about it openly because they will say. "No that's wrong!"?

Aksel:
Yes.

Anthony:
Makes me think of the Soviet Union, in the old days?

Jakob:
Yes and… of course it's… I think that is positive that we all learn that we are equal but we don't learn that we are also unique!

Anthony:
Maybe you need to learn a bit of both?

Jakob:
Yes it's… you need more spectrum because… it's too small! But if you look to Sweden… they are a lot more of a socialist country. Last year Trump said this about them… yesterday they denied it! Everybody denied it! It's so important to have this "standard view" that they denied it!

Anthony:
Do you think that there is a lot of denial in Scandinavia?

Jakob:
Yes, I think so. Maybe, if you admit that we have failed. Then maybe the ground underneath us will crumble!

Anthony:
Maybe society will "break down", in a way?

Jakob:
Yes, I think so. You lose a bit of foundation… I don't know… It's not so easy to (explain)…

Anthony:
Well... I think you've done pretty well!

(AN – Note his phrase "lose a bit of foundation" which is exactly what Amanda was saying about needing something more "concrete"... they are telling you directly... They feel UNSTABLE... and they ARE unstable, which a completely normal logical response to a lack of foundation. We pause for a few moments and a side conversation started between Aksel and his mother, Nora, which will demonstrate this.)

Anthony:
Turning this on for a second... because there was a side conversation going on after I turned off the microphone... Aksel, tell me what was said?

Aksel:
My mum was saying that this thing... about learning something that you don't think is true and wanting to rebel... but not daring to. It means that people are controlled by fear... and then it makes them more suspicious...

Anthony:
And this... exactly what you have just said is what I mean by "trauma response". That paradigm (which you have just described) creates trauma... so that if an outside stimuli comes in, something that you are not used to, then it will be quite traumatic because you already have enough things to deal with, internally. Which is trying to understand and reconcile; "I have to live in a system that I don't believe in, they tell me that I have to act like this... but, wait a minute... do I actually have to say this or that? Or this?" That is obviously fatiguing... it's tiring. So, that's why you really will just do your routine... things that you usually do, because any kind of questioning or outside stimulus from anything external is, in a way is going to be very traumatic because you've just got so much to deal with and especially if it comes from your history, Janteloven and from your school, so if you're thirty, forty, fifty years old... you're well deep in it!

Nora:
And the religion!

Anthony:
What we are talking about right now… so many Norwegians have told me that they are scared to talk and to say how they really feel about what we are talking about right now…

Aksel:
Yes.

Anthony:
They literally say the words "I would never usually talk about this" and I ask them directly "Why?" Firstly they are usually like "we just don't think about it"… but if you think about it, this should be the number one issue in your life? The society and the culture and communities that you live in… because, how can you flourish if people are telling you what to do?

Aksel:
Yeah, well… yeah! I mean… there are some things which are "OK" to be good at I guess… I like skiing! (Laugh)…

(AN – He is being sarcastic he is saying that "skiing" is a safe and approved subject to discuss and be "good" at, without social reprisals… the group burst out laughing.)

Anthony:
Now… escapism… there are certain ways that you can get through this… one of those ways would be sporting activity… one of them would be materialism… that's a big thing here in Norway… or if you talk about blogging or if you are an "influencer"… that's very "acceptable" and a big thing here too, right?

Aksel:
Yeah, yeah yeah!

Anthony:
Sports… people here can talk about sport all day?

Aksel:
Yes.

Anthony:
So it's superfluous conversation? Talking about the weather, for
example… somebody could literally talk about the weather for ten days
and feel completely comfortable… because it's a "safe" subject?

*(AN – Somebody talking about the weather will probably (but not necessarily) not have to
experience being undermined or passive aggressively attacked in Norway. So you will often
notice that many people over compensate, by increasing the level of talking about these
"safe" and "approved" kind of things. Subjects of real life observation, which are risky and
subject to "attack" by the collective and those around you, are often avoided, as a means of
survival by a great number of people in Norway. Interestingly, it is this obvious imbalance
which is one of the main indicators highlighting the problem… talking about superficial
inconsequential things is merely a survival mechanism because speaking the truth might get
you excluded and "punished", directly or indirectly, so it's best to just "shut up" and talk
about the weather and skiing, if you want to live without social disapproval, abuse or the
fear of abuse? However, even these subjects are not completely "safe"… As we will see later
on in the journey, when we speak to the sports experts.)*

Aksel:
Yes.

Anthony:
But the "outsider"… the person who thinks differently… that doesn't
blog, that doesn't talk nonsense and talk about the weather constantly…
then the only realistic option is to be alone and withdraw?… and that is
the solution that I am observing… because you have to let that pressure of
what you just described i.e. having to live in a way that you have been
taught, that they don't believe in to come out in some way. So some
people hike, some people climb mountains, some people do sports, some
people talk nonsense, some people blog, some people become reclusive
but, ultimately too many people it causes to break down, but one way or
the other it is going to come out… because, what you just described… the
pressure from the school onwards… it doesn't just go away. Another way,
by the way… talking about it solves it potentially… but if you never talk
about it and you always keep it inside… I believe that it would cause
some kind of neurosis. If everybody just talked about how they felt and
said, "Do you know what? We're taught bullsh*t… we don't actually
believe their Janteloven"… and there was no fear, then I don't think there
would be such a problem?

Aksel:
Yes.

Anthony:
But the thing is, it doesn't sound like you guys would be completely free to talk publicly or socially about these subjects?

Aksel:
I mean… ah… some of it.

Amanda:
I just wondered… *(AN – turning to her husband)*… you have freedom of speech so why can't you just…?

Aksel:
(AN – Speaking to his wife.) No no no, it's not like you're legally obliged not to talk about it… I mean you can…

Anthony:
Of course you "technically" can… but there will be *consequences* to that, right?

Nora:
Yes!

Aksel:
Yes, not legal consequences… but social consequences.

(AN – Aksel has just confirmed how it works in Norway.)

Amanda:
Ahhhhhhhhhhhhhh!

Anthony:
Yes… and you all know this, you control people covertly, not overtly… this is a very powerful system because we know from Soviet times… if you have a rule saying "you can't say this"… It's much better to say "you are free to say anything you want"… but *if you do say it*, you will be covertly undermined, excluded, passively attacked… you won't be promoted… You'll be outcast… and that is a more subversive way of doing it. That's *Animal Farm* (George Orwell), control, right?

Aksel:
Yes, yes.

Anthony:
That is heavy! So for example, Aksel you are an academic... I know, for a fact... if you said something which is not approved, conformist, doesn't align with the Janteloven, and is against the "Norwegian ideal"... maybe funding won't come your way, maybe you won't get that promotion the next time?

Aksel:
Yes, it's possible.

Anthony:
I'll give you an example, when I walk into the bookshop... all of the PhDs and all of the degrees in Norway have not written a single "serious" book that's available on the shelves on Norwegian culture and development of the people...

Aksel:
(*Laughs.*)

Anthony:
Now there is one book, from the university, where there is one professor who is about seventy years old... he wrote one chapter, in one book, where he addressed some of the hypocrisy in relation to climate change and environmental issues in Norway. That book is not available in the bookshops of Norway.

Aksel:
Oh?

Anthony:
He had to publish it in the UK, it hardly got any traction at all and it was basically ignored... He is a professor at the university with so many Norwegian books... and the fact that he wrote that one in his 70s, after he'd built his career... he had nothing to lose... Finally he said to himself that he will write one chapter of one book?... this is the reason why I believe that I can't find a real self-reflective book by a single Norwegian in the book stores... because anybody in their prime that writes it will

LOSE! Not necessarily legally… but they will be outcast. They will be glossed over for promotions… It's much better to talk about skiing and to talk about sports and talk about all the other stuff… thousands of those books in the Norwegian bookshops though!

Aksel:
Yeah.

Anthony:
Because these things are uncomfortable? Why would anybody ever use their personal collateral? Why would anyone ever sacrifice their career? Maybe in twenty years people will talk about this… but not right now?

Aksel:
Yes.

Anthony:
And so, even I know that I will be attacked for writing this. I know I will, right?

Aksel:
Yes, yeah yeah… they will write about it… the *usual*…

Anthony:
They will undermine me… and I will write about that in turn just as I am pre-emptively exposing it right now. I will say that we need to anticipate, weaponised exclusion and the "usual" because ultimately you *will* just be attacked or ignored for this stuff… but when you can't ignore it… when it's too authentic, when it's obviously the truth… when it's real… you're only choice is then to attack the man and undermine the messenger… that's the way… but these are things that are simply straight out of the communist tactic book… it's the way you destroy dissent… it's actually ingenious. Just tactics. It's not a problem for me but it gets serious when you are an academic and you want to write about one of these subjects in Norway… In how many years, 100 years? 120 years?… or whatever it is… not a single Norwegian has written a single serious non-fiction book about the Norwegian people, it's society or behaviour… except for four or five, or whatever it is… comedy books… even *they* were written by foreigners… calling Norwegians unthinking "psychopaths" disguised as comedy? It's unacceptable. That proves to you right there that there is an

issue with dissent... with just simply speaking about these things... because there is not even one book... not even a single book! That proves it... because a free society MUST include alternative views and dissent.

Aksel:
Yes.

Anthony:
You might have somebody saying "I hate Janteloven, I don't believe in it!" Where are the books about that subject in the bookshops? Just three individuals talking online and two statues!?

Aksel:
Like I said, we do learn in school that Janteloven is bad...

Anthony:
But that doesn't align with your view of the country? So, as we said before... You may "technically" learn that it's "bad"... but you don't *actually* learn that it's bad of course, do you?

Aksel:
True. Yes.

Anthony:
So, that's what I'm saying... and by the way... what you have just described... would instil into you, a kind of schizoid way of thinking... because you have two separate narratives running in tandem... what you *really* believe and what you feel you have to *say* and that traverses the whole of Norwegian society, in my opinion... is there any truth to that?

Aksel:
Errrrr... hmmmm.

Aksel:
Well, what I think is the Janteloven... it is wrong and I learnt it in school that that is wrong... So that's aligns.

(AN – Aksel bursts out laughing. He is engaged in clear-cut doublethink now... which is why he laughs... his mother will dismiss him directly, shortly.)

Anthony:
But you're not "allowed" to say anything publicly against it are you?

Aksel:
Well... I guess you *could*. You could say that Janteloven is bad all you want...

Anthony:
But you couldn't say that at work... because then they will tell you "Oh, he's so up himself!" Right?

Aksel:
People would probably agree that Janteloven is bad...

Anthony:
Would there be any "punishment" for that?

Aksel:
No, I don't think so... I don't think that's Janteloven is popular really.

(AN – His mother is getting angry listening to him speak... she wants to speak, so I turn to her...)

Anthony:
Nora, Aksel is telling us that this Janteloven is *no problem at all* in Norway. Why would he say that?

Nora:
Well... I think that he maybe has been too much in America...

(AN – She uses her tone of voice to completely cut him down and for the first time today Aksel gets animated.)

Aksel:
We learn in school that the Janteloven is dumb!

(AN – He may have read that Janteloven is "dumb"... possibly (I actually doubt this is true)... but he LEARNS the complete opposite and experiences the complete opposite in reality but still refuses to accept and admit that... even as his mum repeatedly tells him that it is a major problem, even though he himself sees that it is an issue and has discussed its problems today, previously... You will now see his

mother describe the pain Janteloven has caused her in her life… monitor Aksel's response… complete emotional shutdown and inability to connect or even comprehend what she is saying – cold and combative – look at the usual method of undermining by "technical" targeted analysis whilst completely disregarding context and her pain… I will raise this with him directly… listen to his response carefully… monitor his mother's response to what he says too, as well as the rest of the room.)

Anthony:
OK, wait, wait, wait… Nora, is this something which is in your life?

Nora:
(Sustained silence.)

Anthony:
Is the Janteloven something which is relevant in your life?

Nora:
(Sustained silence.)

Anthony:
OK, for example… something random… like the *Magna Carta*… or some ancient scroll… if somebody in my country burst into tears and said, "Oh, Queen Elizabeth I… Or Henry VIII… wrote this book… and it's destroyed my life!" people would be like "What the hell are you talking about?" But that has actually happened in Norway! More than once… in front of me… people have burst into tears saying that "Janteloven" has destroyed their lives! I won't give you their names, but I am telling you that is a fact. I will tell you about one woman… she burst into tears… but she actually burst into tears *twice*… she first burst into tears and got upset with me, saying, "How can you say that?!" … and then I told her, "Because you have just told me how much it has destroyed your life and how much people around you have undermined you"… and then she cried again… but started WEEPING! She then said, "Yes, I know I know! This thing called Janteloven…" She then goes on to tell her personal story about how it restricted her and how her community *works*… she was weeping! If somebody in London told me that some ancient prosaic text… from an author from Denmark… has destroyed my life TODAY… people would say that that person is insane.

Aksel:
Oh, but he (the Janteloven author) was critical of it!

Anthony:
If it's negatively impacted your life in any way, directly or indirectly... to such an extent that you would be weeping saying that it had destroyed your life... regardless of the "technicalities" of the text... what we can agree on is that <u>she</u> believed it?

(AN – Aksel is silent.)

Nora:
We have two types of people here: one is the victim and one is the perpetrator!

Anthony:
Nora, I have experienced and observed these things too many times whilst talking to Norwegians all over the country. I feel that there are people who hate this but do not have the courage to say it too. Nora, just so we are clear, would you say that Janteloven has a big impact in the way that people think in Norway?

Nora:
Yes.

(AN – I then turn to everybody in the group individually and ask them.)

Anthony:
Aksel, do you feel that Janteloven has had any impact on your day-to-day life at all?

Aksel:
Probably, yes.

Anthony:
Jakob, has the Janteloven had an effect on your life in any way?

Jakob:
Yes, I think so.

Nora:

Are you asking whether I see Jante Law in action? Are you asking whether I am affected?

Anthony:

Yes, I am asking you as a Norwegian has this Janteloven had any effect on your life, adversely or positively in any way at all?

Nora:

In my life, the both ways, because I hate Janteloven! But I have got strong because of my rebellion… when I was a little girl I was traumatically attacked and abused and because of this I was more affected by jantalaw.

Anthony:

Really? I'm sorry to hear that Nora.

Nora:

I taught my children differently, so it was very useful for me… when you see that things are going wrong, it is only then that you wake up.

Anthony:

I understand but wouldn't it make sense if other people in Norway did what we are doing today? We are having a *relatively* intelligent and emotional conversation *(AN – "relatively"… one must be allowed a moment of humour for oneself from time to time dear reader!)*… this in itself, is very rare in Norway?

Nora:

I'm not sure but speaking for myself, I understand that this is not right and my people… I have to limit myself… my parents they limited me.

(AN – Again, this is so strange, the respondents often differentiate between themselves and others verbally, regularly. They differentiate and clearly state "who" they are speaking for. Are they are so concerned about appearing neutral and not offending or not being wrong that they dissociate even verbally from their own opinion? This would demonstrate the level of potential risk from simply giving an opinion or a direct answer… to constantly add these equivocations, just in case… this would give them plausible deniability, "I said at the time that I didn't know… "probably, "maybe", "could be", "but"… i.e. I didn't say it was actually so!" …it's an incredible mental/verbal tactic to avoid conflict.)

Anthony:
Oh, so you are saying that your parents' attitudes have limited your life?

Nora:
Yes and I know inside of me that this is not right and we have to do it another way… I have to make my life… and my children…

Anthony:
That's one of the most incredible things somebody can say in front of their family… *(AN – Turning to Aksel)* Aksel, hearing your mother say that does it affect your views of Janteloven?

Aksel:
Errrrrrr… well no. Because I just consider Janteloven as just recording their attitudes (i.e. a historical document).

(AN – Note no expression of empathy, kindness or compassion to his mother… Note the passive aggressive "errrrrrrr… well" before he delivers the blow too, implying that the question is stupid.)

Anthony:
She has just said that it has actually affected her though?

Aksel:
Yeah, yeah, yeah… I know but it is the attitudes… It's not like people… Janteloven… and think to themselves "this is these are rules I should live by"… they live by the attitudes and later on they learn, by the way these attitudes are "bad"…, Aksel Sandemose wrote about it, on living with the attitudes again…

(AN – He is undermining her by challenging her technical explanation and understanding of the cause of her pain (Janteloven) whilst totally ignoring her expressed pain, in front of his eyes and ours. I have seen this done repeatedly on my journey in Norway. The rest of the room is impassive and so is his mother.)

Anthony:
Yes but now, your mother has just expressed how it has affected her… So does that's not make the impact a little bit more real? Because me personally hearing what she just said… I do feel like "Wow!"

Aksel:

Yeah... no no... the attitudes are real and I mean you can call the attitudes "Janteloven" because that's what Aksel Sandemose called it when he wrote them down...

(AN – I raised the concept of empathy and compassionate and an emotional response... He seemingly has no comprehension of what I am saying or the implication that he has just undermined his mother and showed zero empathy or compassion.)

Anthony:
Yes.

(AN – He sees that I am not impressed by him...so he gives a little...)

Aksel:

But it is the attitudes that are real and not really the "Janteloven" itself.

(AN – To argue about semantics in the face of somebody expressing vulnerable emotional pain and to argue the smallest detail and technicalities... this is something which happens in nearly every group conversation with the respondents that I have had in Norway.)

Anthony:
Yes, but Aksel, your mum has just said that it is real because it has affected her life?

Aksel:
Yes but...

(AN – The emotional connection is just not there... could the undermining be a reflex response because he can't stop himself, even when I point out his behaviour to his face in front of his mother?)

Anthony:
But how do you *feel* about that? Again, for me, hearing what she said... It makes my heart beat a little bit... It makes me feel. It makes it real...

Aksel:
OK...*but* it's not like her parents looked at the Janteloven and said "what

does the Janteloven say?" It's not like that... it's just like they had these attitudes, they learnt them from a young age...

Anthony:
And then they just pass them on to their daughter?

Aksel:
Yeah, yeah.

Anthony:
And do you think that that is normal?

Aksel:
Yes, well it seems to be normal. (*Laughs.*)

(*AN – There are two things that shock me... firstly his message, attitude and demeanour... but mostly that it is accepted as completely normal by the group. His mother has not reacted in any way whatsoever! He is unchallenged... this is the most telling... is it truly normalised behaviour that is usually not challenged or questioned? It appears so. It appears to be enabled behaviour too. This could be why they are in so much shock when I question them... nobody has questioned their behaviour before... ironically, I think this is why I actually get an answer! They are so shocked and inexperienced with being challenged that they answer as if a school teacher has caught a child in the act of doing something naughty! It's all very bizarre but it's incredible to observe that this is how this group of Norwegians interact and think. We can observe and have a unique insight into what they accept as a normal view of the world.*)

Anthony:
Nora, can I ask you, you have just said that you recognise that it is not normal and you want a different way for your own family?

Nora:
You have many enemies...

Anthony:
Oh, this way of thinking gives you many enemies?

Nora:
And lost friends.

Anthony:

Being "anti-Janteloven" creates a lot of enemies and lost friends in Norway? I understand. This aligns exactly with what we have been discussing today. So, "intellectually" this may be normal and the response to the normal environment... but how do you judge it now, Aksel? Do you think that it is objectively normal or abnormal? Do you think it is wrong or it is right? Or is it good or is it bad?

Aksel:

Like I said, I disagree with many of the Janteloven rules... but I do think that they are normal in Norway.

(AN – Note that he answers for "Norway", not himself (disassociation or avoidance?), even though I clearly asked what "YOU" think; "Do you think that it is objectively normal or abnormal? Do you think it is wrong or it is right? Or is it good or is it bad?".)

Anthony:

Morally... Judging them for *yourself* though... I am trying to get at... From *your* point of view do you think that it is normal? Like thinking about it I would think to myself "this is not normal this is not right... we need to get rid of these completely because it is affecting people" Don't you think that at all?

Aksel:

Well... errr... yeah... I don't think about Janteloven in my life... (*Laughs.*)

(AN – He continues to evade and avoid and then laughs... at himself... he is laughing at himself because part of him knows exactly what game he is playing, I suspect?)

Anthony:

But how about now because we have just discussed it together?

Aksel:

Yeah, well... I...

Anthony:

OK, let me ask you another question. Do you have a reluctance to condemn it? I feel like there is a reluctance to condemn it outright with you... tell me?

Aksel:
OK, OK... if we go through the list of Janteloven rules then I can tell you the ones that I like and the ones that I don't like.

Anthony:
But let me ask you on an *emotional* level... You have just heard your mother say, that the Janteloven has caused her *pain*... it has caused her to *have enemies*... it has caused her to *lose friends*... it has actually *affected her whole life*... isn't that reason enough alone for you to consider rejecting them? Just because of what your mother has just said alone?

Aksel:
Er, no!

(AN – The truth is that his mum is outwardly unaffected... she isn't concerned in the least by what he says... the non-Norwegian only, his wife, looks embarrassed, upset and shocked... everyone else in the room is acting like this is all normal talk and appear happy and jovial.)

Anthony:
OK.

(AN – He sees that I am not impressed by him and laughs and then disagrees with himself... no question was asked.)

Aksel:
No, no. (*Laughs.*)

Anthony:
OK.

(AN – The passive aggressiveness is terrible to witness but the normalisation and the non-reaction by the group in the room and especially the mother is horrifying for me... his wife sits quietly... I address this directly.)

Anthony:
Do you know what's interesting? Tell me what you think about this? I was interviewing a lady and we were talking about enemies, sometimes

you have a husband and wife and sometimes the husband is friends with his wife's enemy... Maybe not a life or death enemy but somebody that his wife does not like... and then she told me, "Just because I don't like her, doesn't mean that my husband should not like her... maybe he has a different kind of interaction with her" It was logical... but it wasn't emotional. It wasn't "I hate her so I want my husband to hate her". Is that "logical" way of looking at things normally in Norway?

Aksel:
Yes!

Anthony:
Yes, that's what it seems... but does that not cause issues with loyalty in relationships?

Aksel:
Yes, remember the thing about chocolate cake "Yeah yeah, er, er, hmmm, er, er, er... I prefer swiss roll"? *You want to have as much in common with your friends as possible.* I think you'll see it especially in kids... They will like chocolate cake, if you do, and they will hate it if their friends do... But if they are both in the same room then you will be in trouble.

Anthony:
So what happens with regards to husband and wife... you "have" to maintain a relationship with their enemy... one of their *enemies*... and it seems like... The wife will just accept that the husband "needs" to maintain an interaction with her enemy? She is not thinking "my husband should be loyal to me and only to me... he should tell my enemy to go away!" It doesn't seem to work like that in Norway?

Aksel:
No, no, no.

Anthony:
In England it's more of an emotional response.

Aksel:
Yeah.

Anthony:
I.e. "If my wife hates you, I hate you."

Aksel:
OK, yeah! (*Shocked laugh.*)

Anthony:
Amanda, I'm going to ask you a question now… imagine that your husband is not sitting next to you… it's just me and you in the room.

(*AN – We are laughing because Aksel puts his arm around Amanda in an exaggerated overprotective way.*)

Anthony:
If I am married to my wife and my wife has an enemy… let's say her name is Holly. So my wife hates this girl called Holly… and I am friends with this Holly…

Amanda:
Hmmm hmmm.

Anthony:
In Norway, as just described, that kind of dynamic seems to be accepted, "Just because you hate her does not mean that I should hate her", and I said that in the UK that would probably be perceived as disloyalty in the relationship because if they are your enemy, then they become my enemy… because I am loyal to my partner. That seems very normal and if my wife or somebody that I loved was friends with my enemy… It would be seen as disloyalty and it would be seen as wrong but here in Norway they are describing it as very different from that and they have described it as just "everybody trying to get along"… and now I'm asking you… In your opinion… Would you see that as disloyalty?

Amanda:
Weeeeeeeeeeeeeell… disloyalty? This word is so serious! (*Laughs.*)

(*AN – Again, note the immediate rejection of the word "loyalty". It is obviously an emotional trigger for her. It's a very simple word with a very simple definition. I gave her the background of the story and asked her a simple question. It's a yes or no. Instead she reacts emotionally to the word, specifically. Expectations of loyalty appear low, so there would be an obvious triggering to the word "loyalty" or "disloyalty", which is why she laughs... and she then falls silent. She cannot answer without exposure. This is the usual technique that we have seen. Whenever you see an emotional disproportionate response to a word and a rejection of the legitimate definition, especially if the word is exactly appropriate... you know that word is true but also that they are sensitive to it because it is true. I would expect an emotional response for the opposite... if the word was NOT true and DID NOT describe the situation accurately but this has not been the case on these occasions... the respondents consistently reject the appropriate words. This is a device of avoidance and it's intentional, in my opinion.)*

Anthony:
By the way, this is something which has actually happened... I have interviewed people where this has happened on a serious level... by the way... the fact that it is taking you so long to even answer this question is shocking me?

(AN – I imply that I am shocked that she can't answer a simple question, simply and in a timely manner... the fact that I called her out elicits an immediate response. I find that directly confronting nonsense usually makes the respondents drop the "act" pretty quickly.)

Amanda:
I think that I will ask him to cut the relationship.

(AN – I had to keep it very calm, logical and ignore her laughing... then her voice changed and she got serious... and finally answered the question appropriately.)

Anthony:
Yes. Of course. But, as they have just explained, in Norway the expectation does not seem to be to cut the relationship because they say that you might have your own "different relationship" with the person. What I am saying is that that is irrelevant because if you are with your wife or you are with your husband then your loyalty should be to him or her, shouldn't it? You don't need to have that person in your life... obviously, it causes your partner pain... why not just cut them out for the sake of your partner's emotions? Is causing pain not acknowledged as a big deal in Norway?

Nora:
It is a big deal *inside* of you.

Anthony:
So it's a big deal "inside" of you but it doesn't change the interaction of your relationships or outcome on the "outside" in the real world?

Nora:
Yes. *(Correct.)*

Anthony:
Amanda, if this theoretical situation happened and it was your husband, would you then feel hurt?

Amanda:
Yes. Because I'd feel that he didn't stand by me.

(AN – She has just described disloyalty… but previously, just moments before, rejected the word "disloyalty". It's a combination of fear, intimidation and peer pressure I think. So by saying the same thing but with less emotive words, she feels more comfortable. However, later in the conversation the older couple state for the record that, in their opinion, "loyalty" is NOT common in Norway.)

Anthony:
Yes, I feel that that would be normal… But that is not considered normal in Norway? Nora has just said that she would feel it "inside" but that she would not say it… I am saying that this all sounds like another level of anxiety…

Nora:
Here in this house we do say it!

Anthony:
But just so I am clear. You are saying that this is not the norm in Norway? It usually would not be said? Is this correct?

Nora:
Hmmm hmmm.

Anthony:
Is that right?

Nora:
Yes...

(AN – She then turns to her husband, in a very accusatory way.)

Nora:
And you can ask *him* about this!

Jakob:
Yeah, yeah *(AN – no viable emotional change or reaction.)*

Nora:
Jakob has learnt this from his home town... he learnt that it should be like that *(AN – i.e. disloyalty, enabling and abuse)*... and then I came into his life, and said "No! It's not OK... you belong to me!"

Anthony:
Now, speaking to many of the respondents in Norway it seems that between them the consensus is that the expectation of loyalty is not there for most of them? So for example, you would not be required to give up being friends with your husband's enemy... there wouldn't even be an expectation that you would and the fact that you insist on that loyalty is not common in Norway you feel, Nora?

Nora:
Yes maybe! If he (Jakob) wants to hurt me... ten or twenty days in the year... then I will leave him!

(AN – Her husband is sitting next to her listening to this, impassively. I then ask about their communication method and suggest that it might be anxiety inducing and fatiguing.)

Nora:
Yes, you get tired! *(Laughs.)*

Anthony:
Yes, you get fatigued?

Amanda:
Yes.

Anthony:
And that's what I'm trying to explain, something which seems "small"... like pretence "I'm just being polite"... in the long term will destroy you... because it would cause you fatigue, anxiety, personality disorders, psychiatric disorders, illness... whatever! In my opinion of course... that's just my personal opinion... "don't show vulnerability"... everything is "OK" and I think that this all comes back to you the Janteloven and the "let's not cause any offence"... "let's not make a scene"... and that kind of thing?

Nora:
And the religion is behind Janteloven!

Anthony:
And the religion also says don't abuse people, I believe? It's all hypocritical. It's all used as an excuse?

Nora:
Yes, if somebody sexually abuses you, you are supposed to "forgive" them the bible says and in Norway we use the bible as the basis that we want to use for life... and ignore the other... this is my understanding of it... the way I see Norway.

Anthony:
Are you saying that with regards to the religious theology Norwegians try and strive towards "turn the other cheek?" Would you say that that is the overwhelming attitude in Norway, which is underlying the society?

Nora:
Yes! I think so!

Anthony:
That's my general observation too, speaking to people around the country... "turn the other cheek" is the attitude I see... why do you think that is?

Nora:
Yes... you should avoid conflict... You don't upset people... and that is the easier way.

Anthony:
But the collateral damage is that victims are destroyed?

Nora:
Yes.

Anthony:
But that's a tragedy. That's a disgrace isn't it?

Nora:
Hmmm hmmm... because if you feel pain then you seem weak.

Anthony:
Yes, expressions of vulnerability and pain are perceived as mental illness here I have been told too many times. If you express vulnerability then too many people say that you are "crazy"... people that just express pain... I have seen this. On the other hand, these people will have learnt that they should not express pain because if they do then they will be perceived as mentally ill and "weak" by so many others. So obviously they will not express pain or vulnerability readily and openly. But if you keep that inside for thirty, forty or fifty years then trouble will come! Trouble comes...

(AN – Amanda has been sitting in stunned silence listening to this interaction! She has been absolutely gob-smacked by this revelation discussion... She then interjects.)

Amanda:
I'm a bit surprised! Because my opinion is that you guys (Norwegians) are so blunt... When you are not happy you say that you are not happy.

Aksel:
Yes, in our family, yeah.

Amanda:
(Then she asked her husband) But not general?

Aksel:
Not really, no.

(*AN – Amanda is absolutely stunned and gob-smacked!*)

Amanda:
Oh! I see… I thought that Europeans were blunt! I thought that if you don't like something you speak out and are not concerned about conflicts… like I just tell you that I don't like you right now… they are so blunt! I think that from my experience it is like this! (*Nervous laugh.*)

(*AN – I suspect that she has been equating passive aggressiveness with "honesty" as it appears many Norwegians do up and down the country. Pain is a reminder of reality; it reminds you that you are alive… so in a way, it is the ultimate "truth". That's why pain and passive aggression is often mistakenly equated with honesty in Norway, in my opinion.*)

Aksel:
She hasn't met that many Norwegian people though… except when she is been to Norway (with us)… Most of…

(*AN – Amanda protests, that she has and does… she needs to convince herself that she was right and is right. She is holding on to her preconceived ideas, even though reality is showing her differently. Aksel will speak to her explicitly in a moment and they will collapse. However, this is often the reaction of immigrants in Norway that I speak to. They can't accept the reality of what is around them and get very upset when reality is described. We will speak to a group later and you will see this for yourself. She is refusing to accept it and would rather stick with her preconceived fantasy. It's painful to admit that you were wrong. It's painful to admit that you were fooled and it's amplified further when you are stuck in a situation with no realistic exit… so best to stick with the fantasy and ignore the truth. I will ask her about this directly later and she will agree.*)

Amanda:
Your extended family seem to express themselves, no? "Lars" and "Michael"… Michael is not mild! Soooooo… errrrrrrrrrrrr… er… I think.

(*AN – Amanda is now realising that she hasn't been perceiving the environment around her accurately. Today, for the first time, she is hearing the people around her talk in a real way about how they really feel and really think, which has shocked her. She is now trying to convince herself that she is right and they are wrong... about themselves! She will ask her husband about this and he will now tell her this to her face! She looks visibly in shock, with her mouth open.)*

Anthony:
What you have just heard seems to surprise you?

Amanda:
Yes!

Anthony:
I will tell you, it doesn't surprise me that you are responding like this... That's why I'm writing a book about it. Remember what your husband said before, that the person on the "outside" gets a different "performance" and the people that are native to this country get a different "performance"?

Amanda:
Ahhhhhhhhhh... ohhhhhhhhhhhhh...

Anthony:
(AN – Turning to Aksel.) Would you agree with that by the way?

Aksel:
Yeah, yeah, yeah!

Anthony:
Aksel, can you just summarise to your wife what I am saying because I can see that you agree completely?

(AN – Aksel turns to Amanda.)

Aksel:
Yes... so, basically if you are a native Norwegian, you will get treated like one, but if you are not, you will get treated like a "foreigner".

Anthony:
So a "foreigner" gets a totally different story would you say?

Aksel:
Yes.

Anthony:
Now, specifically, why have so many Norwegians given me this unique access?

(AN – Aksel turns back to his wife and explains it to her.)

Aksel:
Yes… he has talked to lots of people, he understands how people think in Norway… Yes, he is a foreigner… but he also gets to be on the "inside" because he understands… and this shared understanding, means that we can treat him differently.

Anthony:
Let me ask you this and tell me if I am wrong… The Norwegians that I have met can often speak to me more about their "Norwegianess" than to other Norwegians?

Aksel:
Oh yes, and I think that you have another advantage because you are not part of the local community… you are not going to go and talk to their enemies, about them and stuff…

Anthony:
Nope.

Aksel:
So it's easy to trust you!

Anthony:
Here is the thing, Amanda is also not part of the local community though?

Amanda:
Yes, right!

Anthony:
But she doesn't get the same access that I get. Why is that?

Aksel:
I think it's that she doesn't demonstrate the same awareness.

(AN – That this comment is normalised and treated as a normal thing to say internally shocks me. The rest of the room sits silently.)

Anthony:
Why aren't problems often discussed openly in Norway?

Nora:
Because I think that we are afraid of confrontation.

Anthony:
You mean "conflict averse"?

Jakob:
We spoke earlier about the issue of "loyalty", as you say… and "respect"… *it's a word that maybe we do not use so much…*

Anthony:
The word "respect" is not used so much here?

Jakob:
No, I don't think so… "loyalty"… I don't think that word…

Anthony:
So "loyalty" and "respect" are not familiar in Norway?

Jakob:
Yeah yeah… because (loyalty) is not so common… because my mindset… I have to admit… was that you have like peace with everybody… do I think loyalty and respect… we are not seeing what we are really doing. We are blind in a way.

Anthony:
So, it's a "self-perception" issue?

Jakob:
Yes.

Anthony:
Did your wife educate you, in a way?

Jakob:
Yes, yes! That's for sure! But as you say... your example... *that is almost normal here, in a way because we have to have peace with everybody.*

Anthony:
That is incredible because some people would never admit what you have just said... and you are willing, to admit it in front of your wife. That's kind of like a big thing!

Jakob:
Yeah yeah yeah! But maybe it was a hard struggle.

Nora:
I told him that I expect respect and I told him many times he doesn't understand what that is... many times I get frustrated and angry and he said that he did not want because he was afraid of reactions *(AN – she is referring to him failing to confront abusers in the community)...* and negative.

Anthony:
This is in the past?

Nora and Jakob:
Yes.

Nora:
It is... but sometimes, no...

Anthony:
There is a lot of pressure there... there is pressure... fear... so I know that it is tough but here is the thing,... you have just talked about understanding that it is an issue... that you are working through and that alone is hopeful... and I think it is incredible. By the way I am talking worldwide! Not just Norway...

(AN – They both laugh and say, "OK!")

Nora:
We want to change the world!

Anthony:
Your ability to communicate and talking about it openly is incredible.

Jakob:
I need help from my wife... because when you listen to others... you have another perspective.

Final Note: This is not an isolated group with unusual opinions and viewpoints. This is a normal group of people in Norway who are kindly opening up and telling us about life in Norway and the way in which they have been raised to think.

In fact, I found them to be, relatively speaking, kind and courteous. Let's end with their exact point of view relating to the "right road across twenty-five mountains" scenario because it has also been noted generally across Norway, by others before. For example, in *Xenophobe's guide to the Norwegians* published by *Xenophobe's Guides* by Dan Elloway (on page 13), he makes the point that I have just demonstrated and captured on tape. He states:

"This is quite disconcerting for any foreigner."

He writes when describing what happens if you "ask a Norwegian" if they can walk from a town to the next city that they will simply say "yes" but that "**he will not *think* to inform you that the walk would be around three days**".

Will not think... exactly what the respondents stated earlier almost word for word, regarding the same type of described scenario. Let's move on to the Norwegian town of Alesund...

This is Norway – A Dead Lady under my Window

I walked into a hotel in Alesund, Norway and immediately noticed the usual passive aggressive signs on the wall and one even telling me to 'be happy'. When I went back down to the reception and chatted with the staff and made a joke about it. I asked them what would be so hard about putting up a sign simply saying 'Welcome to Alesund'? What's with all this passive aggressiveness in Norway? They simply laughed.

Another sign in the room said this:

Windy and rainy out there? Good.
This room is powered by water and wind. It's no good just talking about the environment...

Alesund is known for being windy, rainy and stormy and my first night in Alesund was no exception and the wind and rain was just about to kill somebody outside my window that first night. I looked out of window and filmed a massive ship called MS Finnmarken. To my horror a woman had fallen from the deck. While I did not see her fall, I did watch the search being carried out by boats and a helicopter. I decided to go down and it was clear that after about an hour of such hazardous conditions, this person was not going to survive. The wind and rain whipped around me and I was soaked through. However, I did manage to film the helicopter land just a few metres in front of me and noticed that one of the boats which was around the corner had found the body in the water. I watched her attempted resuscitation and even saw the paramedics raise white sheets. There was no chance of her surviving. So imagine my shock to see that the media reported that night that she was alive in Tronheim's St Olavs Hospital. She wasn't pronounced dead until the following day.

I came back to my hotel room completely soaked through and immediately looked at the message on the wall, "*windy and rainy out there? Good*"

Norwegians tweet about passive aggressiveness in Norway

"Olympic Commercial From Norway Is The Greatest Ever. Passive Aggressive media continues"

#loveit S*** @S*******

"With my Norse heritage, I can promise you that Norway would crush it at the passive aggressive olympics"

e**** @l********

"Or as we mostly do in Norway, establish passive aggressive rules prohibiting people from thinking differently. Labelling it as being not loyal"

B**********s @B**********

*"It's just that time of year in Norway where everyone is passive aggressive because of everything being fu**ing cold"*

M**** @M********

"My family came from Norway/England, the type of immigrants this racist regime desires. As someone who's Norwegian/English; just want 2 say I'm glad we've welcomed immigrants from all over the world. It'd be horrible if it were just Norwegians:we can be so passive aggressive!"

@q*******

"Lucky. All I have is a 4 generation matriarchal tree branch straight to Norway and a lot of cooking knowledge and years of unlearning passive aggressive racism and homophobia. I'm so fun at parties lately"

D******** @K********

"So... im in Norway and they ask for tips in the most passive aggressive way"

@********

This is Norway...

A Conversation with a Lawyer

Let's return to Aksel the expert linguist and his American wife, along with the rest of the Norwegian group. After talking for a couple of hours, I suggested that we go for a walk. The group was happy, smiling and almost euphoric. This is often the initial reaction after these kinds of discussions… initially, at least. I even asked Aksel, "Why are you smiling so much?" At this stage though, I wanted to speak to Aksel's wife alone and I dropped behind the group with Amanda to talk… recorder still on… When we were alone, the first thing that Amanda said to me was:

"You're existence here makes me feel not alone!"

What a tragedy and sadly not the first or last time I would hear this on my journey across Norway. After reading to this point in the book, the uninitiated may be forgiven for drawing the conclusion that any *public expression of emotion or vulnerability* is considered a "crime" in Norway. This might make sense on a certain level because by expressing such emotion you are confirming its *existence* to those that may have rejected their expression and mere presence. The "anti-Janteloven" display of emotion, pain and vulnerability is, in itself, of course, a direct threat to the individual or collective who may have fully embraced the "philosophy" and suppressed these things within themselves and attempts to suppress the expression by others. Those are the people who cannot even comprehend the toxicity of their attitudes, actions and behaviour towards the innocent and of those who want nothing to do with *their* "Janteloven"… maybe due to denial, maybe due to ignorance, maybe due to peer pressure or even, let us not forget – even by choice.

To escape this, the unconditioned must conceal their emotions and this creates internal guilt… a kind of self-loathing. They know that when they deny the natural expression of normal human vulnerabilities or when they conceal them, to themselves and others, they are doing something "wrong"… because Janteloven is against human nature. Consequently, on some level, the suppressed will feel "criminalised" within the domain of the Janteloven… so if you could ever get someone to lower their defences, push through their fear and admit how they *truly* feel about their environment and the behaviour of the many Janteloven-conditioned people in it, even if only temporarily, it would probably have a "confessional" tone to it. They know that they colluded and are complicit. They kept quiet. They never protested. They have enabled this too. This is why they might, if you could ever get them to tell the truth and transcend their behavioural normalisation, say something like:

"Yes, I confess…"

Just like Amanda will. For the same reasons, as previously mentioned, let's again start near the end of the conversation… by the way… did you get angry or upset reading what Aksel and the group or by anything which has been said by the respondents in this book so far? If your life has been touched directly or indirectly by Janteloven or if you have simply previously been exposed to Janteloven, you might even be angry at me, I suspect? You might consider every word said against the collective in this book as a personal attack on *you*, every question asked… an interrogation of *you*… if that is you, simply go back to the top of this very chapter and start again. For the rest of you, we're going to jump straight in at an odd moment in the conversation… well, it's all odd… but chronologically, an odd moment. We're talking about an incident which has just happened regarding pizza which will be explained in full by the end of the chapter.

Anthony:
You didn't even get an apology! I'm looking at you strangely now because you said, and I heard you say, that you wanted the beef pizza three times… He went into the shop… He completely ignored what you wanted… He came out of the shop… answered your question with a single word of rejection… laughed in your face… he did not apologise… doesn't that make you FEEL anything?

Amanda:
A little bit hurtful… Yes! It's true!

Anthony:
Here is the thing though, why has it taken so long to make you feel comfortable to simply just say that? Why has it taken such a long time to get through to the truth?

Amanda:
Yes, I confess. It was hurtful.

(AN – Finally the truth! Even though it is not the answer to the question asked. The truth… and a "confession" too… what an incredible phrase. It implies that she was lying all along. She was fighting against herself the whole time… at least she got there in the end.)

Anthony:
Yes?

Amanda:
Just now I didn't feel that it really mattered…

Anthony:
But I am talking about on an *emotional* level… and by the way… even when you purchase a new pizza for yourself later… his act still remains. He still ignored you. He still didn't listen to you… isn't that a core problem for you? That's a core issue? It's not something which can be solved by simply buying a new pizza for yourself?

Amanda:
Yes… yes, it is a core issue. I think in most of the Norwegians (laugh).

Anthony:
You feel so? Please, tell me more?

Amanda:
Hmmm… well I will use the word individualistic… I wouldn't use "selfish" because… yeah…

Anthony:
Yes, it's better not to use the words that you "wouldn't use" and use the words that you do want to use, indeed. Now, when you say "individualistic"… I feel like you're actually implying unkind or mean? Would that be true?

Amanda:
Yeah!

Anthony:
So, just so we're clear… are you saying that you perceive many Norwegians as acting in an unkind or mean way?

Amanda:
Hmmmmmmmmm…

Anthony:
You can tell the truth and say how you feel.

Amanda:
They don't say mean things… but… some of the things they do are quite mean, without knowing that.

Anthony:
Now, I'm not concerned about the "without knowing that" part… but I am interested in the reality of the actions and the consequences to those mean "things" that you've mentioned?

Amanda:
Yes.

(AN – prolonged silence.)

Anthony:
… It seems like you're reluctant to say how you really feel though? You've already said that you have disregarded the word "selfish", so I'm going to ask you again… Do you think that, in your opinion, that a lot of Norwegians actions are unkind or mean, regardless of whether they may know it or not?

Amanda:
Hmmmmmm…

(AN – prolonged silence.)

Anthony:
It's a simple "yes" or "no", I think?

Amanda:
(*Laugh.*)

Anthony:
I'm going to point this out again… it's interesting… do you notice that you're finding it really hard to say how you really feel either way? You can just say, "no" if you wish! I'm curious though… we are alone and I am not Norwegian so why are you finding it hard to express how you really feel about your new country?

(*AN – She cannot say how she really feels… her body language clearly indicates that she thinks "yes"… but she seems to be fighting actually verbalising how she really feels.*)

Amanda:
Because if you judge something, you have to learn about a culture.

Anthony:
Just so I understand what you've said correctly. You are saying that if someone is unkind or mean to you, then you have to learn about that person's culture?

Amanda:
Yes, because they are not… I think that "mean" is related to their intentions… they may not intend to be like that.

Anthony:
I understand but if somebody is mean or unkind to you why would you care about that persons intentions or even about their culture? What has that got to do with it exactly?

Amanda:
Hmmmmmmmmmm…

(*AN – She is stunned and remains in sustained pensive silence. I can see that we are now close to the revelation of truth.*)

Anthony:
Could it be that you're in denial or trying to make excuses do you think?

Amanda:
It's so challenging!

(AN – I am confronting her usually held beliefs and she's finding her own thought process hard to understand which is why she is finding it so "challenging". The question is very simple. The most logical answer would of course be; "Some Norwegians are but some are not".)

Anthony:
I will ask you again, if you don't mind? Are you saying that in your experience a lot of Norwegians act in a mean or unkind way? Yes or no?

Amanda:
I have to say… they do things without caring about people's feelings…

Anthony:
I'm observing that it's painful for you to admit how you feel? You married a Norwegian man, you have connections to Norway now… it's like the "fantasy" is slightly different from the reality, in some ways… obviously there are beautiful things too… but part of you… obviously has a little bit of denial within yourself, you don't want to admit "actually what happened I didn't like… it was mean"… and you know what, maybe it's a case of, "I can't bring myself to say it… because it's too painful"?… is there any truth to what I said?

Amanda:
Yes… it's TRUE! You are RIGHT! It's painful to say they ARE selfish!

(AN – She is beginning to speak consciously, not from what FEAR compels her to do and what she thinks she should say… note that she is now using the word that she just moments ago vigorously rejected and said that she "wouldn't use". A word that she herself volunteered without prompting and then subsequently rejected… and has now accepted as accurate.)

Anthony:
But sometimes you just have to say how you feel… don't suppress what you really believe because you're scared of anybody in a new country… otherwise you will go crazy after a while won't you?

Amanda:

Yeah, but… yeah, you're right! Because… I feel more secure talking to you now, because my husband is inside.

(AN – This answer proves that it is fear, it is manipulation and it is passive aggressive coercion that is manipulating her feelings and limiting her ability to freely express them… both from individuals and the collective, in my opinion.)

Anthony:

Stick to your principles! Because after time… things that are not acceptable and overstepping boundaries in your life… in Norway… will just suddenly start becoming "acceptable" to you. You already said that you are changing in Norway. Now, with regards to what you just said, "I can just go and buy a pizza"… that's not the point… of course you CAN… but you shouldn't have to do that should you?

Amanda:

But you know what… normally when I go back… I will still ask him why! Not because you are here… because I am the kind of person… questions in my heart… I will clarify.

Anthony

Can I ask? You mentioned earlier that it is the Norwegian "way" to just keep it "inside"?

Amanda:

Yes, they just swallow it!

Anthony:

Wouldn't that create extreme psychological pressure?

Amanda:

Right! Yes! I agree.

Anthony:

And that is what I'm saying… some of the stuff that was just said earlier… you said that it was "weird"… but I would suggest that it is actually irrational to think like that?

Amanda:
Yes... yeah yeah yeah.

Anthony:
They were analysing the simplest, little thing and imagine, if that's their thought process analysing something so insignificant like that... imagine what's in their head every day?

Amanda:
Yes.

Anthony:
I am not surprised that anti-depressant use is so high in Norway...

(AN – If a society stigmatises the expression of vulnerability and pain people will not feel comfortable reporting their problems, which must call into question the accuracy of its "statistics". Now, I will give you one example of one woman who would steal her sisters' anti-depressants and encourages her sister to get even more from the doctor to replace them. She is is on no official statistical record in Norway but she exists and I saw the box of anti-depressants that she steals from her sister with my own eyes and I confirmed with the sister that she actually steals them too. I spoke with a doctor who told me that certain reception staff, especially in rural areas, will gossip to the rest of the community if you go to a doctor for depression or a potential mental health issue. I state this so that when disingenuous people quote their "statistics" to try and deny the true less picturesque reality you can understand that many people in Norway are scared to reveal the truth about their inner pain and struggles to their friends, family or even the medical community. Who can blame them?)

Amanda:
I am the *outsider* here and I don't want them to kind of have to sacrifice for me.

(AN – She is married to a Norwegian...she now has Norwegian family... yet she describes herself and considers herself as an "outsider". That is incredible and disturbing... but a typical self-image of non-Norwegians that I have spoken to on my journey... further conversation...)

Anthony:
Earlier when we were talking there were several occasions when you

literally had your mouth wide open in shock. You are also part of the discussion… How do you feel about it? What did you think about what you learnt? Obviously you were shocked at times… what do you think?

Amanda:
I think… weeeeeell… Norwegian culture… it's quite weird!

Anthony:
I understand.

Amanda:
One of my colleagues is from New York and he also thinks that the Norwegian culture is weird… like taking the luggage thing! Is that normal behaviour in the UK?

Anthony:
It's not.

Amanda:
You help your girlfriend?

Anthony:
Of course you would offer to help if you were able otherwise you would probably be perceived as a selfish person.

Amanda:
When I say "girlfriend", I mean just normal friends… just normal girls… Is it OK if you help them take their luggage?

Anthony:
Of course. It's just a normal thing to do.

Amanda:
Yes! Yeah, yeah it's true!

Anthony:
There's obviously a lot of neurotic thinking… things are so often over analysed and it's just complete overload. Somebody does something nice or offers help and it's just like "Oh my God, why did they do that!? Why did they do it!? They're making me feel bad! They think I am weak!?… I

am not weak! They are saying that I am stupid?!... I can carry my things!... it's better that I carry this 50 kg on my own then somebody offer to help me... it upsetting me... they're such a rude person to intrude!". That is just crazy. As Nora just said, she couldn't handle hearing even five seconds of somebody simply saying... "There are twenty-five treacherous mountains that way"... She'd rather ignore it because she was "busy" and it would stress her out.

Amanda:
Yes... and you have a saying in the UK "ladies first" is that right?

(AN – Amanda seems discombobulated. She seems to be using this opportunity away from the group, to ask me questions to gauge what is "normal" behaviour.)

Anthony:
It's said, yes.

Amanda:
But in Norway, no! They don't agree with ladies first! Sometimes back home I say to my husband "Hey! Ladies first"... Or "if you open the door you should let me go first"... and he is like "What!? No!"

Further conversation

Amanda:
I think you have inspired me!

Anthony:
Really? Why?

Amanda:
To think more... that if I am in a foreign country I shouldn't give excuses to not treating people fairly!

Anthony:
And also to not accept things that you don't agree with?

Amanda:
Yes!

Anthony:
Just remember to not forget who YOU are… because you can help too.

Amanda:
Yes! Yeah!

Anthony:
It works both ways. I think that too many people that come to this country simply accept everything because there are a great deal of Norwegians… who don't want to accept anything new from outside of Norway… that needs to change… not just for foreigners, but for themselves, for their own mental health and for their own benefit.

Amanda:
Yes!

That was the end of the conversation. It took me a lot of hard work to get that truth, which you will see now. Let's now go back to the beginning…

Amanda:
Your existence here makes me feel not alone!

Anthony:
Why? Do you sometimes feel alone?

Amanda:
Because I don't understand any Norwegian, so I'm not the only one who don't understand this…

Anthony:
Do you sometimes feel a little bit lonely and isolated when you don't understand?

Amanda:
Yes! *(Laughs.)* Because they just keep talking in Norwegian.

(AN – At this point Aksel, her husband, tried to take her away… I told him "No, no, no, can I borrow her… you guys go ahead… I'm talking to her." Amanda

laughed and said it was fine. I have noticed this all over Norway... often when you start speaking individually... many other people get very uncomfortable, visibly uncomfortable when they realise that they can't influence and manipulate them and they realise that there is a distinct possibility that they will tell me the truth. They often try to passive aggressively stop the conversation... this has happened several times over Norway. I always did the same thing, very politely and directly said, "No, I specifically want to speak with them alone away from YOU. So I can know what they feel without the group influence." I tell them to their face and with a smile... as long as the interviewee wants to be interviewed (which was almost 100% of the time because they are flattered that I want their opinion)... what can the suppressor do next? Nothing. They know that their passive aggressive tricks won't work on me because, as every bully knows, it's always a bad idea to attempt to bully people stronger than you. This is the same tactic respondents will often try in the group discussion. They MUST try to keep authentic communication to a minimum and suppress honest effective communication... they actually try to suppress communication... and they want to reduce the risk of exposure... only THEY want to be interviewed, so they can, in their mind, try to control the narrative. This implies that, on some level, many know it's all a sham at risk of exposure and collapse. However... and this is the beauty... on so many occasions, I have spoken to the people around them separately. This is because almost 100% of the people I asked for an interview agreed straight away and were flattered and emphatically said, "Yes!" Now, because, I'm sorry to say, many of the Norwegians that I met often didn't talk to each other and also many often hid their true emotions and because they had been pouring out their heart and all of the abuse and struggles they have to face in day-to-day life in Norway to me... they then keep very quiet about their interview to those around them. I guarantee anonymity, of course. This means that I have often times, interviewed several members of a group separately BEFORE I interview them as a group so when a bully or someone is passive aggressive they KNOW that I know... but the COLLECTIVE does not know that I know. The bullies do not know that their victim has already told me all I need to know... I NEVER tell or confirm that I have interviewed anybody at all. The only exception is if somebody witnessed or participated in the same discussion. Many of the people speaking, their colleagues, employees, friends, family, children, relatives... have pretty much told me everything about them and they have been happy to! As long as you don't put the spotlight on them specifically, they were happy to aim the spotlight at the people around them and essentially tell me everything... loyalty was so low that it was very easy and very natural. Now, if somebody is trying to stop somebody from talking freely? Let's see what they're trying to hide! After the rest of the group leave us... I mention on the tape "just for the record... now we're alone"... my voice *whispered, like we are talking secretly… I have observed this kind of whispering a lot in Norway. Amongst the Norwegians themselves and foreigners amongst Norwegians and Norwegians among foreigners. So many people seem to hide their true feelings and opinions in Norway.)*

Anthony:

I've noticed this a lot in Norway… when I'm with my friends, they will often speak the whole time in Norwegian and I am just sat there on my own. Does this happen a lot to you too?

Amanda:

Yes! Yeah! That's happened a lot!

Anthony:

It feels rude and you feel so unacknowledged?

Amanda:

Yeah, yeah, yeah!

Anthony:

So, tell me, you have you experienced that? When they *know* that you don't speak Norwegian they still talk in Norwegian? Why would they do that, do you think?

Amanda:

Because I think that some people do not speak very good English so they speak in Norwegian and some other members of his family don't speak good English.

(AN – This is blatant denial and rationalisation. Yes, on occasion, this would be the case but I am talking about when everybody can speak English, obviously. She previously said it happens "a lot" and it makes her feel "alone"… so it's a regularly occurring issue. Her answer ignores this completely and focuses on the exceptions which are irrelevant to the question. No reasonable person would expect somebody who can't speak English to speak English. This is a tactic of denial… you will see more of this soon… I will address this directly.)

Anthony:

But you just said a few moments ago, that it happens "a lot"?

Amanda:
Yes.

Anthony:
So, if it happens "a lot", it's not just his family, obviously? I'm asking...
why would it happen "a lot" when people know that you don't speak
Norwegian, they speak English, but they choose to keep talking in
Norwegian, whereby that you don't understand? Why, do you think?

(AN – This question addresses the real issue. Note that she completely ignores it.)

Amanda:
I can't understand anything!

Anthony:
But you know they speak English?

Amanda:
Yes they do! but... errrrrrr... *actually, I don't mind that much...* but at first
when they just kept talking in Norwegian, I used that time as my personal
time and I just play "twitch" on my phone, on my own.

*(AN – The first thing that she said, totally contradicts this "new" opinion now.
She is not communicating rationally because, in my opinion, she is in denial.)*

Anthony:
Did you feel hurt a little bit?

Amanda:
Weeeeeeeeeeeell... maybe at first! But now I don't really feel that strong... I
don't have strong feelings...

Anthony:
OK, did you feel good?

Amanda:
No, no... normal I think...

Anthony:
OK... I noticed something... tell me what you think about this. I've

noticed something with many immigrants that come to Norway. If something's deemed rude in their home country, they are reluctant to say that it is rude here. So let's just say, for example, that I am sitting at a table with a group of Norwegians and I don't speak Norwegian and everybody knows that I don't speak Norwegian, in Norway an immigrant might be like "Oh well... maybe... it's fine"... but really feel hurt inside.

(AN – These questions get straight to the truth. I had no idea that this question would be played out in front of my eyes, in real time, on tape, in a few moments time... we catch it happening on tape... and then discuss it...all live... read on...)

Amanda:
Hmmm hmmmm.

Anthony:
But if it happened in their home country... they would say "That's rude!" ... straight!

Amanda:
Ahhhhhhhhh.

Anthony:
It's like earlier on... you feel like you're being "offensive", so it's hard to say the real truth in Norway if the truth is perceived as "offensive"? Do you have any experience with that?

Amanda:
Weeeeeell...

(AN – Note that she can't answer these questions logically, maturely or even using normal words.)

Anthony:
Let me put it another way then. If I am German and I speak German and I'm in a conversation with you and you only speak English, and if there were three of us... two of us knew that you did not understand German and, by the way, we also speak perfect English but we just *choose* to speak in German... That would clearly be inconsiderate and rude, would it not?

Amanda:
Yeah, yeah!

Anthony:
If we are talking German for one hour and you are sitting there alone,
then obviously that is rude?

Amanda:
Yes… hmm… hmmmm…

Anthony:
For me that's not even a question… It's just obviously rude… but it
seems that you don't feel the same way?

Amanda:
No, I don't really feel that. Because I think… "OK, it's his family… it's his
place."

*(AN – Obviously, it can be "his family" and it can be "his place" and it can also
be rude at the same time. A physical location and environment has absolutely no
relevance or bearing on a personal objective interpretation of whether a behaviour
is "rude" or not. It is simply a judgement call based on a behaviour. If she said,
"He can be rude because it's his house and his rules and he can act in any way he
wants", then that has underlying logic to it. However, it is irrational to say that
somebody's actions are rude, but that they are not acting in a rude way, due to
merely location. To remain logical she must address reality in a logical way and be
consistent i.e. their behaviour is rude or it is not. She can't say that the behaviour
is "rude" for one occasion and situation but now she is in Norway, suddenly it
is… "eeerrrrr, maybbeeee… errrrrrrr". Has she been so influenced that she is
scared? Has she been conditioned that she is suffering from cognitive dissonance? If
so, we will soon be able to find out… let's continue…)*

Anthony:
It's not just in his family? You said it happens "many times"?

Amanda:
Yes, OK… okaaaaaaaay.

*(AN – It's very clear on the tape that she is completely stunned now. She has now
reached the point where her own logic breaks down.)*

Anthony:
Outside of the family… in real Norwegian life?

(AN – Aksel returned at this point and tried to encourage her to go with him a second time… this time, Amanda herself said firmly, "You guys go ahead I'll catch up with you later", because on a certain level, I suspect that she is intrigued and curious. Part of her desires to know what is going on… we will get there and we will articulate it together shortly after she has worked it out for herself. I see fear in Aksel's eyes. I call this "the look"… I've seen it all over Norway. It's when the eyes glaze, the cheeks go red, the jaw tightens. I address it directly, and say, "Don't worry! Talking about languages and stuff!" and then something incredible happened in front of my own eyes and the tape recorder captured it all! Let's go back thirty minutes though. I was walking with the whole group and we were talking about food and Amanda said that she really wanted beef pizza. We agreed that we should get pizza. We then debated the level of "greatness" of beef pizza. Aksel disagreed and said that cheese pizza was best. Amanda said that she wanted beef pizza and he could have cheese pizza if he wanted. As we walk and talked, just before we got to the pizza place, she said again, for a third time, in front of us ALL, that she wanted BEEF pizza. I myself noticed that she had now said this at least three times. However, I didn't focus on it because there could be no conceivable chance that Aksel could realistically now walk out of that place without a beef pizza for her… it would just be crazy and, although I had just spent time with them and now know how they operate and think, I didn't think that they could do that to her. I say "they" because Benji also heard that Amanda wanted beef pizza and went into the restaurant with Aksel. Aksel walks out of restaurant with a massive smile on his face and four massive pizzas, right in front of her face and passed us both doing the interview… what happens next is incredible… and so is Amanda's reaction…)

Amanda:
(AN – asking her husband.) Did you get the beef one?

Aksel:
No.

Amanda:
Why not?

Aksel:
My wallet. *(AN – Aksel hands her his wallet and walks off laughing.)*

Amanda:
OK… I'll see you… *(Amanda then bursts out laughing.)*

(AN – I was shocked but did not show it. She just accepted it as completely normal! Not even worthy of conversation. In fact, she would soon DEFEND his behaviour and start normalising it as completely normal Norwegian behaviour and totally fine with her. I remained calm and waited for her to say something about the pizza situation… she didn't. She resumed the previous question as if nothing has just happened at all. I went with it as to not influence her, but I was obviously going to raise this shortly. Until then, back to the original question… back to the usual avoidance and tactics and games… question the very clear question etc.… all very predicable now…)

Amanda:
Do you mean with friends?

Anthony:
I mean with anybody.

Amanda:
Let me think.…

Anthony:
Let me tell you what I'm trying to do… I am trying to get you to connect with the *emotion* of what you previously just said. You just said that for once you "feel like you are not alone"?

(AN – Consistent exposure to this type of irrational abnormal behaviour, like what just happened in front of our very eyes, deadens normal emotional responses and reactions. It desensitises normal people in my opinion. Amanda chooses to dampen her own rational response rather than confront the behaviour and the perpetrator. Benji didn't say, "Aksel, your wife wants beef pizza", he remained silent in that restaurant too. We can't excuse this as a bunch of low IQ individuals who don't know better, that would be preposterous… they are grown adults with, at least Aksel, extremely high education levels. He has just proven what he himself and the group previously said about thinking for themselves. Now, that is part one. Then there is part two. Why would an American woman with intelligence just accept that like it's normal behaviour? She acts like everything is normal and will go on to defend it as normal… the question for me… is this conditioning? Is this coercion? What type of manipulation is this exactly? Can I get to some truth

and logic? I know the answer because I can see that Amanda has underlying logic but is easily manipulated and made pliable by this group and is scared to criticise bad acts, it appears… this fear, in my opinion has been INSTILLED in her by the collective.)

Amanda:
Yes.

Anthony:
So, obviously that implies that you feel "alone"?

Amanda:
Yeah.

Anthony:
That obviously implies that the other times you feel alone too. Now, obviously, it is not nice to feel lonely?

Amanda:
Yeah! It's not nice to feel alone.

Anthony:
So… why don't you characterise (it like that)… because if the people around you make you feel alone, obviously, that is not a good thing?

Amanda:
Hmm… you're right.

Anthony:
But my feeling is, that a lot of times behaviour which is considered rude by immigrants… immigrants feel like they are the ones with the problem… it's something "wrong" with them. Do you have any experience with that?

Amanda:
Yes! I think… yes, you are right! Because I think… I'm just travelling here… I am not living here… So, for example if I just started Norwegian then I can't understand all of the things that they are talking about… But they still keep speaking Norwegian! I feel left out!

Anthony:
And that's why you feel lonely?

Amanda:
Yes.

(AN – I will now raise the pizza issue.)

Anthony:
There is something that I just observed and I would like to speak about it with you. Previously you asked your husband three or four separate times "are you just going to get cheese pizza or are you going to get a beef one as well? The beef one is my favourite"… you also said "maybe we should get the beef pizza"… and he has just walked out of the restaurant with a pile of four cheese pizzas.

Amanda:
And gave me the wallet!

(AN – Immediate reflex defence response! Just like in the group discussion, she defends them without thinking logically… it's 100% reflex… she instinctively goes to defend him and excuse his behaviour… she did not even logically compute whether the behaviour was worthy of being defended.)

Anthony:
You asked him "did you get the beef pizza?" and he said "no" and then handed you the wallet… But here is the thing… for me it would have been normal… we're talking about empathy and consideration for others now…

Amanda:
Oh yeah!

Anthony:
You clearly wanted a beef pizza and he could have easily got one beef pizza and three cheese pizzas?

Amanda:
Yes.

Anthony:
But he didn't… He didn't… He didn't get what you wanted he only got what HE wanted. You even said before "I like the beef pizza" and you dropped so many hints in addition as well?

Amanda:
Yes.

Anthony:
And you literally had to say to him "Oh, did you get it?" and he just said "no"… he didn't even say anything other than "no"… So, this is what I'm trying to say… this thing about empathy and sensitivity to other people?

Amanda:
Yes… hmmm.

Anthony:
To me, what I have just observed in front of my eyes… it's like he didn't even consider your feelings at all… he just completely ignored what you said. Now for me, that's just a fact. Now that I have just articulated that… Do you agree or disagree?

(AN – She now realises and starts to think logically… she will also start thinking about why she is acting in this way…)

Amanda:
Yes, I agree with you! Do you know what, I'm kind of so used to it already… at first I would get so furious! At the very beginning when I was with him… and I would ask him afterwards "Hey! You know what I want the big pizza, why didn't you get it!?"

Anthony:
And how long into the relationship would you ask those questions? Six months?

Amanda:
The first year.

(AN – I suspect that she's being over optimistic. I don't see how a normal person, and, with no disrespect, somebody as suggestible as her, could ever withstand this

type of manipulation, passive aggression and subsequent normalisation by so many people around her, for one year... maybe one to two months if you were very strong and a non-conformist... I am sceptical...)

Anthony:
So can I ask you, do you think that this kind of interaction has grinded you down? Because you have changed... because you said that something which you noticed at the beginning but now you realise that the "environment" is not going to change?

Amanda:
I think, it's because, just now... I don't have *that* strong feelings because I know that I am standing in front of the shop and I can just buy the beef pizza myself.

(AN – She has said repeatedly today that she doesn't have "strong feelings". I think she really means: "feelings, any more, like I did at the beginning". Note her response... it's devastating to see what her new environment has done to her.)

Anthony:
But I am talking about from an emotional point... It would have been so easy for him just to listen to what you said?

Amanda:
Yeah.

Anthony:
It just shows that he didn't even consider your feelings or thoughts even though you explicitly told him and I have observed this in Norway many many many times... in fact we have just discussed it for, like, three hours!

Amanda:
(Bursts out laughing.)

Anthony:
I basically just said, "Your mother has just expressed pain because of the Janteloven... she has just told you how much it hurts her..." I ask, "How does that make you feel?" Nothing! He was just like... "I think parts of Janteloven are OK." Imagine his mother hearing that? And they just all sat there like it's nothing and normal?

Amanda:
Hmmmm.

Anthony:
I see an emotional disconnect.

Amanda:
Hmmm hmmm.

Anthony:
Empathy is obviously a challenge?

Amanda:
Yes.

Anthony:
Am I crazy or what do you think?

Amanda:
When I first talked to Aksel I told him that Norwegians are so individualistic!
(AN – in my opinion this is a euphemism.) I think in Norway, maybe it's
Scandinavia... They are extremely individualistic, "I just do my thing I just
eat my food"... just like in the fridge in the kitchen it's just like that... In the
Norwegian house you visit... you can see this level belongs to this person...
this level belongs to this person... *(laugh)*... and then they will say "this is
your food... I will not eat it... Unless maybe you offer or somebody really
wants to eat it"... So then I just thought "You guys are weird!"

*(AN – Ultimately, the word "weird" is meaningless... it's too vague as to be
redundant... even though it is a euphemism often used in Norway. In actual fact,
in my opinion, that's NOT what they actually mean. That is only what they are
saying in a dampened way because they could NEVER EVER describe the
behaviour accurately because they fear reprisal. They can't say, for example, you
are RUDE or you are DISRESPECTFUL or you are SELFISH or you are
ABUSIVE. Instead words are used which are vague and often have a "comedic"
element instead... or just excused... it's actually incredible conditioning by those
who suppress criticism, evade responsibility, accountability and facing the truth
about their own behaviour and actions. We have seen this trick many times
already in this book and will continue to see it regularly. We're going to address
this exact point head on right now.)*

Anthony:
Now I must say that I feel that you just using the word
"individualistic"...

Amanda:
Individualistic.

(AN – Note the child-like repetition and answers.)

Anthony:
... I actually think that that's just you being "polite" because the more
accurate word is "selfish" is it not?

Amanda:
Yes... sometimes when I get angry... I will say... "You're f****** selfish!"

Anthony:
OK then... let me ask you... why did you previously use the word
"individualistic"? Why didn't you just say "selfish"? For example, him not
getting that pizza just now is selfish because he was not thinking about
you, he was only thinking about himself, he talked about how much he
likes cheese pizza... we know that he only cared about what he wanted
and he disregarded what you wanted?

Amanda:
Hmm hmmm.

Anthony:
In any country of the world, that is "selfish".

Amanda:
Hmm hmmm.

Anthony:
So, why are we describing it as "individualistic" and not "selfish", in
Norway?

Amanda:
Hmmmmmmmmm.

Anthony:
It's almost like the language rules are different in Norway?

Amanda:
Yeah.

Anthony:
It's like we excuse rude behaviour when we wouldn't excuse it in any other country of the world?

Amanda:
Yes... back home... we have "individualistic"... and "selfish"... and they are different... errrrr... did the people really *intend* do that...

(AN – She immediately refers to "intentions". This is a method of perpetual avoidance because she can NEVER know his true "intentions". So, instead of looking at behaviour and logically framing it... where she will have to conclude that the evidence points to where it points...she might not like it... but that is reality... instead of facing reality... she ignores the BLATANT behaviour and hyper-focuses on "intention". This is EXACTLY why Aksel is also so concerned and enthusiastic about "intentions", because it, conversely gives him UNLIMITED freedom to act as he pleases without accountability. I have heard this repeatedly in my discussions. "Intention", that's why intentions are often more important than reality...as you have just seen. She is literally ignoring reality and going straight to the "intentions", even though any sane person can see his intentions... he has been telling us about them in detail for hours... he is now carrying them out in front of our eyes... but instead, she is living in denial about it. It is something which you will see almost all immigrants do in this book series. She is not alone in acting this way.)

Anthony:
So you're saying that there is an "intention" behind it?

Amanda:
Yes.

Anthony:
In real life, it doesn't matter if you "intend" or not... the point is, does somebody think about the other person and does the action have a conclusion which incorporates the other person's views?

Amanda:
Hmmm.

Anthony:
And if it doesn't... it doesn't matter what the person thinks or how they
"feel" about it because it's selfish regardless of how they "feel" or their
"intentions". Because they are only thinking of themselves by definition?

Amanda:
Yes. If you think them really bad (laugh).

*(AN – Note that the words change based on how you FEEL and THINK not on
the reality of what they actually describe.)*

Anthony:
No. I am just telling you the definition of the word "selfish". It's when
somebody only thinks of themselves.

Amanda:
Yes... other than other people.

Anthony:
So you said to him, "this pizza... I want to taste this pizza"... and he just
walked in and then he walked out with...

Amanda:
Four cheese pizzas.

Anthony:
With four different pizzas and not one of them one that you wanted. You
must know that he ignored everything that you said?

Amanda:
Yes.

Anthony:
So do you understand? How is that not selfish?

Amanda:
Yeah... but... maybe... I... hahaha... didn't think... about this is a bad

way... I mean it... it's not nice... obviously... yeah...

(AN – It's incredible because her answers are almost exactly like Aksel's when she is confronted with logic. She even giggles like a child at the same moment mid-way through her "answer", just like Aksel did. She instinctively speaks and seems not to be thinking rationally... the words are gibberish... auto-response... it's actually incredible... the question is... why? What is it in this environment that makes someone act in such an irrational way? The answer is on every page of this book... read her answer again... she equates the reality with a "bad" thing so disregards the accurate description of that reality, based on that perspective. She equates the accurate use of the word as using the word in a "bad way" and thus suspends its use as invalid and "wrong". Consequently, her perception of reality no longer matches reality. We have already seen this in several places in Norway but it will feature in our conversations all over the country.)

Anthony:
And this is the point I am getting to... I've noticed with so many immigrants in Norway... behaviour that you would not tolerate in your home countries you rationalise and tolerate here. Why?

Amanda:
Yes. Right.

Anthony:
I have actually seen this with almost all of the immigrants that I have spoken to in Norway. They excuse certain behaviour. So if something happens that is rude... they excuse it... they make excuses. Why is that? Do you observe that?

Amanda:
Because if this was my brother back home in America... and I told him... and I knew that he knew... he would buy the one that I wanted... and at least include me!

Anthony:
Can I ask you, what would you say to your brother, if he came out of the shop with four pizzas that you did not want, after previously telling him what you wanted? What would you say to him? Wouldn't you think to yourself, "I didn't know that my brother was this selfish?"

Amanda:
No, I don't think that "selfish" would come to my mind.

Anthony:
Oh, "I think that he only thinks of his own needs?" What would you
think? What words *would* you use? How would you describe him?

Amanda:
Ahhh... I would say, "Why did you just buy the thing for yourself!? It's not
included me?"

*(AN – Notice that she did not answer that question. This is where the painful
part comes in... to verbally acknowledge that the behaviour is selfish even though
she knows it is... it's now an inner fight for her.)*

Anthony:
Can you not think about how you would think about him if he did that?

Amanda:
Even back home, I wouldn't use this word "selfish"... this word is so strong!

*(AN – This is pure acclimatization to a different type of irrational interaction.
She is answering with irrational answers but is using the same techniques and
logical fallacies as the group which is an indicator that she has been conditioned.
Otherwise, why would she answer, even if illogically... why not in a variant way?
She is answering and pulling out the exact techniques of her peers now. It's totally
sad to see actually... a kind of "Stockholm Syndrome" but on a larger
"Janteloven" size scale? She refuses to use accurate words in Norway because she is
scared to face the truth? It seems that simple. Why? She has told us already. Note
what happens next. She changes again...)*

Anthony:
OK... So tell me something... The word "selfish"... it's literally the
definition of what just happened just now, do you agree?

Amanda:
Yes.

Anthony:
Why are you reluctant then to use the word which described what just

happened? Are you afraid of causing offence?

Amanda:
Maybe! Because even if it was my brother, I would say, "Hey! You are so selfish!" I would say that... because... hmmmm...

(AN – She is obviously intimidated and fearful of saying how she really feels to such an extent where she can't even think it, let alone express it verbally. Note, also, that this is the total opposite of what she said just moments previously. Finally, note that she is with me and we are alone and away from the group and away from anybody that could even be remotely "offended".)

Anthony:
Can I ask you something... is it a bit mean?

Amanda:
Yes, maybe... or just care about yourself.

Anthony:
That's the definition of "selfish"?

Amanda:
Yes, if you really use the word "selfish" then it's really is. Yes.

(AN – This is an illogical response... if you "really" use the word then it "really" is... what word was I really using before then? Actually, she has a point. In my opinion, she was not previously interpreting the word accurately at all. She was interpreting a warped version of the word. She truly wasn't comprehending the actual word itself as she interprets these simple words through a warped lens of conditioning and trauma, which means she responds to the trauma and not the actual definition of the word. She rejects the original word even though she understands and comprehends that it is perfectly accurate and reasonable and appropriate. This is incredible stuff.)

Anthony:
And this is what I was referring to earlier when I was talking about language... normal language... they played mind games and used mental gymnastics to describe things, which are so... for example... "I want that pizza"... he walks in and then walks out with four different pizzas. You ask him if he got your pizza. He says "no"... to me that is a very simple:

selfish. Instead of just saying that, you obviously don't want to disappoint them… you obviously don't want to acknowledge; "You know what? That is quite selfish"… and I understand that it's quite difficult to say in this place… but maybe in a month… what will happen if you have to deal with 100 interactions like this in Norway?

Amanda:
Hmmm hmmm.

Anthony:
And instead of just saying that… because then you would have to concede that regular rude behaviour is simply regular rude behaviour in the country that you are now residing in… so, instead, you gloss over mean and selfish things. Is there any truth to that?

Amanda:
That may happen because I am in a foreign country?

Anthony:
Yes… I suspect that you want it to be a positive experience… so if you experience something that is obviously selfish, you can say to yourself "Oh, it's not selfish… that's errrrrmmmm errrrmmmmnm" and some people even say "Oh, that's just "Norwegian politeness"… when rude behaviour is rude behaviour anywhere in the world and they know that but simply can't face it.

Amanda:
Yes!

Anthony:
Mean is mean everywhere in the world.

Amanda:
Yes!

Anthony:
But you know this! But I am just thinking, why does your perception of reality change when you are in Norway and with Norwegians? Why?

Amanda:
Hmmmmmm…

Anthony:
You said that you wouldn't tolerate that from your brother, so why?

Amanda:
I wouldn't be mean to him… I wouldn't say "you're so selfish"… but…

Anthony:
But you said that you would think that?

Amanda:
Yes… I would think that it's weird!

Anthony:
But why?

(AN – Amanda will now attempt to start thinking logically about her own thought process and how she actually felt and why. She explains that she is confused and doesn't know why i.e. "for some reason"… this is classic a sign of being conditioned and manipulated, of course.)

Amanda:
But for some reason just now, I didn't… Maybe I just assume "it's their culture"… I just don't bother… I have this type of feeling…

Anthony:
Just so you know… I have just pointed this out to you… so obviously that means that I noticed, heard and understood that you wanted beef pizza?

(AN – I pointed out that I, a guest, who am not her husband and have just met her, noticed what she needed and her own husband, did not. I am very slowly bringing her back to seeing reality as it just happened in front of both of us and a more normalised non-Janteloven way of seeing the situation.)

Amanda:
Yes.

Anthony:
I was listening to you… but your husband was not listening to you?

Further discussion

Anthony:
So, now that I pointed that out, thinking about your initial reaction to kind of ignore it or excuse it… "Oh that's just the way they are." What do you think?

Amanda:
Yeah, yeah, yeah… I think… I am giving them excuses. It's TRUE.

(AN – There you have the truth… finally! For her to work it out so quickly, I suspect is actually relatively quick. I observe that immigrants in Norway find it much easier to be convinced by logic. It takes time to break through the conditioning and fear but she has done it!)

Anthony:
Almost all of the immigrants that I have spoken to, also do the same thing. I am now going to give you a theory! I think that the indoctrination and the conditioning of this country could be so strong, constant and pervasive that it even affects foreign people that come here… so that when the reality of their experience does not align with the P.R or the brand that they were sold… the fantasy, which is heavily promoted and constantly repeated… then instead of just saying simply "this guy is rude!" or "I was wrong", then they say…

Amanda:
Is it really brainwashing?

Anthony:
Well, that's an extreme way of putting it but you are influenced?

Amanda:
Yes.

Anthony:
For example, why would you use… if something was selfish… why would

you excuse it? Why? There is no logical reason to excuse it just because you are in this location in the world?

Amanda:
Hmmm hmmm…

Anthony:
What I have noticed is this… many many many people do this in Norway. Something which is rude, they just say, "Oh, that's just the way it is here"… (or deny the reality of what is happening completely.)

Amanda:
Yes… yeah…

Anthony:
That's abnormal isn't it?

Amanda:
I think on the one hand because we don't know the society so well… the society so then we can't judge right away… So that's my opinion.

(AN – Who is this "we"? The collective? Her and who else? Me? Who is she telling what "we" can't do? Note the, "on the one hand"… "we can't judge but then also adds, "right away". She is saying that because she doesn't "know the society so well" she can't judge behaviour and should disregard her own judgement? This would not only be abnormal but also untrue. She absolutely can because people make value judgements every moment of their lives. You don't even have to "judge" but there is no need to warp and deny reality to suit how you "feel" and then change definitions of words whenever you feel like… that is abnormal behaviour. You can simply say, "Behaviour A is rude but in Norway Behaviour A is not considered rude". Yes, this is at least logical even if not a good thing… but it makes sense. She does not do this. She is interpreting reality like this; "Behaviour A is rude. Behaviour A in Norway, is not rude. Therefore Behaviour A is not rude". She must construct a mental firewall in between part 1 ("Behaviour A is rude") and part 2 ("Behaviour A in Norway is not rude. Therefore Behaviour A is not rude."), for this to work in her head?)

Anthony:
What? So let me ask you something… I'll give you an extreme example… If a Norwegian stabs you in the stomach with a knife. Can we both agree that that is "bad"?

Amanda:
Yes, of course. It is illegal.

(AN – What a bizarre response to simply being asked if a Norwegian stabbing you in the stomach with a knife could be considered as "bad":
"… it is illegal". This is incredible. She speedily adds it as a bizarre pre-emptive "defence". I believe that she adds the caveat, "illegal" so she can then go on to later say, "Yes, but stabbing someone is illegal and being rude is not illegal". The speed that she added that as well… whether being stabbed in the stomach by a Norwegian is "illegal" or not is totally irrelevant, of course and simply an attempt to avoid addressing the point directly but all in advance of the point being raised… incredible.)

Anthony:
OK, so here's the thing though… this is behaviour that is not location-based. Just normal principles which human beings hold. So "selfishness"… being "friendly"… being "empathetic"… being "nice"… being "expressive"… these are human qualities, which you should find everywhere in the world?

Amanda:
Yes

Anthony:
For example, why would you not have the expectation that they would be so in Norway too? Why would you then say, "Oh, but it's just the way they are?" Maybe someone should say to Aksel, "She clearly told you that she wanted beef pizza but you went into the restaurant and walked out with four cheese pizzas. Stop being selfish, stop being stupid, listen to your wife and next time get the pizza which she asked you four times for… just get it for her"… by the way… that is literally what should be said. That is completely normal but in Norway it's seemingly not normal behaviour?

Amanda:
Yes.

Anthony:
You ignore the whole thing and remain silent?

Amanda:
He will actually say something like this... something like... "Yes, I thought
about it but then I didn't get it."

Anthony:
What?!

*(AN – This is horrifying behaviour and even more horrifying that it is accepted as
normal.)*

Amanda:
It's true! It's true!

Anthony:
But that's so rude... putting it in your face?

Amanda:
Yes, I asked him... I have to ask for things... because I expect him to
voluntary do it... but he doesn't!

Anthony:
You have to bring it up? So tell me what happens?

Amanda:
So that's why I asked him. "You know for so long that I have talked about
this why didn't you just buy it?"

Anthony:
And what's his excuse?

Amanda:
He will say "Yes, I thought about it... and then I thought... oh, maybe not!"

Anthony:
Can I just say something?

Amanda:
(Giggles.)

Anthony:
That's mean. If you were in the UK or even in Antarctica… a normal human being would be embarrassed to say that!

Amanda:
Hmmm hmmm.

Anthony:
"I thought about it… But I thought not!" That is shameful.

Amanda:
Really?

(AN – There you go. Her new environment has warped her view of normality to such an extent that, just like the many others that we will meet, she literally doesn't know the difference between right and wrong any more. She has just admitted that she doesn't even know. We will have respondents ask us repeated questions like this and say that they don't know if it is right or wrong or if it's different outside Norway… complete moral discombobulation. What is incredible is that it appears that a "Janteloven" culture can discombobulate your perspective and morality, after a short amount of time. Imagine, if she can't recognise bad behaviour and call it what it is, how can she protect a vulnerable person or spot abuse around her? She can't! It's game over! Exactly like the group. They sat silently and said not a word, when lies were told… complete silence… when he was rude… complete silence… they actually encouraged him by laughing.)

Anthony:
Oh come on. You know that?

Amanda:
(Starts laughing.)

(AN – Amanda immediately giggles like a child.)

Anthony:
Do you not know that?

Amanda:
Because… because the thing is… they are so genuine… and say it so sincerely… But when you think about it… you say "that is related to me… just do it!"

433

(AN – "Genuine" and "sincere" are words that have no place here, considering the levels of dishonesty and insincerity that we have seen. More accurate words are "CONVINCED", "MANIPULATIVE" and "BRAZEN". I believe that she means that "they" (whoever "they" are?) believe "their" own lies and that "they" believe what "they" are saying.)

Anthony:
The thing is. You have just described that it's so "naive"… it's so clueless?

Amanda:
Yes!

Anthony:
It's so naive that you fall into the trap of just going that along with it?

Amanda:
Yes, kind of!

Anthony:
Instead of actually standing up and saying "No, it's wrong, I don't like it! Change your ways!"?

Amanda:
Yes.

Anthony:
But that would mean that you would have to do that, to a whole lot of people, I guess?

Amanda:
Aksel has changed a little bit…

Anthony:
But obviously not a lot because of what I've been witnessing just now and today?

Amanda:
But just now… I really want to clarify what just happened!

(AN – What is there to clarify? It was extremely simple, it just happened in front of both of our eyes… there is nothing to "clarify"… she can only try and understand his motivation… Which, well… good luck with that! What can he say? There is literally only one thing he can say… a passive aggressive "beauty"!… "Oh, I forgot!")

Further discussion

Amanda:
Because his awareness is quite low I think!

Anthony:
I have encountered this daily. The emotional awareness and often awareness in general just appear non-existent at times it seems?

Amanda:
Like earlier when we were talking… they analyse so many things behind which is just not necessary!

Anthony:
Well, neurosis is when you make up craziness inside your own head. So when Nora was talking about her being in a "rush" so she can't communicate for three seconds… that was just… Something that would potentially save your life or somebody else's for just two seconds…

Amanda:
Yes!

Anthony:
To be so rigid, that you don't want to hear that… that's not normal?

Amanda:
Yes! I don't ask… so you just don't answer…

Anthony:
That's so robotic. That's like android behaviour?

Amanda:
That's true (laugh).

Anthony:
Humans are organic, spontaneous, you say things, you share things... but the group are not interested in sharing anything. They just want what they want and that is selfish... and that's what I'm saying. I just said it... they want what THEY want... they are not interested in what YOU want?

Amanda:
Yes. Right.

Anthony:
And even if it hurts them... they still don't want to know! That's not logical?

Amanda:
Yes. I wonder... for example, is this common in the UK? Is it normal for a couple that if you want to buy an ice cream that the girl will pay?

Anthony:
It switches, it depends, sometimes one, sometimes the other.

Amanda:
No, the point is not this in Norway... both of them will pick and you queue up separately and then pay for themselves!

Anthony:
Right...

Amanda:
(Laugh.) The thing is that this is the whole society... the word you say brainwash... they find it no problem! Somebody brought it up and said "don't you think that that is selfish?" and then they don't even think about that!

Anthony:
I think that generally the self-awareness levels that I observe here are just so low. I'll tell you something straight, right now... I was basically telling the group that they don't even show empathy... I am *not* saying that they don't *feel* empathy but I pointed out to Aksel, that your mum has just expressed to you how much pain she experienced and you didn't even say "Oh, I'm sorry to hear that!" I basically said, "You haven't showed any

sensitivity to your mum." and they didn't seem to understand?

Amanda:
Hmmm hmmmm.

Anthony:
You guys were all speaking like you were all in separate rooms.

Amanda:
Yes. (*Laughs.*)

Anthony:
I think that the sensitivity and awareness is so low that they couldn't even see that. That shows you how dead...

Amanda:
And you know what! In the end I can't compare. Do you know why? Sometimes I think maybe that it's guys... maybe this is male mentality... because I don't have any comparison!

(*AN – She is describing being discombobulated by the environment and behaviour and trying to rationalise it by blaming innocent parties because she doesn't understand what is actually going on.*)

Anthony:
Just so you know, if you are dealing with individuals with strong narcissistic traits then the victim will always feel like they are the problem because the victim does not have a reference of normality.

Amanda:
Yes.

Anthony:
And this is what I think about Norway: when you come to Janteloven it's like you enter a different world with different rules.

Amanda:
Yes!

Anthony:
Normal morality, normal sensitivity, normal empathy… doesn't seem to generally apply across the board like elsewhere… and because so many people seem to act like it's "normal"… you think that you are the crazy one?

Amanda:
Yes! That's why maybe! The girl just now was isolated and bullied because she was different!

(AN – "The girl just now…"… when we were standing outside the shop a girl approached us and she was very talkative. I said to her, "It's incredible that you are so talkative and coming up to us like this… you are only the second person ever who has walked up to me in this country who doesn't know me and just started talking!" The little girl said: "Nothing interesting ever happens around here!" I then said, "Even so, you're very confident and I think it's brilliant!" She then said, "That's because I say what I think. I've been bullied so much and now I don't give a s***!" This literally happened as I was standing outside the shop in the middle interviewing Amanda… completely random in the middle of nowhere. Bullying is everywhere in Norway. I asked her to wait and then interviewed her too! We will listen to her appalling story later in this series.)

Anthony:
But have you noticed something… that it actually works on you, because when we started this conversation you said, "Oh somebody is speaking and now I am not so lonely"… and you found it really hard just to say that when you finally did. You were excusing it. You found it so hard to simply say that something which was obviously selfish, was selfish?

Amanda:
Yes! The word selfish is so serious…

Anthony:
OK, we can change it to "mean"?

Amanda:
Yes.

Anthony:
Either way it's just a normal word and I had to convince you that that

behaviour was not normal behaviour?

Amanda:
Yes… hmmm hmmm.

Anthony:
You did not realise that it was not normal behaviour? And now you are thinking to yourself "hmmm maybe it is not normal behaviour". Do you need me to point this out to you?

Amanda:
Because I have been with him already for X years and he is changing a bit but sometimes his awareness is still low (*laughs*).

Anthony:
But you said at the beginning of the relationship you would have said something?

Amanda:
Yes, I would have accused him so much!

Anthony:
Yes, but why did you stop? Why did you change?

Amanda:
Because I think… yeah, just now… because I am right now in front of the supermarket… I won't get furious because I can buy the pizza myself.

Anthony:
Yes, but why have you changed? Because this would not have been the case at the beginning of your relationship, you said? What I am trying to get to… I'm thinking *emotionally*. You are thinking in a very "Janteloven" way now. You are saying, "it doesn't matter because if I want pizza I can just go and get it" but I am not talking about that. I am talking about it on an emotional level. You said that you wanted it and he completely ignored it.

Amanda:
Yeah!

Anthony:
And that is the thing isn't it?

Amanda:
He is my husband and he should not ignore me!

(AN – *Finally realisation it slowly dawning on her!*)

Anthony:
It's almost like you are saying "No, it's OK if I want pizza I can just go into the shop". Is that the Janteloven way of thinking and analysing that you've learned in Norway?

Amanda:
Yes.

Anthony:
That is intellectualising it though? Talking emotionally… you told him and he ignored it?

Amanda:
If he told me that it was sold out then that would be fine but nope… he didn't say that!

(AN – *Even him lying and saying that it was "sold out" would be an indication that he actually thought about it and considered it in his mind. This cannot happen because he did not even think of her wishes and request. I have repeatedly observed in Norway that other people's feelings, emotions and needs are too often not prioritised or often even considered, so lies are not even required. In any event, why would you lie if you feel unaccountable and will never have your behaviour called out and confronted? A lie isn't even required or even anticipated here.*)

Anthony:
But aren't you hurt a little bit? He heard you… we know he heard you?

Amanda:
Yes.

Anthony:
You pointed out the exact pizza previously?

Amanda:
I think I actually pointed it out three times!

Anthony:
Yes you did! And he totally ignored it. And you didn't even get an apology?

Amanda:
Yeah!

And that takes back to the beginning of the conversation.

OPINION: Observing the 350 Respondents

Just because many Norwegians accept negative stereotypes about themselves does not mean they're true. Just as people who bully and propagate these stereotypes and describe Norwegians as "strange", "weird", "special" and "crazy" are not correct. I believe that one issue is probably the major challenge in Norway; "amplitude and disparity".

Amplitude and Disparity in Norway

I travelled to the south-west of Norway and found myself at a very special place called an "amphidromic point" (or a tidal node). An amphidromic point is the point in the ocean where there is no or very little tide. The water is level on a vertical plane as opposed to the usual up and down tide you find nearly everywhere else. I noticed something very interesting when I was at this location: it was *so* calm.

Low "disparity" environments often create a "calm" environment and a large "disparity" usually produces problems. Most Norwegians know about amplitude and disparity even though they might not know the actual words. For example, climbing a mountain, as every Norwegian knows, is often tiring which is directly linked to the elevation. It's the deferential that causes fatigue. The same with traversing a fjord. I stayed in a certain area where the shop was about 300 metres away. However, you couldn't get there directly: you had to go around a fjord which added another 3000 metres to the journey. So close, yet so far and a psychological challenge just as much as a physical one. Interestingly, if you look at Norwegian society you may often notice a lot of disparity. For example the following are all examples of an abnormally high differential.

- Drunken behaviour v Sober behaviour
- Polite 'fake' friendliness v Real feelings
- Public beliefs v Private beliefs
- Constant projection of strength v Internal pain and weakness

- National image v Reality
- Calm weather v Extreme weather
- Daylight extreme v Darkness extreme
- Official Statistics v Real life observation
- Treatment of people you do know v Treatment of people you don't know
- Janteloven principles v Real life experience of those principles

In my opinion, those living in constant internal and external contradiction and disparity of extremes would obviously experience fatigue because the extremes can't be reconciled easily by a normal human being, possibly resulting in: **mental illness, fatigue, personality disorder or other adverse effects.** I believe that this is why anxiety and depression is so often found wherever you go in Norway; most people that I met were not left untouched.

This is actually a completely normal and appropriate response, in my opinion because it's a rejection of the *abnormal*. People need reciprocation and to feel accepted, appreciated and safe. Will you ever, as a matter of course, know this feeling in Norway, or is it so rare that you will constantly be triggered and alert and on guard against continued trauma? The anxiety is a trauma response to avoid pain? If you can't avoid it then you become anxious? Avoidance is just a means of controlling your environment which means that "outsiders", "strangers" and new people are obvious potential threats, thus they are to be avoided? Essentially is this just to reduce the risk of anxiety and a logical precautionary protective measure? Is it just a simple survival mechanism? I believe that if this were the case then it is learned and not desired which means that even more discomfort and anxiety would be generated.

It's a cycle and it's a cycle that can be changed. It will take time of course. What is needed is for people to see that they will not be "punished" if they express feelings and emotions *publicly*. Many people might also need to understand their own emotions and reconnect with them and then reciprocation will come naturally. Currently, it is my strong opinion that Norwegian society generally is not a safe space for any genuine interaction and expression, beyond a very thin range of "approved" subjects. I believe that it is a hostile environment which means that the natural and normal physiological and emotional response will *likely* be anxiety and other mental issues as it's the body and mind telling you that something is "wrong".

The pretence needed to cover this pain and pretend everything is alright is fatiguing and exacerbates the toxic mental environment. The pain then elicits responses of trauma which manifest in many people as bullying, abuse and mistreatment, in my personal opinion. Victims are too often silenced because it's not a safe space and denial and cognitive dissonance cycles continue. It's all logical and I believe that if people perceive expressions of vulnerability as "bad" or "negative" then they will not be likely to report them. This is exacerbated when the society places stigma on expression of pain and vulnerability which leads me to question any Norwegian statistic when it comes to voluntary revelations of any kind of emotional issues. People will be reluctant to report pain and mental health issues if they perceive that as a negative thing and if stigma is attached to that expression of vulnerability. Even the statisticians would surely be unconsciously (or consciously) affected by their upbringing if it is influenced by Janteloven to probably be slightly rejecting of the "bad" just by a matter of unconscious bias?

I believe that all of this creates a major problem nationally and *that* is what is too often described, incorrectly, as "weird", "different" and "special". I believe that you observe the effects all over Norway and that it manifests in many ways but especially in high levels of passive aggression.

IMPORTANT: During my journey, I found that the majority of the 350 respondents (both Norwegian and non-Norwegian) were extremely passive-aggressive in a variety of ways, which I will now demonstrate. I suspect that this and many of the other peculiar behaviours observed were almost always a trauma response and a response in part or in full due to being conditioned by the ideology of Janteloven. I believe that the respondents were typical average people from a wide spectrum of society who are fairly representative of typical Norwegian attitudes and views. However, these observations are limited to the 350 respondents only. I will keep this very simple when giving my opinion and stick to "majority" which is 51% of the respondents or more. However, I must state that many of these observations were evident in more than 51%. I call on the Norwegian government, media & those with a duty of care and positions of influence and power, to set up a commission investigating, what I believe are the devastating mental health effects of the passive-aggressive imposition of the 'Janteloven' ideology on the innocent across Scandinavia.

Observation One: Overthinking Answers

Simple questions ought to elicit simple answers… or so you would think.

My observation, in the majority of respondents, was a generalised **overthinking of their responses** rather than a simple direct answer to a simple question. This overthinking **came** across as border line neurotic at times. It was like they were fighting with themselves. The respondents became visibly stressed, some even replied with, "I hope I've given the right answer" or "I hope I haven't got it wrong", in response to a question about how *they* felt. As if they were unable to answer a question about themselves.

In addition, I observed that the majority of the respondents were also obsessed with **moral relativism** and had a "who am I to judge?" attitude, even to the point of irrationality and with no regard to how they appeared. Moral relativism is the view that "right" and "wrong" is dependent on your position and not fixed. There seemed to be an absolute avoidance of stating undeniably and without equivocation that anything was "right" or "wrong". Again as if not permitted an opinion and certainly not wishing to be accountable for one.

This appeared, in the majority of the respondents, as if they were hyper-focussed on their "intentions" and in "avoidance of expressing their own view" – so much so it seems like the majority of respondents have a complex: constantly attempting to avoid **accountability** and **blame**. At the same time it seemed to me that the majority of the respondents were obsessed with the "other". It was like they were lost without something else to compare to or judge against and this is reflected in their answers and opinions of themselves. Repeated and constant answering with a comparison to something else rather than stating something directly and simply. I believe that this insecurity is why the respondents are obsessed with being the "best" country because they don't accept their own country, thoughts and judgements as independently valid or important on a subconscious and probably on a conscious level.

Observation Two: Extreme Lack of Candour

The majority of the respondents were extremely uncandid. They constantly and repeatedly used techniques and tactics that were very transparent and obvious. I easily circumvented these by simply keeping focussed on the questions, identifying any technique and tactic and calling it out to their faces. This actually is one of the main reasons, I suspect, that I was able to build rapport with the respondents because once they respected me enough to drop the techniques when they realised that they weren't going to work on me, they then became *extremely* candid and open. These were just some of the tactics and techniques used by the *majority* of the respondents:

Exclusionary Qualifiers

The respondents repeatedly used "exclusionary qualifiers", even for the most straightforward, unthreatening and simple questions. They were used in a constant and seemingly compulsive way, including: "probably", "maybe", "could be", "I think", "I guess" and many more.

The Straw Man Argument

The respondents repeatedly used fallacious arguments including the "The Straw Man Argument". The respondents would try to give the impression that they were refuting an argument but would simple ignore it and argue a totally different point.

Tu quoque

The respondents repeatedly and compulsively used the "Tu quoque" argument. "Tu quoque" is often used by those who can't answer an argument so they try to turn the tables on you. It's a blatant red herring and an attempt to place the "heat" on the questioner to avoid addressing the point.

Convince vs Convey

The majority of the respondents tried to answer questions by convincing me but ultimately not conveying an actual answer. Often, a respondent would "answer" a question for five or ten minutes with lots of convincing-sounding statements but with no communication of an *actual* answer to the question. If you are not focussed then you might be misled by a long-winded "answer" which sounds convincing but conveys no truth. This was particularly embarrassing for many of the respondents when I listened patiently and then asked them if they wouldn't mind answering the question because they'd just spoken for ten minutes and given no answer.

Verbal and Non-Verbal Disconnect

The majority of the respondents displayed a disconnect between what they were saying and their non-verbal communication. This was transparent and frequent. They would often laugh and smile but display aggressive non-verbals or might smile broadly but be on the verge of tears. There truly was a massive disconnect between what the respondents were saying and what they were communicating with their non-verbals. This made it very easy to identify what was truth and what was not. I nearly always observed laughing, smiling or giggling during any initial expression of pain or suffering.

Deflection

The majority of the respondents attempted to engage in deflection by changing the subject or by trying to change the course of the conversation away from something which would expose them in some kind of way.

Evasion

A number of blatant evasion tactics were observed in all respondents. Respondents either blatantly answered direct, very simple questions with "answers" that were unintelligible, unclear and obscure (**obfuscation**) or they used lots of vague words and long-winded explanations when a simple "yes" or "no" would have been an appropriate response (**circumlocution**). Use of deliberately ambiguous language to conceal or not commit to any answer or position (**equivocation**) appeared to be compulsive in almost every person I spoke to, if not *every* person. The result was the same: no clear answer and a deliberate attempt to avoid answering the question directly.

Omission

The majority of the respondents failed to provide full answers and intentionally left out important information.

Pausing

The majority of the respondents paused frequently for long periods during discussion because, in my opinion, they simply couldn't *construct* answers that I would be convinced by quick enough, and they knew that. This was very interesting to witness because they knew that I knew what they were doing and they often looked panicked but strangely in awe that somebody was challenging them. At this point I observed in almost all respondents what I call 'the look'. It was a look of doom, awe, shock, respect, realisation, fear and surprise all wrapped up in one. It usually came about fifteen minutes or so into the discussion and it meant *the game is up*. This is when we'd usually reach a breakthrough and after that the answers were full of candour.

Observation Three: Manipulation

Trust and Honesty

I need to be clear: I do not consider a high level of trust the same as a high level of honesty. If you do not steal it just means that you are not a thief. It absolutely does not mean that you are necessarily "honest". I think that this is something which is missed by many in Norway. Yes, you can leave your door open and in many places in Norway you will be totally fine and at no risk of robbery. However, it doesn't imply honesty… it just means that your neighbours are not thieves. Norway is a place with high "trust" levels including: very few cameras in museums where nearly every country in world would lace cameras or cordon areas off. You have cabins which are left open and available for public use. I have even seen an open bank vault in a bank in Norway… the bank vault left open! Incredible.

Halo Effect

The overwhelming majority of the respondents attempted to manage my *perception of them* using *very transparent manipulation*. This was a kind of attempt at eliciting a "halo effect" and often included pre-emptive manipulation of trying to make me think they were a "good" person. This often included respondents talking immediately about their charity work, activism, honesty or "moral" position on something or other. This almost always happened at the beginning of the conversation and they didn't know that I considered the whole virtual signalling act as a major red flag and a clear indication of a problem and that this person was going to give me some incredible insights into some of the darker sides of their community, even though *they* didn't know it yet.

Role Playing

Another thing the majority of respondents engaged in was acting and role playing and I mean that *literally*. They would often *fake responses* repeatedly. The way I cut through the "role playing" was so easy… I call it a "truth bomb". For example, one lady was asking me about racism and she said that she was "shocked" to hear that Norway was so racist… she had the whole sad shocked feigned act going on… I then launched the "truth bomb" which was, "What are you talking about? Why are you acting shocked? Norway is the most racist country I've ever been to in my whole life." I delivered it very calmly without smiling. She then dropped the pretence and "shocked act" and we started talking… we talked for a total of FOUR HOURS and predominantly talked about discrimination and racism that she personally had witnessed and experienced in Norway. Just hours earlier she was pretending to be "shocked" at the mere *implication* that racism existed in Norway and now she was speaking for hours and hours about personal experience about that same racism.

A "truth bomb" usually allowed the respondent to immediately realise that they could trust me and be open with me and that they didn't have to be scared to say how they felt because I had taken it to the extreme which "allowed" them to be open and honest. In my opinion many Norwegians engage in a "I'll pretend to believe your BS if you pretend to believe my BS" arrangement, which has now become the norm. It's easily broken with a "truth bomb" delivered directly. Finally, the respondents repeatedly used "perception qualifiers" which really amused me… "frankly speaking" and "honestly".

Machiavellian

The majority of the respondents answered my questions in a very selective and Machiavellian way. What's more many of the respondents were quite aware of this and spoke openly of a *very Machiavellian way of behaving and thinking*. This was done overtly and without shame or embarrassment.

PoLIEness

The majority of the respondents engaged in or implied that they agreed that a "lie" in the name of "politeness" was "honest" and preferable to telling the "truth" if they considered that truth as "rude" or potentially uncomfortable for the communicator's feelings or the receivers' feelings. A "lie" in the name of "politeness" is in no way considered dishonest. To some extent all human beings engage in this but in Norway it is amplified to an incredible level. For obvious reasons, if nearly everything is considered taboo and causes "offence" then potentially any communication of reality can cause offence and be considered "rude". That means that almost any "lie" can be legitimately justified to avoid offending people and being "rude", which then seemingly pacifies the "lie" and renders it "honest". It's a case of incredible mental gymnastics and completely normal in Norway amongst the majority of the respondents. In fact many respondents explained the process to me in detail with no embarrassment and a kind of pride. I also had a type of "honour in war" system described to be by a very old lady. This involves not using information to expose criminal or illegal or immoral activity even if everybody in the community knows about it unless is has come from an *official* source. The lady described that information which everybody knows about is often *not* used and would only ever use "legitimate" information. It seemed very similar to a court of law, however, this is real life and not a court of law so it makes no logical sense to allow somebody to get away with crime because you have evidence which wasn't gathered "officially". It all sounds like enabling to me.

Caught in the Act

Respondents similarly expressed no overt shame or embarrassment when they were caught out telling an untruth. In fact, they either pretended they didn't say it and moved on, or they simply moved on. When I would point it out they would frequently attempt to ignore it and if they couldn't, the most common acknowledgement was a giggle.

Arrogance

I saw arrogance expressed in several ways. I commonly observed arrogant confidence when respondents expressed racist views or views on Norwegian exceptionalism. They were condescending towards me personally and nearly always underestimated me which was advantageous to the whole project. Many often-used phrases like "stranger" and "outsider" to describe guests in Norway and seemed obsessed with projecting a faux nationalism. I believe that the "equalitarian" myth, which has nothing to do with equality, is a demonstration of potential abuse and dominance and in actuality is malignant equalitarianism. I think that even the thought that somebody could be "above" you elicits anger and frustration which is why everybody must be devalued and brought "down", via abuse, gossip, passive aggression, exclusion, etc. This is juxtaposed against frequent celebrity worship, which implies to me that it's, even more, the case of being an *artificial enforced construct* than a natural desire. We find this to be the case in other areas too, in my opinion.

I found many of the respondents to be extremely boastful and cocky. I am curious about whether there is any way that an imposed philosophy or set of rules on a person or group could have adverse mental health consequences for the individual or the collective, concerning, for example, the constant overt and more often than not, covert indirect bragging and boasting that you will often find in Norway and Scandinavia? This can be seen and heard in almost any official literature, brochure or video about almost any region of Scandinavia but especially Norway. Strangely, we often observe shock and horror when this is simply pointed out directly and then, more often than not, an acknowledgement, privately when comfortable or when not feeling confronted in an accusatorial way. Many will reveal it themselves euphemistically or jokily, with phrases like, as an old man in Alesund told me; "All Norwegians think they're kings and Queens" or as a middle-aged man told me in Molde, "You can always tell a Norwegian but you can't tell him much".

Could it be then that if a person or a group is conditioned or forced (through social pressure, education and other ways) to believe that a set of rules or beliefs is true, even if they don't naturally accept them at their core could then cling to them creating a kind of individual or mass reactance? Obviously, most human beings are proud of themselves and brag on occasion and no imposed rule of Janteloven can change that. As I understand it, psychology reactance is when you are told not to do something and you then feel compelled to do the same thing and to do the opposite. If this were the case could there even be a situation where, for example, if you are told all your life, "Norwegians don't brag. Don't brag... boasting is so bad... you are nothing special!" that this could cause an issue and inner conflict? I put this to a Norwegian psychologist who could not even begin to accept that Janteloven exists, let alone comprehend the question and give us an appropriate answer.

However, if it's enforced and social stigma is also attached, i.e. pain, trauma, guilt, shame and even passive aggression, might one ever feel or think, "Oh my god! I am proud of myself! I think I even boasted!? I am a bad person!"? If that were the case then could there ever be a conceivable situation where you have the irreconcilable attempting to be reconciled via denial or even reactance, unconsciously? Where you go the other way to the extreme? Where you may even then brag and boast excessively but not be able to even accept it, be aware of it or conceive of it because of the imposed rule and the pain it's caused you? You can't compute that it's even possible for you to do, so you then do it – a lot. Unconsciously or consciously... could something like that ever happen? To the best of my knowledge, there has never been a study of the psychological effects of Janteloven to find out the facts but I think that it is probable that there is indeed an effect and I can't imagine it being a positive one.

Boundaries

Another thing I noticed is that there is a very clear disregard for people's boundaries. People often demanded to know how much money you earn and probe your private life and gossip about it to the whole town but then get very upset when inconsequential artificial boundaries, like sitting on a bus seat near you, is "encroached" upon. In other words we see very low boundaries but very high inconsequential superficial boundaries… this is why a teacher feels entitled to fondle a student's buttocks and breasts in front of a whole class with impunity but would get upset if somebody sat one metre away from him on the bus. Abuse is internalised and we see a constant reinforcement of "you are nobody"… and I observe that many of the respondents seemed to believe that and actually argued *for* it initially. I also observed and heard the respondents describe major intergenerational tensions within Norway.

Observation Four: Pluralistic Ignorance

A majority of respondents engaged in obvious pluralistic ignorance. They would often admit this after denials but then concede after pointed questions, that they don't understand why "everyone" acts the way they do and they don't like it. Pluralistic ignorance is when a majority of a group *privately* reject the norm but go along with it *publicly* because they believe that everyone else accepts it. The majority of the respondents stated that they hated much of Norwegian culture and Janteloven with all its restrictions but feel that they can only admit that *privately* due to fear and because they feel that they are alone. In fact, many respondents stated that they had never discussed this before or even thought about it before I spoke with them. In fact the majority of the respondents didn't seem comfortable having an opinion of their own on much, other than on a very narrow spectrum of superficial things. It's very peculiar because it seems like many of the respondents experience a faux false consensus effect but choose to live in a consensus reality by choice, anyway.

Observation Five: Predictability

The respondents were without exception entirely predictable. It was like they were speaking from a script with pre-programmed answers but delivered in a very unconvincing way. The respondents, generally dressed the same, acted the same and even looked, generally, the same. There was not a single person who surprised me or said something which I considered unique or "different". None. I want to add one caveat though. The respondents only surprised me with the illogical extent of their views and arguments. Other than that, it was all predicable and robotic I'm afraid to say. That is why it was so easy to expose what they were saying because the respondents often say the same things, use the same words and phrases and have the same positions. It's either pro Janteloven or pro Janteloven with a loathing of Janteloven. It's extremely sad. Norwegian schools on the most part don't enforce a school uniform, like many schools in the United Kingdom, however, it's totally unnecessary because the students nearly always voluntarily wear their "uniform" of almost exactly the same bags and clothes... the teenagers described themselves in this book as being like "clones" for a reason.

Observation Six: Emotions Run High

The majority of the respondents were easily triggered into an emotional response. Almost anything could elicit an extreme emotional response, even something as mundane as offering to buy the respondent a drink. This often elicited a MAJOR irrational response in the MAJORITY of the respondents. It was as if unsolicited demonstration of kindness is taken as a threat and a loss of control and elicits anxiety or irritation: being bought drinks, opened doors, offers of help, compliments, talking too much... etc. Another thing I noticed was that the majority of the respondents were triggered by single words; "bullying", "racism", "abuse" or any perceived criticism of Norway or "Norwegianess". They too often simple couldn't handle it and the response was the same: tight face, red face, glazed eyes. In fact a large *minority* of the group burst into tears or became very emotional and even unstable during the discussions.

I also noticed extremely strict rules with regards to friendships and rigidity in all walks of life. I believe that this is clearly "constriction" and a response to trauma. The respondents appear to restrict and place strict limits on their lives and interactions, in an obvious attempt to reduce their anxiety and pain in attempt to reduce their trauma? They reduce and limit their lives to try to escape pain? This is possibly why many of the Norwegians often state that they don't interact with "strangers" and "outsiders" and literally perceive them as threats... because in a way, they are threats, within their model of reality?

We see this in Norway with so many "rules" both overt and covert... I believe that it's all probably a trauma response; an attempt to regain control. The respondents seem to truly live in a completely controlled environment, self-imposed, in an attempt to keep trauma to a minimum. Nothing is often spontaneous and everything must usually be predictable or is perceived as a threat (and it truly is!) – a threat to the system? It's all a psychological play and performance so you have to express truth very slowly and sensitively if not avoid expressive of truth at all… truth is the biggest threat to a Janteloven society. We see this in the often described absolute avoidance of confrontation and the "head in the sand" mentality which pervades Norwegian society. Four phrases which the respondents constantly referred to were "Façade", "Head in the sand", "Sugar coating" and "Sweep under the rug". If you want to make a friendship, you usually have to pretend that you don't want to be friends. If you want a girlfriend, then you usually have to pretend that you don't want a girlfriend and pretend that you love sports or some other activities that you don't like. There is a good reason why these social rules are so rigid and why the Norwegian bookshops heavily promote books with these "rules". It's because it's all a house of cards and will collapse with the slightest exposure of truth. In my opinion, much of Norwegian society is like a real life "Potemkin village" with many people intentionally choosing not to look behind the façade. I believe that this has serious mental health consequences.

I wonder if this explains in part why so many of the respondents seem so afraid; why I observed many whispering and looking around them to see who was listening when being open and honest about their country and community? This was shocking to me and I often asked them outright, "Why are you whispering?" they would then usually continue whispering. One individual, inside his own house, at about 11pm, a forty-five year-old man alone in his living room with me actually stopped talking to me in the middle of telling me their truth about Norway and then walked to his balcony, checked to see that nobody was listening and then closed the window. We were in the middle of rural Norway in the middle of nowhere and even so… can a forty-five-year-old man not actually say how he feels without fear that somebody is spying on him and listening to him and fearing the repercussions?

Observation Seven: You Cannot Be Wrong?

The majority of the respondents seemed to have major issues with not being able to handle being wrong. They often had challenges even comprehending that they were wrong even when it was abundantly clear… they often couldn't even admit it. In fact, many of the respondents, even when it seemed that *they* knew they were wrong, marched on regardless of logic.

Observation Eight: Immaturity

The majority of the adult respondents acted extremely immature and childish when faced with pointed questions. When a serious question came it was like they turned into a child and repeatedly giggled and laughed. This was very bizarre and it was constant, while they laughed, I would remain impassive. If you're observant you will see that I often intentionally spoke to the adults like they are children in the transcripts. They would also constantly answer with incoherent sentences in a child-like fashion. However, the *actual* children and teenagers communicated, in the main part, **articulately and maturely.** Relativity speaking, the teenagers spoke much more coherently and logically than the adults. In fact I found them to be extremely bright and intelligent, but scared to tell the truth, initially.

Observation Nine: Constant forgetfulness, Selective Amnesia or Disassociation?

A large *minority* of respondents would often say, "I forgot what I just said" immediately after I pointed out something controversial... even if only five seconds later. It was if they were talking but not really listening to what they were saying. When I pointed it out and reminded them what they'd said, they would look shocked but try their best to continue. This happened so many times that I realised that something major was happening in these respondents. This worried me. A lot. It seemed as if they were somehow **disconnected.**

Worse still, was when a respondent would say something outrageous and then moments later say the completely converse thing – with *no apparent awareness* of what they'd said. Again, when I pointed that out they looked at me like *I* was crazy. I could see that often they were genuinely shocked at this, so was it deliberate or was it so intrinsic they were on some kind of bizarre autopilot?

I later noticed that if I said a "trigger" word, that could elicit a change in the demeanour of the respondent. For example, let's say they were talking about how "great" Norway is and then I contradicted them with a trigger word. They would STRONGLY react but then become vacant and then, often, when I pushed my point, would then say the total opposite thing to what they had just been arguing. I also noticed that not only the positions would change but also often the tone of voice. When they regurgitated the "narrative" they would often speak enthusiastically and with very high "happy" tones. They would speak in short quick sentences but when I triggered them and finally got to the truth then they regularly would switch to a more low energy, low pitched voice, much less smiley, more adult-like and with well-formed adult sentences.

You can see this clearly in the transcripts but you can really *feel* it in the room. It was like talking to another person. Later on you will hear about an individual who argued with themselves… out loud, with alternate sounding voices.

Bizarrely, I noticed that I could "snap" the respondents back too. For example, I felt that one lady was getting a bit scary so I just pointed out of the window and said, "Look at that cloud over there!" and then she looked and then she talked about the weather for ten minutes and became comfortable. Talking about the weather was such a comfort to her, like it is to many, because it is "safe" and it grounded her. I regularly did this. Another way is to provide narcissistic supply. This was when I could see that they were on the verge of "breakdown" I would just say how "*amazingly* insightful" they are and this is "*amazing* stuff"… and then they would all too often calm down and become grounded and relax… and then I'd start again.

Now, I wanted to explain this to *myself* because it was scary to witness and I realised that, in my personal opinion, I was probably witnessing a kind of "dissociation". I really felt, in fact, on many occasions that I was talking to somebody with multiple personality disorder. In fact, this is how I framed *all* the conversations and was able to keep very calm, patient and completely empathetic. After 'triggering', I was able to make them forget seconds later acting impassively and sensitively. To me it felt as if one part of them was almost "indoctrinated" by Janteloven, I presume, whilst the other part was them… the real "them". I guess this is what indoctrination does to you? Maybe it makes you split? In this way, at least there is a potential logical explanation. What's the alternative? A majority of the respondents were just mentally ill? No, I don't believe that.

I believe that this is a trauma response and a survival mechanism for many in Norway. They choose to disassociate, thereby losing connection with reality, with their personal identity and to survive take a **collective personality**. They live in a fantasy and a consensus reality where Norwegians are the happiest people on the face of the earth living in the most equalitarian country where they are rich and content and everything is perfect and they are the "best". This could also explain the "bad" memory because without memory there is no identity and thus no personality. Could this be why so many people are obsessed with writing in cabin books which you will find everywhere in Norway? You will find pens and pads, even in the most remote places where you can write your name and date and a few notes. Is this obsession with micro recording even minor trips to the forest and writing a *new* history a conscious attempt at creating a real narrative which previously didn't exist? A new history and narrative which is "owned" by Norwegians completely, without Danish interference and invasions and the spectre of Nazi occupation? This might explain why so many people described an almost non-existent attention span for "complex" or "emotional" ideas and liked to keep things very "simple"... many will admit this outright in this series. In fact, the respondents will often attempt to run away from anything too "complex"... again, some will admit this and use that exact words to describe "this is too complex for me!" when asked a simple question.

The majority of respondents seemed to be in **denial**. It was if the majority of the respondents had a vested interest to perpetuate untruths; engaged in a kind of slothful induction in actuality. I observed that many respondents can't face reality so seemed to withdraw into a fantasy world of delusion with a hyper-focus on irrational Norwegian "grandeur" as a means to regain control of their lives, I presume? When you look at the projection of reality and the reality on the ground (Macro v Micro) you notice that things aren't as they seem necessarily in Norway, including:

1) Happiest country ever v The reality
2) Edvard Munch being a famed Norwegian v Many Norwegian hating Edvard Munch and knowing nothing about him beyond "The Scream"
3) Norway known for being a centre for conflict resolution v Repeated descriptions of problems being ignored and head in the sand and conflict averse as the "norm"
4) Leading Climate change and recycling advocates vs One of world's biggest oil producers per capita
5) No hierarchy v A covert hidden in plain sight hierarchy
6) Low corruption reputation v Moral corruption on an epidemic level in reality?
7) Child rights advocates vs Reality, disgusting under current of abuse
8) Transparent society v Bad acts often simply ignored, unacknowledged or covered up.

Observation Ten: W.A.R.R (Warping And Re-framing of Reality)

The majority of respondents engaged in something which I call "W.A.R.R" which is a warping and re-framing of reality. They often rejected accurate words which described reality in favour of what they *felt* was more accurate regardless of facts.

Observation Eleven: Constant use of Euphemism and Doublespeak

A majority of the respondents seemed to speak in a strange type of "code", which comprised of constant use of euphemism and double speak. They also appeared to rationalise this by engaging in doublethink and collectively, in groupthink.

Euphemism:
Using an indirect word to replace one that is considered embarrassing or unpleasant

Doublespeak:
deliberately using euphemistic and ambiguous language

Doublethink:
accepting *contrary opinions or beliefs at the same time, usually as a result of indoctrination.*

Observation Twelve: The Dictionary is Kryptonite

A small minority of the respondents when faced with the dictionary actually responded with fear and extreme passive aggression. They tried a multiple of tactics to try to avoid hearing the *actual* definition of words, often when it was clear that their warped definitions were about to be proven as factually inaccurate. For obvious reasons, those who engage in doublespeak cannot face a dictionary because it immediately exposes their irrationality.

Observation Thirteen: Extreme Passive Aggression

The majority of the respondents were excessively passive aggressive and described that they lived in an extremely passive aggressive environment. A large minority of the respondents were bullies and bullied with no embarrassment or shame in front of me and whilst being recorded. The respondents often withheld approval from each other. The majority of the groups also described being witness to or aware of criminal activity, including especially sexual abuse in their communities which is ignored and "brushed under the rug". This was one of the most shocking things for me to witness on this journey. The level of passive aggressiveness in Norway is horrifying as is its normalisation. One of the most prominently used methods is actually "negging" (emotional manipulation) and I believe that it's actually perceived by many as *affectionate* in Norway. Passive aggression is compulsive and normalised in Norway to such an extent where even identifying it is often seen as being "dramatic" and "overreacting".

Observation Fourteen: Lack of expressions of Empathy

The majority of the respondents appeared emotionally tone deaf. They often openly attacked and undermined victims, openly discredited victims and openly suppressed victims. On the other hand they were often supportive of perpetrators and often used language which excused bad acts. This seemed to be as a reflex response.

The lack of empathy and sceptically the lack of expressions of empathy in the majority of the respondents was horrendous and horrifying to witness. They would regularly express collective intellectual concepts when they were asked simple questions about how they feel. I had to explain to certain respondents what empathy was as they often couldn't even seem to compute it. Even when I pre-warned them that I witnessed a lack of empathy they too often didn't take the hint. It was like many couldn't compute empathy at all. When I asked questions related to how the respondents *felt*, they would nearly always answer how they *think*. I repeatedly tried to get the respondents to connect to their emotions but it was often like they couldn't do it. This was scary and not nice to witness. It was like the majority of the respondents can't express how they feel *emotionally*. It was like they don't regard their emotions as important or relevant and deprioritise them to such an extent that they can no longer access them. Many didn't even seem to consider their emotions or feelings important. On the rare times emotion was expressed it was nearly always accompanied by some kind of doubt and equivocation.

Observation Fifteen: Social Regulation

The large proportion of the respondents were bullies or if they weren't bullies they were passive bullies. Positive social regulation appeared to be non-existent.

A paedophile seems to be treated like everybody else. Bad behaviour and even criminal activity is not often challenged at all it appears. The respondents would *often* bully and lie and people would so often just sit silently. They too often wouldn't speak up or contradict… complete tacit approval. I sat down with "Hans", a German scientist living in Norway who put it this way;

"Communism is here… It's everywhere! You are watched and you are treated equally to everybody. Even if it's a rapist or murderer, you are treated equally and it's not a good thing. It is not a good thing! Because people are suppressed. They don't want open-minded thinking. They want closed-minded thinking and they want you to do as they say. I no longer feel intelligent, confident or really worth very much. It's like they swapped the class system for an even more oppressive socialist, bordering on the communist, system. Not only in work but also how you dress, your opinions, your ideologies. I don't want this to come across in any way that I support terrorism because I don't. But I think the reason that Anders Breivik and others resorted to such horrific acts is because society never allowed them, from a young age, to express themselves or their right to an opinion that differed to mainstream views. Thus resulting in years of social exclusion and resulting madness that leads them to their crimes. With no outlet to express their views, they resorted to the only way they know people will react. Violence. The same goes for mental health, every country has mental health issues. But it's a complete taboo to even discuss mental health here. The conversation will be quickly re-routed or ignored."

We will meet "Hans" later in this series though. Secondly, there appears to be very little privacy and more shockingly no expectation of true privacy. The majority of the respondents except that "everybody" gossips and will know everything about everyone and describe that as completely normal in Norway. When I stood up against it in the rooms the respondents reacted like nobody had ever stood up for them in their lives and often became euphoric.

Another thing is to think about the disparity of consequence between cause and effect. In Norway if you use the "N-word" socially or express racism or tell racist "jokes", it appears that the likelihood is that on many occasions absolutely nothing will happen. You will probably not be condemned and at best maybe you will be ignored… you might even elicit laughter or giggling. If you contrast that to certain parts of London or New York, if a racist person spoke in those places in the way that they spoke so openly in Norway then there would be a high probability that not only would they not be leaving the conversation with no consequence but very likely they'd be leaving via a visit to the trauma ward of a hospital. It probably would be life changing for them to say the same "joke" in a different country. That's because most other countries have a very clear "social regulation" system. The people *themselves* will often regulate your behaviour. In Norway a paedophile or a murderer can seemingly walk freely and many people will smile and say "Hai, hai!" We will speak to a group later in the series who will explain this exact situation and their thought process. In many places of the world the paedophile or murderer would be treated antagonistically. Norway doesn't seem to have the same social regulation and often the most revolutionary act would be to *ignore* something and that would be an INCREDIBLE statement of protest oftentimes in Norway. I have heard Adolf Hitler excused, Anders Breviek excused but little Greta Thunberg attacked... it can regularly get that preposterous in Norway. Negative social regulation, on the other hand, directed at those who might waver from the "narrative" is obviously strong and apparent everywhere, as described by nearly all of the respondents in this book series.

Observation Sixteen: Cognitive Bias and Blatant Cognitive Dissonance

A majority of the respondents seemed to experience cognitive bias and blatant cognitive dissonance. I really felt like many of the respondents engaged in a cover up and collaboration to normalise abuse to such an extent that they could not face the truth without getting angry, dissociating or getting very upset.

Observation Seventeen: Choice Support Bias

Approximately 90% of the immigrants that I spoke to appeared to be experiencing extreme choice support bias. They would start with the "usual" narrative but non-verbally communicate the opposite. Just talking about Norway would elicit an emotionally unstable response. When I just touched on the subject they would often become aggressive and even degrade their own country. They seemed to be suffering with Stockholm bias. With the exception of one German scientist, I didn't meet a single one that appeared reasonable, observant and balanced who was able to communicate their feelings on Norway in a calm, convincing and logical manner. They tended to start with how "great" Norway was but communicate it in a *contradictory* way. If I asked, "Do you like Norway?" They might say, "Norway is the BEST. I mean, I'm not saying that Norwegians are rude... I mean, yeah, Norway is great." I'd then ask them if they were suggesting that Norwegians were rude? Then they'd usually get very agitated and then after a few questions they'd often be on the verge of tears. The immigrants that I met were nearly all mentally ruined in Norway. In December 2019 a mother murdered her children in Tromso by walking them into the freezing water. She was from Sudan… I can state categorically: too many immigrants are often mistreated in Norway and pushed to suicide and depression by their mistreatment and abuse. The Norwegians "experts" can publish all of their "data" to make themselves feel better but it doesn't change the fact that some immigrants are even choosing to kill themselves and their children in the most horrific circumstances than live in Norway… and that is a fact.

Finally, a majority of the *immigrants* that I spoke to in Norway were extremely racist and discriminatory, to an even greater degree than the majority of the Norwegian respondents. I believe that this could be some kind of self-loathing reaction to abuse and racism that they regularly experience so they project their pain on to others aggressively. It's a hostile environment so they react with absolute shock and thus extreme hostility, especially to other immigrants? They might too often be surrounded by people that, because of their racist views, privately despise them but pretend not to, they might be surrounded by incredible intense physical nature which might seem overpowering, they might be surrounded by extremes of weather, they might often be surrounded by imagery and extreme nationalism where they are repeatedly "reminded" that their country is worse than Norway? Obviously, they would be psychologically affected and those affects are too often clear to see. One way or the other you see it, including with initial excessive over compensation: "Norway is the best! Norway is heaven!" etc.

Observation Eighteen: Depressed, Anxious and Negative

The majority of respondents described THEMSELVES as anxious, depressed, bullied or/and having major dysfunction in their lives. Almost every single story and conversation was based on a personal negative story. I hardly heard a single real nice thing or positive story on my whole voyage. I truly felt like the majority of the respondents were depressed and a large number even seemed quite mean, cold and insensitive. The majority of the respondents looked down a lot, had poor eye contact. The respondents constantly devalued almost everything including their friends, families, jobs… nothing seemed to escape being devalued. Many of the respondents explained their view that expressing vulnerability and pain is akin to "negativity" even if they are the ones in pain. They often described that they consider expression of pain to be inconvenience to others and "others" consider the expression of that pain and vulnerability as an affront and "negativity". I've heard so many people explain this to me with a straight face and looked completely shocked when I explained that it's normal to express pain and vulnerability… many looked at me like I was crazy. I've had Norwegian police officers explain this is detail and it's shocking and horrifying to repeatedly observe and hear that vulnerability truly is perceived as a weakness by so many in Norway. The younger even have words for people that are "emotional" and that words translates as "weak"… more on that later… we'll hear from them directly.

Observation Nineteen: Almost No Interest in History, Travel or Culture

The majority of the respondents had almost no interest in culture, travel or history at all. That is why I describe much of Norwegian nationalism as "faux nationalism". I have travelled Norway more than probably every Norwegian I met. I am embarrassed to say that I have a greater knowledge of Norwegian history than almost every Norwegian I met. The majority of the respondents seemed to have a kind of tunnel vision and little sense of perspective at all when it came to their own country. They too often exhibited an "us and them" mentality and were highly xenophobic but many were also even prejudiced against the next town and others within Norway.

Observation Twenty: Little Self-awareness and Poor Communicators

The majority of the respondents were poor communicators and exhibited extremely low awareness to almost zero self-awareness. I found the majority of respondents to be highly suggestible and easily led. Even though the conversation was being recorded many often seemed to be used to getting away with expressing extreme views. I didn't seem to observe any fear of being exposed or fear of reprisal, even if expressing racist views, criminality or anything at all… except of course when I coaxed the *real* truth from them. Another thing which I encountered constantly is that I don't think I have ever heard an official "introduction". When you meet, you introduce yourself or you are often ignored. Simple as that. I've encountered this repeatedly all over Norway. There seems to be a real fear of interaction and it is too often avoided with obvious pretence. There is also something else I observed on three occasions. I watched it very carefully and I believe that it could happen elsewhere in Norway and it's related to working and over working. On these occasions I noticed that when somebody had done something wrong and they knew that they had… they didn't discuss it with the wronged party. They would just pretend that it didn't exist and often their face would be beetroot-red. However, in a strange kind of penance and demonstration of guilt which seemed to be a non-verbal unconscious acknowledgement, they would clean and clean and clean. Even when the place was already clean. I watched this three times with my own eyes. Instead of discussing their issues and resolving them they were overtly clean the whole house and focus on work… although like on autopilot. It was like a ritualistic display of shame and this is the very strange part… it appeared that this unspoken and unacknowledged action *worked* and was indeed enough to pacify the "wronged" on these three occasions. It was all unspoken and I have spoken to many Norwegians about this very thing and so many agreed that they work to take their mind away from life's problems. Many respondents and nearly all in their mid-twenties described themselves as "workaholics" or constantly working, too. We'll meet many of them in this series.

Observation Twenty-one: Unresolved Nazi History

A large minority of the respondents brought up Nazi Germany and Hitler unprompted. It appears that the spectre of Nazi Germany hangs in the air in Norway. There are many unresolved issues which I suspect need to be faced because it's still under the surface in too many places.

Observation Twenty-two: "Cult" like impression

Carolyn Steber wrote an article for **www.bustle.com**, published 21st June 2018 where she listed the traits of people who would be susceptible to cults, as described below and in my opinion they correspond extremely closely with the many of the respondents I met:

1. *Those Who Want To Feel Validated*
2. *Those Who Are Seeking An Identity*
3. *Those Who Are Followers, Not Leaders*
4. *Those Who Are Seeking Meaning*
5. *Those Who Have Schizotypal Thinking*
6. *Those Who Are Highly Suggestible*
7. *Those Who Constantly Blame Others*

8. Those Who Are Always Angry
9. Those Who Have Very Low Self-Worth

To some extent a majority of the respondents seemed to be conditioned or to be affected by conditioning. Many even appeared docile, low energy, apathetic, submissive, indoctrinated and scared. They often seemed to avoid emotion completely or avoid anything which even hints at an emotional response. Too many of the respondents also appeared to be completely desensitised to abuse, criminality and accepted it as "normal" within Norway. They often described being scared of "negativity"… which seems to be anything they don't like or challenges them. There was an obvious glorification of pain which was almost everywhere. Great pleasure from doing extreme potentially harmful things and social kudos from jumping into the coldest of cold lakes and being in the most hazardous activities… that's how many described that they show their "manhood" in Norway they said. The respondents too often responded to direct questions with an auto-response which you would expect in something like *The Truman Show* or in an episode of *The Prisoner*. It appears that many of the same punishments and alienation exist for those who criticise the "cult of Norway" as in cult-like organisations.

However, the "leader" appears not to be a man, or a God or a thing… it is NORWAY itself, and its glorification is the "worship" apparently. If you go and look at the traits of cult members you will see many similarities to many of the people in this book. If you listen to the punishments they describe for speaking out against the Norwegian "narrative" you will see that it also aligns too.

I was also shocked at first when I realised that nearly all of the respondents who I personally sat down with, seemed to take any kind of *perceived* insult on the *collective identity or country*, as a *personal* insult and affront, but at the same time, took any *positive affirmation of the collective or Norway* as a *personal* compliment. I believe that many of the respondents simply "projected" what they craved the most i.e. "we are honest", being that the truth has been abandoned, "We are transparent", because the reality is hidden, "we are fair!", because unfairness is the norm in their experience of reality.

Another very interesting thing is the extremely high number of young people that you talk to in Norway with an American accent. We have seen an official Canadian government website (**www.international.gc.ca**) state: Anti-American sentiment is also high in Norway:

"One should be prepared for a significant degree of anti-Americanism (though often combined with some hints of admiration towards Americans)."

You will often hear many Norwegians speaking in an American accent, dressing like Americans and obsessed with American culture but simultaneously, and with no apparent awareness of contradiction, pronounce strong anti-American views *at the same time*. The irony of ironies is that there are actually 4.5 million Norwegian Americans living in the US… that's nearly the same as 90% of the total number of people living in Norway!

Finally, a word about displays of nationalism and flags. I made it a habit of counting the flags in the places I visited in Norway so I could compare their frequency. Many Norwegians seem to have a habit of displaying their flag and many even have a flag pole outside their house. However, my suspicion that displays of the flag would increase the closer you got to the capital didn't seem to be the case. This wasn't scientific but I noticed that the closer to the south coast you were the more flags you saw. For example, in one ten-metre stretch of road I counted seven Norwegian flags in a city on the south coast in Norway and that didn't include the man who walked past with a Norwegian flag on his arm. I then travelled around and noticed that the further north you travelled the less you saw the flag. When I visited a city called Tromso I only counted two flags on their whole main road. That is an incredibly low number for a main street in a major city in Norway and I noticed that they were actually hung outside the tourist shop. It appears that displays of nationalism, overt visual displays, change and increase the further you go south. I also thought about the impact of weather and how it might affect flags but I travelled through Norway through all seasons and have seen flags in deepest Svalbard and storms in Alesund, so I don't think that weather has much affect.

Observation Twenty-three: Faux Confidence and Self-loathing

The majority of the respondents seemed to exhibit a kind of extreme guilt, shame and self-loathing. It seemed to pervade all of the conversations but in a very strange way. It was like many of the respondents would often toggle between low self-esteem, inferiority complex, faux confidence and real confidence/arrogance. Could it be a kind of PTSD in a way?

Observation Twenty-four: Logic

I noticed something with almost all of the respondents: they often did not seem to respond primarily to logic but to attention, affection and authenticity. So, I made sure to listen to them and connect emotionally with them and I believe that this was the key to build trust to punch through the nonsense and conditioning and get to some truth and reality. They often just needed some help, guidance and encouragement.

The Threshold Test

I noticed that almost all of the Norwegians that I seemed to meet in London or outside of Scandinavia were often quite gregarious, talkative and outgoing. I found, generally speaking, the total opposite seemed to be true of the respondents in Norway. I put this to a Norwegian who told me, "Yes! That's true! We know that and we even have a word for that. It's called "chartered Norwegians". We go crazy when we're out of Norway." I've asked around but couldn't find another person who had heard of that phrase but I did find another person who agreed but who suggested that every nationality that travels abroad is *different*. To a certain extent I agree but not on this level, I suspect there is an EXTREME difference in my observation and then I thought to myself: is there any way I could prove it? I think I can point to some unscientific data that is quite enlightening and I have called my test; "The Threshold Test."

What is the Threshold Test?

The Threshold Test is very simply how many Norwegian front door thresholds have I crossed over. How many Norwegians have invited me into their homes in Norway in approximately ten years and then look at the data and see if we notice anything… you notice something for sure. In my whole time in Norway I have been invited into twenty-one homes. I then divided the home owners up into categories. Where did I meet the owner? How am I linked to the owner? Did I meet the owner organically inside Norway or did I meet the owner outside of Norway? Was I introduced to the home owner by somebody that I met inside Norway or by somebody that I met outside of Norway?

Here is the data:

21 homes total in Norway
16 linked to London or my accommodation

3 Non-Norwegians in Norway
2 Semi-organic Norwegians

London or accommodation linked

The vast majority of the homes that I have been invited into in Norway are owned by people that I have met in London or their extended family. I also include my landlords and their extended family in this category. In some way these people are linked to my home country and not Norway.

Non-Norwegians in Norway

I have been invited into the home of three non-Norwegians that I met inside of Norway and had no link to London or my accommodation. Organic meetings in Norway who invited me into their homes.

Semi-Organic

I have been invited into the home of two Norwegians which I call "semi-organic". These are Norwegians who I met through a London friend. For example, one of my London linked friends might invite me to a dinner and then they would invite all of us together, including me to dinner at their house. I call that a semi-organic connection because I was invited with my London Norwegian connections. I was on one occasion invited to a barbecue where the invitation was extended to me whilst I was at a dinner. This is the only time I have been invited into the home of a Norwegian person who was at least one link away from somebody that I had first met in London.

Looking at the data in full – No Organic Norwegians have invited me into their homes in ten years

However, if you look at the data it is clear that almost every invitation is somehow linked to my London friends or non-Norwegians. In fact NO Norwegians that I have met organically in Norway have ever invited me into their homes. In fact it's been the *non-Norwegians* in Norway who have invited me into their homes "organically". I have removed one individual from the list and his family's homes for undisclosed legitimate reasons. However, the data is overwhelmingly clear... the people that I have connected with and have treated me with hospitality have been, in some way, linked to meeting me in London and not in Norway or have been linked to my accommodation which is "forced" interaction.

Dating App Study Stockholm vs Oslo

When I travelled to Stockholm I noticed something very interesting indeed. I noticed that the dating app that I had installed got a very different response by simply travelling a few miles across the Norwegian/Swedish border. The difference was incredible. When I travelled to Stockholm I noticed that I had about 2000% more "swipes" in just one week than in Oslo or in actual fact, the whole of Norway over months previously.

Same profile, same pictures, same bio, same everything.

In fact, let me be really clear; I had twenty times more "swipes" in Stockholm in *five days* than in just under *one year* in Norway which including nearly every major city in the country. By the way, I have factored in the population differences between Norway and Stockholm. I also decided to do a little experiment. Do a little informal study. I wrote down the first 100 profiles in Stockholm and the first 100 profiles in Oslo and then compared:

1) I wrote down whether the profile was a white or non-white profile
2) I wrote down whether the profile displayed a national flag or a national symbol
3) I wrote down whether the profile included at least one photo of a national lake or mountain

Well the data was very interesting indeed. Let's start with Stockholm first:

Stockholm 100 profiles:

1) 89% of the Swedish profiles were white and 11% of the profiles were non-white
2) 17% of the Swedish profiles displayed a lake or a mountain
3) 0% of the Swedish profiles displayed the Swedish flag or a Swedish national symbol

I then compared that to Norway's results

Oslo 100 profiles:

1) 93% of the Norwegian profiles were white and 7% of the profiles non-white
2) 33% of the Norwegian profiles displayed a lake or a mountain

3) 18% of the Norwegian profiles displayed a Norwegian flag or national symbol

The results are very clear and apparently align with the conclusion drawn in this book... and one more every interesting thing. There were three profiles in Sweden who DID display their national flag and national symbols... after closer inspection, they were Norwegians on holiday.

Spheres of Influence

I'm going to demonstrate clearly in a diagram how a "bad actor" can get away with his behaviour in a community in Norway and act with impunity and immunity, as described by many of the respondents and personal observation. In fact, this is a real life example. I've had many "confessions" off predators and bullies and talked to people around them and asked them directly, "Why do you cover up for them?" that I feel that I confidently have the answer. I've then put my theory to members of the same community and they agreed with me 100%. You would be shocked at how many people have been in tears telling me how *they* are bullies or perpetrators... one guy even told me how he was accused of rape. I had a guy banging on my door in tears telling me that he has an "issue in his head" but more importantly, I want to know **why and how these people can get away with their crimes and the whole community sit by silently?**

Here is the answer: Spheres of influence.

What are spheres of influence?

Below is a diagram which shows a perpetrator and members of his/her "inner circle"... on this occasion members of his family and extended family. Now, already we have heard from Norwegian after Norwegian that many of the communities are predisposed to "turn a blind eye" and keep quiet about abuse and corrupt acts, so they already get an easy ride. However, due to the fact that people who speak out are often pushed back down then it means that the most shameless of the community can actually exert a lot of influence because they are unopposed by other members of that community.

It might even be because they are shy and just don't want to get involved with drama. However, the perpetrators have no such reservations and, just like an orchestra conductor, they can exert a lot of influence and control the tempo of the community. They say that power corrupts and absolute power corrupts absolutely and that is true. So now we have a perpetrator and maybe he has a daughter or a son and they are ashamed of their father. Will they expose him? Of course not. They will cover up for him because otherwise it would bring "shame" and stigma onto them which Janteloven insists must be avoided one way or the other. Now, why do the rest of the community cover up to?

Well... it's simply fear and I'll explain how it works with a real life example from a small town in rural Norway:

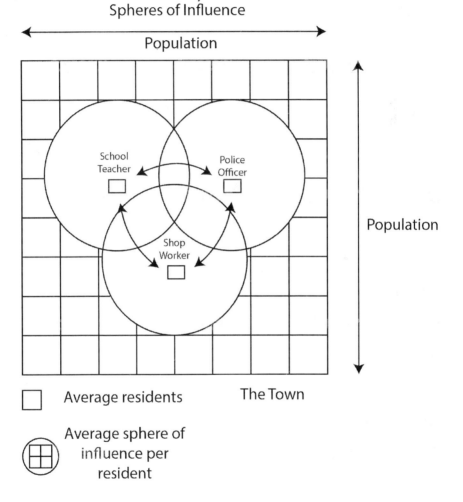

This is a real life example but I've disguised the culprits. Now, let's say you have a predator and he works in the local shop. The local shop is the only shop in the community so it is a "chock point". It is not only a place which is essential but it is also a point where a "bad actor", especially someone who works there can infect the community with propaganda and gossip. That alone is a deterrent for people not to oppose the predator. It's an implied threat… and it will work.

Now let's say that a member of the family of the predator works for the local government or is even a police officer and that person enjoys their influence a little bit too much. Would you oppose the local government official or the police officer if they could actively cause trouble in your life or would you just be quiet and let things pass? You have to worry about the only shop in the community plus trouble from the commune/police force now… probably best to be quiet and let things pass?

Well, how about if another member of the same extended family works in the local school and they all work together collectively to cover up for their perpetrator father because of the stigma and shame it would bring on them if he was publicly exposed. Now, if you oppose any of them you will have potential problems with your children in school, at the place where you get your food and with the police/local government. What would you do? Publicly oppose the predator… along with his whole influential extended family or keep quiet out of fear? An average person in this small community in Norway might have a sphere of influence over 4 – 5 people including their own family but these three individuals, working in tandem exert influence over nearly the whole community now… and that's how they keep things quiet.

The fear that these "bad actors" enforce and influence over a community is often real to such an extent that many people live in fear. For example, I spoke to one lady in her sixties and said, "What do you think of (redacted)?" She said, "He's very nice". I then looked at her and said, "Please don't lie to me. What do you think of "(redacted)?" She then broke down and rubbed her hands over her breasts and body and said, "I hate him! He touches me! I don't like it!" Her husband sat quietly and didn't react. That's how it works… it's a code of silence. This "pillar of the community" is protected by the community who keep his secret due to fear. It's as simple as that. Disgusting… but very effective. I then spoke to many members of the same community and asked them, "Why did you lie to me about (redacted)? Why didn't you warn me?"

They then told me the full story about how they live in fear from him and his cohorts and family because of their individual (and collective) sphere of influence and power they wield in the community.

Observation Twenty-five: Why are ideology and stereotype so heavily promoted inside and outside of Norway?

It's important to acknowledge the damaging contribution of the many non-Norwegians, within Norway, but also around the world, who are some of the biggest enablers of pushing generalisations, rules, myths and stereotypes about Norway and the Norwegian people. To some of them, it seems to be just a money-making scheme, a bit of trivia or more often than not, some kind of "Nordic" fetish with no regard to accuracy or to the real-life consequences that we read about in this book series. I have even seen foreign companies boasting that they've purchased batches of unhealthy Norwegian stereotype-based "guide" books and given them to their foreign employees en masse after moving to Norway to "learn" about Norway and Norwegian culture. There are even companies that charge money to "teach" people about Norwegian culture by propagating these stereotypes, including the oppressive Janteloven so that they may "fit in".

I have observed time and time again that many non-Norwegians in Norway do appear culturally alienated and discombobulated. So what do they do? It would appear, sadly, that instead of describing reality, they so often *enthusiastically* embrace the stereotype version of the "narrative" and Norwegian "rules" *just to gain approval.* They become "experts" and as long as the conclusion is the same; the "Nordic lifestyle" is "great" and "Norway is one of the happiest most beautiful countries in the world"...all is fine... but its faux approval. Are they even able to look past their own fantasies, generalisations and myths to see reality any more? I think that the fact that Janteloven and its consequences as described in this book, which is *everywhere* in Norway, are still taboo and a secret tells you all you need to know about that.

The "Cult of Norway" ideology, myths and stereotypes are very often *encouraged* by too many Norwegians who are quite happy to allow them to circulate and to promote them. It's now not only an industry but completely normalised within Norway. It's also perhaps, a very unhealthy co-dependency because many Norwegians believe these lies which are *imposed* on them. For example, many believe that they are unemotional/anti-social/cold people when of course, it's just not necessarily true. However, many will argue that they're generally accurate with many even emulating these generalisations and stereotypes behaviourally. The stereotypes are not only tolerated but *embraced* and promoted within Norway to such an extent that they are now believed to be true by many. Why is this? I believe that the answer is multi-faceted and complicated but at the very least, in my opinion, they act as a convenient *shield*. They probably now serve to protect against the dark side of Janteloven and Norwegian society being dealt with comprehensibly and consequently revealed, which if widely known might adversely affect tourism and reputation (most importantly it would seem) and in themselves also have value as tourism revenue streams. It's ingenious and incredible misdirection and it truly seems like it has convinced the world and the overwhelming majority of people that visit Norway. If you are focussed solely on trolls, Vikings and Nordic fantasy... on the facade... why would you even bother to look behind it or even want to? Ironically, I think that much of it is unconscious and completely normalised behaviour now.

However, I want the young Norwegians, the silent victims of the charade, like "Seline", "Mathias", "Nina", "Emma", "Ole", "Helene", "Petr", "Hanne" and "Anita" to know that even though many of the adults around them were unwilling or unable to speak up for them, that the foreigners that came here were too focused on imposing their fantasies to see reality, that there are *some* people that have the courage and will speak up for them. Is this book series an indication that the proverbial cracks are now beginning to appear? What will happen when Norwegians themselves start to reveal and reject these generalisations and "unwritten rules"? If these rules have somehow held Norwegian society "together" like glue, what then happens when we start picking at that and shining a light on the bullying and fear? At the moment it's a case of decoding the rules, agree and follow them or don't follow them, and be "punished"... even though nobody will "officially" ever tell you what the "rules" are. However, some Norwegians have written them down... albeit disguised as "comedy", dripping with passive aggression and threatening undertones. You can find evidence of this in almost every Norwegian bookshop and throughout Norwegian media and television. There is no shame or embarrassment either... it is hidden in plain sight and highly promoted. Within the Norwegian bookshop, you can read a sanitised version of all of the unspoken "rules" of Norway, that almost everyone knows, and will often only admit to their existence off the record and privately, nearly always rejecting them as only a "joke" when publicly challenged.

If you go to YouTube and look at the young Nordic vloggers. They will tell you a bit of "truth" about all of these hidden "rules"... but sanitised, warped and varnished into a *positive*. Don't be fooled. These propagated stereotypes destroy the lives of countless Norwegians just as much as they destroy the lives of countless immigrants in Norway too. Fear, ignorance and passive aggression is the glue. How many young Norwegians have to be bullied into the ground for not living up to these imposed ideals and commit suicide before people see that this is damaging Norway? The Janteloven, along with the stereotypes and generalisations, is a psychological prison and I hope that this book series can help redress the balance and unlock those chains, or at the very least, loosen them enough to bring some comfort to those in Norway who need it.

Observation Twenty-six: Finally freedom to speak

I wanted to end this in places *difficult to read* section with its complex interpretations and detailed analyses, by telling you something positive – because it's not all bad. It was upsetting, frustrating, fatiguing… horrifying at times – but something happened in many of those conversations, a moment, a look, a breakthrough – moments you will have read for yourself. That is when I saw something. I felt something – and I realised what a great honour it truly was to be trusted, to have been able to break through some of that façade to get at a bare often painful truth. And in spite of the horrors I have uncovered, is a seed, a possibility of change. As I said at the start of this book, my intention is that through knowledge we can effect change. Let me repeat that… through knowledge we can effect change. We can't do that unless we understand what is happening. But more than that, there must be a need there and that need might be part of what I felt. I felt it when people who had used every tactic there is not to open up *opened up*. And some of them didn't just open up, they blossomed. Once they started to talk to me, like *really* talk to me, they didn't want to stop. Maybe some of it is an inherent need to understand themselves. Was I unwittingly throwing them a rope, showing them that to speak freely, to cast aside the constraints could be truly liberating, a solution even… who knows. This isn't about me, this is about them. But what I do know is that it must be noted here how I met some of the most amazing people in those fifteen months, once I had broken through the walls.

The 'Supermarket' Game

It's a social game, perhaps more correctly defined as a social observation, and it's 'played' extensively across Norway usually with reference to the "bus" or the "supermarket". It happens when two people *who know one another*, see one another in a social context – such as in the supermarket – but instead of acknowledging they have seen one another, they will look away, look at a phone, and not facilitate *further social engagement or conversation*.

A forty-five-year-old respondent, Sigrid, a teacher near Oslo, mentioned that the supermarket *lie* made her feel *guilty* but said that this was an interaction that was very normal in Norway. When I asked if she thought it was an 'act of dishonesty', in the pretence of it, she claimed it was not hurtful because it was by *mutual agreement*. I then asked whether the experience had a negative impact on the mental health of the *participants*. She responded with an emphatic, "No."

As I then pointed out, guilt in itself is a response which at the very least makes a person feel uncomfortable. I further suggested that there could be a cumulative mental health effect with these anxiety-inducing micro interactions. While in themselves "small" moments in this situation, imagine the consequences if magnified in other more *serious* situations. Sigrid then asked me if we had *white lies* in England. This is an interesting deviation – is this behaviour really a 'white lie'? I responded that while familiar with white lies, *what we don't tend to do* is participate *en masse* with specific *mutual agreement pretence*. I pointed out that once one of the participants noticed that the other had noticed them, then the pretence would be dropped and the social engagement initiated. Perhaps the only time we might see no engagement or resultant conversation is if one did not see the other.

According to the first hundred Norwegians interviewed on this subject, the pretence is nearly always by mutual agreement – a form of *acceptable deception*. No attempt is made to change it and only two people responded that they didn't do it but were aware of it as "normal" in Norway.

White Lie vs Pretence

Definition of a "white lie":
"a harmless or trivial lie, especially one told to avoid hurting someone's feelings."

Definition of a "pretence" is:
"an attempt to make something that is not the case appear true."

Analysis of the Supermarket Game

1) During the shop interaction, you have at least two participants.
2) You both see each other, you may both feel anxious, you both pretend not to see each other and then you continue as if everything is "normal".
3) This often elicits a "guilt" feeling, probably because you are essentially "lying", and you know it, but it is rationalised as just being "polite", seemingly to alleviate further anxiety and awkwardness between the two parties, so thus is perceived by many in Norway as a "good" thing?

Real life example as explained by a Norwegian Police Officer

Here is an actual example as described by a Norwegian police officer. I'll include a summary of our conversation below:

Police Officer:
The social interaction is Norway is strange and even I find things weird and strange at times. For example, yesterday I was in the supermarket and an old school friend saw me and I saw him. He pretended not to see me and turned away. We both knew that we saw each other but there is this thing where this is done in Norway. Afterwards, I phoned a friend and told her it was weird.

Anthony:
It's "weird" even though you do it and you know the game? He obviously didn't want to speak to you or he felt like he was too anxious to speak with you? You have admitted that you saw each other and that at least "70% of Norwegians" engage in this behaviour regularly and that "100% of Norwegians" have engaged in this exact interaction in the past. Why did you play along with the pretence and why didn't you just say hello to your friend?

Police Officer:
I didn't want him to feel uncomfortable.

Anthony:
He was uncomfortable already, so what was there to lose? Would he crouch down to the ground and disappear into the earth?"

Police Officer:
No he wouldn't and he didn't do that…

Anthony:
Do you think that this situation is normal when you collude with each other in such a very peculiar way? Why don't you simply change it by acting differently and saying hello?

Police Officer:
I didn't want him to feel anxious.

Anthony:
He already felt anxious. You felt "weird". Maybe you are reinforcing weird behaviour to such an extent that you are normalising it. If you just said "hello" then maybe it might have helped him. What's there to lose? You're both obviously anxious anyway so manufacturing a pretence sequence that generates anxiety to try and relieve anxiety seems futile and illogical to me. You felt like it was "weird" enough to phone your friend but not weird enough to just engage with him, that's very peculiar as well as blatantly deceptive, no? It's not normal, which is why you phoned your friend to express that, right? Next time would it just be easier to quickly say "hi" and move on? It would save a lot of anxiety, stress and pretence it seems!

Possible Mental health effect and the consequences of the above interactions: Pretence vs a White Lie:

1) A white lie by definition elicits very little emotional response and no follow-up of "confusion".
2) The pretence in the mutually agreed "supermarket" interaction, however, generates a feeling of "guilt" that can be sustained after the interaction.
3) Though fully aware of the 'game' no efforts are made to stop it.

4) Pretence and acting can be fatiguing if engaged in regularly.

Regardless of Sigrid's attempted explanation that this act is merely a white lie, there is a clear difference between the pretence involved in the mutually agreed "supermarket interaction" and the collaboration of the collective and a white lie, which would have no lasting impact (emotionally or psychologically – by definition).

One of the first things that was repeatedly cited as a 'Norwegian trait' by many of the Norwegian respondents, and often emphasised strongly, was *honesty*. However, this contradicts with this behaviour that is engaged in, in a widely normalised way in Norway, according to the respondents themselves.

Only two people out of the approximate hundred told me that they refused to engage in this kind of social pretence. Is it possible perhaps, that many of these people in Norway do not consider this concealment and deception as dishonesty but rather a form of survival mechanism? This was actually explicitly stated by many Norwegian respondents under questioning.

This is Norway – "I am appy"

When I checked into my room at my hotel in Kristiansand I noticed a gigantic vertical sign on the wall facing my bed, next to the television. It was about 6ft high and this time it proclaimed: *"I AM HAPPY"*.

It struck me as a strange thing to put on the wall of a hotel room although it surely appears that many in Norway are obsessed with proclaiming themselves *"Happy!"* No wonder Norway is so often voted towards the top of the "happiest" country in the world list so frequently. Of course, if you get points for simply *saying* that you are happy then Norway must be given the gold star. Or at the very least share it with Denmark or another Nordic country, every now and again. If you could be happy from simply saying that you are happy, smiling with the biggest grin or showing off the spoils of your "blessed" life then, surely, Norway would indeed *actually* be the happiest country on earth. It's like some kind of hope that if you repeat something enough that maybe it will come true.

Back in my hotel room, somebody smashed off the "H"… so it now said:

"I AM APPY".

This is Norway…

A Conversation with Oil Industry Workers

I interviewed two Norwegians, "Ingrid" (who is twenty-five years old) and "Raj" (who is eighteen years old). Raj was born in Norway but his parents were born in Asia before moving to Norway. Raj is educated at an international school within Norway. They're both going to give us an insight into Norwegian life and attitudes. Ingrid is seemingly the quintessential twenty-five-year-old Norwegian and appears representative of the twenty-five-year-olds that I met on my journey, with a couple of exceptions. Raj is extremely intelligent, insightful and not typical of the usual type of eighteen-year- old that I met in Norway, generally. However, he is typical of the general intelligence levels of those that I met who are educated at international schools, in my opinion...

Anthony:
You said that some people give you back-handed compliments and are rude to you?

Ingrid:
Yes, if they are rude in some way then I told them that the shoes that they are ALL wearing are very nice.

Anthony:
To be clear, you are referring to the conformity and the fact that they "all" look the same?

Ingrid:
Yes!

Anthony:
And how do they respond to that?

Ingrid:
They say, "Oh thank you!"

Anthony:
They don't even get it?

Ingrid:
No! (*Bursts out laughing.*)

Anthony:
Like clones? And you are not?

Ingrid:
Yeah!

Anthony:
That's incredible, because you are literally saying, "You're a clone" and they take it as a compliment?

Ingrid:
They're like (*AN — she puts on a fake sarcastic voice.*) "Oh, yes thank you, I like my shoes!"

Anthony:
By the way, just to be clear, you said that you like to be "different" and that it makes you "happy"?

Ingrid:
Yes.

Anthony:
Would you say that people are rude to you a lot for being different?

Ingrid:
No, not many but… they're kind of like "Did you buy that at the child store?"

(*AN — Many respondents will deny as a matter of reflex and auto-response but if you rephrase the same question without the "trigger" word ("rude"), but with words that describe the same action but are interpreted as "softer" by the respondent, they will usually always confirm the affirmative quite readily.*)

Anthony:
Do many people in Norway often try and use humour as a way to insult
sometimes?

Ingrid:
I think so, I think so, yes.

Anthony:
I've noticed that a lot of people bully with "humour"?

Ingrid:
Yes, yes they do, yes yes yes! But it's probably, the way I have gone in life, like
my friends, the girlfriends, when we went to school… they went to a regular
school and I went to a school with only boys, in class because I wanted to
work in this industry.

Anthony:
The oil industry?

Ingrid:
Yes, to work in the oil industry, so I went the other way so I didn't get that
pressure.

Anthony:
Do you mean the pressure from school of having to look good etc.?

Ingrid:
Yes… because the boys were like, if I showered three times a week, they were
still like "Oh you smell nice today!" And they just wore sweatpants and oil
from top to bottom, and I am like… here I am comfortable!

Anthony:
Is it tough emotionally to be different in Norwegian society? Do you ever
find it hard to be different, because I guess that humans like to feel
comfortable with their surroundings and if you are different in a way you
won't be accepted?

Ingrid:
Yessssssssssssss! Yes!

Anthony:
Is there any truth to that?

Ingrid:
Yes there is… but I would rather stay alone at home with my dog than be around people that I don't like and feel comfortable around.

Anthony:
So this life choice that you have picked, it sounds good but it sounds very hard?

Ingrid:
Yes!

Anthony:
Because you are different to everybody else and everybody else is not brave enough to be different?

Ingrid:
No! That's true! It's sometimes hard…

Further discussion

Anthony:
Would you say that conformist behaviour, like everybody dressing the same way and saying the same thing, is that the case in Norway?

Ingrid:
It's big in Norway! Yes, it's big in Norway because they get the pressure when they are fifteen to have the same bag, everyone should have a Michael Kors bag, everyone should be like this and this and this, and they have to go home and ask their parents to get it. I spoke to some boys earlier who just liked to brag about what brands they had on or they had at home.

Anthony:
That's peculiar?

Ingrid:
Yes! And I was like when you get older I hope you care about more than just

brands… And he was like *(AN – and she puts on a sarcastic voice)* "It's important to know your brands!"… And I was like, "Wow, OK"… we have all of these influences, showing off Gucci bags but I make my own clothes and get a lot of compliments!

Anthony:
Now, what's this thing about the Janteloven and you're not allowed to be different all about? Because it sounds like you have made a life choice to be unique?

Ingrid:
I haven't really thought about it, when I was a child all of the other girls chose pink swimsuits and I chose blue, and my mum was like "Are you sure?" And I was like "Yes!" And it had like a red bow… I don't know I've always been like…

Anthony:
Being unique… is that usual in Norway?

Ingrid:
I don't think so! No!

Anthony:
Have you actually confirmed that with your own eyes though?

Ingrid:
Yes! I know people that rent more expensive cars than they own that when they go to the holidays in the cabin… they went in the expensive cars so the neighbour thinks that they have so much money!

Anthony:
And how old would those people be?

Ingrid:
Twenty-five to fifty maybe… and when they buy the cabin they ask how big the fireplace is because they want theirs to be bigger than his fireplace… and same with the cabin… and same with the…

Anthony:
Does this happen a lot?

Ingrid:
Yes! Drive a fancy car as well... you drive like an a******!

Anthony:
Many Norwegians have told me; "Oh, we're all so equal and we don't ever show off..." but you have just told me that, in reality, that is nonsense?

Ingrid:
Yes! I think it is b*******!

(AN – At this stage we are joined by Ingrid's work colleague, Raj. He has been listening and interjects at that moment...)

Raj:
It is pretty much b*******! I think that in Norway we have this fake sense of modesty.

Ingrid:
Yes!

Raj:
Like we kind of want it so but deep down we just want to brag about... It's a d*ck-measuring contest.

Anthony:
There is a word for that and it's called "pretence" I think?

Ingrid:
Yes!

Raj:
Definitively!

Anthony:
Now, I can see that you trust me but I suspect that if you didn't trust me and you didn't think that I knew all of this and what I was talking about, then you wouldn't probably tell me this? So in a sense it's collusion? And we are all involved in this charade?

Ingrid:
Yes, yes yes!

Anthony:
My thing is this: there are no real books on Norwegian culture which are not "hilarious" comedy, humour or stereotypes?

Ingrid:
Yes, that's true!

Raj:
That's true.

Anthony:
I think that there is a good reason for that. I don't think that people often want to go deep and are prepared for the mirror to be turned in Norway. Would you agree with that?

Ingrid:
Yes.

Raj:
I would say so, yes.

Ingrid:
Yes!

Raj:
Can I ask you a question?

Anthony:
Of course!

Raj:
Don't you think that conformity is prevalent in all westernised cultures?

(AN – This is a very good question. This young man was one of the first people to ask me an intelligent question… or a question for that fact! If you notice, when I talk with the respondents… they often showed almost no interest in me or my thoughts.)

Anthony:
I do but I think there is a difference in Norway. For example, with the
United Kingdom, we have aristocracy, royalty and true *inequality*... but
the difference is, is that it's overt... everybody knows it. Everybody knows
it... i.e. *you're* at the "bottom"... *you* are powerful and *you* rich... *you're*
royalty. Now, in Norway you have the same thing but the people often
seem to *pretend*, which will have a psychological impact. That's unique to
Norway. Because over there it's clear... you are rich... you are powerful...
you are "better"... and everybody "knows" that. But in Norway, the
pretence of "oh, we're all equal"... in my opinion that disparity between
reality and what many pretend to think and what you "should" say and do
has a psychological impact based on the history, geography, jantalaw and
all that. In Norway many people have told me that they lie to themselves
about this. Does that make sense what I said to you?

Ingrid:
Yes, yes!

Raj:
Yes, I understand... because we live in this sort of illusion.

Ingrid:
Yes... Like when they rent a lot of expensive cars and use a lot of their budget
in the Easter holidays... a lot of their budget to rent expensive cars just to
show off!

Anthony:
The thing is that many people would never admit that publicly and so
many people collude in this fantasy... but here is the thing though, do
you think that there is a consequence in participating in the illusion?

Raj:
Definitively! Because, we're adding on to it...

Anthony:
Exactly, so being part of it will fatigue you psychologically? This is what I
observe and I also observe that no one, no PhD in Norway that I can find,
has ever even looked at this properly or in any way that I can see, at all...
and I think that there is a good reason for this... it would make complete
sense. Am I on to anything?

Raj:

Totally! Definitively! I have already thought about this myself… I put a lot of my time into philosophy and existentialism, but what you're saying is true… It's funny because I recently read *American Psycho* and it's all about conformity and consumerism and materialism and being obsessed… and when you talk about it you can just draw similarities just left right and centre.

Anthony:

I'm noticing that when I speak to most people in interviews, I have to encourage them to say what they really think but it takes me time to get them there, because at first they just usually talk nonsense… strange isn't it?

Raj:

They say something generic.

Anthony:

Yes, aren't initially honest. They often just say what they think I should hear… and when they realise that I don't buy their nonsense… *then* they usually tell me the truth…

Raj:

I completely agree with that actually.

Further discussion

Ingrid:

Some of the Norwegian stereotypes are correct. Like Norwegian dating as well. Because when you're really drunk you meet someone and then you go back home and have sex and then you think whether you like the person and whether you want to date the person.

(AN – I have found that it is most the respondents who regularly propagate stereotypes about themselves.)

Anthony:

I think that there are underlying issues with the stereotypes. For example I think that many Norwegians are often told so many times that they don't express emotion, don't express emotion, don't express emotion, and then the Janteloven… you don't express emotion you don't express emotion, that when somebody makes a joke and calls you a "psychopath" then you just laugh?

Ingrid:
(*Bursts out laughing.*)

(*AN – That tells you everything you need to know about that.*)

Anthony:
I think that there are people in Norway that need somebody to say "No" we can share emotions, if we want to share them and it's OK to do it.

Ingrid:
Yes, and I think that we don't do it on purpose. I went paragliding in the Alps and the guy who did it with me didn't think that I had a good time because *I just sat there silently* and he asked me, "How was it?!" and I said "It was fine"… but he didn't believe me!

(*AN – Reasonable people communicate not only in words… if your words and behaviour don't align; reasonable people assume that something is wrong. This is just a normal human response. If you want to pretend that you don't know that then you are wilfully ignorant, passive aggressive or worse… let's continue and see where this goes.*)

Anthony:
Because you didn't express it?

Ingrid:
I didn't express it with laughter, loud sounds like the Americans when they express.

Raj:
Do you know what's weird?

Anthony:
Go ahead…

Raj:
I often find myself more expressive when I speak in English than in

Norwegian. Like genuinely! Like I speak fluent Norwegian and I speak fluent English... But I often feel like I become more expressive when I speak in English then when I speak in Norwegian. That's why I often I just prefer to speak in English.

Anthony:
The stereotype seems to be that Norwegians don't express how they feel for some reason?... But I think it's just a case of so many are not encouraged to and when many try to be expressive it is suppressed?

Ingrid:
Yes!

Anthony:
You often get into trouble for it or more specifically get an insensitive response to it? If they express any vulnerability then they are too often smashed and bullied... or excluded... So why would anyone voluntarily express how they feel when they know they won't be treated in an insensitive way?

Ingrid:
Yes! I have a sister and we always tell her to stop feeling so much because she feels a lot... "Ahhh! All these feelings... Just stop!"

(AN – Ingrid was telling me this like it was POSITIVE thing. She was proud of it.)

Anthony:
Let me tell you something... I think that that's a terrible thing.

(AN – Ingrid misinterpreted what I just said. She interpreted me saying that that is "terrible" as agreement that her sister was "terrible" for expressing "feelings".)

Ingrid:
Yeah, it is terrible! It's kind of she always feels something about something about something and it's just too much for me to take!... and now she got the result from her doctor because she has gluten allergy... and she said that's probably why she "felt" so much, so I think... I hope that it will go over when she stops eating gluten.

(AN – I almost can't believe what I am hearing… her doctor said she "feels" too much because she eats gluten? Her sister tells her to "stop feeling… because it's "too much to take"?)

Anthony:
But when you say that she stops "feeling" what do you mean by that? Because you could only feel what you can feel. It's not a conscious thing when you *feel* something. Do you mean how she expresses the feeling?

Ingrid:
Yes!

Anthony:
Just to be clear do you understand what I just said?

Ingrid:
Yes! It's just because… she shows it! She cries… she tells us about it… and it's too much for us! Because we don't want to hear it.

(AN – This is unpleasant to hear but it is much more horrifying that she is brazen and proud enough to say it with no self-awareness to how she sounds… to a guest with a tape recorder recording. I'm sorry to say that her behaviour and attitude is not untypical.)

Anthony:
Of course, whatever the doctor and medical experts say is what should be done without doubt or exception, as they know best but aside from that generally, with regards to the "feelings", could it be that she is also not crying necessarily just because of what she "feels", but is crying for the reception that she knows she will get for expressing how she feels? So she would consequently feel "crazy". Because she might perceive the world in a different way that is contrary to society and the people around her… and if she can't communicate her feelings… I don't think they're just going to go away?

Ingrid:
No but, now we thought because she has she got a diagnosis… *because we don't express…* "Oh, that explains why I feel so much."

Anthony:
But she does express because you said that you don't like it?

Ingrid:
Yes, she does express.

Anthony:
But you guys don't like it?

Ingrid:
We... er... hmmmm...

Anthony:
You get uncomfortable?

Ingrid:
We comfort her and we listen to her... sometimes it's just... she cries so much.

Anthony:
Can I ask you something, do you ever get to the point where you solve any of the issues which upset her?

Ingrid:
Yes.

Anthony:
Really?

Ingrid:
Yes.

Anthony:
And then it gets better?

Ingrid:
Yes, but then she talks about something else...

Anthony:
Oh, so she just moves on to the next one?

Ingrid:
Yes, she just gets sad about that… she thinks about this, and I just… she shouldn't think so much! She's in a relationship and she thinks about all the outcomes of the relationship and she cries when the relationship is good because she thinks it can end.

(AN – "Thinking" and "feeling" are being used as derogatory words is this context.)

Anthony:
Does she have anxiety as well?

Ingrid:
No, but she can get anxiety with gluten allergy and that may be why?

Anthony:
Could she just also be sensitive and expressive as well?

Ingrid:
Yes… but in our family we don't do that. (*Laughing.*)

(AN – Ingrid's tone is derogatory and demeaning of her sister… she is laughing at her sister… note her apparent fixation on "gluten" as a catch all solution to her sister expressing "feelings".)

Anthony:
But here is the thing, let's just say that you are a "normal" person, you haven't got a personality disorder, or a medical issue, you're not neurotic, but you just express how you feel a bit more than others… You might be perceived as having an issue that needs to be "diagnosed" in Norway? As you just said, the expression of emotion is uncomfortable for the people around them?

Ingrid:
Yes.

Anthony:
So in a way, it is the person who is expressing who would need to tone down their natural being and behaviour to compensate for those around them? So obviously that will cause them distress?

Ingrid:
Yes, erm, but, er, when we have like the, when we have Christmas and such and she has to leave early, she will cry! She chooses to leave… yet she will cry about leaving! (*Bursts out laughing.*)

Anthony:
Are you saying that it's not logical?

Ingrid:
No, we're happy… and then she's suddenly crying?

Anthony:
Speaking generally only, could any of this maybe even be linked to community and society as well?

Ingrid:
I think that she has too much spare time! Because she has, she works two weeks on and then she has four weeks off.

Anthony:
Does she work in oil as well?

Ingrid:
Yes… yes! She's got money! She's got a house! She's got a boyfriend! I think that she's got too much time on her hands that she can worry about anything.

Anthony:
Is this a general Norwegian issue?

Ingrid:
Maybe.

Anthony:
A very old lady told me that the "Norwegians have got too much money and when you have too much money you have to find things to worry about". Do you agree with her?

Ingrid:
Yes! Because she has time to worry about how her nose looks, how her hair is or if she's gained a couple of kilos. I don't get time for that! Because I study

and I work, and I have to worry about money because I work part-time and I have to do all of this but she can just sit at home and she can just look at herself in the mirror and she can just scroll down Instagram and look at all the things she doesn't have!

Further discussion

Ingrid:
Yeah, but when my grandmother passed away and the day before the funeral, I was writing a speech about my grandmother and then she was crying about her boyfriend not liking her Instagram picture… and I was like "Our grandmother is dead and he is going to be buried tomorrow, and you're crying about this?"

Anthony:
Understood. Speaking to many people I am often noticing a possible disconnect between emotions and the ability to express them verbally?

Ingrid:
Yes.

(AN – Her voice is getting louder and more emotional now.)

Further discussion

Anthony:
But is it the normal situation in Norway?

Ingrid:
Yes!

Anthony:
I'll give you an example. I think that five or six students committed suicide in Kongsberg in one year.

Ingrid:
Yes.

Anthony:
Have you heard about that?

Ingrid:
Yes.

Anthony:
I spoke to so many people about this and do you want to know what people have said to me? The majority of people that I have spoken to have described or implied that the manner in which they killed themselves as "selfish" or "inconvenient" to people.

Ingrid:
Yeah.

Anthony:
Because they jumped in front of a train and "delayed" the train for example… I can't remember exactly. None of them seemed to show any embarrassment or shame in telling me that. They just told me. I myself have had to explain to them it might be an idea to think about the state of mind you would have to be in to commit suicide. And then sometimes they'd realise and say "Oh yes, maybe you are right." It wasn't natural to them, it seemed. I asked a Norwegian teacher who told me straight out that "Norwegians don't think from other people's perspective". If it is "normal" then that's when there would be psychological issues? Anyway… Did you speak to your sister about this?

Ingrid:
Yes.

Anthony:
And what did she say?

Ingrid:
She just cried even more! When everybody else is crying she can't cry but when everybody is crying she does not cry…she loves her grandmother and she was very sad but at the funeral she sees everybody crying and she can't cry. When we had the big terror attack in 2011 our whole family cried… but she could not cry. So, I don't know why but whenever everyone else cries she said that she feels that she can't cry… Because everyone else is crying… That she

has to kind of support and help us when we are crying… But we only ever cry about things that you should cry about!

(AN – What an odd thing to say… "We only ever cry about things that you should cry about!")

Anthony:
Is normal expression of empathy, feelings and emotion not "normal" in Norway?

Ingrid:
No.

Anthony:
But that's not normal?

Ingrid:
No, it's not normal.

Anthony:
So tell me about that?

Ingrid:
I don't know!

Anthony:
Really?

Ingrid:
I just—

Anthony:
But do you feel it though? Obviously you notice it with your sister?

Ingrid:
Yes, because she cries so much.

Anthony:
So, you *really* think that empathy, feelings and expression of emotion is often not communicated normally in Norway, at all?

Ingrid:
Empathy is.

Anthony:
But I really mean expressions of empathy... expressing it verbally, for example?

Ingrid:
Yeah yeah, but when people are in trouble and need help, then I help them.

Anthony:
Yes, but expressing it *verbally*, for example?

Ingrid:
Aahhhhhhhhh...

Anthony:
Like talking and describing your emotions, communicating, expressing... what I mean is *communicating* empathy?

Ingrid:
But but... I don't know... how do you do that?

(*AN – This line is the breakthrough of the whole book, in my opinion.*)

Anthony:
I'll give you an example: somebody tells me that his brother died two weeks ago. I then reply, "I'm really sorry to hear that do you want to talk about it?" or "Let's go for a walk" or... would those things happen in Norway?

Ingrid:
Errrrrr... yeahhhhh... hmmmm.

Anthony:
Do you think so?

Ingrid:
Yeah.

(AN – Raj interjects, as she is struggling.)

Raj:
I would do that! But I hang out with English speaking people…

(AN – I turn to Raj and say, "Now let me ask you straight out… the things that I just said, I think are normal, would they happen in Norway? Please be straight.")

Raj:
With *me* personally, yes.

Anthony:
But typically in Norway what would that happen? Would you often hear, "I'm sorry to hear that, let's go for a walk and talk about it… come around to my house etc.?"

Ingrid:
If they know you well enough, then they will, yes.

Anthony:
But this is what we're talking about… It's not how "well" you know the person, it's; would you treat every human being in that way? Not just your friend, not just your mum, I'm talking about *any* human that you meet?

Ingrid:
I would probably say that "I'm sorry to hear that" but I wouldn't want to talk about it. I wouldn't invite them to talk about it… But if somebody came up to me and told me that I think it would be strange… But I would help them if they needed help…

Anthony:
Why would it be strange?

Ingrid:
Because that's nothing you tell a stranger! Because if somebody came up to me on the bus and told me that their brother died I would say that I'm sorry to hear that.

Anthony:
And that's it? You would say nothing else?

Ingrid:
Yes. Maybe I would ask how they died… I don't know!

(AN – I have found that talking to a great deal of the respondents about hypothetical emotional subjects, they'd often get upset and confused. Even though it's hypothetical and of no consequence.)

Anthony:
But you wouldn't in a way try to connect with them emotionally to show them that you know how they feel?

Ingrid:
Hmmmm… No! Probably not.

(AN – I then turn to Raj, speak directly to him but first tell Ingrid that she will probably be interested in what we are just about to say…)

Anthony:
If somebody tells me that, even if I don't know them, I will tell them that "I'm sorry to hear that man." I might even give them a hug! It totally depends. I'd be flexible. I might ask them how they are feeling and ask them what happened or whatever is required… Now, Raj how do you feel about what I have just said?

(AN – This is the only time that I regret giving an example… I said "giving a hug"… this is too extreme and an impossibility here… it's so out of the question that it will invalidate the point completely because just the thought of that would probably panic her… I should have said "touch on the arm" or something less "threatening" She panicked when I merely suggested that. Many of the Norwegian respondents seemed panicked and exhibited blatant anxiety when I asked them to even just think about an emotional expression and connection/communication with somebody they don't know very very well.)

Raj:
I would have to agree! But it's way easier to do that in English than in Norwegian.

Anthony:
Right, because you said previously that you can communicate more expressively in English than in Norwegian is that right? Why?

Raj:
I don't know… That's just how I feel. I feel like it's easier to express myself properly in English than Norwegian. Culture and language go hand in hand so when I speak in Norwegian, you kind of assimilate to that Norwegian culture you conform subliminally… That's what I would say.

(AN – An incredible insight.)

Anthony:
Unconsciously?

Raj:
Yes, Unconsciously.

Anthony:
Now, Ingrid has just said straight out, I think it would be "strange" to do that… do you think it would be strange too?

Raj:
Not really… I talked to a homeless person. I was waiting for a bus and he came and he came where the stairs was for some reason… And then we got into a conversation and then he told me how he was addicted to heroin… For me just talking to people is just normal. I enjoy talking to people in general.

Ingrid:
But I can talk to them!

Anthony:
Yes, but just not about emotional things you said? Talking about that initial reaction, what you said previously was that you *may* ask them how they died but then you would stop, didn't you?

Ingrid:
Errrrrr… it depends on how they answer.

Anthony:
Just so you know from a different perspective… we might continue the conversation; we might communicate emotionally to that person, because it could be important to us that *they* see that we are connecting with them emotionally and to show that they actually care about them and their story on an emotional level?

Ingrid:
Yes but it isn't because I don't care about them, it's just because it makes me uncomfortable.

(AN – Her point is very clear, the priority is "me", how "I" feel and "my" comfort.)

Anthony:
Yes.

Ingrid:
I don't like to hug people, I have had a boyfriend for five years and he just received his first hug from my mum after his grandmother died, because she thinks that that's worth the hug. *(AN – Raj bursts out laughing.)* Yeah. We don't hug.

(AN – With regards to her boyfriend not getting a hug for five years and only a death being "worth" a hug… that is EXACTLY the same thing that Ole implied with regards to racism. Thresholds which are very very high… death is worth one hug after five years. Ingrid just said those words as if it was normal… "after his grandmother died, because she thinks that that's worth the hug… We don't hug". I need to stress that Ingrid is a completely "normal" woman… she is not crazy… she is educated and working in a professional place. I just met her and we are talking normally… this is normal behaviour for her… this is all just normal, she is not embarrassed and the tape recorder in front of her face. she just stated; "We don't hug" and a death is worth one hug… after five years of no hugs… that is normal for her… I think that that tells you all a lot of what you need to know about the culture that she lives in.)

Anthony:
OK, we'll move away from hugs… Let's only talk about verbal communication. I'm told that it often doesn't even seem to go to the point of talking to somebody in depth, about anything other than the

weather or possibly sports, unless you really know them well, and I'm asking, if that is true, why?

Raj:
We do have this group of people who are kind of like that in my class! Me and my friends... well I was going to say that I was enlightening my friends, but, then that would give me a God complex!

Anthony:
Please feel free to have a God complex!

(AN – Raj has undermined himself and took it to the extreme... enlightening his friends...which is quite a reasonable normal thing... is all of a sudden categorised as him having a "God complex". This shows his perspective of things... why? Because Janteloven requires you be "equal" and he is aware of that expectation and that he is being "naughty" by educating his friends... so he must undermine himself... we know the procedure by now... if you know a little bit more than your friend then you must think you are God and "superior" and... "What's wrong with you? How dare you?! I'm not dumb? You're not God! You can't teach me! We are equal! There is nothing that I don't know that you don't know... we're all equal!"... you get the point. Janteloven is a killer of education and learning too, evidently.)

Raj:
It's more like I made them see the stereotype. And when we hang out with people like the stereotype, we actually make fun of the people by making fun of the stereotype...

Anthony:
Now, do me a favour, explain clearly... you enlighten them?

Raj:
Well, it's like I try and make them see that all of us are way too similar! Our interests. These are Norwegians and they are all the stereotypical, you know the chick squad! You know Starbucks, the clothes la da dee la da da.

Anthony:
Really?

Raj:

They find me amusing because I'm a talkative guy but what my friend's find amusing is that I ironically compliment them… Ironically, that's the thing…

(AN – He means that he is making fun sarcastically.)

Anthony:

So do you mean that if they have the Michael Kors bag, you will say "Wow! That's the amazing new incredible Michael Kors bag that you have… is that the brand new latest Michael Kors version that you have it's so incredible! Oh! I see that you've got the gold trim too!"?

Raj:

Yes! If they bought it because of the hand craft and equality for example, that would be fine but they don't… they buy it simply for the logo. They just want the status.

(AN – Status in an "equalitarian" society.)

Anthony:

Do they get that you are making fun of them?

Raj:

No! They don't that's the funny part!

Anthony:

Can I just say, that's incredible! Because Ingrid mentioned that before too didn't you?

Ingrid:
Yes!

Raj:
Yes, that's why I love this!

Anthony:

So you are pointing out their superficiality and materialism and they don't even recognise it?

Raj:
No!

(AN – Just to be clear, he is saying yes, that they don't recognise it.)

Anthony:
Doesn't that show a real disconnect between perception and self-perception because that means that they don't even think about how they are perceived?

Raj:
I would say… but I'm also very indirect with this… I'm not so "in your face" with it… I make very slight remarks. My friends notice it and they just laugh! They laugh their a*ses off… but they don't notice it.

Anthony:
That's interesting.

Raj:
And I've been doing this for a year!

Anthony:
Just so you know, this is something that I have experienced as well, for example, I would probably have to point out to somebody after they have told me something horrible… "You are a horrible person", or they would just keep on going and tell me more and more with no shame. No shame! One twenty-two- year- old girl told me that "Norwegians will only be friendly with someone when they can get something out of them"… otherwise they will not get to know you… She said this… And then asked her, "How do you think what you've just told me is perceived by a non-Norwegian?" She couldn't answer… She was just talking nonsense and got passive aggressive… I then thanked her for the answer but told her that I'm specifically talking about perception and imagination and again asked. "How do you think what you have said is perceived by somebody else?" She could not answer it.

Raj:
Well they would technically be sociopathic. Correct?

Anthony:
Just so you know, that is something which seems quite normal... I will ask "How do you think a non-Norwegian might feel about what you have just said? How do you think they might perceive you after saying that?" The best answer I seem to get is, "I don't know." So that's what I'm talking about... why am I observing apparent high levels of disconnect between expressions of empathy and also low levels of perception?

Raj:
I also feel like a lot of people lack self-awareness... Not to put myself on a pedestal but I think that I am relatively self-aware for my age.

(AN – Constantly undermining... an auto-response?)

Anthony:
Yes, you are. Generally speaking though, why do you think we might encounter what appears to be extremely low levels of self-awareness in the Norway?

Raj:
Well self-awareness is the antonym of conformity. If you are self-aware you will not be conforming.

Anthony:
So consequently, as this is probably one of the most conformist societies that there is, you are going to have low self-awareness? Maybe that's why when you go to the library or you go to the book store and ask for a serious book about Norwegian culture, beyond the usual travelogues and history books, you hardly have a single book offered which is not a joke or stereotype?

Raj:
I haven't read a proper book on other cultures at all but I do find a lot of articles on other cultures rather than Norwegian culture... but we are only a country of less than six million people as well.

Anthony:
But there are countries in the world with even fewer people who are self-reflective, no?

Raj:
Good point.

Further discussion

Anthony:
Your PhD's have studied other cultures more than they study their own culture it seems. There are Norwegian books about the Polynesian culture but there are almost zero serious books about the Norwegian people and culture that I can find in the bookshops… and that's crazy. I want to read a book about Norwegian culture… and I think one of the main reasons might be because real life is nothing like the narrative we are given in the stereotype books?

Ingrid:
But a lot of the stereotypes are kind of true!

(AN – I too frequently encountered Norwegians that had a self-loathing view of themselves collectively and often individually. Many people in Norway are seemingly conditioned to believe that the stereotypes are "kind of true!", as Ingrid is stating now.)

Raj:
I think that the stereotypes do have some basis of truth to them that is often hyperbole.

Anthony:
The truth is that those stereotypes elicit an emotional response, but there is another layer. I'm sure that at least some of the people want to reject those stereotypes about Norway and Norwegians… for example, there may be an underlying genuinely held believed "truth", as you suggest, about those stereotypes but they are not actually real and true… in the true sense of the word! They have been projected and imposed on people, but I think that some people must actually want to break out of it. For example: "We don't express how we feel."

Ingrid:
Yes.

Anthony:
Well actually that's fluid… One day you might want to express how you feel! You're not a robot… and that means that if that is repeatedly reinforced, that you don't express emotion, don't express emotion, don't express emotion… then in 100 years, you probably really won't express emotions! But if somebody says, "Do you know what… it's OK to express yourself"… and that's why I think that these stereotypes are quite dangerous, because they compound what's already there, and so many people are often afraid to go against them.

Ingrid:
Maybe…

Raj:
I would say that in Norway we do have this kind of immigrants' stereotype… that immigrants listen to hip-hop and wear clothing and I had this experience in tenth grade… I wanted to just break free! And I just went, for some reason, and this is really weird, I went into like classic clothing, suits like proper business… and listen to classical music and now I genuinely love it! I just feel like myself in it! But it's basis was to break out of that stereotype. That was kind of what forced it, maybe not forced it but kind of made it flourish… But now I'm doing it just because I love it.

(AN – A few moments ago, he was portraying those stereotypes as just harmless and "hyperbolic"… now he has stated that those same stereotypes and his rejection of them forced him to change his life and appearance drastically. He wanted to "break free"… the implication of those words is clear… he felt restricted and imprisoned by them. So something which is just a "joke", just harmless, just "hyperbole" is enough for somebody to feel imprisoned by and secondly is powerful enough for them to change his life and appearance. He doesn't recognise this himself, and attempts to trivialise the same thing that forced him to literally change his life.)

Further discussion

Anthony:
Now, you have just given me an incredible point of view, but I've noticed that often in Norway I only get one point of view, there seems to be very little dissent, but I find that when you speak to somebody for more than

five minutes that their *actual* point of view is often opposite to what they told me in the first five minutes. And this is the whole point of this book that I'm writing... the surface... I think I'd like the reality of what people *really* feel and think... and the big question is, why the fear?

Ingrid:
Yeah! If you stay here in Norway and say what you vote politically... If you vote for the far-right then you are a racist! You are a racist, and that is it. Even, though you think that the political things that they do are good and right But you're still (labelled) a "racist", so you can only vote for the left side and then you are a "good" person.

Anthony:
But that means that you have to hide how you really feel?

Ingrid:
Yes!

Anthony:
So pretence and politeness are a barrier to the truth in Norway?

Ingrid:
Yeah!

(AN – We begin to talk about something specific, which I must conceal for confidentiality reasons... it's a kind of "propaganda" video that all three of us have watched. We discuss that it is totally the opposite to what they actually feel but that they themselves encouraged me to watch it and directed me to it originally.)

Raj:
But what I think it does is it sells a story, and I think with all products the aim is to sell. So I think that this is just a story that appeals to people.

Anthony:
Just so you know, I think that that is one of the most apt observations I have heard in Norway. There are a lot of stories that present things in a certain way, for the benefit of tourists and people but it's almost like an initiation, when you really know how it is then you know it's just a fictional "story" to sell, as you have just admitted. And that is something

which seems to be everywhere in Norway... and when I'm speaking to people and then they suddenly tell me the truth about how they really feel, which is the total opposite of what they are forcing me to watch, or were previously telling me, or read and that they themselves were promoting as "true"... I'm like "OK, that's not what you said at the beginning?" And they're so often just like, "Yes but now we know you!" This implies that they can *now* be honest with me.

Ingrid:
(AN – Ingrid bursts out laughing because that's exactly what she has just done.)

Anthony:
So coming back to pretence... that pretence and acting in a way which is contrary to how you really feel is tiring and fatiguing and eventually it will cause psychological issues, over time, lots of these micro interactions over time you'll eventually just want to scream?

(AN – Ingrid explained that she totally disagrees with the video even though it was Ingrid who enthusiastically encouraged me to watch it and told me that it was "really good" initially. She actually told me that it was "not to be missed". After talking about it now she explained that she "hated" the video and it was totally wrong. I then expressed that that behaviour is dishonest... now you will see her get passive aggressive in response to that exposure... she will start talking about "English" people. We notice that both Ole and Aksel also, when they had their dishonesty exposed did the same thing.)

Ingrid:
For example, English people they always say, "How are you?" and you expect the people, to say "fine", but what do you say when people say "I'm not good"... if I say I'm having a s***** day, how would they respond?

(AN – She is unconsciously becoming passive aggressive and defensive.)

Anthony:
You asked how would you respond to it... If you said that you had a really bad day and let's say that we only had twenty seconds... maybe I would acknowledge and say "I'm sorry to hear that", even if you just give them five or ten seconds of "I hear you", I hear and understand that you are going through a bad day... I know that when I go through a bad day it's not nice... You can actually communicate that in ten seconds... It's

OK you don't owe them anything.

(AN – Note that I completely addressed the issue she raised and answered the question. She is now unprepared... she will continue the attacks and try again... she wants a reaction... she won't get it from me.)

Ingrid:
We say about English people that they are superficial polite.

Anthony:
100%.

(AN – Note that I agreed with her statement, which was actually about HERSELF. She didn't directly state that English people are "superficially polite". She only stated that "we" (her) SAY it, which I am very happy to agree with. Her passive aggression will now increase again.)

Ingrid:
Because my aunt is married to an English guy and his mother and father-in-law, hates our family but she doesn't tell us! And he doesn't tell us but after we leave... they trash talk us! And we get to hear that from my aunts... So now when we meet them... we don't want to talk with them... Because they're like "oh how nice to hear..." *(AN – Spoken in a fake voice.)*

Anthony:
Now, that kind of pretence is going to be fatiguing because you don't know where you stand... you don't know whether they're lying or they're pretending. There could be a difference between Norway and England though... because you would get the pretence but then you would probably eventually get attacked for it and called out for it in the UK. That's rarely the case in Norway though, right?

Ingrid:
Maybe after a couple of drinks!

Anthony:
Why the need for a "couple of drinks" though?

(AN – She will now escalate the passive aggressiveness towards me but indirectly, of course.)

Ingrid:

Because, yeah because I have some English friends, and I think that they are polite until you know them, and then they are like the most rude people I have ever... One guy was telling me "Oh, my girlfriend is so fat!" And I was like, "What?" ... "You can't tell me that!" And they tell me that they're thinking of like cheating on her and they like do! There is a stereotype the English guys are always cheating and rude and rude. (*Laughing.*)

(AN – One interesting point... read what she said to him... "You can't tell me that!"... she did not tell us that she said, "Don't tell me that!" or "You shouldn't tell me that!" or "I don't want you to tell me that!" ... she said the one thing which is, technically speaking... not actually true... obviously... I am pointing out the non-confrontation and non-regulation. She did not technically condemn what he said at all.)

Anthony:
Do you know what a valve is?

Ingrid:
Yes.

Anthony:
Sometimes they would be told (to their face) "Do you know that you're horrible and a piece of trash", and sometimes it would probably be like a public shaming... so it could happen quite regularly to that person in their life. Now, let's say that same person is in Norway. Would they ever have to face the consequences of their behaviour publicly? Privately they might have to, possibly but even then... probably not? What they would never be is likely called out on it public?

Ingrid:
Yeah, that's true.

Anthony:
We're not very far away from each other (the UK and Norway) but that difference in handling these situation means that everyone else in the community might have to collude... do you know what I mean?

Ingrid:
Yes, because I've met English guys that don't like my sister... and they tell me

"oh, your sister she's so nice!" (*AN – in a sarcastic voice: fake*)… and I'm like… "you don't like her!"

Anthony:
Do you tell them?

Ingrid:
Not when it's my colleagues, nope… because I have to work with them… but then afterwards, "You don't like my sister?" and they will say… "We had some issues but that's OK"… and I'm like… "You're lying!"

Further conversation…

Anthony:
Say what you just said again? What's your "aim"?

Ingrid:
My aim is to tell men what to do in the oil industry.

Anthony:
Tell me why?

Ingrid:
Because they always look down to me because I am a woman working in an industry where mostly men working.

Anthony:
What does looking "down on me" mean specifically? Can you give me an example please?

Ingrid:
Yes, when I did the security course the travel offshore in Norway, you have to do… A security course… And when you had to put out the fire it was like me and forty guys. And first someone was like, "What are you doing here?"

(*AN – Sexism is VERY common in Norway… acknowledging and admitting sexism in Norway is VERY uncommon. Pretending that sexism doesn't exist or promoting it as virtually non-existent is VERY common in Norway though, I observe.*)

Anthony:
Really!?

Ingrid:
Someone's like "You're really young"… but that wasn't actually the Norwegian guys. They were like "Oh, this is full, please take this one, this one is much lighter that one has already been used."

Anthony:
Implying that you are not capable?

Ingrid:
Yes, of carrying…

Anthony:
Were they obvious or did they try to be subtle?

Ingrid:
I think… I think they were trying to be "nice!"… But in a wrong way… You have to practise climbing up into the lifeboat, and often I hadn't even touched the top before some guy, pushed me up and another guy had pulled me and pulls me in. And I am like, "This is nice of you but when an emergency happens are you going to be here to help me then?" I have to learn for myself!

Anthony:
Did this happen a lot in your experience of the oil industry?

Ingrid:
Yes, when I close a valve one of my colleagues would come and double check it because I am female.

(AN – SUGGESTION. This is subtle but important. She is now talking about her experiences with "valves"… Why do you think that is? Do you remember that earlier I asked her" Do you know what a valve is?", in an unrelated point… now she is, indirectly, informing me that she sure as hell knows what a valve is. The point is… she is talking about her experience with valves… she will even talk about details of a valve. Incredible Nina, earlier… she repeatedly used the word "minimised" after I had said it a couple of times… this is suggestion and many of the other respondents seemed to be VERY susceptible to suggestion.)

Anthony:
That is undermining you.

Ingrid:
Yeah! And some of my work is to check that it's not under pressure so you have to open a valve and then close it again, small valve… And then he wanted to have a guy come and help me!

Anthony:
Did he do this in front of your face?

Ingrid:
Yes!

Anthony:
How did you feel?

Ingrid:
I said, "Do I need a dick to open a valve?" And they were like *(AN – in a friendly fake voice)* "Oh no… you can probably help me."

(AN – Note that my question was not "What did you say?", it was "How did you FEEL?", which not actually answered.)

Anthony:
So tell me how has this translated into your "aim" now?

Ingrid:
Because now I want to tell them what to do… All these men that have treated me bad!

Anthony:
Can I just say that I'm sorry that you've experience this.

Ingrid:
I think that it is funny… because it gives me good stories.

(AN – Her inappropriate treatment is now described as "funny"… by herself… undermining and minimisation. Something which has, also, like Raj, directed her life and goals is suddenly a "joke" because it gives her "good stories"… this is a

seemingly complete inability to communicate honest emotional pain.)

Anthony:
How long on the journey are you to being able to "boss" men around?

Ingrid:
I have one year left.

Anthony:
What is the word specifically here?

Raj:
Sexism... it's misogyny.

Ingrid:
But I don't think that they always do it, I think that they actually wanted to help me I think they had daughters my age and they actually wanted to help me... But they aren't helping me!... We had one here two days ago and they wanted to ask a man a question... And not a female... Female had like five years of experience, and had worked there for one year.

(AN – Note that as soon as the behaviour was identified and characterised for what is was: "Sexism"...she minimised her experience immediately... the actual word... was too much... too triggering... I think the reader will see the pattern now.)

Anthony:
Can I ask does that happen a lot in Norway?

Ingrid:
Yes, I think so, think so...

(AN – She confirms that sexism happens a lot in Norway.)

Anthony:
How about ageism? I noticed that many Norwegians make reference to age?

Raj:
Yes they do! I really feel that.

Anthony:
There is a lot of ageism I feel?

Ingrid:
But what do you mean by "ageism"?

Anthony:
I mean when someone says, "Oh, you're too young to do that" or "you're too old to do that"... That kind of stuff. What do you feel about that?

Ingrid:
My father broke his knee and they told us that we don't operate on people that old... He's such an old man...

Anthony:
How old?

Ingrid:
He was seventy-one; if he was thirty then they would have fixed his knee... It's not worth it because "you are old"!

Anthony:
Doesn't Norway have the money to do the operation?

Ingrid:
Yes but we do not want to spend it! (*Laughing.*) We have a problem in Norway where old people live too long... The best thing for Norway is that people die just when they are about to become a pensioner because after that they only cost money and don't do anything for the land of Norway I think people think.

Raj:
They become a cost.

Ingrid:
If they die they are not a cost but if they live they are cost.

Anthony:
You saying that, considering the wealth I have just seen today... demonstrating how much wealth Norway has... It can be afforded?

Ingrid:
Yes, yes, yes.

Anthony:
So why do they do that?

Ingrid:
I don't know (*sigh*).

Anthony:
You guys have a lot of unanswered questions don't you?

Raj:
Norway is one of those places where socialism is supposed to work... But I do not feel the effects of that socialism... But that's me, I'm eighteen and I haven't had the benefits.

Anthony:
Tell me more?

Raj:
I don't know... I mean sure we do have some great public transport that is supported by the government, and we do have free schooling,

Ingrid:
Free dentist... free doctors! (*Laugh.*)

Raj:
But you get better treatment if you go to the private doctors than to the public doctors.

Ingrid:
You will never be homeless, unless you are a drug addict and don't want to live in the house you get... You will never be homeless, like you will in England... You can go from having a house to being homeless in a short amount of time! So you will never be homeless in Norway.

(*AN – This is delusion. The area that we are talking in has, I believe, the highest number of homeless people in the whole of Norway! Unfortunately this is a widely held opinion. If you want to know more about this denial see, "A ban on beggars in Norwegian cities is not the answer to homelessness: Norway's dirty little secret is out: how did one of the world's richest nations grow so mean as to consider banning begging on its streets?" by Professor Harald N Røstvik, Guardian Newspaper, 12th February 2015.)*

Anthony:

(AN – to Raj)... So you are saying that you don't see this so obviously in your life?

Raj:

But that could also be my adolescence?

(AN – Undermining himself.)

Anthony:

But that's no problem though because it's still valid?

Raj:

That's just me... but perhaps I'm just taking it for granted?

(AN – Undermining himself BUT exhibiting self-reflection.)

Anthony:

Imagine that you in a big house and everybody tells you, "Goodness you are so lucky to live in that big house! You are so lucky! You are so lucky!" But imagine if *you* didn't really feel that you were lucky for living in your house? Because sometimes it's only when you lose something that you realise what you had, but because you don't have a comparative and you don't really know? When I travel around Norway... look at the wealth! Look at the houses! People have got a second home; people have got a boat... And I'm like "This is incredible!"... And they're so often like "Is it'?"... and I'm like "Yes!"

Raj:

I think that that's the normalisation of things and when you have something you just want something better.

Anthony:

OK.

Raj:
I just think that it's something that's in human nature that we just can't abandon.

Ingrid:
I think... I know that I am spoilt!

Anthony:
Oh really?

Ingrid:
Yes, yes, yes I know that I am lucky.

Anthony:
But not as much as your sister?

Ingrid:
No, because she is older than me... And she has the err... the oil crisis... Went down when I finished one of my studies, so I didn't get a job so therefore I was forced into being an engineer... People were telling me oh you an engineer? (*Tone of voice change*)... And I am like, "I am going to show you and I am going to boss you!" (*AN – she is becoming increasingly passive aggressive.*) Yes! Because you can't tell me what I can't do! But I know that I am spoilt.

Anthony:
Really?

Ingrid:
Yes... Really spoilt... I am! I really am!

Anthony:
That's amazing. You're lucky.

Ingrid:
Yes I am! I think I am. I think I'm very lucky... when I watch my car out there I feel very lucky... (*AN – she is laughing and smiling smugly*)... When I go home I feel lucky... When I see my dog I feel lucky...

Anthony:
Do you also have that feeling of being lucky, Raj?

Raj:
I do sometimes I have that feeling of I need to work harder, work harder, work harder... But I do, feel that it's OK for me to be trapped in that mentality until I get a proper job... And then afterwards be more like analytical. I feel like having this hunger like this perpetual hunger is helping me reach the goal that I want... In the short term but when I have achieved that goal then I think that maybe I can sit back and be more analytical.

Ingrid:
I feel that everything I have got in my life, accept my education and how I behave, I have gotten... Mostly for free. Because, my parents worked in the oil industry my granddad was a wealthy man, so I feel that I have gotten...

Anthony:
And how do you think that has been for your personal development? Do you ever think about it? I can see that you're thinking about it now!

Ingrid:
Errrr... I do... I think I am kind... I think so!

Anthony:
Do you think you have missed out on anything for being "spoilt"?

Ingrid:
Err... no. Because when I was in apprentice my house was paid for my electricity was paid for, by the company... then I felt lucky! But when I didn't get the job because of the oil crisis... I was like oh, I had to move back home and I had been living the good life... Like an eighteen-year-old, I could just use my pay on fun stuff!

Anthony:
You could just use your money to do whatever you wanted to do?

Ingrid:
Yes, because I didn't have to pay all the bills... (laughs)... So when I move back home I didn't have all the money, to get paid I had to search for a new job, I had a new job that I didn't like and I thought that this is good for me,

because I thought that if I had been like my sister like from eighteen-year-old having all that money, then I would be like her! She doesn't look at money as an issue.

Anthony:
So what you're saying is that, relatively speaking, you had a period of hardship which taught you about the value of money?

Ingrid:
Yes, yes.

Anthony:
Which your sister did not have making her more "spoilt" and "materialistic"?

Ingrid:
Yeah, yeah, yeah! Because I had the ability to move back home with my mum… And not all people have that. They don't have a place to go home to.

Anthony:
I think that what you have just said shows an incredible insight and I have not seen that too much amongst most of the twenty-five-year olds that I have spoken to?

Ingrid:
Because we get everything we want here in Norway (*giggle*).

Anthony:
A bit spoilt?

Ingrid:
Yes… We are!

Raj:
I mean… I would say that I'm spoilt as well!

Ingrid:
A Norwegian walking in London, walking down Regent Street, I would say "We own the street!" … Because of the oil industry…

(AN – When asked what are the "traits of a typical Norwegian?" a very large number of the respondents answered or suggested that "Norwegians don't boast" and are very "humble".)

Raj:
Yes.

Further conversation…

Ingrid:
When I… in my manuscript in this company… when you yell on the speaker that we are closing… we say, "We're closing" but when we speak it in English, we say "We are closed… thank you for visiting."

Anthony:
Do you think that's because English people need to feel special?

Ingrid:
Or else you would think I'm "rude", yes… "She is very rude… She didn't thank me for visiting her!" *(AN – she's speaking in a sarcastic voice.)* I think it's weird!

Anthony:
We need extra sensitivity, which you guys don't need, do you think?

Raj:
Yeah, like… I don't say it… but that's just me.

Ingrid:
But I do! And I have to be *extra* polite when I deal with *them* I have to be *extra*.

(AN – Note that Ingrid has phrased this as "us" and "them".)

Anthony:
That must be so tiring for you?

Ingrid:
Yeah it is! Because in Norwegian when you trip you say the word s*** but in English it is not the word s***… It's the Norwegian one and when I do that

in London people say "oh my God she is so rude!"… And I say that it's rude in English but in Norwegian it's alright.

(AN – In actual fact, this rationalisation is actually correct on many levels. This is why she can't understand what the problem is… she, in her mind, has been completely reasonable and saying normal things today.)

Anthony:
Is that true?

Raj:
Yes.

Anthony:
So tell me what you think it is? Oversensitive? Are "they" *(AN – people from the UK)* melodramatic?

Ingrid:
I think so! I think so! That's what I mean about the fake thing because in Norway we can just say "we are closing" but in English you NEED "thank you".

Anthony:
So, do you think that the expectation for that politeness is not here? *(AN – in Norway.)*

Ingrid:
Yeah.

Raj:
I would say that it's not here at all!

Ingrid:
In school, in the English language you say, "Thank you."

Anthony:
And "please"? I have actually been told that Norwegians don't have a word for please? Is that actually the case?

Ingrid:

Yes, but I say it when I go into a restaurant <u>but some don't and that's OK!</u>

Anthony:

It's a totally different paradigm if you don't expect that politeness, but we do, but you are saying that it is a weakness that we expect that?

Ingrid:

Like when they call you "love" in the shop that makes me feel uncomfortable... Because when I was in London when I was seven, I was like "All of these people love me, Mum, that's creepy!"... And she was like they don't "love" you they just say that. They don't mean it that's just a thing you say. Like "darling" as well... I don't like it. (*AN – she sounds very passive aggressive and menacing now... her voice lowers*)... Because I think it's fake... Because you don't love me! You don't know me! You don't love me! When you're in the shop and someone says "love"... That's a big thing!

(*AN – She is getting angry at the thought and this is appears like a response to some kind of trauma. Her response is disproportionate, abnormal, literal thinking, no understanding of nuance and seems to be triggered by certain other cultures and behaviour etc.*)

Anthony:

A lot of things are merely greetings, you know?

(*AN – Ingrid leaves us and I continue speaking to Raj alone.*)

Raj:

<u>I just got a flashback</u>... Because I grew up in a British School... a British School... And you do get raised in this superficial politeness and if you are not polite you get shunned by the teachers. My teachers were very strict about being polite and you don't have this in Norwegian schools at all. You have Mr and Mrs and this thing with royalty like you have Sir... You have the Queen but in Norway you just called the teacher by their name... like their front name but in England that would be like, ludicrous! Would be lunacy!

Anthony:

And that means that expectations would be different because rudeness in one culture would not be rudeness in another culture? But I also think that if you do not have politeness for so long then you will not expect politeness. Secondly, if you don't have politeness for so long and somebody is polite to you, it might upset you. Because you don't know how to emotionally and psychologically respond. Do you understand what I just said?

Raj:
No I do! I get it.

Anthony:
For example in London like Ingrid just said, if somebody gives you a greeting at the market and says, "Alright mate do you want a fruit?" because she's not used to that type of colloquial use of language... It might upset her! And this is when it comes down to simple flexibility. When you have a world view, you probably just know, that this is merely a greeting, they are not saying they literally "love me"... It's just a greeting... It's an intellectual exercise and if you have world experience you will know that, but if you don't and especially if you have an insular society then you could be triggered by anything and everything! And foreign people from a different culture could probably really upset you if you're not used to different styles of interaction other than your own very rigid one?

Raj:
That is definitively a danger of having a homogeneous society I'd say.

Anthony:
And I think this is what we've been discussing today, that many people, for example, do you think that those from the international schools, the ones with a more world view can more often understand that people communicate differently?

Raj:
And one thing I forgot to mention! We get kind of looked down upon by the Norwegian kids... And that's mainly because we speak a different culture. We are both literally and figuratively looked down upon!

Anthony:
Norway says that everything is "equal" but obviously it is not... because obviously, how can they look down on you if everybody is on an equal level? How is it possible to look down upon you if you all live in an equal level system?

(AN – Breakthrough question.)

Raj:

I think, the whole thing of equality is b*******! That's my opinion. It's the same thing with superficial politeness in the UK but here it's being "equal".

(AN – And there it is as clear as day.)

Anthony:

But here's the thing, nobody writes books about that and nobody says that publicly, people rarely say it privately and when they do say it I usually have to work very hard to coax it out of them... It takes so much time and probing for them to say it. So many people are living a lie?

Raj:

That's true.

(AN – Said very slowly... he is experiencing realisation.)

Anthony:

You're living a lie?

Raj:

That is true.

Anthony:

Because when you are walking around and you are not treated equally, for example when you are undermined at school, part of you is saying, "Oh, but we are equal... so I can't be undermined."? Yet you *are* being undermined.

Raj:

I mean, I've never had this thing about equality because I know that some people will look down to me, some people will look up to me, some people will put me on a pedestal... I really don't give a s*** I really just live the life the way that I want to live...

(AN – Note that this is almost exactly what Olav the pilot said? Almost WORD FOR WORD... note that they are almost exactly same age too. Both expressed anger at exactly the same moments... same words... same frustration, shown at the same time.)

Anthony:
Exactly! And anyone that thinks that the King and the Crown Prince live an "equal" life to you or me, lives in a fantasy world too.

Raj:
They don't! They live off our tax money! They have a sheltered life!

Anthony:
And also, they have a hereditary line of descent, and they have titles… Your Highness or Your Majesty… But that is obvious, it's just simple logic… however for some reason many Norwegians that I speak to can't see the obvious?

Raj:
It's subliminal manipulation but I feel that this does exist on the international plane because where there is hereditary there will be an imbalance of the public. That's how they keep in power.

Anthony:
But here is the thing though, with Queen Elizabeth we all know that we are not treated "equal" with her, but here though, many Norwegians surely must know that they are not treated in an equal way to *His Majesty The King of Norway* yet I have met so many who *say* that they are treated exactly the same as the King and are equal to the King… and I've seen people get upset if you even imply anything otherwise… it's the weirdest thing?

Raj:
I feel like the media portrays them as "equal".

Anthony:
Yes but people believe it? And I have seen the cognitive dissonance when I point out that they are not "equal" with the King of Norway in a great many ways!

Raj:
They do have these privileges.

Anthony:
Of course! There are lots of things like that… But there is this cognitive

dissonance. There are many things, and that's the thing which I'm very curious about... But it takes a lot of time to even discuss it because you have to go on a journey... You won't get there in a few minutes...

Further conversation...

Anthony:
What was the quote before you said that you'd rather be lonely than be?

Ingrid:
With those people.

Anthony:
And who are "those" people? You were talking about the superficial and materialistic gang?

Ingrid:
Yes, yes.

Anthony:
Tell me what you were saying about your boyfriend you said that you were talking about this yesterday?

Ingrid:
Yes, yesterday, I rang my boyfriend that I don't have a lot of friends... And he was like "You can try to get friends... You can go out and try to get." And I was like hmmm..." Now I think about it I don't want to be with them... they just to talk about make-up and purses... I would rather be alone at home with my dog... Yeah... So I don't have a lot of friends.

(AN – Many of the twenty-five-year-olds that I spoke to said the phrase "I don't have any friends" or "I need more friends".)

Anthony:
So listen, this is what I pointed out right at the beginning. I asked isn't this lonely?

Ingrid:
Yes, it is! Because it is hard on your mentality.

Anthony:
Because it's hard on your psychology to know that you are different to the people around you?

Ingrid:
Yeah it is!

Anthony:
So how do you... mentally, what do you do to survive?

Ingrid:
I don't know... I knit a lot. I make my own dress and I tell everyone that my mum is my best friend, and also my sister because they are more like me talking about the things that I care about, we have mutual interests.

Anthony:
Oh, so your family are... so you have somebody to talk to?

Ingrid:
Yes, my mum is just like me.

Anthony:
If you didn't have her what would you do?

Ingrid:
I don't know... I have a boyfriend?

Anthony:
But to talk about these things you would need to have someone like minded to share them with?

Ingrid:
Yes yes... probably, I see a lot of things coming up with younger people they create these groups to meet and get friends but I think it's more of a superficial thing.

Anthony:
Contrived?

Ingrid:

Yes, they make friends with people they don't have anything in common with… They don't actually like them it's just that they don't want to be alone. But they will feel alone because they can't talk about things tell them because they won't understand! My dog… She understands. That's why I love her and I have a T-shirt which says, "No, I can't… I would rather spend time with my dog."

Anthony:

There is another way of looking at this though… You're saying that your dog gives you more than the friends and society around you?

Ingrid:

Yes yeah!

Anthony:

Is that true?

Ingrid:

Yes!

Anthony:

So let me put it another way, your dog gives you more emotional support than the friends that you *don't* have in society?

Ingrid:

Yes… But now I sound lonely! (*Laughs.*)

Anthony:

Don't worry. It's alright. How you sound doesn't matter as long as it's the truth? And that's OK?

Ingrid:

Well it's true I would rather spend time with my dog then with a lot of people.

Anthony:

And you said that you don't have a lot of friends anyway?

Ingrid:
I don't have a lot of friends.

Anthony:
So you'd rather time with your dog then nearly everybody?

Ingrid:
Yes! Because I'm sick and tired of friends talking about their hair talking for hours and hours about… like one friend I had she was only going on going on going on about her cheating boyfriend… but she didn't want to dump him and she didn't want to end it… But then I was like "well then I can't help you and this is getting tiring"… I don't want to listen to it.

Anthony:
So, basically you are not getting any fulfilment from those materialistic and superficial people because they're often not on your wavelength?

Ingrid:
Yeah… like I said earlier, all of my girlfriend's they chose the school where all of the hot boys were going but I chose to school what I wanted to do with my future, and that's when maybe I discovered that maybe I don't fit in with these girls.

Anthony:
How many people like you are there? Percentage wise… Out of that whole group?

Ingrid:
I don't know…

Anthony:
If you had to guess?

Ingrid:
Maybe 1 or 2%.

Anthony:
So 98% are superficial or materialistic?

Ingrid:
Yes and they want to fit in and I understand it because it's hard not to fit in, but… I don't care!

Anthony:
Thank you so much, because that is an incredible statistic… Now… *(AN —turning to Raj)* if you had to guess?

Raj:
Of eighteen-year olds?

Anthony:
Of eighteen-year olds and then the whole of society, in Norway… What would you say are the number of people like you in society?

Raj:
OK… For eighteen-year olds, like me?

Anthony:
Yes, open it out to every eighteen-year-old you have interacted with in Norway.

Raj:
I mean…

Anthony:
Who are the people that desperately strive to look inside or to understand the world that they live in… who fight conformity?

Raj:
Oh I understand! I've never met anyone like that.

Anthony:
Have you ever met anyone and thought he is unique or she is unique?

Raj:
Not in a Norwegian School.

Anthony:
So give me a percentage… What would be the percentage of the non-

conformists where you think "wow they are unique", in Norway, in your opinion what's the percentage? Ingrid said one to 2%... What do you say? Would it be 0%?

Raj:
No no no... There is always a percentage.

(AN – Very true... this young man is intelligent.)

Ingrid:
(AN – Ingrid turns to Raj and says...) Don't be such a Norwegian person!

(AN – This means that on a level some people DO understand that the stereotype about being "straightforward" culturally, as is often promoted is not true... this phrase has been said in front of me several times on the journey, when people don't answer questions directly and are teased by their associates.)

Raj:
Thinking... Realistically... Probably about 1%.

Anthony:
So basically it's very few?

Raj:
Only a few...

Anthony:
Now spread it out to everybody that you've met in Norway ever... Have you ever met any non-conformist and said wow they are unique? Maybe by their world view or their outlook... What would be the percentage of non-conformists?

Raj:
Probably 2%, but then again I feel that there's probably a lot of people who don't bring it out.

Anthony:
Do you think that there could be a percentage who actually hate being conformist... But they just don't say it?

Raj:
Yes! I *seem* conformist… to about everyone… until I speak… I don't tell everybody that I'm not a conformist… because when you fit in… you have power, in a sense. When you fit in and yourself aware that you fit in then you have power.

(AN – This is what Janteloven does to an otherwise extremely intelligent young man…)

Anthony:
So you do what you have to do to survive?

Raj:
Yes, when you're a wolf in sheep's clothing… You feel like you have power amongst sheep, so therefore I know that I can conform pretty damn well.

(AN – Incredible! Look at the categorisation of the people around him… "SHEEP"… "WOLF"… incredible!)

Anthony:
But you can't share that because they will then use that against you, is that correct?

Raj:
Definitively! But I do like ironically mock them.

Anthony:
But don't you think that literally, like you just said, that is like a "wolf living amongst sheep"? You can't show your real side?

Raj:
No no no.

Anthony:
Because if you do it will be used against you in some kind of way? Is that right?

Raj:
I had a friend like that, and he became my best friend and he was just like that.. He didn't fit in… And then people looked down on him… I mean

people would hang out with him but I realised that the bonds that people had with him were superficial.

Anthony:
But it seems like that "98%" is very materialistic and superficial anyway?

Raj:
Yes, I would say so.

Anthony:
But maybe 50% of the 98% resent the supposed super superficial and shallow proportion?… But they just never say it? And then some of the others might just *really* be superficial and materialistic?

Raj:
Yes, they just live in their own world.

Email follow-up questions with Raj

(AN – I later followed up with Raj a few weeks later. I sent him a list of questions and he kindly answered them. His answers speak for themselves and I believe that they give a very clear insight into what Norwegian culture and Janteloven.)

Anthony:
You answered all of my questions with intelligence and with confidence. However, are you aware that when I mentioned the word "racism", you verbalised that you would not say that Norway is racist, you turned to look and see who was around you (i.e., looked behind) and you became uneasy? This is the only time in the whole discussion you became visibly uncomfortable. This is something which I am often noticing whenever I mention racism, especially to non-white people in Norway, they commonly look uncomfortable and very commonly turn their head to look behind them. This is absolutely typical! Considering your confidence during our discussion, why did you become uncomfortable at that stage and specifically, why did you turn around to see who was behind you? You did not do so at any other stage of the discussion, only when talking about racism. Are you afraid to discuss this?

Raj:

Intriguing observation, however I do have a theory as to why I might have acted this way. My initial thought was that I quite possibly could have checked behind me to *(AN – redacted)*, as they often wait quietly until they are noticed to request any form of aid. I do still stand by the fact that racism is not an intrinsic aspect of the Norwegian culture, and is not practised by the majority of Norwegians. If Norway was to be culturally racist, then I would not be solving the problem at all. Personally, I am guilty of occasionally judging residents of Norway based on their culture and their level of articulation regarding the Norwegian language. I am quite aware that these characteristics are inaccurate when judging one's intelligence (assuming that intelligence gives an individual a higher value in society). To elaborate on this, I judge those conformed to the ghetto culture as having less societal value, than those who have conformed to the Norwegian culture. However, such judgement is not unique. Well, do you believe that beggars have equal societal values as CEO's who drive the economy? A major stereotype of the ghetto culture, is that they purely live off our welfare benefits (through an organisation called NAV), thus being a cost to society. This ostensibly irritates the majority of people. If someone white was to say this, they would be labelled as a racist. However, since I am brown, I can say these things without being socially ostracised (which I find highly amusing). I have tested this paradox in my grade, where I have made the majority of the white people in my grade say the controversial word "n*gga/n*gger" *(AN – I have edited these derogatory words. Raj did not.)* They were all initially discomforted by the thought, however with time it became normalised, very much to my own amusement. Regardless, I personally disregarded my own culture and fully assimilated into the Norwegian culture in fifth grade (when I transferred from the British International School to a Norwegian public school), and I have continued to be assimilated ever since. However, it was initially into the immigrant/ghetto culture, rather than the true Norwegian culture itself. I was stuck in this culture until 9th grade, when I consciously made the shift into becoming more like a "true Norwegian" in regard to mannerisms, behaviour etc. This shift included taking up interest in sophisticated clothing, classical music, literature etc. The very antonym of what the immigrant/ghetto culture represents. Personally, I now associate the latter with hoodies, baggy pants and vulgar rap. Thus now, after talking to me, one realises that I am culturally Norwegian, and any prejudice (if there was any from before) is effectively brushed away. To be perfectly honest with you, I do believe that this appeals to Norwegian snobs rather than the average man. To answer your question directly, racism is not a prevalent issue in Norway. However, there is slight discrimination based on one's culture. To answer your question regarding my unexpected uneasiness, that was merely due to my slight fear of my colleague overhearing me. Although my opinions might be seen as being racist by some, I am aware that I would not get publicly criticised for it by anyone. However, it would quite possibly give a bad impression of me to other people. Conformity, in my opinion, is double-edged sword. I would say that I seem incredibly conformed to the culture that I am very much a part of. However, that does not jeopardise my self-awareness. As nauseating as it sounds, I would identity myself as a wolf in a sheep's clothing surrounded by sheep. Perhaps that is slightly induced by my male ego. Regardless, once you truly seem conformed to the culture of your acquaintances and you are appealing to them, they will slightly lower their guard. False truths and false relatabilities truly harvest power. History has testified to this fact, a prominent example being how Joseph Stalin kept his dictatorial power. Once someone has lowered their guard, it is incredibly easy to earn their trust. After earning a close level of trust with the majority of the people in a group, you truly have social power. This is the basis of me wanting to seem conformed. It exudes an aura of relatability and friendliness. This ties in with me wanting to seem truly conformed to the Norwegian culture, as aforementioned in the previous question. It has more to do with people's perception of me and how it gives me social leverage, rather than genuine discomfort.

Anthony:
Were your parents born in Norway and have they or yourself ever experienced any racism or discrimination in Norway? If so, do you feel pressure to keep it quiet or to not complain or protest about it? Were you born in Norway and how does your heritage affect your life in Norway and your identity? Can you tell me about your identity as it relates to Norway, please?

Raj:
My parents were born in (redacted), and as far as I am aware of, I do not believe that they have experienced any form of racism. I was born in Norway and I have lived there throughout my short life. On the contrary to my parents I have experienced instances of slight racism, not by ethnic Norwegians but rather by other minorities. The pretext of the two episodes were in luxury boutiques. In both instances, I received an unwelcoming look. However, once they were aware that my watch knowledge was immense their attitudes changed completely, and instead of indirectly being shunned away I was offered champagne etc. The first episode was with a Chinese saleswoman,

who ironically knew less about the product she was selling than I did. I presume that she had a superiority complex, living in the illusion of being superior, however in actuality suffering from intellectual inferiority in the context of watches. The second episode was when I got the classic "look" from a Hispanic woman who had come in the boutique with her husband, her husband being the actual customer. I do not feel any pressure to keep such information in secrecy, however by my own nature I do not care about such situations. If allowing some people to revel in the illusion that they are superior to me, by so means be it. It does not matter to me because I am well aware of my social and intellectual prowess.

Anthony:

You mentioned the self-awareness levels of the people at your school when you made fun of their materialism and shallowness. You mentioned that they were so shallow and had such low levels of self-awareness that they did not even realise that you were making fun of them. I asked you why this was and you said that you did not know. Now that more time has passed, do you have any idea as to why their self-awareness levels would be so low?

Raj:

I have a hypothesis that their self-absorption and constant worrying over trivial problems might have caused their social intelligence to drop. However, I am quite self-absorbed myself, as being self-absorbed it a necessity to be ruthlessly effective (so long one does not expose their self-absorption).

Anthony:

Do you think that Norwegian society is an enlightened, self-reflective, philosophical society or do you think it is materialistic, narcissist or shallow? Please tell me more either way?

Raj:

I personally believe in the latter, though people who are not truly conformed to the Norwegian culture might opt for the former opinion. Then again, I believe that the notion of materialism is inevitable in a capitalist society (I am by no means a communist, if anything I support capitalism). Due to the prevalence of materialism, narcissism occurs naturally, as one values one's possessions in a higher regard than other human beings. This naturally leads to a hierarchical system based on materialistic progress, which is intrinsically shallow.

Anthony:

I observe that if you criticise anything "Norwegian" often many Norwegians take this as a *personal* offence. Why do you think that any Norwegian would take offence to something unrelated to them or something on a national level which they have nothing to do with? Do you think that the Norwegian peoples general sense of identity and ego are so often intertwined that many cannot accept criticism? Do you have any thoughts or perspective on this possible suggestion?

Raj:

I believe that this ties in with the notion of "group identity", and henceforth national pride. Furthermore, I do not think that this offence-taking is something that solely occurs in Norwegian culture, but with any culture where one must truly conform to have any form of social influence. Perhaps it has partly to do with Norwegian ego, however considering the Oil-boom and the security net caused by the Oil Fund, if this ego does exist there is true reasoning behind it. Additionally, if such an ego existed, it would explain why Norwegians feel that they are superior to other national groups, likewise to the American tourist stereotype. Attacking a national group in that regard, would be proposing that the group is inferior to other national groups and cultures.

Anthony:

Do you think that the Norwegian collective exhibits any kind of inferiority complex or low self-esteem, which some say manifests as "arrogance" etc.? If so, why?

Raj:

I believe that the Norwegian public exhibits a superficial inferiority complex to seem humble. However, their true opinions differ vastly to this superficiality. Due to the materialistic nature of the Norwegian society, and the superficial inferiority complex, they might give the impression of being arrogant to other cultures upon further analysis. This is due to the behavioural traits that are favoured in regard to moving up the materialistic hierarchy require arrogance.

Doping in Norway

I sat down in a place near Oslo with an extremely respected and highly educated sports doctor and had an incredible conversation about skiing and the Norwegian doper, Therese Johaug. I like the doctor very much and felt like he is probably the most candid person I met with on my trip. Even though I disagree with his conclusion I respect him and believe that he has intellectual integrity.

Anthony:
Therese Johaug... we were just talking about Therese Johaug. The last few years I have been here, she has had issues with crying and doping and lip gloss and blah blah blah. So we have just discussed that there is a "missing link" there is something missing to this story?

Dr Sebastian:
The Federation can't be telling all that they know about this. There is a big missing link there.

(AN – This is an indication of intellectual integrity. We immediately have an identification of potential "missing information". This is rare to hear on the journey... I rarely heard a respondent call into question any Norwegian institution or any public narrative prior to me coaxing doubts out of them.)

Anthony:
Reading the story... I'm seeing her press conferences I remember thinking straight away that, "This has to be a joke... lip gloss... this is amusing!" Although we don't know... what in your opinion could be the two "missing" links?

Dr Sebastian:
The first one: lip gloss was a cover story and the second one, I mean that this serious doctor that went down to the local pharmacy, and purchased this box with a big red triangle saying doping, outside the box how could you do that?

(AN – Again, this is refreshing… we have an individual who is simply questioning the obvious and implies straight away with his use of the words "cover story" that something is not adding up… he is aware of that…so already, we can have a relatively normal conversation because he is indicated that his level of intelligence and insight… he is a not stupid. He has asked a very pertinent question: "How could you do that?".)

Anthony:
So, do you think that he was so negligent that he was probably drunk or something else?

(AN – This was a face-saving question by myself… I didn't want to come out too hard and I wanted to give him an opportunity to explain the story from his own opinion.)

Dr Sebastian:
We cannot really say but we cannot really understand how it's happened.

Anthony:
So, with regards to what actually happened saying that the "cover up" was with regards to how substance got into her system? Or are we saying that the "cover up" is because… Is there any chance that she, for example, doped? And then that initiated a cover up?

Dr Sebastian:
I think that the Norwegians do not believe that the Norwegian skiers are doing doping. I don't believe that either.

Anthony:
Because Norwegians don't need to do that really?

Dr Sebastian:
Because they are strong and I think that, to be honest, to do cross-country skiing in Norway you have to be dedicated in your sport, from early in school so they are strong.

(AN – Just as a quick observation, I believe that there is a case to make for the fact that when a person prefaces a statement, especially when it comes to a question of integrity or pride, with "to be honest", then it could be an indication of some kind of unconscious or conscience resistance. On this occasion, if this is the case, it

would be unconscious because this individual is not only honest but probably the most honest person that I interviewed on my whole Norwegian journey. He is honest and I respect him... honesty doesn't necessarily make you correct though, let's not forget... let's continue...)

Anthony:
This is the thing though, this makes this very strange. What is this lip gloss and what the hell is this Doctor doing giving her this?

(AN – Again, I am being very gentle. This is seemingly perceived as a personal issue for Dr Sebastian, so it's important to be sensitive. Dr Sebastian's position: Main story correct, some details of story wrong. My position: Main details wrong probably means details of story are wrong too. So now let's look at how "invalidating" the "wrong" is and if it's wrong enough to invalid the whole narrative, in his mind.)

Dr Sebastian:
Yes, it's unbelievable.

(AN – Exactly... It is NOT believable... so where will he go next? Let's continue... I will start to point at some pertinent issues and see where we go...)

Anthony:
And she was banned for like, two years, is that right?

Dr Sebastian:
Two years and of course, the people in CAS in Switzerland had to punish her because they could not have faith in this story because there is a missing link there.

Anthony:
100% of the people that I've spoken to in Norway have said that they think that she did not dope. It's 100%... it's unanimous. So that would then mean that the doctor did something to fail her... or do you think that it could be that she did something?

(AN – The question is loaded because I have just pointed out two things that don't reconcile...1) She was banned for doping and punished for it. 2) 100% of Norwegians respondents believe that she did not dope, even though she was found guilty of doping, banned for doping and punished for doping. 3) The suggestion is

clear: This is not logical… subtext: How do you reconcile those things Dr Sebastian?)

Dr Sebastian:
But of course they are both responsible because when you are an athlete you are responsible for what you are putting into your body. Although, you are there in the Alps training resting sleeping, training again in the evening and then you have a doctor there that is taking care of this so why shouldn't you trust the doctor? But of course this does not take away her own responsibility.

Anthony:
Is she the biggest sports star in the country? You know she's a beautiful and a big sports star?

Dr Sebastian:
Yes, but her friend that just retired last year, she probably has more…

Anthony:
What's her name?

Dr Sebastian:
I've forgot her name already.

Further conversation

Anthony:
Now, with regards to skiing, what does it mean to Norway? Is it the National Sport in your hearts?

(AN – I am gently suggesting; could this make ones perspective biased/unclear when it comes to admired Norwegians stars caught doing bad acts? This is why I mentioned "heart"…emotion over reason.)

Dr Sebastian:
Yes, I think you can say that skiing is the national sport in Norway.

Anthony:
Now, what is this saying that Norwegians are "born with skis on their feet" or something like that?

Dr Sebastian:
Norwegians are born with skis on their feet… Were… Not anymore, maybe!

Anthony:
Tell me a little bit about that… What do you mean you mean "not anymore"?

Dr Sebastian:
Because there is a lot of people in Norway now that hardly learn to go skiing and the ones that do, do it one way or the other, doing it a lot and of course they are very skilled, but back in the old days the common transportation of people to go to school was Skiing.

Anthony:
OK… practical?

Dr Sebastian:
I did that myself.

Anthony:
How long was that?

Dr Sebastian:
It was about 5 km, each way.

Anthony:
Wow! So, you ski to school on skis and then you study and then ski back home after school. How did you feel about that?

Dr Sebastian:
Well it was the most…

Anthony:
Efficient way to get to school?

Dr Sebastian:
Yes, because no one was driving us and there was no bus. We could walk along the road which is more time consuming… yes.

Anthony:
Is this why you're such a good skier and became a sports doctor, would you say?

Dr Sebastian:
Well, part of it yes. And also we did a lot of skiing out playing like jumping downhill or cross-country. And all of the kids did that back in the old days.

Anthony:
So even if you didn't have to ski to school then you'd probably be an amazing skier? Probably?

Dr Sebastian:
Yeah, I, yeah… we did a lot of skiing.

Anthony:
Now, chess! I have seen a player called Magnus and he has made big impact in the world. In fact he is very much a representative of Norway on the world stage just as a name right?

Dr Sebastian:
Very much.

Anthony:
What do you think about that and what do you think about chess about what he's doing?

Dr Sebastian:
I think that Magnus Carson is incredible. Of course, he has won a lot is the number one chess player at the time. And he really has increased the interest around chess in Norway. Before him not so many really cared. But in the recent years when he has been winning just like in the skiing events a lot of Norwegians watch it on TV. And will often say that they can't do this now because they have to go back home and watch Magnus Carlsen play!

(AN – These are national pride issues… not just sporting achievements, note.)

Anthony:
I remember watching it with my good friends in Kongsberg. He is a Doctor too actually. Very generous and cool family. I like Kongsberg…

We watched it was being broadcast on NRK 1 prime time and they put a lot of effort and promotion into it.

Dr Sebastian:
Oh, yeah!

Further discussion

Anthony:
So there are so few chess grandmasters so to have one in Norway is obviously a big deal. Would you say that it's a big deal?

Dr Sebastian:
Yeah.

Anthony:
So, I'm guessing that that's a big source of pride? Because that's what it seems like…

Dr Sebastian:
Yeah, I mean… Norwegians, we support our athletes…

(AN – What an incredible way to end the conversation… an incredibly insightful conversation.)

An alternative perspective from Finland, "Onni", Fifty years old from Helsinki

When Finnish athletes were caught doping, Norway gave them no mercy. I asked a Finnish individual with knowledge of these matters for his thoughts and opinions of Norwegian doping issues. Here is what he said:

Anthony:
I have noticed that 100% of the Norwegians that I have spoken with have said that they disbelieve that Therese Johaug is a doper. Even though she was found guilty of doping. I am wondering why it's 100% and without a single dissenting voice. Any thoughts on it?

Onni:

Well, we Finns have our own history with doped skiers. The Lahti 2001 thing. I think we as a nation grew up and lost our childish view of clean sports. I think many Norwegians know Johaug is a cheater but they refuse to admit it. She's too much of an icon for them. Some just have a blind spot. I'm absolutely sure the doping in Norwegian skiing is an organised thing and has been like that for a long time. (Redacted) and all. Almost every Norwegian skier supposedly has "asthma". What a coincidence! (Smiley wink face emoji)

Anthony:

Do you think that many Norwegians are in denial? It appears that so many really believe that it's all a conspiracy and that she's 100% innocent. Or do you think that they're lying to themselves? There seems to be very little dissent on much in Norway I am finding... any thoughts on that? Finally, you mentioned that the Finnish "lost our childish view"... are you saying that many Norwegians are naive?

Onni:

I think Finns and Norwegians are pretty much the same when it comes to something else than skiing. It's serious in Finland too but it's a CULT in Norway. They don't want anything to smear it. I'm sure it's partly denial and partly just a cover up.

Anthony:

Incredible! If it's "partly cover up" that means that people are aware of what they're doing, no? How and why would they do that?

Onni:

I'm pretty sure it's run by *(redacted)* nationally or whatever it's called. Just like it was in Finland when the sh*t hit the fan in 2001. Johaug is the only high-profile skier who has been caught. It was pretty clear to anyone with a brain that she did not get the steroids from a lip balsam like they claimed.
(AN – We note his use of the word "cult", "denial" and "cover up".)

This is Norway – The Racist Anti-racist

Mary is a self-proclaimed anti-racist. She is so anti-racist that she gets angry at racist people. She even said, "How can people be racist?"

I found that the anti-racists were often even more racist than the self-proclaimed "proud racists" in Norway. I would rather speak to a "proud racist" then a delusional anti-racist any day because at least you have a basis of reality to communicate on... something fixed. When you speak to these "racists" you soon realise that many of them are just angry at not being heard and if you listen to them, respect them and actually connect with them as human beings, then those "racists" will often treat you with more respect and kindness than many others.

I can say with absolute certainty that the proudest most ardent "racist" that I met on my journey was one of the kindest and respectful people to me *personally* on my journey across Norway. I can also say that, there is no question... the most racist disrespectful people were the self-proclaimed "anti-racists" who hate racism in all forms... they were the worst of all.

Mary was struggling and about to have a panic attack when I met her. She'd ordered a veggie-burger and was convinced that it was actually a meat burger. I called over the waiter who quickly put her mind at rest – it was 100% veggie. Initially placated, Mary moved on to her next subject... Norwegians!

After a brief discussion on racism, I pointed out that if you ignore racism then it's not going to be resolved and asked her why they don't speak about it? This simple question then triggered an argument... but not one involving me. An argument involving only herself.

It was horrifying and scary to witness. I have seen this type of thing before in Norway... in fact I've seen a similar thing many times. A respondent will sometimes say something and then a few seconds later, with a completely blank look on their face, say the opposite thing, a counter attack against *themselves*. If

I point this out they generally look confused... might even start speaking gibberish that you can see for yourself in the transcripts. On this occasion it was different. Multiple opposing arguments with somebody arguing with themselves, with no prompting or questioning is horrifying to witness.

I just walked next to her and listened carefully. Here is the conversation:

Mary:
As a coloured person, have you experienced any racism in Norway?

Anthony:
Yes, almost daily. Norway is the most racist country I have ever visited in my life.

Mary:
It's funny you say that! My American friend who's black mentioned something about that! I told my friend at work not to bring it up to him actually.

Anthony:
Why would you not discuss it? If you keep quiet but just whisper about it behind his back, it's not going to help solve the racism he has to live with is it?

Mary:
The thing is, I've had some bad experiences with people from different races... I'm not trying to put down what you're saying! But, I'm just saying... I have had bad experiences from other races so I that—"

(AN – I interrupted her.)

Anthony:
What's that got to do with what I just said?

Mary:
Oh no no no! I'm not trying to dismiss what you're saying or anything or link it to you guys!

Anthony:
OK. What has it got to with me?

Mary:
Nothing! Nothing… I just think that sometimes when you see someone…
(AN – She then stopped herself speaking and changed tone completely.)
Maybe I am linking it… but how can anybody think that way?! That's so racist! It's just wrong!

The 'Staring' Game

This is another social observation; one I experienced directly and one that happens regularly in Norway, according to many of the respondents. If you are perceived as an "outsider" as I was as a visitor to Norway, or look slightly different… you will almost certainly be stared at, especially outside the major cities. Can this be regarded as blatant curiosity, interest in the newcomer, perhaps? Or is there more behind this behaviour? Interestingly, the American *Scribner's Monthly* reported the same thing back in 1876, from their Norwegian travel report (*The Century* illustrated monthly magazine v.11 1875-76 page 423):

"A trait of an isolated and untravelled race; for if one appears in some remote inland hamlet or sea-port, he is stared at and commented upon as though a rare specimen of natural history."

This staring behaviour doesn't only apply in the street or in a public place. I witnessed it time and time again while working on this book from the cabin I'd rented. I became aware of an almost constant stream of Norwegians boldly walking up to my cabin window, cupping their hands and staring directly in. They couldn't see me until they were only 50 cm or so away. When they did see me, they strangely all reacted in the same way. They'd jump back, as might be expected, but then they'd behave as if *they had never seen me and that I had never witnessed their actions.* Not just one or two – all of them behaved in ways I would not have expected.

For example, one time I shouted, "Hey!" through the window at a lady who simply turned and walked slowly away as if nothing had happened. Another time a man responded by looking up at the sky while standing next to my window as if that was what he'd been doing all along. What was odd to me though was the blatant lack of apology, acknowledgement or even initiation of a conversation once "caught". This didn't happen just once or twice – this happened over and over again.

While it is tempting to interpret this behaviour as rude, it's apparent from how many times this happened that this seemed to be *normal behaviour* in, at least, this small part of Norway. If regarded as a social norm then perhaps it is not perceived as rude? As a consequence, I started to film these observations. It wasn't long before I caught two people 'playing the game'. With camera rolling, I spoke to them directly, asking them what they were doing. A lady of around forty years old with her ten-year-old child, giggled in response, so I asked again. When she still didn't answer, I asked a third time: *why were you staring through my window?* What was confounding was her response to this, and her overt expression of shock as if my comment was not directed at her. She said, "It's so bad that people do that."

I captured this behaviour a number of times. I then asked a nearby local what she thought about it. She *acted* genuinely shocked and asked if many people had engaged in this to which I explained yes I had witnessed it a lot. While expressing shock, as if it was a new concept to her, it was pretty obvious that she was aware if it – I assume not only because it was *normal behaviour* in her community but also because we had discussed it previously, as it related to her own partner's privacy, which was encroached upon by a local voyeur.

This is Norway – Wrong!

I climbed a mountain in the west of Norway with an acquaintance. It had a ridge on one side that is the old border between Norway and the old Swedish Empire. I made sure to put my left foot in "old" Norway and my right foot in "old" Sweden. I asked my acquaintance what year Sweden took over this territory and my acquaintance giggled and said, "I don't know." This certainly did not surprise me. I didn't know that the Swedish Empire had extended that far west and read up on it later.

A few months later I was driving with my Norwegian friend, an accountant. He's a pillar of the community, experienced, extremely well educated and a good man. We were talking about Sweden and Norway and I told him about my mountain experience and that I had stood across the old Norwegian/Sweden border and he abruptly interrupted me: "Wrong!" I looked at him and assured him that I had personally stood on it with my left foot on the Norwegian side and my right foot on the old Swedish side. Again he said it again. "You're wrong!"

His response confounded me because he is highly educated and we were discussing the geography of his own country. I explained to him exactly where I was and that I physically stood on the border and he cut me off and abruptly dismissed me even though he had not been there himself.

I realise now that this demonstration is a reaction I saw often when someone was challenged – too many do not like to be wrong.

I decided to take up my phone and to pull up the history of Sweden which had an animated video map. The map changed and changed and changed and then I told him to watch… I then paused it at year 1658. I knew not to say a word. I knew not to challenge him but to just let the facts speak for themselves. He looked at the screen. His face went red and he replied, "OK… right." I actually got an acknowledgement… that is rare in my experience in Norway. We will soon see an almost identical situation where we will see a much more bizarre response.

This is Norway…

This is Norway – Wrong again!

I needed to take a bus to the airport and I was unsure of which bus stop to wait at. I was in a rural area and buses were infrequent. It was important as I needed to catch a flight. I messaged my local friend. I asked her which bus stop, on the left or right hand side of the street. She replied with an emphatic "Right". I actually verified this again to be quite clear as my gut was telling me something contrary.

The next day I took my case and off I went, although still felt unsure. So much so that when I got to the bus stop I took out my camera phone and filmed the bus stop that I was standing at and said, "I'm standing at the bus stop on the right. Are you sure I should be going in the opposite direction as the bus stop down the road over there?" (I then turned the camera around in the opposite direction). "I think that is the right way to the airport?" I asked. Very quickly I got a one word reply: "Wrong." I then thanked her for her help and then got a reply: "Have a nice flight".

So I waited until a bus appeared when I told the driver I was heading for the airport. He laughed and said "No! This is the opposite direction… you need to cross the road and walk along and wait at the next bus stop in the opposite direction." So my adviser had advised incorrectly and my saving grace was the bus due in the other direction was later, therefore I was still able to catch it on time. When I messaged my friend to tell her, unsurprisingly, as expected, there was no apology, not even an acknowledgement. What she did was send me a photo in reply. A photo of a door frame and a mop. A door frame and a mop? Nothing else. This kind of bizarre behaviour is not unusual in my experience, especially when somebody is shown to be wrong… it's often just shut down or start acting irrationally. Never to be discussed again.

This is Norway…

A Conversation with Two Receptionists

I never intended to interview these two hotel receptionists. In fact I just chatted to them and explained what I was doing and told them I just wanted to talk to them as human beings, rather than under interview conditions, because this was all getting too crazy. However… when they started talking I realised that I had to get them on the record and interview them! I asked them if I could record the conversation and they enthusiastically agreed.

Interestingly, the non-Norwegian, Ilona, was very confident and opinionated and this shocked me. According to many non-Norwegian respondents that I have interviewed, it's usual for them to feel intimidated and not be honest about their views, in front of Norwegians, they say. This is especially the case when the non-Norwegian is in the minority in the discussion. I have observed pack behaviour many times on my journey.

However, on this occasion the Norwegian was in the minority and couldn't rely on others to back her up if she said something illogical or irrational, like is usually the case in our group discussions… or if she didn't like something that she heard from her non-Norwegian colleague. On the other hand the non-Norwegian colleague was obviously encouraged by my presence so felt "safe" to speak. However, the fact that she spoke so "directly" genuinely shocked me and obviously shocked her Norwegian colleague too.

However, on this occasion, she'd agreed to be recorded and she had nowhere to escape. Her face was shocked to hear these views. In fact there was obvious passive aggression between the two of them. Before we started recording, Signe was already agitated. She was agitated because she couldn't accept that any Norwegians that I had just met would speak to me. She repeatedly said, "But why would they speak to a stranger?" and "Why would they speak to an outsider?!"

I explained why and I explained that her country had many issues and that some people actually want to talk about them and "get them off their chest".

She became even more agitated at that! She couldn't comprehend what I was saying. I then told her that almost every person I spoke to seemed to have an issue or expressed that they were depressed or abused or bullied and then she said, "Yes, but you've only spoken to depressed people and not happy people!"

As soon as she said this stupid comment I knew that she was agitated because I was telling the truth and I knew that she had issues too. I then decided that I was going to prove it. I said to her, "No, I have spoken to different types of people from all age groups from all over the country."

She then tried to undermine me more with, "Yes, but have you spoken to young people too?" I explained that I have and gave her a rundown of the demographics and ages. Now, she was in full retreat and it was my turn.

"I'm really glad that you mentioned about happy people because I can finally talk to a happy person! So tell me, you said that you were happy, right? Now, I can finally add somebody that's happy to my list... that's great!" She replied with a downcast face, "No, I didn't say that I was happy..." I replied, "Oh, I thought you were a happy one that I could add to my list? I've noticed that a lot of people talk about happy people but are not happy themselves. Are you sure that you're not happy? It would be great to add a "happy" Norwegian to my list! I've been pleading for people to tell me happy stories from their lives and people just don't have anything to say it seems... but if you have something to say, please tell me now and I'll be happy to publish it!"

At this stage she realised that she wasn't going to be able to control the narrative. I could see that she was upset and then she started talking about her life. She confessed that bullying was a problem and that "everyone" was bullied in Norway. She confessed that she was leaving work and that there were issues with discrimination in her town, she then talked about the challenges about being honest in her job interview because the potential employers don't like change and don't like people that think for themselves.

And there you go.

That was the break through.

We chatted a bit more and then her non-Norwegian colleague said something incredible. She had noticed that her colleague had had to concede and do a total 180 turn on what she had said... this was obviously empowering for her to witness. Now, at this stage I explained what I have observed repeatedly: disassociation. Signe had just done it now. She didn't like that she was proven wrong and became "vacant". I told them both that I've have seen people react like that all the time in Norway, often when what they say is proven to be nonsense. I explained that many people literally just "forget" what they said a few seconds after they spoke even. Ironically, at that exact moment as the tape recorder is turned on, Ilona immediately said that she just "forgot" what she said five seconds before, as you will now see…

Anthony:
What did you just say, Ilona?

Ilona:
Now, I have to think about it… hmmm… I'm not disassociating from what I just said!

Anthony:
Are you sure?
(AN – I am laughing now.)

Ilona:
Yes!

Anthony:
Are you sure you're not dissociating?
(AN – I am laughing even more.)

Ilona:
No! Because actually… I mean it… It's actually rude to tell the truth!

(AN – Ilona had previously, just seconds earlier, said "I have discovered that it's rude to tell the truth in Norway"… she said with a little bit of venom and her colleague looked shocked. Her colleagues face went red with rage.)

Ilona:
See! I remembered!

(AN – Said with a little smile and back to a normal friendly voice.)

Anthony:

Now say what you said just before that? You said "I came to Norway..."?

Ilona:

Yes, I said that I came to Norway and I realised that it's rude to tell the truth!

(AN – When she says the words "rude to tell the truth" she has a little bit of aggression in her.)

Anthony:

Explain what you mean?

Ilona:

Well, I mean, for example... It has to do with looks as well *(AN – she is already retracting because her colleagues face looks furious)* yeah, like... I do believe that people are actually talking behind your back, because it's rude to say it like frankly to your face.

Anthony:

OK?

Ilona:

But it's OK for them to actually think it.

Anthony:

OK?

Ilona:

But not tell it to your face.

Anthony:

But now we need to define what's "true"... and this is where it gets really weird. For example, it works if you say to yourself "I am not honest and I lie as a mechanism of survival in this society to make it work better"... That makes sense and that is totally rational but what is not rational is to say, "I lie but I am honest"... Obviously high level of pretence and acting is not truthful behaviour... many people in Norway have actually argued on tape that not telling the truth is not being dishonest.

Ilona:
I don't agree with that.

Signe:
But you can make an honest mistake… You tell something that was right…
That's what I was thinking about…

*(AN – Note that it is Signe who immediately interjects to defend this
attitude/behaviour.)*

Anthony:
OK, Ilona, you just said that "it's rude to tell the truth in Norway"?

Ilona:
In my opinion, yes.

Anthony:
Do you mean that telling the truth is *perceived* as being "rude" in
Norway?

Ilona:
As harsh criticism.

*(AN – This is incredible. Ilona has already said that saying the truth in Norway is
"rude" but has now added that the truth is perceived as "harsh criticism" in
Norway too.)*

Anthony:
This is the issue… It's all about how you define "truth"… because if it's
not the dictionary definition, everybody could be offended by everything
and anything… because there is no fixed level of truth… It's subjective…
It's your opinion of what is the "truth", so it will constantly be the lowest
threshold and trying to cause the least offence, because if you can't tell the
truth to someone… then you don't live in reality?

Ilona:
Yes! But it depends… If it's an "offensive" truth then I find it rude to tell
somebody… but if you are talking about family friends or close friends or
whatever then they just have to handle it.

Anthony:
OK, well now we come onto another thing, which is who gets what level of truth? If somebody is considered a "stranger" or an "outsider"... during my discussions it appears that politeness is more important than telling the truth to a perceived "stranger" or "outsider"... but if you know somebody better than you can be "more truthful" with them... So it seems that "truth" is not solid... it's fluid... It's all about what people define as "truth"... even if I get the dictionary out, even if I speak to a linguist... I realise that there really is something here... It's all about what triggers them... what hurts a person... it could be truthful... It is about what they are triggered by... for example if somebody is subjected to an assault and then that is referenced...

Ilona:
It will be offensive yeah! (*AN – she interrupts quickly.*)

Anthony:
No. It won't necessarily be at all. For example, in court, a judge or a lawyer would have to reference it, wouldn't they? That's not "offensive"... He or she is just doing their job... but if the truth is perceived as an "attack"... which I do think seems too often the case in Norwegian society, that many people seem to just choose to be quiet and "not to go there", because maybe tomorrow you have to face the person... so I will withdraw from saying anything which is potentially "offensive" which, of course, is usually the truth?

Ilona:
But now depends on what you decide is the truth and your side of the truth or not. Because maybe she is a really nice person (*AN – She refers to her colleague*)... but in my head I am like, "Oh my God she is really full of s***" (*AN – I am shocked listening back to the recording of the passive aggressiveness between these two receptionists*)... But if she will ask me "what do you think of me?" of course I will not tell her that I think that she is full of s***.

Signe:
And I know... sugar coat the truth.

Anthony:
Yes, and this is why you never really know where you stand? It must be discombobulating to live like that, because if someone is nice to your face

and in addition to that, they don't tell you the truth. Obviously you don't have a strong foundation in your interactions… and I believe that you can see the effect of this if you talk to people long enough. I have heard many in Norway using phrases like "concrete" and the need for "foundation"… "I need to know a bit more"… "my husband doesn't tell me what I need to know… I asked him whether I look good in this dress and he doesn't say anything!"

(AN – They both start laughing.)

Ilona:
You know that!

Signe:
We are used to it already! *(Laugh.)*

This is Norway – We are Stable not Spontaneous

I liked to ask random interesting questions on my Norwegian voyage and one that I regularly asked Norwegians was, "What's the most spontaneous thing you've ever done in your life?" I asked an older man this and his answer saddened me. He explained that Norway is a very boring place and that Norwegians rarely do anything spontaneous. I pushed him and said that you *must* have done something spontaneous in your whole life… how about in your twenties? We were having a real heart to heart and he was being 100% candid and said, "I haven't, we really don't do that, it's all very level here."

Later, I was driving from Sweden to Norway and there is a T junction… the left road to Stockholm, several hundred kilometres away and the right road to Oslo. I was in the car with three other people, one man and two woman. All Norwegian and all around forty-five to fifty years old. I playfully said, "Let's be spontaneous! Let's drive to Stockholm!" They said, "No!" I knew that I was asking for the impossible but I wanted to see their response. I said, "Left… do it, turn left… let's be spontaneous… we only live once!". "No, we're going home" one of them said. As we approached the T junction I said, "Last chance! This is it… we can still turn left and do it. It would be an adventure!" The car turned right and off we continued to Oslo.

I then asked them, "Hey! What's the most spontaneous thing you've ever done in your life?" Now, these are the type of questions that really mess up so many people here! Just trust me on that. I asked them each individually. First person's took her time and then replied boastfully, "we are stable not spontaneous!" Now, with much help and assistance we finally got to one time where one of them picked up a hitch-hiker twenty years ago. That was it. I then turned to the passenger next to me and asked her, "What's the most spontaneous thing you've ever done in your life?" She looked very pleased and said, "I have something! I booked a ticket to Jamaica the day before!" I was completely shocked. "Wow!" I said, "I'm so impressed, that's great!" And then I realised…

she answered "booked a ticket", so I said, "You flew the next day?" She answered, "No, I went in the summer a few months later." That's more like it... so nothing too. The other person in the car also gave no answer.

That night I really got thinking about the people I was with and Norway in general. I really didn't want to become normalised to these Janteloven attitudes, culture and behaviour and I really thought about that T junction sign... "Stockholm 500Km" (or whatever it was). That night I booked a plane ticket to Stockholm for the next day... and I went. When I arrived I sent a photo of the beautiful Stockholm National Gallery with the words, "I took the left road."

I received the reply; "You are crazy".

This is Norway...

A Conversation with a Hotel Receptionist

Milena is a white woman from a large European nation and is married to a Norwegian man. She is the manager of a hotel which is part of one of the largest hotel chains in Scandinavia. After she got chatting with me she began describing racism that she heard in Norway and then went on to say how people that are racist are so bad and the "usual" speech. She then spoke these words, in front on her Norwegian colleague, who didn't react in any way at all, in fact, she acted like it was the most normal thing in the world to say:

"I say nig*ga. There is nothing wrong with it because it's only a word... ni*ga.. When my daughter hears me say it she freaks out... but I don't mean it in a racist way because it's just a word!"

Just before she said this she made a joke and belittled people from her *own* country, implying that they are "stupid" too. Here is the next part of our conversation...

Anthony:
Please say what you just said again?

Milena:
He said that the best thing that foreigners can do in Norway is to go and hang themself.

Anthony:
Was that person Norwegian?

Milena:
Yes.

Anthony:
Roughly how old?

Milena:
Seventy. In northern Norway.

Anthony:
Why did they say that?

Milena:
I have no idea.

Anthony:
What do you mean you have "no idea"?

Milena:
Maybe he is offended by all the immigration?

Anthony:
Did you actually hear that?

Milena:
Yes. Didn't say it to me directly but he knew that I was a foreigner.

Anthony:
How many people were in the room?

Milena:
Quite a lot.

Anthony:
I am trying to work out the context of somebody saying that?

Milena:
Partially Norwegians there were a lot of Norwegians… The other ones they
gave him a look.

Anthony:
Did anyone confront him directly and say, "Don't say that!"?

Milena:
Yes.

Anthony:
And what happened?

Milena:
He just shut up.

Anthony:
Did the others in the room speak up?

Milena:
Yes.

Anthony:
Really! What did they say?

Milena:
They told him to stop talking bullsh*t.

Anthony:
Did you get an apology?

Milena:
No. He didn't say it directly to me; he was just talking different things, just out in the air... It wasn't said to me or to anyone... It was just said out...

Anthony:
But obviously it was very passive aggressive because they knew that you were there listening?

Milena:
Yes, maybe.

Anthony:
What do you mean "maybe"?

Milena:
(*Laughs.*) I don't give a s*** about what people are saying!

Anthony:
But don't you think that that is passive aggressive?

Milena:
Yeah, yeah, yeah... It is, it is.

Anthony:
If somebody said this at work to your work colleague... They would be reprimanded for that, wouldn't they?

Milena:
Yes.

Anthony:
They would have to be! You wouldn't let them away with that, would you?

Milena:
Nope.

Anthony:
You would punish them... they would get a letter or a warning?

Milena:
They would... if it happens in the workplace.

Anthony:
Can I ask you something? We can clearly say that that was inappropriate, right?

Milena:
Yes... It is... of course it's inappropriate behaviour... so it's not acceptable... at least by some people.

(AN – I asked the repeatedly because it seemed like she was defending it and justifying it in a way which I have seen many times through Norway on my journey... so I was very silent when I asked the questions and waited for her answers... What happened next is unbelievable. We then continue talking about racism and she said that she uses the word n*****.)

This is the direct quote:

"There is nothing wrong with it because it's only a word... ni*ga.. When my

daughter has me say it she freaks out… But I don't mean it in a racist way…
Because it's just a word"

And then she said…

"But some people are racist and mean it in a racist way and apply it to people,
which I don't do."

(AN – I went for a walk and when I came back I got talking with them again
and I got talking with Milena. She told me that her husband was Norwegian.)

Milena:
The number one TV show in Norway is the boat the Hurtigruten (ferry)!

Anthony:
From where to where?

Milena:
From Kirkenes to Bergen, I think… but the train!

Anthony:
The train?

Milena:
The train from Oslo to Bergen! They made it because the one with the
Hurtigruten was so popular!

Anthony:
I heard that there was one which was just filming a fireplace… did you
hear anything about that?

Milena:
Yeah, yeah, yeah.

Anthony:
I think that one was a top show as well?

Milena:
Yeah (*laughing*)… I know the picture I know what you're talking about!

Anthony:
Just to be clear for the recorder... This is a camera on a boat or a train where it is travelling, it's a normal journey?

Milena:
Yes!

Anthony:
It doesn't go on an adventure?

Milena:
Nope.

Anthony:
It's just on the sea or on the track?

Milena:
Yes!

Anthony:
OK... Now, you just told me that your husband was watching this... and you told me that you "freaked out"... is that true?

Milena:
(*Laughing.*) Yes!

Anthony:
What was your reaction when you saw your husband watching this? He is Norwegian right?

Milena:
I was like "what the f*** is this?"

Anthony:
And what did he say?

Milena:
He was like, "It is nice... it's Norway... It's nice to see."

(*AN – This is a very noteworthy comment.*)

Anthony:
What was he watching exactly?

Milena:
Hurtigruten.

Anthony:
The boat?

Milena:
Yes.

Anthony:
And you said that you "freaked out"… what were you thinking?

Milena:
I was like what are you watching!? If you want to go out and see the sea go out and see the sea! Why would you sit by the television and see this?

Anthony:
Why do you think that somebody would actually sit and watch that?

Milena:
I don't know.

Anthony:
No, no, no… you're too intelligent… I don't believe that…

Milena:
Maybe he was tired or sometimes people *space out or something?*… I don't know…

Anthony:
What you have just said is incredible. You have just referred to disassociation… I think that you have answered the question exactly and given the psychological drive behind it. You said that he or people "space out"… that's disassociation… that's a way you can relax or you can disassociate from trauma too, for example… so in a way it can quite relaxing to watch that?

Milena:
But isn't that why people watch TV series, the movies?

Anthony:
Well, here's the thing, would it be different if your husband was watching a HBO TV show? I assume it would be different to watching a simple train ride or a bus ride from his own country?

Milena:
Yes, yes.

Anthony:
So what's the difference between the two?

Milena:
Action... and he watches so many documentaries... so many documentaries... it's crazy.

Anthony:
I have a possible theory, tell me what you think... I think that the ultimate aim of these TV shows is disassociation... so that you can relax and get "away" from normal life... Escapism.

Milena:
Yes.

Anthony:
What's interesting is that somebody might watch a movie... or an action adventure... but here these shows go straight to the hmmm... in a way, they bypass the pretence, like the viewers don't even need to watch a story... "I can just watch anything"... and it can be literally *anything*, even the most boring thing... it takes you directly to the relaxation and escapism so you don't even have to waste time pretending to be interested in a story... like, bypass the story... let's get straight to it?

Milena:
Yes! Like lots of times people listen to the sounds of the rainforest... Have you not heard? Go onto YouTube and type in sounds of the rainforest... three hours!

This is Norway – Queen of Africa!

I was in the back of a car going to a dinner. One of the occupants of the car was describing the people who we were going to visit. When they started talking about a certain man, they brought up his wife and said, "She is black… she is the Queen of Africa!" It was said in a stupid voice as the others in the car laughed. When we arrived I immediately noticed that the lady, the only non-white person in the room was sat on the end of the table and was being completely ignored. I got up from my seat and walked around the table and knelt down next to her and started talking. Her husband was sitting opposite her and when I came over, started engaging.

The conversation went to how he had retired young, which I thought odd, I didn't quite understand what that meant… and then I worked it out… he was bragging about his wealth. Then we started talking about his relationship. I asked his wife about her life and life in Norway and we had a little chat about our experiences and she said, very emphatically, "I am not treated the same here!" I told her that I know exactly what she was talking about. She then said it twice more but in a more agitated fashion; "I am not treated the same here! No! I am not treated the same here as in other countries!" At this time, I looked at her so she understood that I understood and I could see that she her calmed down.

Then something unbelievable happened. Her native Norwegian husband undercut her and started talking about how he understands her treatment because certain types of immigration are bad and that it gets too much for Norwegians because people take advantage of the system and that Norway does too much already. He completely cut his wife down in the most emotionally tone deaf way.

This is Norway…

A Conversation with a Receptionist

Julia is a receptionist in Svalbard. She is from a western European country and is friendly and smiles a lot. We got chatting and she started recounting the "usual" Norwegian "narrative". I asked a couple of pointed questions and got the usual startled "look" and a change of direction, so I asked her if I could interview her for my book… she happily agreed. After I began to point out that her "narrative" didn't quite make sense, she tried to explain that Norwegians "can't be wrong" and how that was some kind of *virtuous* thing… I let her explain herself before asking her a couple of questions. Julia is approximately twenty-seven years old and here is our conversation…

Anthony:
I'm in Svalbard and I'm talking with Julia… Please don't worry, this will remain anonymous and I'll disguise details… So we've just been talking about the Norwegian skier who was banned for doping, and Julia, you just said that "Norwegians have to be the best and they can't accept being wrong"… What do you mean?

Julia:
They are so… They have such high standards that they set themselves I think, it's so unrealistic.

Anthony:
OK, I'm going to tell you what it sounds like right now.

Julia:
(AN – Julia knows what's coming and bursts out laughing.)

Anthony:
You have just given me an equivocation and an excuse.

Julia:
(AN – she abruptly stops laughing and speaks in a serious voice.) There is no excuse.

Anthony:
Yes, so what you're saying is... it's a virtue? Surely it's not a virtue?
Maybe you can start again, Julia?

Julia:
They just think that they are the best at everything!

Anthony:
Thank you for being honest. Let me ask you a question... I'm writing a
book and part of it is about the assimilation of immigrants in Norway... I
found that many are not comfortable telling the truth initially about their
experiences in Norway, it appears because of possible fear and
intimidation. I'll give you an example: it's unconscious... and you did it
just now? You said, "Oh... they have such high standards..." No. You
"think that they are the best at everything", as you just stated, no? It's
very simple. You just stated that explicitly?

Julia:
They think that they are the best.

Anthony:
Now can I ask you, why didn't you just say that initially?

Julia:
That's what I think it is! That's what I think they think. They have these high
standards, because of I don't know history or whatever... that they think they
have to reach this... And they just present themselves as that...

Anthony:
Again, here is the thing, you are giving me... You are from *(AN –*
redacted – non-Scandinavian European country of origin)... You are not
Norwegian, right?

Julia:
(AN – She burst out laughing.)

Anthony:
Why are you giving me a Norwegian perspective's potential psychological
motivation about how they might or might not think? I asked you about
why *you* didn't say what *you* just said, *initially*?

Julia:
(AN – Julia face looked shocked that I am asking her challenging questions.) Well I don't know… That's just what I see…

Anthony:
No, but that's not what you *see*, that's what you *think* that *Norwegians* might think and feel?

Julia:
(AN – she now gets comfortable very quickly and breaks through the initial resistance and starts talking candidly)… I am projecting, to them… Yeah!

Anthony:
Yes. Here is the thing… why aren't you telling me what *you* think and feel, first? Why are you telling me what Norwegians might or might not think or feel? That's the question!

Julia:
They are very self-obsessed. *(AN – she bursts out laughing.)*

Anthony:
But here is the thing though, do you understand… this is subtle… why didn't you tell me *your* point of view from *your* perspective, first?

Julia:
(AN – she bursts out laughing.) I have no idea! *(Laughing).*

Anthony:
I have an idea. I know. I've seen it happen all over Norway.

Julia:
Yes?

Anthony:
If I ask an immigrant, "What do you think?" they will often tell me what a Norwegian thinks or feels…

Julia:
First?

Anthony:
And then they will try and make it "positive" too… then I probe them a bit, and then they change and tell me what they *really* think… and that is very unique to Norway, I feel. People, regularly seem to undermine their own opinion and they take the collective…

Julia:
Ahhh.

Anthony:
Another thing… I think it's just simple embarrassment too. For example, somebody told me, on the mainland, "You can never be homeless in Norway… except if you are a drug user." It's so brazen. It's so preposterous… and it's so delusional… that you are embarrassed to deny what they're saying, because they truly believe what they are saying so much.

Julia:
There can't be another way!

Anthony:
Yes, then you just be quiet… and if you are in that environment for too long then you would actually acclimatize to that behaviour, I suspect? What do you think about what I have just asked?

Julia:
I think you might be right.
(AN – she bursts out laughing.)

Anthony:
OK. If we start again, and I say, "What was this you were saying about Norwegians having to be right all the time?" Tell me about that?

Julia:
They are up themselves!
(AN – she bursts out laughing.)

Anthony:
How do you survive? I'm going to make some guesses now… I'm guessing that you have to keep your real feelings and thoughts inside? Because I

presume that you can't say how you really feel to many people around?

Julia:
I've said it to *some*... but only to the ones that I don't think are like that!
(AN – *She burst out laughing.*)

Anthony:
Because?

Julia:
Because there are a lot of Norwegians who aren't like that.

Anthony:
Do you know what's really ironic? Do you know when somebody is innocent, and they take the "guilt" for the guilty... and you're like, "You don't actually have to apologise!"

Julia:
Yes!

Anthony:
Is it anything to do with that?

Julia:
Yes! (AN – *she bursts out laughing.*)... That's exactly it! (*Laughing.*)

Anthony:
They will take the blame when they don't deserve it.

Julia:
Yes.

Anthony:
I'm guessing that you couldn't say it to the *real* guilty ones because they would have a breakdown or something?

Julia:
You couldn't say that to them, no.

Anthony:
Tell me why? Why couldn't you?

Julia:
Not that I couldn't, but I wouldn't, because it's not me. I wouldn't do that to them on a personal level. Collectively, I would do it, but not on a personal level... Because I'm (AN – redacted: mentions her home country. She bursts out laughing.) I'm too polite!

Anthony:
That's another thing... It's politeness?

Julia:
We're too polite... I just think it's a (AN – redacted: mentions her home country) thing.

Anthony:
Do you know that you said that "Norwegians think that they have to be the best"? That would mean logically that somebody has to be "worse", wouldn't it? Putting other people down passive aggressively?

Julia:
Yeah.

Anthony:
I've see that kind of thing a lot in Norway, for some reason?

Julia:
Yes, they do.

Anthony:
Is that true?

Julia:
Yes...100% true.

Anthony:
So, tell me! Why would you be polite to somebody that is putting other people down?

Julia:
Because "treat other people as you would like to be treated"?

Anthony:
I agree with you to some extent but don't you think that there could be a little bit of enabling going on? For example, let's say that somebody is delusional and they think that they are the "best"... and they put everyone around down... and then no one ever tells them. Ever! They go through their life thinking that they are the "best"... they put everyone down... and everybody gives tacit approval... tacit approval...

Julia:
It happened so much! I've seen it so many times...

Anthony:
In Norway?

Julia:
Everywhere... Even elsewhere, also.

Anthony:
Don't you think that that alone could be a justification for speaking out against it?

Julia:
Yes... and I think that there are times when I have done it... and there are times when I have not done it... Sometimes it's just not worth it.

Anthony:
Not worth it because it happens so much? Is it quite a big thing here?

Julia:
Yes.

Anthony:
But then again... how can you? It might mean that you'd have to have like a small battle every ten seconds?

(AN – she bursts out laughing.)

Julia:
But I think it's something which happens more on the mainland Norway, than here because it's more diverse here.

Anthony:
Because you have a higher level of immigrants then you have a higher diversity of attitudes... and environment?

Julia:
Yes, because I think there are more Norwegians here that are not like that... Of course there are loads that are! A lot of younger people here are less likely to be like that... The younger generation...

Anthony:
Have you never got the urge just to say to someone who acts like that, "You are not the best stop putting other people down!"? Have you never felt the urge?

Julia:
No.

Anthony:
Is it just not worth it?

Julia:
I don't want to say that with anyone here... I don't want to say that at work... (*laugh*)... to guess I probably wouldn't say that... But to friends I probably would.

Anthony:
Just to state the obvious... Why wouldn't you say that at work?

Julia:
Because I wouldn't be rude to (*redacted*).

Further discussion

Anthony:
I spoke to somebody yesterday in *Longyearbyen*... We had the same thing

that we just had at the beginning… and then I told her that she can just speak to me openly… and she looked like she was going to burst into tears.

Julia:
(AN – she starts laughing at this comment!)

Anthony:
She said "I need to get away! I can't take it anymore."

Julia:
(AN – Julia bursts out laughing.)

(AN – This is very strange but something which is so common in Norway in my experience. When somebody expresses pain or hurt, many people so often just burst out laughing or giggle. It's like the environment could be so hostile that people can't emotionally compute other people's pain so just laugh at them? Julia has now laughed twice at somebody's emotional distress. I was not laughing or smiling when I said it either. During a certain 2019 documentary on a landslide that killed members of this same community in Svalbard, one of the residents recounted the tragedy and is seen literally giggling to camera as he does so. In my experience it is very usual to see giggling and laughing at pain in Norway. However, something really interesting which I noticed "out of the corner of my eye" is something very peculiar and linked to this. The Norwegian manager of Manchester United, started smiling and giggling on TV interview a few moments after his team were smashed by their rivals Arsenal. The fans were furious and the Manchester United player Robbie Van Percey called his behaviour out on BT Sport. He said that he shouldn't be smiling after that kind of performance; "Now is not the moment to smile" (VIDEO Title: "Now is not the moment to smile" Robin van Persie doesn't hold back on Ole Gunnar Solskjaer" 363,794 views, 2 Jan 2020, BT SPort 2.53 Million subscribers) Ironically if you look at the comments underneath the video, the top comment is incredible because it is linked to what we have been looking at in this book: fear and denial. The top comment with 3.7K likes says, "Finally someone that's not scared to speak the truth". Ironically, even though Solskjaer was smiling like a Cheshire cat after his team's annihilation, he did decide to react and show some anger towards Robin van Persie for calling his behaviour and attitude out though! People did notice this and we can see it with comments like, "Ole hopeless in post-match interviews, smiling, giggling…" and "RVP (Robbie Van Percey) just said what a lot of fans think. Ole's press conferences, quotes, sound bites and body language after a loss are maddening sometimes… Misplaced positivity comes off badly" and "He's more annoyed here than

he was when his team lost to Arsenal"…again, this is something which we have seen repeatedly. People too often getting angry at exposure but not at the terrible thing being exposed. The same Ole Gunnar Solskjaer was again in the news when the Telegraph published an article (14th February 2020) by Ben Rumsby entitled "Ole Gunnar Solskjaer should not have picked a player charged with rape". In Norway, the alleged rape victim stated, as reported by the Telegraph article, that he was not "fit to lead" because she didn't think that he "has the values to manage a hugh football club – or people at all". I have repeatedly seen and heard stories from Norwegian after Norwegian that alleged perpetrators and perpetrators are too often supported, elevated and supported in Norwegian society.)

Further discussion

Anthony:
Last question… You mentioned that Norwegians don't like to be wrong or something?

Julia:
I think that they just don't think that they are wrong.

Anthony:
OK.

Julia:
(AN – Julia bursts out laughing.)

Anthony:
OK, let's look at the distinction here; It's not that you don't *like* to be wrong but that you just don't *think* that you *are* wrong, kind of thing?

Julia:
They just don't think that they are wrong! *(Laughs.)*

Anthony:
Obviously, Norwegians are wrong on occasion, I presume? So how does that work logically?

Julia:
I don't know. I really don't know.

Anthony:
How do you interact with someone who is illogical? If you pick one example: somebody who is wrong but can't accept that they are wrong... how do you interact with that person in Norway?

Julia:
Errrr... You just let them think that they are... There is no point.

Anthony:
No point?

Julia:
It's not worth my time, I'm just like, "OK" (*AN – she bursts out laughing.*)

Anthony:
Can I ask you: is there any residual psychological effect on you? For example, do you ever feel frustrated; do you feel angry, upset?

Julia:
Frustrated probably... but also just... (*AN – makes a sound*)... they are delusional.

Anthony:
Norwegians are delusional?

Julia:
It's a totally different way of life here... My own country self, back home, would be, "My God this is so stressed they are driving me insane." But here I don't care.

Anthony:
Do you ever feel like you are treated like you are dumb here?

Julia:
Yes, sometimes! Yeah. (*AN – Julia bursts out laughing.*)

Anthony:
Thank you so much for this, this has been incredible.

This is Norway – Feeling Silenced in Norway

Almost every **non-Norwegian** resident I spoke with repeated an *initial* highly exaggerated insincere narrative about how "amazing" Norway is and how "great" Norwegians are. I had to navigate through their initial pretence and conditioning to get to the truth… it had to be **coaxed** from nearly all of them, but when they started they couldn't stop saying how they *really* felt living in Norway;

"I did my Master's degree I was quite excited coming to Norway, the first thing that struck me was our international welcome week was separate to the Norwegian one… we were not allowed to be part of the Norwegian welcome week. So we were totally segregated. They segregated us between Norwegian and International… There is no mixing so if you go into town now… In the debutante events an organisation groups there is not a single non-Norwegian, because they keep us segregated from the Norwegians. It's shocking, also… They keep us separate from all of the Norwegian students in accommodation. If you go to the oldest and most horrible accommodation… That's where the international students are, you have a floor of Nepalese, a floor of diverse African communities, a floor of Europeans… It's segregated."
"Hans", German Scientist, twenty-eight years old. Lives in Norway.

"I have to say… they do things without caring about people's feelings. Yes… it's true! It's painful to say, they are selfish!"
"Amanda", married to a Norwegian man.

"I think that they just don't think that they are wrong… errrr… You just let them think that they are… There is no point… But also just… They are delusional… It's a totally different way of life here… My (redacted) self-back in the (redacted: "home")… Would be "my God this is so stressed they are driving me insane"… But here… I don't care anymore…"
"Julia", Hospitality worker in Svalbard.

"I came to Norway and I realised that it's rude to tell the truth… I do believe that people are actually talking behind your back, because it's "rude" to say it like frankly to your face."
"Fiona", Alesund – Hotel Receptionist.

"He said that the best thing that foreigners can do in Norway is to go and hang themselves."
"Stacy", Receptionist, a Norwegian man told her what should happen to foreigners.

"Some of them won't even reply to me! They'll just turn walk away! They'll almost just, "I've just wiped you out you've just disappeared… can't talk to you!"…I kind of just… Put it down to like… It's fine. I'm used to it… I know how you're going to react… Usually, it depends on the individual because sometimes they are younger… Sometimes they're like quick "OK. Cool. thanks"… they can't engage in a conversation! or they just shut down… They can't talk! I just accept it cos that's… errrrr… that's just… I've had that experience so many times that that's just the way Norwegians are… I kind of look down on them a little bit. It's a bit like "well that's really sad"… That's a real shame for you. You try to make yourself out to be like this but actually you're really not very nice and polite."
"Oliver", Former Norwegian resident, married to a Norwegian woman.

"They are a bit cold and you never know what is inside… They are going to show you a façade…"
"Dominica", National landmark employee, Norwegian resident from Russia.

"Norwegians are not normal inside the head."
"Brad", American Bar staff employee – Kristansund.

"The Swedish hate the Norwegians! We are jealous of them because now they have got money and love to wear their fur scarves! But they need to remember that just a few years ago they were peasants in the fields just like us and they shouldn't forget that! We have the perception that the Norwegian language ALWAYS sounds happy and joyful! I can understand Norwegian. They're known for being "happy" ALL

the time and when they speak they speak as if they don't have any problems at all. They always have a big smile and like to show how "fit" they are and that they "love" hiking and climb mountains and everything's "perfect" all the time. They don't have anything else so they have to always smile and pretend that everything is happy. They are known for this and known for never being sad… everything is always smiling and "happy"… they never show what goes wrong on the outside."
"Nora", from Stockholm, Sweden.

"It's so hard. So lonely here. Not nice"
"Sufian", a refugee from Afghanistan in tears telling me about his bullying in Norway.

"Norwegians are the most dishonest people. They are not good. Thank God I am leaving!"
"Lynn" – Polish woman in Oslo.

"I know I'm just a nig*a to them but I don't care, I was the first black man here and everybody knows me."
"Pedro" – seventy years old, Norway.

"I'm 33 and from Britain. I came here to go and work and it was lifelong dream for me. I have never met such dishonest people."
"Stacy" – from the UK in the north of Norway.

"In my opinion Norway seems like the best country to live in when it comes to better salaries and social system. On top of that it has a stunning landscape and offers so much from big cities to the possibilities of exploring nature in so many different ways… to the outside world Norway presents itself as the friendly highly educated northern people who welcome everybody and offer opportunities to live here. In fact, that's not true… Norwegians keep everything totally to themselves. Sharing with strangers is not on their top priority. Helping people you don't know is not on the to do list… finding a job with an education from another country is very difficult. Everybody speaks English, but if you don't learn Norwegian fast enough you will not be totally accepted. They are all friendly towards your face, but as soon as you turn around the gossip starts… Of course there are exceptions!! I've met some Norwegian individuals who are different! But the majority doesn't want to get out

of their comfort zone, doesn't want to change routines. Everything needs a scheduled to be fun. Norway is full of people who have a good education but think way too much inside the box and are not willing to share to grow more... Anyway, I believe I can make a change."

"Laura", Austrian – thirty-year-old personal trainer.

The last line is just so sad. If "Laura" thinks she can change anything by propagating lies publicly, whilst keeping her truth about how she feels about her new country inside, then she is in for a depressing future.

This is Norway...

This is Norway – An Ice Cold Beer

Two Norwegian residents who live in the middle of Norway kindly invited me on a barbecue. They were not Norwegians but have half-Norwegian children and they have lived in Norway for a long time. When I was with them I noticed something incredible. So many Norwegians were saying "hello" to them when they passed on the pathways. I said to my friend, "You do know that it's rare for Norwegians to say anything to me when I pass them when I go walking… so many people usually look away actually. I've been here for months and I've heard more Norwegians say "hello" today than in the many months, I've been here." She burst out laughing and said, "Maybe it's your energy… they always say hi to us!" and that was the best logic she could muster. I looked at her and realised what I was dealing with and decided to let it go.

Later we had a barbecue and I appreciated it.

I was with her husband alone and the nature was beautiful and I said, "This is perfect! Thanks very much!"

He then smiled and said, *"It's not perfect. It would be perfect if we had a ni*ga serving us ice cold beer."*

He then laughed. I had liked him. Pity.

This is Norway…

A Conversation with an Educational Leader

I had the privilege to sit down with a Norwegian educational leader in Oslo. He is not only an educational leader who is respected in Norway but also involved in education policy internationally. After the conversation, we are joined by his daughter who wanted to join the conversation... I spoke with her alone. "Christian" is fifty to sixty years old and his daughter is fourteen to sixteen years old.

Anthony:
I'm just sitting with Christian and I just mentioned to him that I seem to be noticing a possible clear and shocking pattern... Basically, many of the people around the age of twenty-five-year-olds I have interviewed are demonstrating a shocking level of shallowness, superficiality and apparent lack of insight which is not a case with many of the sixteen-year-olds or the over fifty-year- olds, for example... it's seems to be especially the twenty to thirty age group? I am shocked at the apparent lack of comprehension and understanding and the ability to be so easily triggered I have repeatedly observed. I have just mentioned this to Christian who is an expert in education and he says that he notices exactly the same thing... Is that true, Christian?

Christian:
Definitely the same thing. I see it all over in both genders... what I was thinking. Is it because like social media? They use it to the same extent as the young ones but they are not critical. So it seems like they go where the entertainment goes but they take in everything so everything has equal value and they don't use it critically. Like if you do a Google search and everything has equal value to you, you will be drowned in s*** and shallowness and you won't be able to find the depth of what you really need. And then I am thinking: is it because they don't apply the critical thinking into it? Are they just bombarded by the amount? Because the younger ones fifteen and sixteen-year-olds are growing up with it.

Anthony:
You mentioned that there was a clear difference between ages and you
mentioned that the fifteen and sixteen-year-olds... they have critical
thinking?

Christian:
They have critical thinking and also they are more careful. They consider
things. They do the teenager stuff but they have their hiccups when it comes
to social media but also they are better at asking whether it is right what they
are actually bombarded with. But also the exposure of themselves and not
thinking what's that leads to...

Anthony:
So, you're saying that there's no accountability, or insight for the twenty-
five-year-olds? It seems like many that I speak with don't seem to have
basic levels of perception of what they are saying, doing or how they act.
They might say stuff, but so many don't even consider how they are
perceived? That's what I'm noticing. What do you think about that?

Christian:
I think that they know what they're doing but they don't know that it is
wrong because they are the generation that grow up and they feel entitled.
You have the adults who I kind of spoiling them.

Anthony:
How old are the "entitled generation" would you say right now? What's
the age group of that entitled generation?

Christian:
I would say between twenty and thirty years old.

Anthony:
I am noticing a massive difference between the insight and, actually, the
maturity level in the responses. I actually feel that when I speak to most of
the twenty-five-year-old respondents, if you just ask them one question
about the way they act, then they too often can't take it... they so often
just "shut down" but if you ask any question about nonsense like
Instagram then they can talk for hours?

Christian:
Yes, yes.

Anthony:
Is that observation correct or am I wrong?

Christian:
There are always individual differences.

Anthony:
Obviously, but I'm speaking generally though?

Christian:
Generally, I would definitely say so. Considering the background, they grew up with parents that were not so ready to talk about their emotions, the feelings, especially here in this part of the world... is like you keep your mouth shut about struggles and then you said you just give them the glory and in a way I think that that's why they grow up feeling entitled because after the war you know when families grow up and it was like it was really important to show off that you did well, and you do well, you had everything, and your children should be only children happy playing around and actually they failed to... actually failed to teach them about resilience. That is the thing... there is something between the twenty and thirty-year-olds that have got a lot of things like money and materialistic things but it's like they know nothing about resilience because they didn't have to buy... the parents were fighting for them and they just got it and they feel entitled and they... I see it. I see it in the young people that apply for working, and started working with me as well, you know when we pushed him a bit they, they know everything about their rights but they don't they don't know anything about what are the expectations and then they really think "What? Can you really be this demanding?"... this is why you know... this is what we do everything!

Anthony:
What you are saying is correlating with my observations and because I have a broad unscientific "outsider" viewpoint, I basically wanted to pass my observations by an expert. Let's just get this on the record, you are an expert in education and have worked with this age group, for how long?

Christian:
Oh... this... is... twenty-five years.

Anthony:
From my perspective you are an expert in dealing with many different age groups and how old to how old?

Christian:
From six to eighteen but I deal with parents and I deal with leadership with the adults so I—

Anthony:
So, through the job you work with all ages?

Christian:
Yes, I would say that I more or less cover everything from six to sixty-five.

Anthony:
And would you say that what we have discussed today... is there validity to my observations?

Christian:
I would say so, Anthony, yes.

Anthony:
OK, now, I am going to raise a point that I have been dealing with in the last fifteen minutes before our interview today. I'm going to tell you and then I'm going to ask you for your response... and I want to ask if my thoughts on it are correct and are aligned with your thoughts on it. Is that OK?

Christian:
OK!

Anthony:
I interviewed a twenty-two year-old girl called Elise. By the way, the only real group who generally asked for anonymity in advance are the twenty – thirty-year-olds... most of the other people don't care if they're recorded at all. I think that's interesting... anyway, back to Elise. When asked what the top five Norwegian traits are she answered this:

"We only care to know other people when it will profit us."

I then asked her: How would a non-Norwegian feel about this, do you think? And how do you think that is perceived? Are you aware of how this is perceived? Is this something to be proud of?

Now this is what she said:

"I think that Norwegians find it hard to fit in because we have so many unwritten rules and if you don't follow them you are quick to be judged. I think it depends on Norwegians view of other countries and if they are open to new impressions. If they are and perhaps have travel to some themselves, they are more likely to act inclusive towards foreigners, most likely don't know a different way and are excluding experience without thinking that there is anything wrong."

I then said: Thank you Elise. Can you please answer the specific question about perception though? I specifically ask this because I am noticing that when I ask a high number of the Norwegian respondents, about perception, for example "How do non-Norwegians perceive x y & z behaviour?", I usually get unrelated answers. This question is about empathy, perception and self-reflection. She then talked about some random foreigner thing which is totally unrelated to what I asked… and then she said:

"If you don't like my answer then you don't have to write it in your book!"

She was obviously upset…she got very angry and passive aggressive. She then started talking about social anxiety which had nothing to do with the question or answer. Then I said to her, "Do you feel that my question was invalid in relation to your initial answer?"… but it was like she couldn't compute what I was saying at all and that was it… I got no answer to that. She actually got offended when I pointed out that she didn't answer the question. I am really finding it tough to get the overwhelming majority of the twenty – thirty-year-olds respondents to get any idea of how they perceive themselves. Why might his be?

Christian:
But that brings me back to what I said about the entitlement and that they always start with the ego way and they think that everything should go their way.

Anthony:

Let's be specific now, so she literally just said that *"We only care to know other people when it will profit us"*... She admitted that. I asked her "How do you how do you feel about that and how do you feel you are perceived?" She got angry... and it's almost as if she had never thought about that, she just wrote it down... she couldn't even tell me... When I asked her if she could answer it, then she got upset. Do you think that she realises that that is not a nice way to think?

Christian:

No. No, no, no, no... I think she got upset because she didn't know what to say. She didn't have the ability to reflect in the way that you asked her to do. Because, like you say, in her perception...

(AN – The educational leader is confirming exactly what I have repeatedly observed.)

Anthony:

Is this normal for Norwegian twenty to thirty year olds, in your experience?

Christian:

Many! Very many! And I think that it's the particular age group that that will happen because the older ones have learnt this because of the hard way because of what happened to them, because they had to deal with things and had to fix things for themselves... So they learnt the hard way how to do. But the young ones... the really young ones are asking about what the (twenty to thirty-year-olds) do because they don't want to be like them! And another thing that we need to remember is that empathy can be taught... And people think that it's a given but empathy can be taught.

(AN – This is absolutely shocking... but many others have actually told me exactly the same thing. We will be looking into this and we will have a sixteen-year-old tell us exactly why they "don't want to be like twenty –thirty-year-olds in Norway" and what they don't like about the groups general behaviour and attitudes, later in the series.)

Anthony:

I am finding that I have to explain. First I had to point out what perception and empathy was, and then she didn't get it and then I literally spelt it out then she still couldn't comprehend?

Christian:
But still… you've already lost her there because she is upset because it didn't go… she expected some adulation and whatever… she wasn't prepared to actually think and that would be a typical traits for that age group because they don't really care so much about what is right like within a common core "right", but they care about being right. They shut down their brains.

Anthony:
Shut down to avoid getting challenged?

Christian:
Exactly and I find that even… even in long discussions even if they realise halfway that maybe they were wrong "Oh!" … They will still defend their view!

Anthony:
I noticed that usually the younger ones around sixteen-year-old usually don't have any shame in changing their view?

Christian:
Because they have an open mind to it.

Anthony:
Yes… now one more thing on this… just as a Norwegian now. It sounds pretty mean… "Only open up to people you can profit from.." just help me out here, that's not a good trait? Is that right?

Christian:
For Norwegians or any other nationality… that is mean.

Anthony:
Thank you. Good, I am glad to hear that!

Christian:
Yeah!

Anthony:
The thing is though that so many actually think that this is normal?

Christian:
Yes, because it's a shallow way of behaving and not having the ability for self-reflection… They're not at a point where they can help themselves.

Anthony:
Do you think that I was right with the question of perception and to challenge her on it?

Christian:
Absolutely!

Anthony:
It's almost like some of the respondents have never been pushed to self-reflect at all and often react negatively but… it's so selfish. Do you relate to that at all?

Christian:
I completely agree with what you're saying.

Further discussion

Anthony:
The thing I… the moment you point out their contradictions then so many seem to shut down?

Christian:
That says a lot about the personality but it also speaks about the generation, that this is the way people around them behave.

Anthony:
There's no accountability?

Christian:
No, and that's my main point here you can't really blame, "Oh because my friend is x y z this way" because as long as you are a thinking human being you should seek to go deeper inside and if you would have asked me when I do stuff I don't do things to get profit myself at all, I am actually the opposite…

Anthony:
The fact that anyone would proudly say what she said and not think that's not a good thing to say... that's crazy!?

Christian:
Yes. Yes, but that's what I'm saying. They are entitled people.

Anthony:
But they don't have any perception that they sound so mean and selfish?

Christian:
That's because they haven't been corrected. They haven't been corrected by their parents. So *(AN – redacted)* hasn't been corrected by *(AN – redacted)* parents so what kind of upbringing is that... when you don't correct selfishness like this?! And they need to learn.

Anthony:
In a weird way, do you think that our conversation has affected her way of thinking at all?

Christian:
Well, it's certainly an input but the first time around? I don't know...

Further conversation.

Anthony:
How do you think she will respond, if she chooses to respond?

Christian:
I think that you will get a quasi-answer... you'll get an answer but not an answer to it. It also depends where she is on the process because she will like all of these people experiencing life... They will go through the feedback of all the other people either verbally or just by their reaction. These guys will learn that this is not the way to live life. So depending on where she is and how many inputs has got... But it doesn't sound (good) from her first response, just the fact that she's not only upset but the fact that she's even expressing it in the answer, that takes a bit of courage as well, because if you had only been upset you might have been like "ooh" and just back off... that reaction as well a lot about the human mindset. People that are reflective would never take it out in that way. They would go the humble way...

Anthony:
Here is the thing though, accountability. I actually pointed out the 'appallingness' of what she said as a Norwegian "trait"… Now, if someone says to you "Christian, you're a Norwegian and another Norwegian told me that a Norwegian trait is that you only do stuff when you get profit out of it"… Aren't you offended by that?

Christian:
Yes! Exactly. I am.

Anthony:
It's not good for Norway?

Christian:
The thing is like, no matter what's the nationality I am offended by those type of people… she doesn't get it. She doesn't have the ability to understand because she doesn't have that depth yet.

Anthony:
Does this surprise you at all? Out of all the age groups fifteen, sixteen, forty, fifty, sixty, seventy: not much have said anything positive about the demographic twenty to thirty year olds… why?

Christian:
There are definitely people within that age group that I think are amazing but those individuals arise as the odd ones out because they are so reflective.

Anthony:
Yes.

Christian:
I know people that are in their mid-twenties that are brilliant but they are different.

Anthony:
Different? You mean that they're rare?

Christian:
Yes, they are the rarity.

Anthony:
Please speak to me about the group in general rather than the exceptions and the rarities... Why would so many be saying the same negative general thing about the twenty to thirty year olds?

Christian:
They say it because what happened as a brilliant idea in the upbringing. You've got to remember that the parents were like we're not going to put our children through the hardships... And things come easier to the kids so they, so they grew up thinking that they are the centre of attention for everything... The most important thing in the entire world... us. We just get this and if we cry out louder I'll get even more. This is what I'm saying... they forgot resilience. These kids were never left alone to sort out arguments with their friends, whatever, because parents got in sorting them out... fallout at school... parents came in to sort it out. So, they are not trained in social interaction or self-reflection... when they have felt pain all out somebody else has come to fix it... They have never really had to go into that deep mode... Where I have to figure out what I am doing wrong here. I am not saying that they are never going to understand it but I am saying that these guys were brought up in a way that they were not taught.

Anthony:
Has anybody ever spoke directly to their face?

Christian:
Oh, yes... there has been a lot of focus on that in the last years.

Anthony:
From?

Christian:
From both the media and in school and a lot of psychologists talking about it.

Anthony:
Oh really? But it's a little bit shocking and peculiar to me that in so many discussions with so many twenty to thirty year olds, I have hardly seen or heard any awareness or certain qualities, but with fourteen/fifteen, fifty year olds, I have?

Christian:
That's quite typical but it's not only Norwegian it's a worldwide thing...

(AN – Would you agree with this?)

Further discussion

Anthony:
But don't you think that the money situation in this country, for example, so many have the means to buy whatever they desire... Do you think that that could exacerbate the situation within that age group in this country?

Christian:
Definitely, but you will see it even more in America... In parts of America. In Britain, as well, you will see it in Britain as well. But it's definitely linked to areas where you have wealth or where you have middle class wealth. Where the middle class got stronger... and you have the same thing we see in young generations now growing up with suddenly to parents are working instead of having mum home and being the parent, always in contact to parent working... so they're more left on their own but they have a TV... the parents probably have a bar so they can steal them alcohol, they have money to buy and do whatever so materialistically... they have a lot of things and people are saying to them that they I have nothing to complain about... because you are so much better off than us in the old days, what they don't have is that adult contact that shaped them as humans.

Anthony:
I have one point with regards to this... I have not seen this anywhere else at such high levels. I really think that if I spoke to a stupid English skateboarder bully... I really think that they would at least have the reflectiveness, i.e. "Yeah! I'm mean... but I don't care! Get over it!". But I haven't seen that in these particular conversations. It seems that so many of the respondents don't seem to *know* what they're saying... don't seem to think about how they are perceived or that what they are saying might even be potentially perceived as bad? What do you have to say about that?

Christian:
It's definitely got a bit of a Scandinavian touch to it... And I think that you

would find Danish people even more aggressive in that style.

Anthony:
Really?

Christian:
Yes.

Anthony:
You are referring to not having that reflective quality?

Christian:
Yeah yeah.

Anthony:
Now, how about when these people are caught out for example? For example, if you go to your student and say, "You've just told me this, you're acting in this way, think about what you're saying and how you're acting". That acknowledgement of "oh wait a minute, they have just pointed this out to me, I'm going to change my ways". I am not seeing that at all. The awareness is not there? So that's what I'm very curious about. Are you saying that many are just spoilt?

Christian:
Spoilt and left alone... Lack of training because like, in that social interaction which there has been a lot of focus on within the young ones, into the schools because you recognise parents are not feeling that rule.

Anthony:
So the young ones are benefiting from the mistakes of the twenty to thirty-year-old generation?

Christian:
Yes, I think so because the thing is like, that's why the jobs in the schools have changed so massively, the teachers don't just teach any more, maybe 80% of their job is psychology... and really development

Anthony:
Do they not get that from their parents?

Christian:

No, because, they spend more time at school than they actually spend with their parents… So I think that that trying to fill in the gap which happened.

Anthony:

So, in actual fact, there are actual consequences financially and, for example behavioural for the next generation?

Christian:

Oh yeah.

Anthony:

This is actually causing an effect?

Christian:

Of course! If you see it like the different decades, generations they have different pros and cons.

Anthony:

Tell me? You said that it's even worse in Denmark or something?

Christian:

Yes.

Anthony:

What does that mean?

Christian:

Because they are really into, "me" thinking.

Anthony:

What do you mean?

Christian:

Danish people… not as in bad… like or bad rude people… they're like "I am who I am and I am entitled to be whatever!" *(AN – sarcastic voice.)* It's like that's how it is and they are very like…

Anthony:

Are you saying that Danish people "don't feel guilty" if it's something bad?

Christian:
No shame! No shame…

(AN – At this point Christian had to run off to a meeting… but we were joined by his daughter who is about 15 years old and was listening to the end of our conversation… her name is Laila and she said to me, with regards to Elises comment about profiting from people, "but we do think that"… let's see what Laila has to say about all this…)

Anthony:
Listen, we've just had an eavesdropper on the conversation! Her name is Laila! Laila, you just said, "But we do think that." What was it exactly that you said?

Laila:
We only get to know people when we profit something, who you can like profit something from. *(AN – She agrees with the statement!)*

Anthony:
Then I'll ask you the same question I asked Elise, and you gave me a very clear answer, which was?

Laila:
That people would perceive it as very rude!

(AN – Listen to her intelligent answers and compare them to many of the older people we have talked to.)

Anthony:
And then I said that that's a normal answer and I said to you that certain people are reacting angrily and they get angry when I say that that might be perceived as rude?

Laila:
Yes. International people and people that come here… don't know that we think that way. So if somebody was to suddenly "Oh! This is how Norwegians think… then they would think "what!? These b*stards… they're just rude!"

Anthony:
(*Laugh.*)

Laila:
You kind of need…

Anthony:
The whole picture?

Laila:
Like you've got… because now, you've got… now you basically know everything about the truth of Norway!

Anthony:
(*Laugh*)… **Go on…**

Laila:
They won't know the whole social situation of our whole country, right?

Anthony:
Of course.

Laila:
But that one thing will sound so bad… but if they knew the rest… I think that either, they'd be like "Oh my God that's terrible!" Or they would probably understand somehow?

Anthony:
But let me ask you… You are fifteen years old and you have insight and self-perception… How come so many people that are twenty to thirty cannot even understand what you have just explained very simply?

Laila:
I don't think there brought up very well… their parents…

Anthony:
Is the observation that something is rude, rude in itself?

Laila:
What do you mean?

Anthony:
Well you just said that "anybody that heard that would say that it is rude, because it is rude"… I agree with everything that you have just said but just so that we are on the same page… pointing that out… could that legitimately offend them?

Laila:
Hmmmm… I think it would offend people that do it. Because I, personally don't feel that I use people… Yeah I have to pretend to be friends with idiots, even though I don't like them… but I don't use them… unless… or… *(laugh)*… I don't use anyone… I don't use people so that I can get something from people. I'm just friends with my best friends.

(AN – Laila started to say that she doesn't use people… unless… and then she realised and laughed and changed direction really fast.)

Anthony:
Do you think that this has triggered them because they are guilty for thinking something which is really mean?

Laila:
Err… yeah! They know! Because everybody can act stupid… and some people are just idiots… But everybody somehow in the situation is aware of what they are doing and I think that that age group, that you are talking about, a lot of them actually do that thing; using people just to get something out of people, and I think they know and I think, they get offended because when you ask them, they say "are you saying that I am doing this?!" Yet they know they are! And that's why they gets offended you know.

(AN – To see a young person answer with such clarity, maturity and self-perception and intelligence honestly is incredible… high critical thinking levels… it is bizarre if you think about. The children interviewed so often seem to speak like adults and many of the adults seem to speak like children.)

Anthony:
So basically… their bad behaviour has just been caught out and they don't like it?

Laila:
Yes!

Anthony:
Here is the one thing that I'm interested in: when bad behaviour like that has been caught out, a normal person would admit it because they have been caught, but some individuals are in it so deep that they don't even have shame, that they've been caught? What do you have to say about that?

Laila:
Yes. I know. I think that some people try to hide it, because it might ruin their image?

Anthony:
It's almost like they're *proud* of being shallow, fickle and using people, because they don't demonstrate any shame when they do that?

Laila:
I think that's the people that end up at the top by doing that are proud... but the people, who aren't getting anywhere, but are still doing it, I don't think they're proud, but I do think that they are too ashamed to admit it.

Anthony:
Oh, so they keep saying it hidden internally? Are they are confused?

Laila:
Yes!

Anthony:
And so it's easier to keep saying the same thing and almost be proud then to stop, think about the way they think, and do the right thing?

Laila:
Yes!

Further discussion

Anthony:
When they tell me this... and tell me these things, it's as if they don't think that I'm going to say, "Wait a minute, that's mean?" It's as if they think that they're just not going to be challenged at all? Why do you think that is?

Laila:
Yes… I think that they're so used to not hearing it… I think that they're aware of what they're doing but I think that they don't know or remember the pain that it might cause to somebody else, because they are used to being… because everybody has treated them like this sometime or somewhere, so I like think… That they're so used to hearing it themselves that they don't think about the consequences to somebody else.

Anthony:
Wow! Thanks Laila! Incredible… you're a genius!

This is Norway – Racism Excused by my Norwegian friends

What I describe to you now was pivotal moment on my Norway voyage. A Saturday evening in a major town in Norway. I am walking with two Norwegian friends on a midnight walk. One of their friends pulled up next to us on a bike and asked, "Where are you from?" I told him that I'm from London. He then said, "You're not from London. People from London are white."

By this time I had encountered enough open racism in Norway, had people giggling and saying the "N-word" in front of me so many times that I wasn't going to let this go. I challenged him to stop being a rude racist idiot. He actually started arguing and said that he "wasn't being racist". I told him to move on… but what happened next broke my heart.

One of the two Norwegian friends who had just witnessed everything turned to me and said;

"You'll probably disagree but he isn't racist and I don't consider what he said as racist."

Those words will forever be etched in my heart. I looked at my two friends and then I knew that they lived and have been brought up in a racist society where racism and discrimination is so normal that it doesn't have an understandable meaning to them any more… even if it happens in front of their own eyes to their friends.

This is Norway…

A Conversation with a Charity Worker

I spoke with twenty-five-year-old charity worker "Karl" on a rainy day in a place called Møre og Romsdal. I was genuinely shocked to hear that nearly 8% of the population of Norway give money to the charity he works for to children abroad. He was happy to be interviewed…

Anthony:
Karl, tell me about what you do?

Karl:
We recruit people to help one child each to get food and to get supplies and stuff like that in mainly Africa but also in South America and in Asia… We've been doing this, not me personally, since 1937 and we are one of the biggest charities in all of the world.

Anthony:
Let me ask you something because something that you said shocked me.

Karl:
Yes?

Anthony:
The charity was founded in Spain and you said, yes?

Karl:
Yes?

Anthony:
And I asked you how many Norwegians support a child abroad and you said?

Karl:
400,000.

Anthony:
OK. That's mind boggling. That's just under nearly 10% of the population of Norway support a child abroad!

Karl:
Yes, is it 7 or 8% or something… It's pretty many…

Anthony:
That, to me sounds incredible… nearly 10% of the population support somebody abroad financially?

Karl:
Yes.

Anthony:
What do you think about that?

Karl:
I think, Norwegians are nice people, and we like to help and also we have the luxury to help in Norway, of course…

Anthony:
OK.

Karl:
We have a lot more privilege then most of the world and most of the people, of course, in Norway know that… So therefore lots choose to support… We had another campaign a couple of weeks ago called care which helps women and children and also a lot of people support that… So I recommend checking out that as well…

Anthony:
Is that inside or outside of Norway?

Karl:
That's both… every year in Norway they have one big TV campaign for charity…

Anthony:
There was one a couple of days ago right?

Karl:
Yes!

Anthony:
Yes I was speaking to someone on Svalbard who raised a lot of money for charity there.

Karl:
Wow!

Anthony:
Yes, a week ago or something, I was there talking about it... but anyway... what's shocking to me is 400,000 people... that's a lot of people! Proportionately, that's a lot... I don't see, proportionately, that many people in the rest of world would donate that much?

Karl:
I don't have all the numbers in the world, but yes.

Anthony:
I don't see how many other countries can compete with that... We have the National Lottery and we have other charities in the UK but 10% of the population to one charity?! *(Laugh.)* I also presume that many of the people that give money to charity abroad probably give money to charity domestically too?

Karl:
Oh yes... To the Red Cross for UNICEF or others... to name a few... Norway has 171 charities, which are registered and you can also check out the numbers online, and see how much goes to administration costs.

Anthony:
Can I ask you, how old are you?

Karl:
I am twenty-five.

Anthony:
And what makes you want to do this?

Karl:
I started with another charity work when I was younger... high school I
worked for Red Cross for two years...

Anthony:
How old were you when you started working for them?

Karl:
Seventeen, eighteen... and it was work that had more meaning to me
compared to a lot of other stuff.

Anthony:
Let me ask you a controversial question... I've met a lot of people in
Norway... a lot of different ages... all over the country... and many of the
twenty to thirty-year-olds age group describe *themselves* as spoilt, superficial
and fake... mostly... this is how they often describe themselves speaking to
me! "We know that we are spoilt and all of our friends are fake blah blah blah."
Now, considering that you work for a charity, and as you said you want to do
something meaningful, do you feel different from your peers? Do you think
that they have the same priorities as you, generally speaking?

Karl:
I'm not sure; I'm not sure what goes in their mind.

Anthony:
Do they also support charities as well or is it only you in your friend group?

Karl:
Most people that I work with are kind of my friends but not most of my
friends who are friends from childhood... a few of them.

Anthony:
Would you say quite a few of them or not so much?

Karl:
Not so much.

Anthony:
So I'm guessing that your newer friends are charity workers as well but
you're normal "growing up" friends, probably not?

Karl:
Not so much, I feel that.

Anthony:
How do you feel about that?

Karl:
It's OK... people find their own passion. Passion for your work is important either way, so...

Anthony:
Is it ever lonely?

Karl:
Lonely?

Anthony:
Yes, is it ever lonely standing up for something you believe in and trying to help people?

Karl:
Maybe 50/50... but I feel that most people have good intentions... but it's my job to get people to act on those intentions.

Anthony:
Oh! So people have got good "intentions" and it's your job to get people to act on those good intentions?

Karl:
Yes

Anthony:
Instead of?

Karl:
Instead of just being passive, make sure... it's not just chat.

Anthony:
Thank you so much for talking!

Afterword: The Tip of a Giant Iceberg

This book series contains a lot of difficult to read, hard to take in, complex analyses and discussion based around the hundreds of people I interviewed. I appreciate it is not an easy read and I have tried to break up the conversations with discussion as much as possible to help. This is only Volume I – there's a lot more to come. This is no more than the *tip of a giant iceberg.* I have intentionally steered clear of the domestic drama and stories of corruption and abuse that I constantly encountered on almost every part of this journey. We will touch on this in the forthcoming volumes. We're now going to broaden out and talk to other Norwegians from different walks of life, in the Arctic and other areas of Norway in the next three volumes and let many of them describe their lives in their own words. The purpose of these books, as I set out at the start, was not to deliberately cause embarrassment but to anonymously reveal the truth for the benefit of all involved. The only point to doing that is if there is a positive outcome. I believe that positive outcome is change and I believe with knowledge that is possible. But we need to go deeper, which we will do with Volumes II – IV.

Source Notes

Professor Harald N Røstvik from Stavanger
https://www.uis.no/article.php?articleID=101970&categoryID=11198
https://www.amazon.co.uk/CORRUPTION-Nobel-Way-Sunshine-Revolution-ebook/dp/B00SH5CAA8
"Differences Between Tight and Loose Cultures A 33-Nation Study" :Michele J. Gelfand.
Michele J. Gelfand1,*, Jana L. Raver2, Lisa Nishii3, Lisa M. Leslie4, Janetta Lun1, Beng Chong
    Lim5, Lili Duan6, Assaf Almaliach7, Soon Ang8, Jakobina Arnadottir9, Zeynep Aycan10,
    Klaus Boehnke11, Pawel Boski12, Rosa Cabecinhas13, Darius Chan14, Jagdeep Chhokar15,
    Alessia D'Amato16, Montse Ferrer17, Iris C. Fischlmayr18, Ronald Fischer19, Marta
    Fülöp20, James Georgas21, Emiko S. Kashima22, Yoshishima Kashima23, Kibum Kim24,
    Alain Lempereur25, Patricia Marquez26, Rozhan Othman27, Bert Overlaet28, Penny
    Panagiotopoulou29, Karl Peltzer30, Lorena R. Perez-Florizno31, Larisa Ponomarenko32,
    Anu Realo33, Vidar Schei34, Manfred Schmitt35, Peter B. Smith36, Nazar Soomro37, Erna
    Szabo18, Nalinee Taveesin38, Midori Toyama39, Evert Van de Vliert40, Naharika Vohra41,
    Colleen Ward42, Susumu Yamaguchi43
https://science.sciencemag.org/content/332/6033/1100
Associate Professor Vidar Schei nhh.no:
https://www.nhh.no/en/nhh-bulletin/article-archive/older-articles/2011/june/norwegians-give-each-other-little-room-for-manoeuvre/
The Guardian by Sindre Bangstad, "Norway is in denial about the threat of far-right violence"
    (16th September 2019)
https://www.theguardian.com/commentisfree/2019/sep/16/norway-denial-far-right-violence-breivik
Kathrine Jebsen Moore, entitled "Does Norway have a far-right problem?" (Spectator, 23rd
    September 2019)
https://blogs.spectator.co.uk/2019/09/does-norway-have-a-far-right-problem/
Norway Today, "Racism in Norway: Bad FAFO research?" (26th May 2019)
https://norwaytoday.info/culture/racism-fafo-research/
"Norwegians impolite? Forget it!" Sciencenorway.com published (11th March 2017) from the
    Norwegian School of Economics (NHH), written by Sigrid Folkestad
https://partner.sciencenorway.no/forskningno-nhh-norway/norwegians-impolite-forget-it/1443593
The Local Norway "Norwegians are polite – in their own special way: Researcher" 27th March
    2017
https://www.thelocal.no/20170327/norwegians-are-polite-in-their-own-special-way-researcher
Curt Rice, "Why international students should not come to Norway" Huffington Post (26th
    October 2015)
https://curt-rice.com/2015/10/26/why-international-students-should-not-come-to-norway/

www.newsinenglish.no May 20th, 2019 "Survey indicates underlying racism"
https://www.newsinenglish.no/2019/05/20/survey-indicates-underlying-racism/

Dr. Davidicus Wong entitled, "Racism on our vacation a reminder people see us as 'The Others'"
for "Burnaby Now" (4th February 2019)
https://www.burnabynow.com/opinion/racism-on-our-vacation-a-reminder-people-see-us-as-the-
others-1.23622371

Science Norway (sciencenordic.com) "Care but no caring", 24th May 2014.
https://sciencenorway.no/ageing-forskningno-norway/care-but-no-caring/1386635

"Pupils with low grades feel less supported by teachers" norwegianscitechnews.com Veronika Søum
(26th Feb 2019)
https://norwegianscitechnews.com/2019/02/pupils-with-low-grades-feel-less-supported-by-
teachers/

J Russell Mikkelsen (editor/curator of Estimated Time of Arrival) "What's Weird About Norway: A
touchy-feely guy's view of a touchless, feel-less nation" 19th September 2013 medium.com
https://medium.com/@jrmikkelsen/whats-weird-about-norway-b1a51c79a3d0

Yngvil Vatn Guttu 28th March, 2017 www.norskbloggen.no "How Norwegians avoid saying
"please""
https://norskbloggen.no/en/say-please-norwegian

"Norwegians urged to stop bragging", 23rd January, 2013 (www.newsinenglish.no – Views and
News from Norway/Aasa Christine Stolt")
https://www.newsinenglish.no/2013/01/23/norwegian-bravado-can-be-annoying/

The Nordic Page (www.tnp.no) "Norwegians Believe Norwegian Culture Is Better Than Other
Cultures"
https://www.tnp.no/norway/panorama/norway-norwegians-believe-norwegian-culture-is-better-
than-other-cultures

John Olav Ytreland "The Norwegian Personality Disorder" 21st February 2018
https://johnsgarret.wordpress.com/2018/02/21/the-norwegian-personality-disorder/

"Oslo, Norway ranked 12th out of 459 cities worldwide: Selfies" Time Magazine (time.com, Chris
Wilson, 10th March, 2014) https://time.com/selfies-cities-world-rankings/

The Norwegian referendum: "Dissolution of the union between Norway and Sweden" on 13th
August 1905
https://www.royalcourt.no/seksjon.html?tid=28690

"Migrants not particularly prone to depression" sciencenorway.no article by Steinar Brandslet (15th
July 2019)
https://partner.sciencenorway.no/depression-forskningno-health/migrants-not-particularly-prone-
to-depression/1567357

"Depressive symptoms among migrants and non-migrants in Europe: documenting and explaining
inequalities in times of socio-economic instability" Author details: Gkiouleka A1, Avrami L2,
Kostaki A3, Huijts T1, Eikemo TA4, Stathopoulou T2. 1. Department of Sociology,
University of York, York, UK.2. National Centre for Social Research, Athens, Greece.3.
Department of Statistics, Athens University of Economics & Business, Athens, Greece.4.
Department of Sociology and Political Science, Centre for Global Health Inequalities
Research (CHAIN), Norwegian University of Science and Technology (NTNU),
Trondheim, Norway".
https://www.researchgate.net/publication/329156178_Depressive_symptoms_among_migrants_an
d_non-migrants_in_Europe_documenting_and_explaining_inequalities_in_times_of_socio-
economic_instability

Andy Skuce www.skepticalscience.com "Living in Denial in Norway" (28th February 2013) https://skepticalscience.com/denialnorway.html

Gram Franck "Why I love Norway but Hate Norwegians" https://medium.com/@askgramfranck/why-i-love-norway-but-hate-norwegians-b6deeaa2b927

"New Book Leaves Norway's 'Heroic Role' in the Holocaust in Tatters." By Ofer Aderet, Published 22nd December 2018 Haaretz (www.haaretz.com) https://www.haaretz.com/world-news/europe/.premium-new-book-leaves-norway-s-heroic-role-in-the-holocaust-in-tatters-1.6766712

Dan Solomon Texas Monthly www.texasmonthly.com published (20th October 2015) "Y'all, Norwegians Use the Word "Texas" as Slang to Mean "Crazy"" https://www.texasmonthly.com/the-daily-post/yall-norwegians-use-the-word-texas-as-slang-to-mean-crazy/

Export Credit Norway (www.eksportkreditt.no) "Norwegians perceived as arrogant abroad, by Norwegian team" https://www.eksportkreditt.no/en/case/common-mistakes-made-by-norwegian-companies-operating-abroad/

The culture website www.theculturetrip.com (22nd November 2017 by Danei Christopoulou) "The eight Types of Norwegians You'll Meet on Tinder". https://theculturetrip.com/europe/norway/articles/the-8-types-of-norwegians-youll-meet-on-tinder/

visitnorway.com "death diving" https://www.visitnorway.com/media/news-from-norway/how-these-insanely-wild-dives-became-a-phenomenon-in-norway-and-went-viral/

Forbes.com's senior contributor David Nikel "Norway's 'Time-Free' Island Was Just An Elaborate P.R. Stunt" https://www.forbes.com/sites/davidnikel/2019/06/26/norway-tourism-bosses-slammed-for-fake-news-pr-stunt/

www.theconversation.com published an article entitled "Is life in Norway as happy as it's cracked up to be?" 24th July 2017 Nathan John Albury http://theconversation.com/is-life-in-norway-as-happy-as-its-cracked-up-to-be-76516

"Told that Norway is the West's most anti-Semitic country, diplomat lashes out at Israel" Raphael Ahren. Times of Israel https://www.timesofisrael.com/at-jerusalem-panel-norwegians-spar-over-israel-and-anti-semitism/

Dr Manfred Gerstenfeld interviewed Norwegian journalist Eirik Veum from the Norwegian Broadcasting Corporation, NRK, author of The Fallen about Norwegians in the SS and other Nazi units, in an "OpEd" for www.israelnationalnews.com published 21st January 2014.

"Book lists 16,000 Nazi collaborator suspects" by thelocal.no, 13 March 2014 https://www.thelocal.no/20140313/norway-to-publish-list-of-16000-ww2

The Guardian "Norway to restage 1914 'human zoo' that exhibited Africans as inmates" by Bwesigye bwa Mwesigire, 29th Apr 2014 https://www.theguardian.com/world/2014/apr/29/norway-human-zoo-africans-as-inmates

Andreas Slettholm (aftenposten.no, 27th May 2015) "6 out of ten are negative about having a Muslim in the family" https://www.pewresearch.org/fact-tank/2017/11/29/5-facts-about-the-muslim-population-in-europe/

The Jerusalem Post (jpost.com, 21st November 2013) "Norway unwilling to confront war crimes" https://www.jpost.com/Jewish-World/Jewish-News/Norway-unwilling-to-confront-war-crimes-332485

"Raise a monument over the graves of the Nordic country's Nazi soldiers" Norway's VG newspaper (By Jon. H. Rydne – updated 16th November 2017)

Richard Orange local.no (6th November 2013) "Norwegian camp guards shocked SS with brutality" https://www.thelocal.no/20131106/norwegian-camps-guards-shocked-ss-with-brutality

"Merciless Norwegians" or "Ruthless Norwegians" Eirik Veum author: tanum.no. https://www.newsinenglish.no/2012/10/23/debate-flies-over-new-war-book/

https://www.un.org/en/ Encyclopaedia of the Holocaust, based on research at Yad Vashem.

Ina R. Friedman, author of The Other Victims: First Person Stories of Non-Jews Persecuted by the Nazis (Boston, Houghton Mifflin, 1990) wrote (www.socialstudies.org/)

"In From the Cold" for The New Yorker (18th December 2005) Jeffrey Frank https://www.newyorker.com/magazine/2005/12/26/in-from-the-cold

Knut Hamsun's Wikipedia page (en.wikipedia.org/wiki/Knut_Hamsun)

The Goebbels Diaries, 1942—1943, translated, edited, and introduced by Louis P. Lochner, 1948, pp. 303–304).

"Frontfighters: The Norwegian Volunteer Legion of the Waffen-SS 1941-1943" by Richard Landwehr (based on the book Legionsminner-Trekk Av Den Norske Legions Historie, assembled by E. Jul Christiansen Furum in 1943 and originally published by Viking Vorlag, Oslo, 1943 and an English language translation published by Roger Hunt in 1986)

The UK's Independent by Andy McSmith (7th August 2009) "Rehabilitated: Nobel Prize winner who fell for Hitler" https://www.independent.co.uk/news/world/europe/rehabilitated-nobel-prize-winner-who-fell-for-hitler-1768518.html

The Guardian "Knut Hamsun commemorated on Norwegian coin" by Alison Flood https://www.theguardian.com/books/2009/feb/03/knut-hamsun-norwegian-coin

"Al Pacino pulls out of 'Nazi' Knut Hamsun play" https://www.thelocal.no/20150526/al-pacino-snubs-nazi-hamsun-drama

The Daily Telegraph article by Richard Orange (www.telegraph.co.uk: 27th May 2015)

Science Norway (sciencenorway.no) "Norwegian industry complied with German war efforts" by Hanne Jakobsen (11th April 2013) https://partner.sciencenorway.no/a/1384738

James Sorg (SGT U.S Marine Corps) Walter Cronkite TV special (CBS News) and 2006, old news reel, James Sorg made a speech to the "Robert H. Jackson Center".

Quisling to Bjørn Foss, 8 May 1945, Dahl 1999, p. 367, Dahl, Hans Fredrik (1999). Quisling: A Study in Treachery. Stanton-Ife, Anne-Marie)

Bratteli & Myhre 1992, p. 198, Bratteli, Tone; Myhre, Hans B. (1992). Quislings siste dager)

YouTube's "Vidkun Quisling: The Man Who Sold his Country to the Third Reich" (Biographics Video Hosted by Simon Whistler) https://www.youtube.com/watch?v=4ZO-jEDVStA&feature=youtu.be

"What is typically Norwegian?" "Easy Languages" posted a YouTube video, hosted by Sindre Garcia https://www.youtube.com/watch?v=86CvfPPd778

Norwegian court: "Many people share Breivik's conspiracy theory, including the Eurabia theory." https://content.sciendo.com/downloadpdf/journals/njmr/3/4/article-p205.xml

"Winning Fair and Square? Norwegian Ski Supremacy Driven by Doping" https://sputniknews.com/amp/sport/201610141046332640-norway-doping-skiing

Sciencenorway "Doping scandal covered very differently by Swedish and Norwegian media" by Nancy Bazilchuk (22nd May 2019). https://sciencenorway.no/communication-and-media-culture-forskningno/doping-scandal-covered-very-differently-by-swedish-and-norwegian-media/1554435

Aftenposten.no (article by Petter Fløttum,Bernt Harald Burnevann, 5th August 2019)

Ingvild Tennøe Haugen "Chapter 9, A Nation Betrayed – The Dramatic Coverage of a Doping Case, Ingvild Tennøe Haugen, MA student, Department of Journalism and Media Studies Doping in Norway"

Carolyn Steber wrote an article for www.bustle.com, 21st June 2018 https://www.bustle.com/profile/carolyn-steber-1908755

Expressen's sports (www.expressen.se) commentator Lasse Anrell excerpt

Sports journalist Johan Esk (www.dn.se), of Dagens Nyheter "First, Martin Johnsrud Sundby and now Therese Johaug. Now it's definitely time to put Norway in the same bunch of cheater states."

Twitter @SpordePorttila (Twitter: 20th July 2016)

Youtube.com:

Title: "Norway – Is It The Perfect Economy?" (800,376 views)

Title: "Norway: A Socialist Paradise?" (106,221 views)

Title: "American REACTS to Norwegian Lifestyle | Norway Is Amazing" (35,245 views)

Title: "Why you should visit Norway – Unspoken paradise" (255,245 views)

Title: "VLOG, travelling to Norway, Norway day one, most beautiful country" (14,069 views)

Title: "Why Norway Has The Best Educational System In The World" (39,771 views)

Title: "Why is NORWAY so RICH? – VisualPolitik EN" (990,264 views)

Title: "Norway's tips for achieving happiness | DW English" (62,563 views)

Title: "Norway's Stolen Children?" (406,417 views)

Title: "Typical things about NORWAY | PART 1" (308,238 views)

Title: "Norwegians are racist? Life is difficult in Norway!" (506,095 views)

Title: "Norway – The Happiest Country of the World" (207,076 views)

Title: "Norwegian men make the best husbands" (22,496 views)

"Oslo, Norway Terrorist Attack: Video Footage of Explosion and Camp Shooting Aftermath (07.23.2011)"

BBC news "How Norway turns criminals into good neighbours" on 7th July 2019 https://www.bbc.com/news/stories-48885846

"Norway top two coffee consumption in the world" - worldatlas.com https://weaverscoffee.com/blogs/blog/the-worlds-top-coffee-consuming-nations-and-how-they-take-their-cup

"Bergen Police whistle blower" - Bergen police whistle blower Per Terje Engedal revealed massive failures which caused him to leave his job, as reported by vg.no.

Tidsskriftet.no, the Journal of the Norwegian Medical Association, 7th May 2013 "Are 72 % of all Norwegian doctors depressed?" https://tidsskriftet.no/en/2013/05/editor/are-72-all-norwegian-doctors-depressed

The Local (thelocal.no) published an article entitled "Norway celebs slam 'racist' nightclubs in Oslo", 29th December 2015 https://www.thelocal.no/20151229/racial-discrimination-at-seven-out-of-eleven-oslo-bars

Mari Bore Øverland thesis "Making friends with Norwegians takes too much time: the role of social capital in highly skilled temporary migrants' aspirations and opportunities for citizenship enactment"

The Local (www.thelocal.no) 29th August 2016 "Expats say it's not just Norway's weather that's cold" https://www.thelocal.no/20160829/expats-find-norway-a-cold-place-and-no-its-not-just-the-weather

InterNations Expat Insider survey https://www.internations.org/expat-insider/

"Lawsuit against Utøya memorial by locals" - The Guardian, 21st June 2017 https://www.theguardian.com/world/2017/jun/21/norwegian-government-backs-down-over-memorial-to-breivik-victims

Daily Mirror, "Sick supporters: Twisted killer Anders Breivik receives thousands of letters a month from fans" by Nick Owens and Ben Griffiths (26th August 2012) https://www.mirror.co.uk/news/world-news/anders-breivik-killer-gets-thousands-1280055

"Utøya memorial defaced with Swastika on anniversary of attack" thelocal.com (23th July 2019) https://www.thelocal.no/20190723/utoya-memorial-defaced-with-swastika-on-anniversary-of-attack

https://www.straitstimes.com/world/europe/utoya-memorial-defaced-with-swastika-on-anniversary-of-attack-in-which-77-died

"Norway: Anti-refugee Soldiers of Odin patrol in Stavanger" Ruptly, 30th April 2016 Youtube.com

Marcus Guiliano "Farmed Norwegian Salmon World's Most Toxic Food" (25th March 2017) YouTube.com

"This is a Nazi system" – MEP on Norwegian foster care system": Ruptly (14,580 views, YouTube.com, 30th May 2015)

The New York Times 9th July 2014, by Andrew Higgins: "A Harsh Climate Calls for Banishment of the Needy" https://www.nytimes.com/2014/07/10/world/europe/a-harsh-climate-calls-for-banishment-of-the-needy

20th March 2010 The Guardian newspaper: "The Norway town that forgave and forgot its child killers" by Erwin James and Ian MacDougall.

"Norway's dirty little secret is out" Professor Harald N Røstvik, The Guardian newspaper (12th February 2015).

"The truth about living in the so-called utopia of Scandinavia according to Kiwis who live there" by Lorna Thornber (January 22nd 2018 www.stuff.co.nz)

Professor Harald N Røstvik, Stavanger, Norway, Financial Times (www.ft.com) 29th May 2015); "Norway: not such a social democratic model society."

"Ukrainian Norwegian chamber of commerce" (nucc.no) "Working with Norwegians" by Karin Ellis (30th January 2018)

Karin Ellis, "working with Indians" (ellisculture.com)

Canadian "Global affairs: www.international.gc.ca."

Michael Booth for The Guardian newspaper, published, 27th January 2014 , "Dark lands: the grim truth behind the 'Scandinavian miracle'".

"Norway's Silent Scandal" & Norway's hidden scandal (BBC News)(BBC – Our World, 2018) by Tim Whewell

"Norway's Stolen Children?" SBS Dateline (www.sbs.com.au/news/dateline) 2016 documentary

"The Bjugn abuse in 1992 in Bjugn, Norway: "Collaborating Against Child Abuse: Exploring the Nordic Children's Home Model" (by Susanna Johansson, Kari Stefansen, Elisiv Bakketeig, Anna Kaldal)

Norwegian newspaper VG (vg.no) "Boasted of abuse, not arrested" (13th October 2017 by Håkon F Hoydaleinar, Otto Stangviknatalie, Remoe Hansen)

"Norway child abuse: Man held over assaults on 300 boys" (BBC News bbc.com 21st November 2018)

Amanda Taub vox.com (24th February 2015): "Is Scandinavia all fun and reindeer games until winter comes and throws everyone into deep depression?"

"Depression and Anti-depressants: A Nordic Perspective" – NCBI (www.ncbi.nlm.nih.gov) A Vilhelmsson, 26th August 2013

Official mental health website of Norway: www.fhi.no Health Status in Norway 2018 – FHI

Lars Petter Teigen for foreignpolicy.com (19th September 2018) "Norway's Green Delusions"

The Guardian, Alex Godfrey 'Before you know it, it's not a big deal to kill a man': Norwegian black metal's murderous past (22nd March 2019)

BBC World Service, Norway article by Linda Pressly (22nd March 2018)

16th December 2018 "Norway's rules about everything – Interview of the authors of 'Norske standarder'" afroginthefjord.com

The 100 Unwritten Norwegian Social Laws https://mallofnorway.com/the-100-unwritten-norwegian-social-laws Egil Aslak Aursand Hagerup, Elise H Kollerud, Cecilie Øyen, Ann Kristin Vangen (ISBN: 9788293622062)

"When the Roses turned Black. Seven years after Utøya Survivors Receive Hatred and Death Threats" afroginthefjord.com – 30th July 2018

"Soccer: Hegerberg 'mentally broken' by Norway national team experience" www.reuters.com.

"Gender issues are ridiculed and sabotaged in the military" by Elida Høeg, KILDEN KJØNNSFORSKNING.NO, Cathinka Dahl Hambro for sciencenorway.no published 30th October 2019

"Academics hide, play dumb, don't care or over-perform" by sciencenorway.no by Georg Mathisen/Nancy Bazilchuk, 25th October 2019

"Norway Justice Minister's Partner Arrested With Accusation of Setting Their Own Car on Fire" www.tnp.no.

"Norway ex-minister Svein Ludvigsen guilty of sexually abusing asylum seekers" On 5th July 2019, BBC News

"Why is the suicide rate not declining in Norway?" by Øivind Ekeberg, Erlend Hem for tidsskriftet.no (16 August 2019)

"Norway hit by biggest welfare scandal in its history" dailysabah.com (6th November 2019)

"Use of painkillers in Norway has multiplied in 15 years" by norwaytoday.info by Tamara Lopes, 25th November 2019

Norwegian Princess's boyfriend, "Norwegian media, you are bullies" https://norwaytoday.info/culture/durek-verrett-apologizes-to-norwegians/

Oskar Aanmoen, Royal Central https://royalcentral.co.uk/author/oaanmoen/

"Who is the greatest and known Norwegian philosopher?" https://www.quora.com/Who-are-the-greatest-Norwegian-authors-and-the-greatest-Norwegian-philosophers

"The Law of the Jante" Author Michael Booth, Paris Review entitled, "The Law of Jante" (11th February 2015) https://www.theparisreview.org/blog/2015/02/11/the-law-of-jante/

"Norwegians give each other little room to manoeuvre" https://www.nhh.no/en/nhh-bulletin/article-archive/older-articles/2011/june/norwegians-give-each-other-little-room-for-manoeuvre/

Independent.co.uk "The lawyer defending the indefensible" by Tony Paterson, 15th April 2012 https://www.independent.co.uk/news/world/europe/the-lawyer-defending-the-indefensible-7645968.html

www.vg.no: "Geir Lippestad's law firm has grown strongly following the July 22 case" www.vg.no (30th Janaury 2014) by Jarle Grivi and Morten S Hopperstad entitled "Lippestad becomes a police officer"

By Stanley Milgram, Volume 205, Number 6 of Scientific American in December 1961 (republished scientificamerican.com 1st December 2011: "Which Nations Conform Most?").

"Utøya survivors experienced that the treatment programme disappeared too quickly and that the support system was not proactive enough" NRK.NO

"Survivor-held-for-17-hours-after-attacks", news24.com "Psychologist: Understand why the police arrested Utøya victim – Sorry, but understandable that the police did what they did, says psychologist Atle Dyregrov." https://www.vg.no/nyheter/innenriks/i/51Bv1/psykolog-forstaar-hvorfor-politiet-paagrep-utoeya-offer

Kate Taylor businessinsider.com (18th April 2018) "Norwegian teens celebrate a bizarre, month-long holiday full of drinking, sex, and wild dares".

The Sun newspaper: "THE KIDS ARE ALRIGHT inside the debauched world of 'Russ', when Norwegian school leavers get drunk, naked and very rowdy Russ is a national tradition involving outdoor sex, pimped-out party buses and insane quantities of booze" by Benedict Brook (news.com.au George Harrison, 27th November 2016)

www.thaiexaminer.com: "Norwegian killer accepts he's going to Thai prison after violent killing of UK man at Phuket hotel" by James Morris and Son Nguyenin, Thailand (31st August 2019):

"Norway apologises to its World War Two 'German girls'" The BBC 17th October 2018

"Inclusion and delusion" Malin Donoso Martnes (Microsoft Business Applications MVP) blog on linkedin.com (1st October 2019) entitled "Inclusion and delusion"

"Pensioner Frode Berg pressured by Norwegian intelligence services to spy is imprisoned and convicted in Russia and 'hung out to dry'" BBC NEWS: "Home for Christmas: Jailed Norwegian spy released from Russia" (2nd December 2019)

"Norwegian Spy Jailed by Russia Is Free. He's Angry, Too, but Not at Moscow… Anton Troianovski, New York Times, 28th December 2019.

"Instagrammers love this iconic spot, but there's something they don't want you to see" CNBC.com by Monica Buchanan Pitrelli (1st December 2019)

"Outcry in Pakistan over Quran desecration in Norway: Pakistan summons Norway's ambassador" - GulfNews.com (24th November 2019)

"Yes Norway, that's racist" by universitas.no (by Indigo Trigg-Hauger, 23rd February 2018) https://universitas.no/sak/63784/yes-norway-that-s-racist/

Local travel brochure from Atlantic Road area, for "Averoy, Eide, Fraena"

"Norwegian values and society page" (www.norway.no/en/uk/values-priorities/norway-today)

https://www.lifeinnorway.net/norway-falls-in-2020-happiness-rankings/

https://time.com/collection/guide-to-happiness/4706590/scandinavia-world-happiness-report-nordics/

https://worldhappiness.report/news/finland-again-is-the-happiest-country-in-the-world/

Scribner's Monthly published in 1876

Norwegian traits" and you can find it on pages 419 – 423 - The Century illustrated monthly magazine v.11 1875-76.

www.international.gc.ca

https://www.visitnorway.com/media/news-from-norway/the-happiest-country-on-earth/

The Xenophobe's Guide to the Norwegians (Xenophobe's Guides) Reprint by Dan Elloway (ISBN: 9781906042431) www.xenophobes.com/the-norwegians/

About the Author

Anthony King is a choreographer who started teaching dance at the world-famous Pineapple Dance Studios, London in 2004 and has authored seven books on a variety of subjects, from Dance to Asperger's to Music History. He has taught stars from music, sport and film including Emma Watson, Miss World, Harry Potter, various members of royalty (European and Middle Eastern), Pink Floyd, Top of the Pops, The Jonathan Ross Show, Richard and Judy Show, Britain's Got Talent, BBC's EastEnders, BBC's The Office, and the England football team. Choreographed fashion shows for Vidal Sassoon, Anthony has starred in and choreographed commercials for Sony PlayStation, Maverick Media, Warner Music and more. Anthony is the original choreographer of the west end musical, Thriller Live. Anthony has held dance team-building events and workshops for the world's biggest companies from Twitter to Google, HM Treasury Department, Lego, Capgemini, Anglo American, PwC, Bonnier Publishing, King (creators of Candy Crush), City Sprint, Red Bull, Cisco Systems, TK Maxx, American Express, Proctor & Gamble, Metro Newspaper group, Rimmel London and many more. He has been interviewed on most of the world's national and international media including Sky News, BBC News, BBC Breakfast, Channel 4, Channel 5, ITV, ITV 2, CNN, ITN, BBC Radio 1, Capital FM, Choice FM, BBC Radio London and many more. His online lessons have been viewed over 35 million times as well as being featured on YouTube homepage on numerous occasions. His classes have been described by The Sun newspaper as 'Hot!' Elle magazine have featured his classes as the 'NEXT BIG THING' as well as "dynamic and charismatic" by the London Lite. The Financial Times of London has recommended and featured Anthony's classes and he has been featured as a contributing writer for magazines including More! magazine as 'Celebrity dance tutor'.

If you'd like to contact Anthony personally with regards to seminars, consultations or just to talk about any subject from this book please email: emailanthonyking@gmail.com or see www.anthony-king.com for more details and to watch the documentary: *The Secret Norwegian: Breaking the curse of Janteloven.* If you'd like to support Anthony via a paypal donation you can do so here: emailanthonyking@gmail.com

Also by the Author

Living in a Bubble: A Guide to being diagnosed with
High Functioning Asperger's as an Adult

The Dancers' Study Guide: A dance guidebook of dance history,
health and fitness, performance lessons, tips and advice

The Personal Development Book For Performers

Michael Jackson and Classical Music

Anthony King's Guide to Michael Jackson's Dangerous Tour

Anthony King's Guide to Michael Jackson's HIStory Tour

Michael Jackson Fact Check – Fact checking the Michael Jackson 'experts'

Dance Like The Stars

The Secret Norwegian Volume One

Coming soon

The Secret Norwegian Volume Two
The Secret Norwegian Volume Three
The Secret Norwegian Volume Four
The Secret Dane: Denmark in Conversation
The Secret Swede: Sweden in Conversation
The Secret Finn : Finland in Conversation
The Secret Icelander: Iceland in Conversation